# UNDERSTANDING OUR BIBLICAL AND EARLY CHRISTIAN TRADITION

*An Introductory Textbook in Theology*

Jean Laporte
and
Finian Taylor

EMText
Lewiston/Queenston/Lampeter

**Library of Congress Cataloging-in-Publication Data**

This work has been registered with the Library of Congress

An EMText volume
ISBN 0-7734-9668-8

A CIP catalog record for this book
is available from the British Library.



The Edwin Mellen Press
Box 450
Lewiston, New York
USA 14092

The Edwin Mellen Press
Box 67
Queenston, Ontario
CANADA L0S 1L0

The Edwin Mellen Press, Ltd.
Lampeter, Dyfed, Wales
UNITED KINGDOM SA48 7DY

Printed in the United States of America

# UNDERSTANDING OUR BIBLICAL AND EARLY CHRISTIAN TRADITION

*An Introductory Textbook in Theology*

# CONTENTS

# PREFACE

The present book is intended for undergraduate students and their teachers, and for many who, like myself, consider it worth while to pursue truth all their life. It was developed for an introductory course, which would lay the Biblical and Historical foundation for the study of Theology.

The first half (Chapters I through IX) is Bible oriented, but does not pretend to be an analysis of the Biblical books and periods. It introduces readers to the modern science of the origins of humankind, prehistoric magic, Egyptian and Greek notions of afterlife, our experience of evil and of God -- all interacting with their Biblical parallels.

Chapter IX deals with the "historical Jesus," and explains the methods and results of the most important exegetes of our time.

The chapters of the first part (I - IX), for which the Bible is the primary text, are shorter than those of the second part (X - XVI). This section deals with early Christianity up to Augustine and Gregory I. The primary texts for this period are not readily available. Therefore, in addition to some exerpts, substantial summaries are given of many of the early Christian writings, which, in their original form, are long, diffuse, and scattered in diverse publications -- often not translated into English.

The final chapter, dealing with unity in Early Christianity, does not consider the later developments of the papacy, and has no comment on these controversies.

Each chapter is accompanied by a questionnaire and a very elementary bibliography. The questionnaire is meant as a guide to reading, and challenges the students' understanding of the section. It should be considered as a basis for further questions from the students of the teacher, and can encourage a lively and free discussion.

I owe a debt of gratitude to all those who have inspired and aided in the preparation of this book. Thanks to Dr. F. Ellen Weaver, my wife, for our long discussions of the ideas in this book, and for technical cooperation. I also thank Dr. Finian Taylor, who was associated with the preparation of this book, not only carefully editing it, but everywhere providing the advice and inspiration of a young college teacher. Dr. Alfred R. Martin provided information for updating Chapter I.

Jean Laporte
University of Notre Dame
18 May 1989

## LIST OF ABBREVIATIONS

| | |
|---|---|
| ACW | Ancient Christian Writers, ed. J. Quasten & J. C. Plumpe. Westminster (MD) and London, 1946, etc. |
| ANF | Ante-Nicene Fathers. Buffalo and New York. |
| FC | The Fathers of the Church, Ed. R.J. Deferrari, CUA. |
| LCC | Library of Christian Classics. Philadelphia and London, 1953, etc. |
| LCL | Loeb Classical Library. London and Cambridge (MA), 1912, etc. |
| LNPF | A Select Library of Nicene and Post-Nicene Fathers of the Christian Church, ed. by |
| Ph.Schaff 1886-1900. | and H. Wace. Buffalo and New York, Reissued: Grand Rapids, 1952, etc. |
| SPCK | Society for Promoting Christian Knowledge. London. |

Quotes from The New English Bible, Oxford University Press 1970.

# CHAPTER I

## THE BIBLICAL NARRATIVE OF CREATION AND MODERN THEORIES OF HUMAN ORIGINS

Regarding the discoveries of modern science about the origins of humankind, what should be the position of a cultured Christian who wants to remain faithful to the Bible and to Christian teaching? Many do not raise the question. Others take it as already answered and do not care. How do they resolve the contradictions appearing between Bible and science regarding the origins of humankind? Do these discoveries really prove the materialistic philosophical thesis which denies as useless and irrelevant the affirmation of the existence of God and of the immortal soul? One of the first and most popular contentions of atheistic materialism is that the Bible is lying concerning creation. It affirms simplistically that humankind is the descendant of monkeys, and that, consequently, there is no God and no spiritual soul.

The present chapter is written for those whose faith is shaken by these questions, and, more particularly, for the younger generation whose belief in science is a priority, a priority worthy, indeed, of appreciation and respect. It is an introduction to the scientific, philosophical and religious problem of the origins. The reader will find elsewhere the up-to-date status of scientific research on evolution and human origins.[1]

The first section deals with denominational statements concerning evolution. The second deals with examples of traditional interpretation of Genesis I-III (Creation and the Fall), destined to show that the rigidly literal exegesis of today fundamentalists in all denominations is not the way the Bible is to be understood. The awareness of chronological problems in the modern times justified the claims of modern science regarding geology and human origins, and led to a clearer distinction between the word of God and obsolete data pertaining to past local cultures. The third section discusses the physical and archeological evidence attesting the human identity. The fourth section deals with the theory of Evolution as applied to humans, and presents several theories of Evolution with their impact on the problem of the appearance of reflective thought. The conclusion focusses on the question of the creation and fall of the Adam, i.e., on the question of monogenism versus polygenism. Two

---

[1] For a succinct but serious account and discussion, see Matt CARTMILL, David PILBEAM, Glynn ISAAC, "One Hundred Years of Paleoanthropology," *American Scientist* (July-August 1986), Sigma XI, 11p.

important appendices follow: the conclusion of Ch. Darwin's book, *The Descent of Man*, and a succinct presentation of the system of P. Teilhard de Chardin, the former appendix being an example of atheistic materialism, the latter, the case of a materialism, or science, open to theism.

The confrontation with modern science in the present chapter is meant to purify our approach to the Bible from irrelevant interference between Bible and science in the rest of the book.

## I. DENOMINATIONAL STATEMENTS ON EVOLUTION[2]

First, it is good to clarify what traditionalist Churches admit and what they leave to free discussion regarding the origins of humankind. For example, for Roman Catholics, in the encyclical letter *HUMANI GENERIS*, August 12th, 1950, Pope Pius XII stated about evolution and polygenism:

> The teaching of the Church leaves the doctrine of EVOLUTION an open question, as long as it confines its speculations to the development, from other living matter already in existence, of the human body. In the present state of scientific research and theological opinion, this question may be legitimately canvassed by research, and by discussion between experts on both sides...
> About POLYGENISM (several independent origins of humankind), which leave the faithful no such freedom of choice, Christians cannot lend their support to a theory which involves the existence, after Adam's time, of some earthly race of men, truly so called, who were not descended ultimately from him, or else supposes that Adam was the name given to some group of our primordial ancestors. It does not appear how such views can be reconciled with the doctrine of original sin, as this is guaranteed to us by Scripture and tradition, and proposed to us by the Church. Original sin is the result of a sin committed, in actual historical fact, by an individual man named Adam, and it is a quality native to all of us, only because it has been handed down by descent from him.[3]

We must note that nothing is said of the origin of life through a particular act of creation, probably because in the past

---

[2] John W. KLOTZ, *Studies in Creation. A General Introduction to the Creation-Evolution-Debate* (St. Louis: Concordia 1946-1973), pp.58-63.

[3] A. FREMANTLE, *The Papal Encyclicals in their Historical Context* (New York: A Mentor Book, 1956), p. 287.

Christians generally accepted the ancient idea of the spontaneous origin of life, which has been refuted by the experiments of Pasteur (1822-95). In addition, we must note that *Humani generis* does not possess the character of a dogma which Catholics should properly believe, or even the mark of infallibility which may be attached to papal teaching under certain conditions. It remains a "prudential statement" subject to revision and improvement. The papal statement is motivated by objections which do not have the same force or implications today. Since 1950, the scientific knowledge of human origins has progressed very much, and the same is true of the interpretation of the biblical text and of the doctrine of the original sin. At least, *Humani generis* allowed scientific discussion of the theory of evolution.

For Presbyterians, there is no conflict between science and the Bible. *The Confession of 1967* 9:29 points out that

> the church has an obligation to approach the Scriptures wit literary and historical understanding... for the Scriptures...are conditioned by the language, thought forms, and literary fashions of the places and times at which they were written. They reflect the views of life, history, and the cosmos which were then current.[4]

Thus, for Presbyterians, the Genesis narrative represents a religious, not a scientific explanation about cosmic and human origins.

For Anglicans, again there is no conflict between science and the Bible, because the intentions of each are quite distinct. Conflict can only arise when the procedures of one are misappropriated by the other, e.g., when the procedures of science are misappropriated by biblical literalists so that the Bible becomes a book of science. When the Bible and science are properly understood in their own way, they actually support one another and are necessary to one another.[5]

Among other Protestant denominations (Lutherans, Baptists, etc.) the issue is still debated regarding the interpretation of Genesis 1-3, while still other groups are pure literalists who read the Scriptures without any consideration of modern science or critical biblical interpretation, for example, the "creat-

---

[4] "The Confession of 1967," *Journal of Presbyterian History* 61:1 (Spring, 1983), p.190.

[5] Consult commentaries on Article 9 of the *Thirty-Nine Articles of the Church of England*; see also W. Taylor STEVENSON, Jr., "Science and the Bible," *Anglicanisme and the Bible*, F.H. BORSCH, ed. (Wilton: Morehouse Barlow, 1984), pp.169-201.

ionists." These fundamentalists are many, and thousands of hours of television are for their preachers a powerful pulpit.

## II. THE CHALLENGE OF THE BIBLICAL NARRATIVES OF THE ORIGINS (Genesis 1-3)

The biblical narratives of the human creation and fall are far from being childish stories or simple tales. They offer a very dignified notion of God, as being unique, omnipotent, creator, supremely intelligent, just and good. These narratives also offer a very noble notion of humanity, as created according to the image of God and responsible for their acts. From the practice of the good, humanity derives spiritual growth and happiness, whereas moral evil stands as a source of condemnation. According to the biblical narrative, humanity chose evil!

Christian tradition has considered these narratives as the foundation of the doctrine of the original sin. This dogma also relies on other bases, for instance, David's confession of his sin in Psalm 51, "I was born in sin," and the classical Greek theory of the "Ages of Life," the first of which is subjected to the flesh before the coming of the age of reason.[6]

Biblical interpreters always found a meaning worthy of God and useful for the life of the soul. Often a "spiritual meaning" was added. For instance, Philo of Alexandria, a Jewish contemporary of Jesus and of Paul, compared the trees of Eden to virtues and vices growing in the garden of the soul, and yielding fruit suited to their nature, good or evil. And the snake symbolized pleasure, which is the source of temptation.[7]

When you were a child, you probably heard that the snake symbolized the devil. This interpretation is a "spiritual" interpretation, i.e., a meaning suggested by reflection, but not plainly stated by the letter of the text.

The Christian doctrine of the original sin is connected with Genesis 1-3. In its classical formulation, the original sin is an inheritance of evil from our first parents, transmitted through human reproduction. It chiefly consists of the soul's servitude under the power of the devil, a servitude of which the Saviour redeems us through the sacrifice of his death on the cross and through the sacrament of baptism. According to this view, Christian life appears as a constant fight against a living enemy, the evil spirit, against whom we must win the victory of faith and virtue with the help of God. This view, however, does not represent the totality of thequestion.

### Ancient and Modern Fundamentalism.

---

[6] ARISTOTLE, *Nichomachean Ethics* III,15,1119.

[7] PHILO OF ALEXANDRIA, *De opificio mundi* 150-150.

Until the time that the natural sciences had drawn up their own methods and performed their own achievements, the biblical narratives did not encounter any serious contradiction. But nobody thought of asking these narratives what we mean today by astronomical, biological, or paleontological science. The mistake was to yield to this temptation in the modern times, and to find in the Bible statements "for" or more often "against" scientific conclusions in these areas. Of course, every "concordism," or attempt at reconciling the Bible with scientific data, failed, either when the six days of creation were identified with geological periods, or when the progress of evolution from lower forms to higher forms was read into the biblical order of creation. The Bible did not really need such a childish defense. Actually, the Bible has something radically different to teach.

The tendency to interpret the Bible according to the letter --right in principle-- can become abusive when the reader does not directly look for religious or moral teachings, but tries to derive from the letter of the Bible all kinds of data loosely related to them. Abusive interpretation takes literally figurative language (for instance, the anger and threats of God, or the promise of a wonderful material prosperity in the messianique time), or blindly follows obsolete ancient science, deriving questionable notions of biology and medicine, and teaching all these things indiscriminately as the word of God to be literally received and obeyed today.

Fundamentalists are not better believers because they accept the letter without critical sense. But they can be very good believers and Christians. However, they may deceive themselves when they assume that their literal rigidity is the best defense of the faith of their children against the challenge of modern science.

### Awareness of Chronological Problems.

The Bible gives many numerical figures for the lives of the patriarchs, which depend more on a mysticism of numbers than on the astronomical clock. At least, never does the Bible make the addition of these numbers! An early Christian writer about 180 A.D., Theophilus of Antioch, made this addition, and found 5695 years, without, he says, taking account of the mention of months and days, which was not always given.[8]

Only recently the idea came about that the earth could be more than 7,000 years old. Already in the eighteenth century, the naturalist Buffon (1707-88) surprised the world when he proved, by a famous experiment, that life had existed on earth for at least 75,000 years.

---

[8] THEOPHILUS OF ANTIOCH, *To Autolychus, Book III*, 28.

Nowadays the origin of life is commonly fixed at 4.6 billion years. The principal divisions of geological time are: the Precambrian, which began 4.5 billion years ago; the Paleozoic, which began 570 million years ago; the Mesozoic, which began 230 million years ago; and the Cenozoic, which began 65 million years ago. The origin of humans (of the genus *Homo*) dates back nearly 2 million years.

New data is brought forth every year or so by scientists, which contributes to a more realistic chronology of the earth and of the development of species. They want us to see the origin of humankind always earlier. The figure given 30 years ago was 600,000 years, but now it is more than three times this number.

## III. THE THRESHOLD OF HUMANKIND

If humankind dates back to the Australopithecines of the late Tertiary period, almost 4 million years ago, the PROCESS OF HUMANIZATION, however, started long before this time. Humanization is more accurately associated with rapid increase in brain size, first seen in genus *Homo* around 2 million years ago. Less closely associated to the humanization process is the standing position (upright posture), which is only seen in the hominid ("human") line of evolution. It is first observed in *Australopithecus afarensis*, 3 millions years old.

Abbe Breuil (1877-1961) had the opportunity to examine a series of *Australopithecus* in southern Africa in 1924 and on. These beings presented a cranial capacity amounting to 400-700 cc. It is possible, although not certain, that they gathered stones, used fire and rod. They lived during the Tertiary period, more than 3 million years ago. We note the South African fossils of *Australopithecus africanus* (pre-*Homo* hominid), 3-2.5 million years ago, and *Australopithecus robustus*, 2-1.5 million years ago.

The human step, i.e., the step is manifested by the appearance of reflection, which is the characteristic of the human mind, whatever use its owner makes of it. Previous to that stage, there existed beings more or less akin to humans by the analogy of their bodily and animal structure. This human step may correspond to the appearance of the Neanderthals (*Homo sapiens neanderthalensis*), early forms of our species, 75,000 to 35,000 years ago. They buried their dead, sprinkled them with flowers and buried tools with them, presumably for use in an afterlife.

The materialist La Mettrie (1709-51), in the eighteenth century, supported the idea that monkeys could be brought through training up to the human level. But,even in the context of a very primitive civilization, a monkey cannot get any education but only some artificial skills provided through training and repetition, because it does not, as a human being, exercise reflection. When expecting the coming of an enemy, certainly the most evolved monkey can get excited and, when the opportunity has come, may use the weapon it happens to have in hand. In the same circumstances, a human being would probably take advantage of the allowed time to adapt and prepare weaponery in the hope of a more comfortable victory. Mimicking can be effected in a monkey. It is possible to excite its instincts and to produce in its "mind" an association of sensory images. But it is impossible to provide a monkey with real education and progress. Their average cranial capacity stands around 400 cc, and does not rise above 600 cc.

In the case of skeletons which have been discovered, in addition to criteria of cranial capacity and other anatomical human features, we must also consider the presence of reflective activity as it may appear in the production of weapons, fire, or ritual burial. If this individual manufactured tools (not only used available objects), mastered fire, and especially buried the dead (which is most contrary to animal behavior), we can conclude it was a human being. However, Jane Goodall showed that chimpanzees actually make simple tools.

The other anatomical features referred to above are, for instance, the upright posture, the use of hands, the reduction of the jaw muscles which facilitates the growth of the brain, the characteristics of the human dentition (teeth), and the presence of a chin. All these features contribute to the development of the human species, particularly the cooperation of the brain and of the hand in creative activity.

## IV. THE THEORY OF EVOLUTION AS APPLIED TO THE CASE OF HUMANS.

The existence of similarities, and the order of succession, between the human species and the animal species which are next to humankind invites us to suppose an actual kinship, and to link up humans with animals.

We must, however, acknowledge that humans manifest an important stage of development above monkeys. The young monkey and a child manifest much similarity in the humanlike shape of their head. It has been successfully tried to bring up a young monkey and a human baby together for a while, but it has been observed that the monkey becomes an adult much earlier than the child. The monkey becomes an adult and is able to have offspring much earlier. On the other hand, the monkey stops much earlier in its intellectual development. Its brain does not develop after a few months. Its skull is definitely fixed, while its head and the other parts of its body continue to grow. This development, is called "differential growing", and brings about monkey-like features. The same phenomenon of differential growing also appears in the later development of humans, but it is less marked and does not influence our intellectual activity.

Human cerebral capacity is much larger than that of monkeys, even the higher ones. The human brain is also much more regionally specialized than in monkeys. The question here is not with the sensory organs, but with the number of connections of neurons of the grey matter in the brain. If modern humans own twice more cells than "hominids," they also own four times more cells than chimpanzees, and eight times more cells than macaques (a type of monkey). Since the relations between the cells of the grey matter multiply with the number of these cells, one more division of these cells seems to be enough to make possible the elaborate biological mechanism necessary for the activity of the human mind.

The discovery of human fossils happened like an adventure, and took place in complete disorder, accompanied by many mishaps. Some early discoveries were challenged, and the fossils were thrown away to rubbish. The 40 *Sinanthropus* probably disappeared in the Japanese sea in the beginning of World War II. It has been supposed that the Neanderthal skull owed its flatness to a punch given by an enemy, and belonged to a Cossack of the Russian army in 1814. An early Neanderthalian jaw found in Mauer (Germany) in 1908 had been photographed under an angle which falsely gave it a monkey-like look. The Java *Pithecanthropus* found by Dubois in 1891 came out of its boxes only 40 years later. And the affair of the Piltdown-man --a fraud committed in England in 1911-- was exposed by evolutionists only in 1952. It did not fit the physical evidence.

The early name given to "hominids," *Pithecanthropus* ("monkey-man") was misleading. In that time, people were more interested in demonstrating the origin of humans from monkeys than in pure science, and did not avoid premature conclusions. *Pithecanthropus* was looked upon as providing the desired "intermediary", or "missing link" between monkeys and humans.

The contention of the materialists, however, that *Pithecanthropus* was the "missing-link," was seriously challenged when it became obvious that *Sinanthropus* was much earlier and had more human-like features. The classical distinction between *Homo faber* (the Neanderthalian) and *Homo sapiens* (the type of Cro-Magnon and modern races), also was biased, since the Neanderthalians, representing *Homo sapiens* neanderthalensis, were capable of rational activity: they cut their stone-tools and even prepared the tombs of their dead, providing them with food for their long journey in the hereafter. Discoveries have since then multiplied, and their contexts are now properly investigated. Therefore, it is possible to determine the features and the order of the chief early human races.

But where in nature is found the key to the mechanism of evolution?[9] Lamarck (1744-1829) held that evolution was a

---

[9] Concerning human origins and evolution, the author acknowledges the advice and up-to-date information of Dr. Alfred R. Martin, I.N.C. Lisle, Ill.

result of adaptation to the environment, and that the acquired features were hereditary. As evidence, he pointed out the different shapes which the same plant takes in water and on dry ground, and the blindness of sea-monsters in the ocean depths.

Darwin (1809-82) said that a population of variable organisms unconsciously compete for limited resources. Those individuals which just happen to be best adapted at exploiting limited resources are better able to survive and reproduce, thus passing on their "genes" in greater frequency to the next generation. Thus, the essence of "Darwinism" is *differential reproductive rates.*

The 19th Century evolutionists inherited from Aristotle the principle: *natura non facit saltus* (nature makes no leap), a principle which they held as sacred. The progress accomplished this way could only be very slow, and the particular improvements very small. On the other hand, on account of their very insignificance, these changes seemed to be achieved easily, almost automatically, without requiring the intervention of a divine Creator. All these observations served the same purpose which was to prove that religion is not necessary in order to explain the origin of humankind or even the constitution of the world, and that there is no radical difference between the most developed animals and humankind, since nothing noticeable can be found between the primates of the Tertiary period and the hominids.

However, recent discoveries indicate that the mechanism of evolution seems to be different, and to have proceeded through changes, i.e., through "leaps," the very opposite to Aristotle's principle! And these changes seem to have been transmitted through heredity. This observation has been made on plants first. In 1886, a Dutch man, Hugo de Vries, observed sudden changes in certain flowers (punctuated equilibrium or evolutionary saltation). Twenty years earlier, an Austrian monk, Mendel (1822-84), had studied mutations in peas, and thereby discovered the laws of heredity. It belonged to genetics to give the decisive answer.

The appearance of new forms is the result of some modification in the elaborate system of chromosomes in the seed when two cells come together for fecundation (usually due to polyploidy). It has been possible to produce such variants artificially, through chemical methods, for instance, on fruit flies, a species which reproduces very fast and so makes observation easier. Extraordinary results, especially monstrous ones, have been obtained, as much on plants as on animals.

Therefore, it sounds more scientific to think of sudden variations rather than slow and imperceptible improvements. In addition, the sudden variation theory resolves the difficulty of the slow appearance of new organs, the usefulness of which would become effective only thousands of years later. Evolution should rather be represented as "revolution," particularly with the coming of humans, because of the appearance of the process of reflection.

But the creation of the soul by God does not mean that it is not also the product of nature and of evolution. It implies that the soul exists by a special creative will of God, the Creator of all.

Modern biology and paleontology do not deal with the problem of creation. They only deal with what metaphysics (the study of ultimate philosophical reasons) describes as "appearences," or "phenomenon." Evolution does not explain the creation of any new being, but it simply explains how more sophisticated structures and activities may appear in a species. The methods of research are those of modern science, and the result is confined to the "phenomenon." On the other hand, modern science is not directly concerned with affirmations or negations historically attached to philosophy or even theology (for instance, the historical character of the story of Adam, of the creation in six days, of the age of Methuselah, of the Deluge, etc.).

## CONCLUSION

Some people fear that, if the hypothesis of evolution is taken for granted, we could hardly find a difference radical enough between the soul of the first humans and the type of thinking of a chimpanzee. They wonder whether so primitive and rough a soul could raise philosophical and moral problems, reach the idea of God, make a distinction between good and evil, be able to commit the original sin!

Many scientists believe that aspects of human personality can or will eventually be reduced to chemical/mathematical descriptions ("reductionism"). For example, there is a chemical in the brain which elicits feelings of love. The same chemical is found in chocolate. Several brain chemicals can cause feelings of well-being and relief from pain. Several personality disorders (for example, schizophrenia) are due to chemical imbalances, etc. More complicated aspects such as learning, emotions and intelligence are harder to reduce, but they too may be reducible. There are even chemicals which stimulate memory.

However, between animals and humans a spiritual gulf lies, and we should not underestimate the importance of the gap. Humankind is different from animals because of its spiritual nature. It can be interesting to examine human nature according to sociobiology, to measure sensory reactions, to study humans just as we do animals, but its ultimate definition belongs to philosophy. Philosophy, indeed, and not biology, is the applied science of human nature. According to the well known expression, the soul is not to be found "at the point of a scalpel."

Human nature is defined more properly from its higher part, i.e., from the mind and its faculties. From the time of Plato, philosophy observes that, through reflection, the human mind turns into a center of activity, and acquires a certain autonomy from senses and body. The mind seems to become a being by itself, and the individual man or woman becomes a "person."

Moreover, souls show an intellectual and spiritual development which differ widely from one individual to another. Some even look hardly awake to personal thought and moral judgment. However, nobody would deny that they own this power, at least radically. We may think that it will turn into activity sometimes, at least when they appear before God. Do we suppose that the souls of the first humans, who possessed reflective thought, were not able to reach any sense of right and wrong? Of course, we must take into account the difference of civilization, but we are wrong when we assume that life is simple among primitive groups; actually, their way of life is very elaborate and sophisticated.

We must also remember that moral judgment is not the privilege of "cultured" people, but of intelligence, and that God casts his light upon every one coming into the world. If there existed a genuine perception of God in these ancient civilizations, we may consider that it took place in the moral judgment, where is found the notion and internal "reality" of the Better (I am tempted to say, the "Sovereign Good," or God). In this sense I incline to ascribe to the first humans the perception of God together with moral judgment. And I would add that the appearance of moral judgment does not necessarily correspond in time with the appearance of reflection. Of course, on this primitive level of civilization, moral judgment does not mean the same catalogue of sins or good deeds as in our own civilization. It might have been a moral duty to eat the brain of an enemy, or even of one's grandfather!

The question of MONOGENISM (only one Adam) and of POLYGENISM (several independent origins) probably will never be answered by science. The "mutants," or "intermediaries," which are the earliest representatives of a new species, are very few. As being only a few in regard to the thousands and millions born in a settled and fixed species, they have, according to the theory of probability, little chance of having been preserved and discovered. The fossilisation of a skeleton is an unfrequent phenomenon, which depends on the conjunction of many chemical and physical circumstances.

Therefore, we cannot expect that science will ever contradict the thesis of monogenism properly speaking, even if many a scientist, on biological grounds, favors the "polygenist" option. Actually, science is not interested in this particular question, which has been raised by theologians from their own point of view, because this question does not lie within the reach of science, but only offers a theological interest, not a primordial one.

On the other hand, open-minded science may favor a kind of "Monogenism." Teilhard de Chardin (1881-1955) likes the idea of a first human appearance as the fruit of the psychological development in the unity of a tribe of primates during the Tertiary period. Instead of "Monogenism," he suggests "Monophyletism" (only one tribe). In any case, the leap from animal to human nature should not be underestimated.

On the other hand, we must frankly admit that the first human was a sinner, if we identify human origins with the appearance of reflection, or, more exactly, with the appearance of moral judgment, as explained above. And is not evil the necessary counterpart of the good, which cannot exist without the possibility of evil? But we should not try to imagine the case of "Adam": such attempts to concretize the first human can only lead to a tasteless fictional story.

Human origins seem to correspond to the coming of sin on earth, and the first tool was a weapon. A 900 gr. brain (750 cc) is enough for correct behavior, and the rest is used for misdeeds. Monkeys do not kill, or roast the members of their own species. The first act of Prometheus (a name given to the demiman of Komdraai in Transvaall) can be considered as the first act of the earliest humankind, but we cannot help admitting that this act was the act of Cain.

Although reflection opened to humanity the way to truth, goodness, and perfection, it seems that evil was actually the first conquest of our intelligence.

## APPENDIX I

## THE THEORY OF EVOLUTION AS APPLIED TO HUMANKIND BY CHARLES DARWIN

### The Biological Evolution.

"By considering the embryological structure of man and the similarities which he presents with the lower animals,...we can partly recall in imagination the former condition of our early progenitors; and can approximatively place them in their proper place in the zoological series. We thus learn that man is descended from a hairy, tailed quadruped, probably arboreal in its habits, and an inhabitant of the Old World. This creature, if its whole structure had been examined by a naturalist, would have been classed amongst the quadrumana, as surely as the still more ancient progenitor of the old and of the new world monkeys. The quadrumana and all the higher mammals are probably derived from some fish-like animal. In the dim obscurity of the past we can see that the early progenitor of all the Vertebrata must have been an aquatic animal provided with branchiae, with the two sexes united in the same individual, and with the most important organs of the body (such as the brain and heart) imperfectly or not at all developed. This animal seems to have been more like the larvae of the existing marine Assidians than any other known form."

THE DEVELOPMENT OF INTELLECTUAL FACULTIES.

"The high standard of our intellectual powers and moral disposition is the greatest difficulty which presents itself, after we have been driven to this conclusion on the origin of man. But every one who admits the principle of Evolution, must see that the mental powers of the higher animals, which are the same in kind with those of man, though so different in degree, are capable of advancement. Thus the interval between the mental powers of the higher apes and of a fish, or between those of ant and scale-insect, is immense; yet their development does not offer any special difficulty; for with our domesticated animals, the mental faculties are certainly variable, and the variations are inherited. No one doubts that they are of the utmost importance to animals in a state of nature. Therefore the conditions are favourable for their development through natural selection. The same conclusion may be extended to man; the intellect must have been all-important to him, even at a very remote period, as enabling him to invent and use language, to make weapons, tools, straps, etc., whereby with the aid of his social habits, he long ago became the most dominant of all living creatures."

"A great stride in the development of the intellect will have followed, as soon as the half-instinct and half-art of language came into use ; for the continued use of language will have reacted on the brain and producted an inherited effect; and this again will have reacted on the improvement of language. As Mr. Chauncey Wright has well remarked, the largeness of the brain in man relatively to his body, compared with the lower animals, may be attributed for the chief part to the early use of some simple form of language, - that wonderful engine which affixes signs to all sorts of objects and qualities, and excites trains of thought which would never arise from the mere impression of the senses, or if they did arise could not be followed out. The higher intellectual powers of man, such as these of rationation, abstraction, self-consciousness, etc., probably follow from the continued improvement and exercise of the other mental faculties."

THE DEVELOPMENT OF MORAL FACULTIES.

"The development of the moral faculties is a more interesting problem. The foundation lies in the social instincts, including under this term the family ties. These instincts are highly complex, and in the case of the lower animals give special tendencies towards certain definite actions; but the more important elements are love, and the distinct emotion of sympathy. Animals endowed with the social instincts take pleasure in one another's company, warn one another of danger, defend and aid one another in many ways. These instincts are highly beneficial to the species, they have in all probability been acquired through natural selection."

"A moral being is one who is capable of reflecting on his past actions and their motives, of approving of some and disapproving of others; and the fact that man is the only one who certainly deserves this designation is the greatest of all distinctions between him and the lower animals. But in the 4th chapter I have endeavored to show that the moral sense follows, firstly, from the enduring and ever present nature of the social instincts; secondly, from man's appreciation of the aprobation and disapprobation of his fellows; and, thirdly, from the high activity of his mental faculties, with past impressions extremely vivid; and in these respects he differs from the lower animals. Owing to this condition of mind, man cannot avoid looking backwards and forwards, and comparing past impresssions. Hence after some temporary desire or passion has mastered his social instincts, he reflects and compares the now weakened impression of such past impulses with the ever present social instincts; and he then feels that sense of dissatisfaction which all unsatisfied instincts leave behind them, he therefore resolves to act differently for the future, - and this is conscience. Any instinct, permanently stronger or more enduring than another, gives rise to a feeling which we express by saying that it ought to be obeyed. A pointer dog, if able to reflect on his past conduct, would say to himself, I ought (as indeed we say of him) to have pointed at that hare and not to have yielded to the passing temptation of hunting it."

THE BELIEF IN GOD.

"With the more civilised races, the conviction of the existence of an all-seing Deity had had a potent influence on the advance of morality. Ultimately man does not accept the praise or blame of his fellows as his sole guide, though few escape this influence, but his habitual convictions, controlled by reason, afford him the safest rule. His conscience then becomes the supreme judge and monitor. Nevertheless the first foundation or origin of the moral sense lies in the social instincts, including sympathy; all these instincts no doubt were primarily gained, as in the case of the lower animals, through natural selection."

"The belief in God has often been advanced as not only the greatest, but the most complete of all the distinctions between man and the lower animals. It is however impossible, as we have seen, to maintain that this belief is innate or instinctive in man. On the other hand, a belief in all-pervading agencies seems to be universal ; and apparently follows from a considerable advance in man's reason, and from a still greater advance in his faculties of imagination, curiosity and wonder."

"I am aware that the instinctive belief in God has been used by many persons as an argument for His existence. But this is a rash argument, as should thus be compelled to believe in the existence of many cruel and malignant spirits, only a little more powerful than man ; for the belief in them is far more general than that in a beneficent Deity. The idea of a universal and beneficent Creator does not seem to arise in the mind of man, until he has been elevated by long-continued culture."[10]

A BRIEF CRITICISM OF THE THESIS OF DARWIN.

Although modern science has greatly improved our knowledge of biology and paleontology, the general structure of the theory of evolution of Darwin is still good today. Prehistory has confirmed its outlines and is now a science supported by lots of discoveries. The development of the mind outlined by Darwin is not wrong, as we can imagine through our knowledge of the primitive peoples of our time. But, in the time of Darwin, science was poor, therefore boastful ; the fewer the facts, the bolder the conclusions! Darwin's conclusion about a continued progress was unfounded. However, he was right when stressing the importance of natural selection (through mating) as the key to evolution, but he failed to recognize that the basis was much deeper, in genetics.

The philosophical conclusions he draws from the assumed absence of a serious difference in the gap between human and animal, which amounts to a rejection of the spiritual nature, are not necessarily supported by the evidence presented. They are Darwin's own philosophy, which is the atheism and materialism of mid-nineteenth century northern Europe and England. No surprise, then, that he found his conclusions supported by the evidence, since he saw the evidence through the eyes of the same conclusions, like all those who work with an unconscious bias.

## APPENDIX II

## THE SYSTEM OF TEILHARD DE CHARDIN

A Jesuit who spent all his life on scientific research in geology, Teilhard de Chardin was known not only, as a scientist, for instance for his participation in the discovery of the *Sinanthropus* of Chou-Kou-Tien near Pekin, but also as a philosopher, as the supporter of an all inclusive system of evolution: scientific, philosophical, theological. Teilhard died in 1955. His challenge raised enthusiasm, but also the distrust of authorities more comfortable with obsolete positions. He became the spiritual leader of the generation following his death after the publication of his writings. The present disappearance of Teilhard was a necessity, but his message should be heard. Many scientific positions of Teilhard may have become obsolete today, but this does not deeply alter his system itself. And philosophers know

---

[10] Charles DARWIN, *The origin of Species. The Descent of Man* (New York: The Modern Library), pp. 911 ff.

that different systems have their relevance, including materialism, which remains basic for our science-oriented generation.

Teilhard's basis is a subtle kind of materialism: for him, matter is not inert, but always shows to the observer some structure and activity, which Teilhard considers as elementary psychism. For Teilhard, all living species, and ultimately humankind, are a sophistication of matter through the process of evolution. But, once arrived at a certain threshold of sophistication, matter becomes able to think (Teilhard says: "the Earth thinks"), and hopefully to survive after death.

In his system, Teilhard remains in the field of PHENOMENOLOGY (whence the title of his book, *The Phenomenon of Man*), without interference from the biblical, theological, or philosophical literary tradition. Although the proof for immortality in Teilhard can be found in Plato, Teilhard prefers to speak the language of a Scientist, and to rely on the data and background of science.

He notices that evolution is following a line of direction toward more autonomy, more intellectuality, more complexity, more unity. He calls the apex of this evolution the OMEGA point, and the whole evolution consitutes the HUMAN PHENOMENON (the human being is the best synthesis of the cosmos).

Consideration of the Omega point leads to a double hypothesis: is the Omega point without a present or actual existence, just as the apex of a future progress? or is it already and independently existing? In Teilhard's opinion, the first hypothesis --purely scientific-- provides a good principle of order and classification, but the second hypothesis provides a METAPHYSICAL CAUSE which explains the orientation itself of evolution toward unity and intellectuality.

Teilhard compares the Omega point of the second hypothesis (the reality of Omega) to the PRIME-MOVER of former systems of thought, like Aristotle's and Aquinas.' In his opinion, this direction is the concrete way of progressing, not an obscure force moving lower things toward higher perfection. The qualitative AHEAD (Teilhard says, THE PRIME-MOVER AHEAD) is added in order to make clear that, just like the Prime-Mover of Aristotle, the Omega point is a FINAL CAUSE, and not a kind of initial "kicking." But the Prime Mover ahead of Teilhard is the principle of a change from lower to higher forms, and not a principle of static being and classification as in Aristotle and Aquinas. The difference is precisely evolution!

Of course, to affirm the existence of the Omega point (as intelligent, personal, one, perfect, and Cause of all) is not a bare syllogism (a syllogism derives the less from the more, not the more from the less), but an act of faith, a BET. It is not possible, indeed, to prove the existence of God just like 2+2=4. There is still a place for faith, for the noble risk of faith!
The notion of risk is part of the human thinking and action: a businessman would not contradict this idea.

Now, starting from the acceptance of the existence of Omega, Teilhard becomes a theologian in his own terms, that is, as a philosopher of science. Cultural, providential, prophetic preparations can be considered as the influence of the shining Omega-God. Thus the incarnation of Omega becomes meaningful and possible: since we are ready to receive God, God also is ready to become human and to achieve the most precious synthesis for the benefit of all, Christ.

In order to become human, God must be born just like any one of us, because there is no other way for assuming the flesh and the spirit in this world of ours. We may add that Christ was born in the right time and in the right place: in the civilization of the Bible. To be incarnate does not mean to just take body and soul, but also to inherit a civilization, just as we did when we were born. Christ thus became the leader of a SPIRITUAL EVOLUTION, a perfectly oriented leader on whom we can rely since he is the Omega-God himself. The death of Christ, according to Teilhard, teaches us the right way to die, namely, trusting God, and in hope, over against the Existentialist despair (of Camus or Sartre).

Teilhard was deeply interested in a philosophy of the PERSON. We must remember the importance which he grants to the appearance of reflection as a function and as the threshold of humankind. With the appearance of reflection, which is the key to all problems, the external or physical progress of humankind matters less than the intellectual and spiritual progress, which becomes the favourite field of active evolution. Humans are the "arrow of evolution" because they are able to think, and evolution, with the coming of humankind, becomes more an affair of the within than of the without.

The Omega point itself is in the within, that is, not far from any one of us. For this reason, we are in the process of centering on the Omega point within ourselves. Teilhard compares a person to a cone cut somewhere between the basis and the apex, but close to the apex. The cut is still a circle, a surface, not yet a point: we are centered, not yet a center. We shall become a center when our evolution is perfected, that is, when, through faith, overcoming the doubt caused by the destruction of the major part of ourselves through death, we join Omega-God, and, adhering to God, we become one with God.

The problem of the PERSON offers another aspect: a sociological aspect. The religions of the past have been destroyed by changes in civilization, and Christianity has been badly shaken, indeed, but purified. Because of its personalistic character, Christianity is able to be the religion of tomorrow. God is a Person ; man (woman) is a person ; and there is a relation between humans and God. More particularly, Christ is God who became human and assumed our "evolution." Teilhard criticizes the totalitarism and the "earthly" character of modern political and economic systems, in which the State enslaves individuals and turns them into a mere piece of the great social machine. People have thus no other end but to serve the community, and they lose all meaning and right when they cease fulfilling this service. They live for the sake of the community, like bees in a hive, not for their own sake. Their personality is denied, destroyed, but only if they live for the sake of God, do they recover a transcendence of sorts, and escape the totalitarism of modern society.[11]

Teilhard conferred on ACTION, on human endeavour, a true religious value. Action is no longer merely an opportunity to exercise and to acquire virtue, but remaining itself without value. Spiritual masters even considered failure as more fruitful than success for the soul. With Teilhard, to change the world, to improve the world, to do anything in the bodily realm is a positive value. This emphasis laid by Teilhard on action as a spiritual value agrees with the thought of our times. It also offers a spirituality to blue-collars and scientists who want to find a spiritual value in what they are doing, and do not like to hear that all their endeavour is trash or even contrary to the will of God and the order of creation.

During World-War I, Teilhard served as a stetcher-bearer on the most bloody battlefields. It was a challenge for the heart and the mind of the thinker. So much suffering on the battlefield represented an immense force of love, but suffering, in order to be love, to be consecrated to God, must be liberated and rightly directed.

Going beyond many spiritual masters who immediately turn any suffering into a cross offered up to God, Teilhard distinguishes three steps: 1) there are "passivities" (handicaps, sufferings) which we must resist and overcome, or consider as the sign of a poor orientation which must give place to a better one; 2) there are "passivities" which we must sublimize, because we must "live with them": they are to be offered up, and it is a precious way to serve God; 3) there are "passivities" which are such that they invite us to say a "Good Bye!" to the world, and to extrapolate, that is, to join Omega-God in a movement of hope, faith and love (in the hour of death).

Coming now to Teilhard's notion of the resurrection, we should first be aware of the necessity not to oversimplify the doctrine of the Church concerning the resurrection, and we should know, for instance, that the most materialistic view is not the most orthodox of all! Coming to Teilhard's discussion of the resurrection comes less as a surprise when we know the complexity of the problem. Some people think that Teilhard evacuates the reality of the resurrection, when, actually, he is offering an answer which suits his general system and should be interpreted accordingly.

---

[11] H. de Lubac, *The Drama of Atheistic Materialism* (New York: Meridian Books, 1963), represents the kind of situation which Teilhard was confronting. Teilhard and Lubac exchanged views.

Before investigating his notion of the body of the resurrection, we should explain his notion of the human body, and compare the body of birth to the body of the resurrection. According to Teilhard, the ordinary notion of the body is unsatisfactory, and a more sophisticated notion must sustitute for it. Even the dichotomy body-soul does not agree with Teilhard. He prefers a "cosmic" notion of the body: THE UNIVERSE AS CENTERED ON PETER, OR ON PAUL, OR ON ANDREW, ETC. In the Incarnation, the Universe becomes centered on Christ-Omega: by the Incarnation, Omega-God entered the world. The only way for Him to enter the world was through woman, through the womb. In addition to what He is as God, Christ was thus made a fruit and a synthesis of the Universe. He became the product of the long history of the Universe and of the human society, i.e., a man of his time, both receiving from, and reacting to, his time. As such, as well as because of his divine origin, he became a wonderful guide, a master for humankind. Without birth, His presence would have been a mere shining of ideals over our minds, but not a person, a model, a Savior.

In order to understand the resurrection of Christ, and our own resurrection, we must understand the Teilhardian notion of the body of the resurrection as the highest synthesis of the Universe, a synthesis which is of the same nature as the Universe, i.e., evolved and sophisticated matter which has reached the level of thought and is concentrated enough to continue its movement of centration instead of falling apart through dispersion.

We borrow the comparison of an apple-tree (and take some liberty with it). An apple is growing on a branch of a tree on which it hangs by means of a stem through which it receives protection and food. When the apple reaches its maturity, the stem dies out and breaks, but the apple, which seems also to die, contains the seed of a new tree. The seed is the highest synthesis of the tree, which is itself potentially existing in the seed. Like the apple on the tree, our body of birth is the highest synthesis, which contains the whole nature of the Universe and of Evolution. But only death reveals what we are: not element, but synthesis, not part, but the whole, not the lower and more quantitative part, but the more unified and stronger part, the one which is so well unified that it can last by itself without the support of the rest, and find its fitting partner in the Omega-God ahead.

The rest of the world can continue its way, and the body, like the stem and the flesh of the apple, can die, but the man or woman who dies in faith is reaching his/her end. Those who do not believe and do not hope, when they die, have no direction where to go: they are "scattered." They may represent the last failure of Evolution (the "tangential"), whereas those who still keep the power of the flying arrow represent the success of Evolution (the "radial"). According to Teilhard, success and failure are represented by these two words, or the law of unity and synthesis.

Should we conclude that Teilhard is just putting an end, a dead end, to evolution when people have reached the Omega-God? A linear diagram might suggest it. But the "cone of evolution" has its apex not in space, outside, but in the within, as the mysterious partner of a dialogue. Assimilation to the Omega-God could seem a boring end, if Omega was just our own unification, but it is not so, since this end is a partnership, and the communication between God and us, which all want to enjoy, in understanding and love.

Teilhard observes that assimilation to the Omega point does not mean the reduction of all to one only Individual, be it human or divine, but, in a personalistic system, a point is a place of meeting where every converging line preserves its own identity. In this regard, Teilhard admits that, for a while, his mind has been conquered by the cosmic and mystical character of Oriental religions (Hindouism and Buddhism), but that, later on, in spite of its depth and beauty, this religious system appeared to him to be impossible because it included the negation of the EGO. And Teilhard considers that Christianity is right when it maintains a religion where at the end we still find the PERSON, and a communication between God and men.

## QUESTIONNAIRE ON THE HUMAN ORIGINS

1. Do you know people (old or young) who strongly affirm the literal meaning of the biblical narratives in Genesis in a fundamentalist manner, or others who doubt and reject what they consider as the biblical teaching?
2. What is the position of Christian denominations regarding evolution and the origin of humankind?
3. Why is *Humani generis* more negative about "polygenism": is it a condemnation?
4. Is it better not to discuss these matters at all from the pulpit? in special meetings with parishioners? in a high school classroom? in a college or university? with members of other Churches?
5. Is not there something shocking in the famous formula, "Humanity goes back to Monkey"? What grounds for, or against, this affirmation were merely superficial?, or more serious?
6. Knowing that the human hand can serve many purposes (the hoof of a horse cannot because it is adjusted to one job only), how could the use of the hand (an unspecialized instrument) influence the development of the brain and make articulate language possible?
7. Explain (with a simple illustration rather than scientific reasons) how could an additional division of the cells of the brain cells of the "grey matter," multiply the possibilities of mental processes enough to make possible the exercise of reflection, which we find, it seems, on the level of "hominids"?

8. Compare the parallel development of a human baby and of a little chimpanzee: what was observed?
9. Explain the process of reflection. How is this power the key to all human problems, including those philosophical and religious?
10. How can we try to resolve, the delicate case of those who do not seem to reach the level of personal thought because of a lack of education or because of mental handicap?
11. What is the advantage, and the weakness, of the method of a naturalist (biologist) for the study of the human species? Why do they often tend toward materialism?
12. What are the discoveries of Lamarck, Darwin, Hugo de V-ries, Mendel, regarding evolution? How can we say that the solution to the problem of evolution belongs to genetics? Can genetics influence the future of humankind?
13. Is it necessary to affirm, or to deny, an important anatomic or physiological change between the "last primates" and the "first humans"? Is it the problem of one, or of a few individuals, or of a group? Do you know the position of Teilhard de Chardin about it?
14. Is it possible to show that "evil" goes back to the first human being? How is the discovery of evil just the counterpart of the discovery of the morally good?
15. How would you present the first chapters of Genesis to your children, according to their age and mentality?
16. How would you describe the human origins in a science-fiction novel of your own composition?
17. How does Darwin explain the origin and functioning of the intellectual faculties of the human mind? Do you agree with it?
18. How does Darwin explain the origin and functioning of the moral conscience? Do you agree with it?
19. How would you answer Darwin's criticism of the notion of God?
20. Discuss Teilhard's notion of matter as a psychic element which, through sophistication, can evolve and ultimately reach the level of humankind.
21. Compare the Omega point of Teilhard to the Prime-Mover, or Final Cause, of Aristotle-Aquinas.
22. Why, according to Teilhard, the necessity for God to be born as a human? Why not a more spiritual type of intervention for our salvation?
23. Are our action, or our suffering, automatically a religious value? From what has suffering to be, as it were, "liberated" for that purpose?
24. What happens of the "unfinished human person" at death? (cf. the cone cut close to the apex)
25. Do you think that Teilhard's theory of the resurrection can be conciled with the classical theology of the resurrection as represented by Paul, I Corinthians 15?

## BIBLIOGRAPHY

BOWLER, J.Peter, ed. *Evolution. The History of an Idea.* Berkeley: University of California Press, 1989.

CHARDIN, Pierre Teilhard de. *The Phenomenon of Man*, tr.B. Wall. New York: Harper & Row, 1975.

____. *Christianity and Evolution*, tr. R. Hague. New York: Harcourt, Brace, Jovanowich, 1959. (Includes *How I Believe*).

____. *The Divine Milieu.* New York: Harper & Row, 1959. (Includes a biography of Teilhard).

HAWKES, Jacquetta & Sir Leonard WOOLEY. *Prehistory and the Beginnings of Civilization.* Vol. I. New York: Harper & Row, 1963.

RAHNER, Karl. *Sacramentum Mundi.* "Evolution" (pp.475-88); Monogenism" (pp.874-77).

# CHAPTER II

## PREHISTORIC MAGIC AND THE BIBLICAL WAY OF ETHICS

The biblical revelation is an absolute, firm and clear affirmation of God's Being, and of the need for morality, without any compromise or contradiction. The Decalogue (Ten Commandments), which sometimes seems trivial to the modern believer, finds its beauty, its depth, and its originality when inserted anew in its historical context. It represents a revolution in the history of religion, because, while all other religions of antiquity compromised with the routine of idolatry and magic, the people of Israel and, later on, Christianity, resolutely fought against these low forms of religion and resisted their insidious temptation. This fight lasted until our own times,since today, if ancient sorcery and magic have definitely been uprooted, we are still threatened by the illusion that we can reach our end by ways other than the way of the moral good.

After stating the teaching of the Bible (Exodus, Deuteronomy) on Idolatry and magic: a strong repudiation of such practices as contrary to the will of God and to the Law of Moses, a first section analyzes the magic, sorcery, and superstition of the Middle-Ages and their survival until our time. From this observation, it becomes possible to better decipher and interpret the remnants of prehistoric magic. The passage from magic to idolatry under the form of astral worship, attests a progress of religion toward a more spiritual understanding, but it also reveals the huge size of the obstacle, which the ethical "revolution" of the Bible had to remove: the weight of millenaries of magical practice. Ethics still has to struggle today for its recognition as the most essential value in religion.

### THE STRUGGLE OF THE BIBLE AGAINST IDOLATRY AND MAGIC.

The Bible denies any truth or value to idolatry and magic, and condemns them with uncompromising energy. As a God of justice, the God of the Bible asks humanity for righteousness in their deeds and thoughts. Nothing can dispense us from our duty of doing good and avoiding evil, and there is no other way to please God. The most genuine way to serve God, the most authentic worship, is obedience to his will, i.e., the accomplishment of moral duty. Ethical behavior is as important as the worship of the only God. On the one hand, there is no right worship of God without good deeds; on the other hand, our first duty is to acknowledge and serve God.

Often in antiquity, cultic practices were understood as a way, not properly to serve God, but to assure His cooperation, and to compel Him to help us. Although a primitive notion of religion, this idea is not bad in itself, since we are in need of everything, and particularly of moral help from God. But often people tried to influence God in order to achieve their evil purposes. Prayer, then, turned into magic, i.e., into a means to subjugate God and to compel Him, or, more exactly, to compel all kinds of supernatural powers (spirits or demons), to do what we want, even if it is a wicked thing.

The experts in this art are called magicians, sorcerers and witches, and this art is called magic and sorcery. Superstition is very close to magic and sorcery since it is an unbalanced trust in saints, relics, and all kinds of more or less sacred things. It happens when these things are seen as the most reliable means of obtaining the advantage which we seek from the deity. Superstition, therefore, substitutes for genuine prayer which, instead of forcing the hand of God, affirms our own subjection to His will: "Thy will be done on earth as it is in heaven!"

The Bible condemns as idolatry, sorcery and magic the religious practices of the former inhabitants of Palestine, the Canaanites. The Bible also considers as idolatry the religion, rituals, and animal cults of Egypt. In Israel itself, the Bible passes judgment on kings according to the way they tolerated magic and sorcery, or resolutely fought against and destroyed these practices.

1) CONDEMNATION OF IDOLATRY IN THE BIBLE.

The first commandment of the Decalogue (Exodus 20) prescribes the service and worship of the one only God (Redeemer of Israel from Egypt and Creator of the world) and proscribes all kinds of idolatry.

Deuteronomy enlarges on this teaching and forbids the religious practices of the surrounding nations:

> When the Lord your God exterminates, as you advance, the nations whose country you are entering to occupy, you shall take their place and settle in their land. After they have been destroyed, take care that you are not ensnared into their ways. Do not inquire about their gods and say, "How do these nations worship their gods? I too will do the same." You must not do for the Lord what they do, for all that they do for their gods is hateful and abominable to the Lord. As sacrifices for their gods they even burn their sons and their daughters (Deut.12:29-31).

> You shall demolish all the sanctuairies where the nations whose place you are taking worship their gods, on mountain-tops and hills and under every spreading tree. You shall pull down their altars and break their sacred pillars, burn their sacred poles and hack down the idols

> of their gods and thus blot out the name of them from that place (Deut. 12:2-4).[12]
> If so be that, in any one of the settlements which the Lord your God is giving you, a man or woman is found among you who does what is wrong in the eyes of the Lord, by breaking his covenant and going to worship other gods and prostrating himself before them or before the sun and moon and all the host of heaven --a thing that I have forbidden, ...then bring the man or woman who has done this wicked deed to the city gate and stone him to death (Deut.17:1-8).

Even one's relatives must not be spared (Deut. 13:7-12).

2. CONDEMNATION OF MAGIC.

> When you come into the land which the Lord your God is giving you, do not learn to imitate the abominable customs of those other nations. Let no one be found among you who makes his son or daughter pass through fire, no augur or soothsayer or diviner or sorcerer or necromancer. Those who do these things are abominable to the Lord, and it is because of these abominable practices that the Lord your God is driving them out before you. You shall be whole-hearted in your service of the Lord your God (Deut.18:9-13)[13]

All those who give their son to Molok, either passing him over the fire, or even burning him alive, as a sacrifice to Molok or Baal,[14] and generally all those who practice magic and necromancy, should be cast out from the people and put to death.[15]

3. SOME FAMOUS CRIMES AGAINST THESE LAWS.

King Manasseh "built altars for all the host of heaven in the two courts of the house of the Lord, and he made his son pass through the fire, he practiced soothsaying and divination, and dealt with ghosts and spirits.[16] King Saul consulted a necromancer.[17]

## RECENT SORCERY AND SUPERSTITION.

1. PRESENT INTEREST OF THE QUESTION.

---

[12] Cf. Ex.23:24; 24:13.

[13] Cf. Lev.19:31.

[14] Lev.20:1-7; Lev.18:21.

[15] Ex.22:17; Lev.20:27.

[16] 2 Kings 21:5.

[17] 1 Samuel 28.

One person out of two believes in magic, and three out of four are able to quote instances of magic. Here we refer to practices known under the names of spiritism, taboos, healing, casting of spells, telling of fortunes, etc. However, we do not consider as magicians the bone-setters whose art does not claim dependence on the supernatural.

As an example of modern magic, we may quote the French newspaper LE FIGARO, January 23 1959: *Le Mans*, "The jury in La Sarthe has yesterday sentenced I. G. to 5 years in jail, for she had, under the pretext of conjuring a spell, obliged her brother, 18 years old, to swallow a large quantity of corrosive salt. M. died after a few seconds from suffocation. Before the sentence, Mr. Vaissiere, the defense-attorney, gave a compassionate plea for his client."

2. DREADFUL KINDS.

Some kinds of sorcery and superstition are simply expensive disasters for patrons, who should be glad if nothing worse happens. An example of this type is enough. In 1856, the court of summary jurisdiction in Bourges sentenced, under the name of "The Somnambulist Healer of Charost", the woman Petit. Here is one of her prescriptions: "Go to Sainte Solange (Cher), on April the 24th; take a bath in holy water at 4 a.m. Stay in this bath for 18 minutes; then, go to a warm bed and stay in it for 6 hours. Take a bottle of 30 year old wine, melt 11 small white sugar statues of female saints in this wine, boil all of it, and drink it at prescribed times."

Other kinds are more dangerous for the patrons' health, because of the medicine used by the practitioners: spider stock, grease of Christians, scrapings of human skulls, distilled juice of the brain of a hanged man. As for a handbook, there is the "Small Albert" and the "Great Albert". Some famous proceedings during Louis XIV's reign attest to it, and the king himself, without being aware of it, drank such mixtures.

Others finally may lead to murder. The practitioner at first looks for the origin of the spell cast upon the patient. For that purpose, he uses several techniques of divination, the most serious of which consists of recognizing the face of the "enemy" in a water pail. Then, he proceeds to break the spell. Finally, if it is required, he punishes the person supposed to be the cause of the evil.

For this purpose, he may resort to *imitative magic*. The magician believes that, if he cuts, or hurts an image or a puppet representing the "enemy," he imposes on the enemy a similar wound. If he decides to occasion a tumor in the head, he makes a dough puppet, the head of which he perforates with a nail before putting it into the oven. It is better if, previously, he has inserted a piece of the enemy's garment into the puppet. If he wants the "enemy" to suffer all life long, he buries the puppet in a cemetery, or in an oven, a slaughter-house, or casts it into a well.

Of course, the magician may use more efficient devices than mere symbol. It may happen that a sorcerer is an expert in poison. It has been related that a sorcerer excited a snake with a piece of garment containing the enemy's smell (the snake and the piece of garment were put together in a box which was exposed to fire for a while). The sorcerer, then, let the snake go at the suitable time, when the "enemy" was passing by.

Leaders of wolves, when they were not legendary, seemed to have used means involving nothing supernatural, simply hides of female animals in heat. Sometimes the "evil eye," or a threat, are sufficient. Frightened, the victim plays the game, and executes point by point that from which she feels hopelessly unable to escape. Terrorized, she gives up and dies, sometimes in the very circumstances foreseen by the magician.

Sometimes, in return, the sorcerer becomes the victim, as the numerous sorcery court proceedings in the past centuries give evidence. For instance, in 1616, three sorcerers in Sancerrois (Cher) were sentenced to make an apology before the church in Brecy (Cher), only in their night shirt, with a burning torch in their hand, then were hanged. Their bodies had to be burnt, and the ashes cast to the wind. Three others perished in Paris on Place de Greve.

These violent reactions find their explanation in the fact that sorcery had turned into a social plague, and everybody, even the victims, believed in it. In addition, the devil was regarded as playing a role in it. Usually, the Church acted with more prudence and circumspection than people today imagine. In any case, the ecclesiastical inquirer was satisfied with acquiring the information belonging to the religious domain. But sorcery was considered a social crime, and its practice was repressed by social pressure. Obsession with sorcery influenced the mind, and, by reaching a high degree of tension, was able to carry out dreadful consequences. In this regard, we can admit that, when Voltaire discredited sorcery proceedings, he contributed to destroy sorcery itself, and thus served a good cause.

## 3. Benign forms of bygone superstitions

In New Guinea, as it was told, if you wish to conquer the soul of a girl, take some earth in her foot prints, fry it in oil, and say: - "I burn the liver, the heart, the feelings of my beloved girl, so that she becomes burning, madly enamored of me, and she burns as this sand burns."

In Berry (France), the girl who wants to get married looks into a pail of water, on the feast of St. John, and sees her future groom's face on the surface which, after being stirred, turns still again. The groom can do the same in order to know his future bride.

Sacred objects themselves become magical agents. Baptism is not only the way to become a Christian, but also a necessary condition for the efficiency of the healer-woman's work when she breaks the spell binding a child. Gospel texts are recited over people for several reasons which are not all unworthy. But the assistant priest in Saint-Marcel (Indre, in Berry), who had sworn he would never indulge himself in such a ministry, fearing he might offend his pastor, felt obliged to recite 70 gospel texts over only one person representing his whole village!

Often in Notre Dame of Chateauroux, the priests found in their mail-box the equivalent of a $5 note and a letter asking them to "do a journey" (pilgrimage) to Our Lady in their own church with the given intention, usually to pray for a healing. Nothing here deserves any reproach. But, since this type of "journey" was often prescribed by a healer-woman together with other things, it was not free from superstition. Often "journeys" to saints were attached to quaint religious customs. These saints, especially the healing saints, are not as holy as their divine Master. They preserve something of the small deities or geniuses of pagan antiquity. They are irritable, fanciful, hard to please. But, if they are given the prescribed worship, they may become benevolent and use their power in healing the disease depending on their specialty. When somebody is ill, the first thing to do, therefore, is to diagnose "what saint is angry with them." After this diagnosis, the patient makes a "journey" to this saint, or sends a representative to its sanctuary.

Here is, for your convenience, a list of the healer saints in Berry: Saint Anna in Nohant-en-Vic for nurses lacking milk because she suckled the Holy Virgin; Saint Apolline for toothaches because in her martyrdom her teeth were extracted; Saint Eutrop for dropsical subjects ; Saint Aignan for people suffering from hair diseases (play on words in French: saint-Aignan for the "teigneux"); Saint Orban for the eye tumors (Orban = orbillons, a play on words); the precious blood in Neuvy-Saint-Sepulcre for nose-bleeding; Saint Aout for hearing (Aout = "ouie", or "hearing", a play on words); Saint Clara for the sight ("clear" for "Clara"); Saint Genou for gout (a disease in knees); Saint Phalier and Saint Greluchon in case of impotence. Saint Acaire is invoked for bad tempered women (Acaire = "acariatre", "peevish"); but Saint Raboni may "rabonnir" or "better" impatient husbands ; Saint Langouret for languors (aching) ; Saint Firmin for fever which makes your legs flinch (Firmin = "firm") ; Saint Fiacre for piles ("fics") ; Saint Marin and his wet cap for "rechignoux", or whimpering children. In case of doubt, you may order a Mass of the Holy Spirit or of all the saints.

As an example of a pilgrimage to a saint, once upon a time there was a little child discontented and moody. His parents took him to St. Marin, a holy place near Argenton-sur-Creuse. They first washed the woolen cap of the child in the chilly water of the holy fountain, and put it on the head of the stony statue of St. Marin. Then, they read the prayer written on a wooden pannel, at the feet of the saint. Finally, they put the cap back on the head of the child --who miraculously ceased murmuring. The healing had a lasting effect since one warning was enough in case of the child's relapse: "Back to St. Marin?"

### 4. THE DEFEAT OF SORCERY AND SUPERSTITION.

The advent of science, especially of medicine, largely contributed to discredit these practices. The modernization of life in the country also changed the mentality which supported them. The development of large towns, uprooting billions of people, destroyed among the population any ideas that were bound to local superstions. We may say that these forms of sorcery and magic have almost completely vanished today, and we cannot regret it.

But is the disappearance of sorcery and superstition the effect of a development towards the better in the mentality of people, i.e., according to the principles of the Bible and of the Gospel? If it is merely a surrender to change and necessity, and not an improvement of the moral conscience, then we are only expected to cope with new perils. For instance, the material, quasi-magical powers of science and technology today, which morality can hardly control, heavily influence the future which threatens us. And we cannot, of course, as the past generations did with their sorcerers, burn the scientists or the political leaders which possess these dangerous powers.

## RELIGION IN PREHISTORIC MAGIC.

In prehistoric magic we find almost everything we mentioned about ancient and medieval sorcery. However, we should avoid unfavorably judging the people in prehistoric times. We perceive in their magic, closely mixed with lower forms of science and philosophy that are presently obsolete and even shameful, a positive value: the slow acquisition of the main elements of religious thought. And, for this reason, we must study them with a friendly spirit, and not with the approach of an inquisitor. We must understand that truth has come from error, or rather from darkness, as a statue comes from marble, or metal from ore. Axe and chisel have, little by little, changed the rough marble rock into the more and more perfect shape of the statue.

In a similar way, religious thought has developed under divine influence. Our forerunners in those remote ages have shared in the gigantic fight for good and evil, and prepared for their children better times. In their spiritual effort they are near to us, and we love them.

### 1. RELIGION IN THE EARLIEST TIMES.

The only evidence of religion (in the spiritual sense) we may ask the earliest people for is reflection and intelligence. Our documents from such remote ages are necessarily poor, and when they do exist their interpretation is difficult. Even burial rites - the most obvious evidence of primitive religion - are testimonies wrapped in much darkness. But what would, indeed, people think of our civilization, if they only had as evidence remnants of cemeteries, foundations of a few buildings, and heaps of garbage? Often also, wealthy monuments in our cemeteries reflect less faith than the simple mostly vanished tombs of the middle-ages or of past generations. Even the presence of signs of worship, shrines and idols is misleading. Authentic religion may have existed without expressed doctrines and defined rites, apart from, or independently of material objects of worship.

Here I mean by "religion" a mode of thinking, earlier than, or parallel with, the settled religions, which distinguishes between right and wrong, or good and evil. Even if it is the law of the clan, it imposes itself as obedience to moral duty and conscience. Whatever were the simple or differentiated, rough or purified forms of this obedience, it had a religious character. Its most suitable name would be "natural religion," which does not exclude a supernatural dimension.

The crossing of the moral threshold is the bridge of spiritual and religious life, and this crossing is possible with the possession of the power of reflection. As soon as persons enjoy reflection, they can raise themselves to the level of moral activity, and reach some implicit or explicit knowledge of God involved therein. Then, they have become what we mean by a "religious animal." However, I do not mean that the moral and religious dimensions of humanity appeared at the same time as reflection.

In the epoch of Pithecanthropus, a form of religion may have existed which reminds us of some present primitives. According to W. Schmidt, C. A. Blanc, Abbe Breuil, etc., the selection of the skulls in Chou-Kou-Tien near Pekin (Sinanthropus), and particularly the trepanation ( seemingly a mark of cannibalistic mutilation) which these skulls presented, are evidence of a burial rite and therefore of religion, but this thesis is accepted only with much caution.

In the stage of Neanderthal, funeral rites are unquestionable. The skeletons of Le Moustier, La Chapelle-aux-saints, La Feyrassie, had received an intentional burial. The tomb had been dug and covered with stone deposits. Tools were added at Le Moustier, and even, at La Chapelle-aux-saints, a thigh of a reindeer and a leg of a bull. At La Feyrassie, seven cups dug in the rock also attest to a funeral rite. Furthermore, these skeletons are oriented according to the solar axis. They are bent back in an unnatural position (La Feyrassie). G. de Mortillet noted that, "as soon as religious ideas appear, funeral rites also appear."

## 2. Funeral worship in the age of the caves.

Intentional burials with tools, weapons, ornaments, bent position of the skeleton, its orientation according to the solar axis, funeral offerings, reappear in the later epochs, in the age of caves or of reindeer, with the type of Cro-Magnon. We can mention the caves of Grimaldi, les Eysies, Laugerie Basse, Urithi (in the Landes), La Combe-Capelle, Chancelade, etc. Prof. Testut compares the position of the skeleton in Chancelade with that of some Peruvian mummies. He writes, "This man also (Chancelade) could have been submitted to a similar treatment, bent back over himself, firmly bound with ropes or flexible reeds, or even sewn in a hide bag." This mode of burial is found among many ancient and modern peoples, particularly among present Eskimos.

## 3. Funeral worship in the Neolithic and Bronze Age.

A study of the burials belonging to this epoch revealed customs found among the primitives of our time. The tribes characterized by the tulip-shaped ceramic of the Michelberg pattern buried their dead, either alone, or a few together, seated and drawn up, under the ground of their huts. This astonishing position shows that they have been bound, probably soon after death. By this, people proposed to prevent the spirits of the dead from coming and troubling the living. Fear of a corpse contact, and maybe also the worship of the ancestors, occasioned the twice-made burial. In the first ceremony, the body was allowed to lose flesh ; long afterwards, the bones of one or of a few dead were gathered together in the same place, a kind of bone-receptacle, such as our dolmen (prehistoric monuments in the form of huge stone tables) are. These places of burial became sacred places. If the dead person was buried in his/her hut, this hut was burnt, and the place was considered as the indwelling of invisible powers.

Dolmens are not necessarily or only tombs of chiefs. Their exact meaning was probably very complex, and is far from being perfectly known. The thousands of *tumuli* (small artificial hills) are usually collective burials. Often they are surrounded by a deep ditch, which isolated the dwelling of the living from that of the dead. Important furniture was deposited with the bodies. The dead went to their tomb with their jewelry and their weapons (broken or folded to become harmless to the living), and even with some food at hand or placed in a pot near their feet.

For instance, the wonderful bronze *situlae* and *oenochoae* (pitchers) imported from Greece in the Hallstadt tumuli served this purpose. Probably also funeral offerings were brought and sacrifices performed over these tombs (dolmen or *tumuli*), because large fire-places are found thereon. We can therefore assume that the purpose of these offerings and sacrifices was to maintain the existence of the dead in the hereafter.

### 4. Magic of destruction and hunting.

A fact strikes the thoughtful visitor as one enters the painted caves of Altamira, Niaux, Fond-de-Gaume, Le Tuc d'Angoubert, Les Trois Freres,etc. These paintings are found, not only far from the entrance, but often beyond difficult passageways. Therefore, these works of art were not destined to be seen by all the members of the tribe, but were reserved to a few initiated, and a preoccupation with secrets and mystery dominated their creation.

These caves were not museums, but sanctuaries. When the earliest discoveries of prehistoric paintings took place, the first impression was an admiration for their artistic quality, and they were simply considered as a proof of pure love of art. But a deeper study revealed that this art was utilitarian. The paintings in the caves were works belonging to imitative magic. The fact of painting, carving, or drawing an animal was the first procedure for hunting this animal.

The people of the caves believed in the existence in each being, in addition to material and visible form, of an immaterial counterpart, a spirit, a soul (if we do not confer on these words their philosophical modern meaning). This counterpart could be caught through its picture, and people thought that the harm done to its picture affected the same animal represented there. We find in this case the well known technique of charming, such as we observed in ancient and modern sorcery. It is therefore possible to say that the paintings and drawings of the prehistoric caves are magic works, destined to make easier and surer the possession of the desired game. As an evidence, the pictured animals are often pierced with an arrow, covered with wounds, or mutilated.

### 5. Magic of fecundity.

Besides destructive magic, there was a magic of fecundity. Some paintings offer neither arrow nor marks of mutilation. And the animals do not appear individually, but in couples, with the difference of sex very strongly marked. The clay bisons at Le Tuc d'Audoubert, the bull and the cow at Le Fourneau-au-Diable, the reindeers scenting one another at Teyjat, the horse and the mare at Le Rock-de-Sers, belong to the magic of fecundity. The hunter of the age of reindeer tried by such representations to increase the multiplication of his game by compelling the natural forces of fecundity, in which he believed, to work for him.

This magic was also applied on the human level. There were initiation rites performed on young people, for instance the initiation dance which apparently took place in the cave of Le Tuc d'Audoubert, and which is found also in some modern primitive societies. In this section are to be classified many representations of sexual organs, and the famous female statues called "Venus," which have been found from the Ural to the Pyrenees. On these statues, the features of motherhood are strongly exaggerated in order to show the importance people granted to motherhood for the prosperity of the tribe.

In the epoch of dolmens, the belief in a great Mother-Goddess of fecundity developed, the worship of whom seems to have been almost universal. Very stylized figures, often reduced to the form of an anchor, are seen on dolmens in Brittany. This Mother-Goddess was apparently also the protectress of the tombs and the guardian of the souls of the dead, to whom perhaps she promised a new birth. In addition, she was given the task of making the land fertile. This Great Mother's religion lies at the source of the Creatan, Egyptian, Phoenician and Babylonian paganism. The Bible had to cope with this worship. The religion of the Great Mother continued during the first centuries of Christianity in the mystery religions.

### 6. Solar worship.

The worship of the sun, which is the basis of the Egyptian religion, probably existed as early as the epoch of dolmens. The megalithic laying out of *menhirs* (erected stones) in the form of a *cromlech* (crown) and of a straight path oriented according to the solar axis were apparently gigantic temples of the sun. This solar worship might have been associated with a worship of the dead and the presence of tombs. The secret of this religion is perhaps to be found in the significance of the Egyptian temples, the arrangement of which is similar and suggests many common features.

Many megalithic monuments are covered with cups, bowls and basins cut into the rock. The stone of Ilkey (County of York) presents several of these cups, surrounded by concentric circles. Often these cups seem to go back to a more remote antiquity. The discs of burnt clay found in the district of Gard and of Aude are earlier than dolmens. In the reindeer age the tombs are usually oriented according to the solar axis. On the contrary, in the lake-dwelling tribes and in the bronze age, skeletons are oriented in any direction, but the burials are often collective, and the general shape of a *tumulus* is a circle. This arrangement may present the form of rays starting from the center, and thus suggest a solar worship. Like the course of the sun, human life has its orient and its occident, and everybody wished that, after the night of death, like the sun they might know the morning of a new birth.

### 7. The prehistoric spiritualist mentality.

The reindeer-age hunter believed in a certain hereafter, an apparently vague form of survival, but one that supposed a continuity of the soul for sometime. He believed in the existence of supernatural powers. There is no evidence, however, he had arrived at the idea of a supreme Being, presiding over nature and life, unique and almighty. Apparently, like some modern uncivilized tribes, he believed in the existence of spirits: the reindeer's spirit, the bison's spirit, the bear's spirit, etc., and the human spirit as well. He tried to convince, calm, or tame these spirits, both those belonging to the living or the dead, and especially, it appears, those of the dead. This concern explains both the honors paid to the departed, and the surprising security measures taken against them (corpse tied up, ditch dug around a *tumulus*, bronze sword broken and iron sword folded). The sorcerer was entrusted with this mission of dealing with spirits in the tribe, and he enjoyed a power parallel to that of the chief, whom the sorcerer provided with advice and guidance.

This religious form of the belief in the spirits is known as ANIMISM. Can we say that these people believed in God? They did not possess a purified notion of the deity, but, all around them was a world full of supernatural beings. They were SPIRITUALISTS.

With the beginning of agriculture, people lost something of their regard for the spirit of animals. They learned to domesticate certain animals, and regarded them as their servants, soon denying them the possession of a spirit, and granting themselves the monopoly of spirit. On the other hand, they realized the importance of natural forces, especially that of the sun, which is the source of all fecundity. As a consequence, people worshipped the sun, and also the moon, the stars, and the elements.

However, the privileged position granted to the sun inclined the thought of people towards the idea of a unique God, of an almighty Creator, the author and ruler of everything. For instance, Pharaoh Akenaton adored the sun, indeed, but under the form of its disk, its immaterial element. But the Bible reduced the sun to the level of a creature, and prescribed the adoration of the Creator of the universe and of the Creator of the sun itself.

## CONCLUSION

The people of prehistoric times may be granted the merit of discovering the main truths of religion: God's existence, the survival of the soul, the spiritual nature of the soul itself. Their animism, magic, idolatry were apparently closely mixed with these discoveries, but we cannot reproach them with the imperfection of their notions. Justice, on the contrary, leads us to pay them homage for the elements of truth they acquired for us.

However, to maintain these lower forms of religion after the coming of the biblical revelation --as the pagan religion and the medieval sorcery have done-- is nonsense. To remain in these poor ideas and practices is to sin against the spirit. Not to surpass our forerunners is to be unfaithful to their effort and to betray them. We are, therefore, morally obliged to rebuke all kinds of idolatry and magic, of sorcery and superstition. We belong to the religion of the Decalogue, which we may consider as culminating in the evangelical law of love.

The biblical struggle for the moral way of serving God, which led to the Decalogue, should always remind us of the danger of regarding morality as a trivial part of religion --a kind of "profane," or "civil" religion--and of pursuing pure philosophy, or, on the contrary, of considering that worship and the accomplishment of ritual is enough. Without faith and morality, even our sacraments are nothing but illusion and magic.

Isaiah reminds us of the importance of justice toward others, since God refuses to listen to those who neglect this essential duty and suppose that they can please God with sacrifices and prayers:

> The offer of your gifts is useless, the reek of sacrifice is abhorrent to me. New moons ans sabbaths and assemblies, I cannot edure. I cannot tolerate your new moons and your festivals; they have become a burden to me, and I can put up with them no longer, I will hide my eyes from you. Though you offer countless prayers, I will not listen. There is blood on your hands; wash away the evil of your deeds, away out of my sight. Cease to do evil and learn to do right, pursue justice and champion the oppressed; give the orphan his rights, plead the widow's cause.[18]

Early Christianity pleaded their own cause against the pagan persecutors by showing that they were good neighbors and good citizens because they believed in the judgment of God, and because their goal was to reach perfection. They gave evidence of their courage in martyrdom, modesty, charity, and they worshipped the only real God, the one who cannot be deceived.[19]

## QUESTIONNAIRE

1. Give a definition of religion, superstition, idolatry, magic, sorcery, a spell, exorcism, taboo, totem, omen, astrology, a medium.

2. Mention practices of idolatry and of magic noted or condemned in the Bible.

---

[18] Isaiah 1:12-17.

[19] JUSTIN, *1 Apology*; ATHENAGORAS, *A Plea for the Christians.*

3. Why were magic practices considered as offending God? Give several reasons.

4. Is there in U.S.A. an interest in horoscopes, prophecy, omens, fortune-tellers, astrology, etc.? Do you know of interesting cases of those who make such predictions?

5. Is there today a form of superstition or of magic of a half-scientific type, for instance, abuse of medicine, success of healers, exaggerated fear of germs? Do you know the novel, *Dr. Knox* ? Do people today simply laugh at the devil?

6. What might have been the religion of Pithecanthropus or of Neanderthal? funny? serious? conscious? unconscious?

7. What is animism? How can you explain that a civilization of farmers might bring about the end of animism which was a "religion" of hunters and, to some extent, of cattle-breeders?

8. Are children naturally "animist"? Give examples of their personifying things or animals.

9. For what reasons were the dead granted honors, food, sometimes weapons?

10. Do many today believe in re-incarnations, or other forms of survival? Do you know people who believe in ghosts?

11. What devices would people in the past use for diagnosing a disease, or the author of a spell, or a secret love?

12. What is "imitative magic"? Give examples of it from prehistoric times and from recent sorcery regarding magic of destruction and magic of fecundity? Is it a beginning of science?

13. Mention examples of solar worship in prehistoric times and in antiquity. Was it a progress over animism? Was it genuine religion?

14. Should we take a position of hard criticism and of contempt against ancient magic? Or should we rather consider it as an imperfect development of science, philosophy, and theology, accompanied by a suitable ritual? Was it effective? Can we consider magic and sorcery today as respectable?

15. What is the difference between "sacrament" and "magic"? Are our sacraments sometimes understood as magic? Give examples.

16. Can we consider the data of these ancient cultures and forms of religion (the theory of the "patterns" of Carl Jung) as liable to

reappear today under the form of dreams, poetry, strange reactions, sometimes carrying along some meaningful message?

17. What is the message of the prophet Isaiah in his first chapter?

18. Is worship, or ethics, the more important feature in our religion?

20. Can certain people serve God adequately through ethical life only?

## BIBLIOGRAPHY

FRAZER, Sir James George. *The Golden Bough: A Study in Magic and Religion.* 1 vol. abbridged. New York: Macmillan, 1950.

HAWKES, Jacquetta. *Prehistory.* Cf. Bibliography ch.1.

LAISNEL DE LA SALLE. *Souvenirs du vieux temps. Le Berry.* 2 vol. Collection: *Les littératures populaires de toutes les nations.* Paris: G.P. Maisonneuve & Larose. Vol.I, pp.383-412.

RUSSELL, Jeffrey Burton. *Witchcraft in the Middle-Ages.* Ithaca: Cornell, 1972.

# CHAPTER III

# THE EGYPTIAN BOOK OF THE DEAD AND BIBLICAL HOPE

The four major questions which every one should raise and answer are: -Who are you? -Where are you from? -Where are you going to? and, -How are you going there? The two latter questions lead us to raise the problem of the hereafter. If everything vanishes for us when we die, then religion, morality and duty lose much of their importance. Saint Paul even writes, "If it is only for the present life that we have put our hope in Christ,we are the most unfortunate amongst men... If the dead do not rise again, let us then eat and drink because tomorrow we shall die!"[20]

Atheistic materialism, provides humanity with a goal, which is either individual earthly happiness, or collective earthly welfare, but there is nothing in it above humanity, and nothing after death. Christianity, also, promises humanity a hope and goal, which are eternal happiness in the company of God. According to the Christian faith, the way to reach this goal is the practice of the moral good as taught in the Commandments and the Gospels.

However, the people of Israel in the Bible did not conceive of this hope all at once or immediately in a perfect manner. They had to fight the temptation of despair inspired by Babylonian skepticism. They also had to oppose the insidious temptation of illusion and error represented by the Egyptian dream about the hereafter. Without going dangerously aside to the right or to the left and because of their fidelity to God, the people of the Bible succeeded in deepening and enlightening this hope with the help of divine inspiration. The adventure of this tenuous hope in Israel until its marvelous transfiguration in Jesus is a wonderful story. The efforts devoted to its preservation make it more invaluable. We must thank divine providence for having spared us the temptations of the ancient Jews, and for having received this hope far more developed and evident. The danger which we can recognize in the Egyptian novel about the hereafter incites us to understand, perhaps excuse, the great discretion of the Bible concerning things after death, and to see it as an additional merit of the Scriptures.

## THE EGYPTIAN MYTHS OF RA AND OF OSIRIS

### 1. The wealth of ancient Egyptian literature.

---

[20] I Cor. 15:19, 32.

We inherit from ancient Egypt a copious literature, consisting of mythological texts, of popular tales, of wisdom writings, of religious hymns, of funeral rituals, etc. This literature is written on papyrus, and preserved in coffins, or painted on the walls of the funeral monuments, or engraved on the columns of the temples. The most interesting part of it is represented by the *Book of the Dead*.

The Egyptians seem to have progressed very far into philosophy and theology. According to certain scholars, we are only repeating what they said before us, and even our metaphysical speculations concerning the Trinity find antecedents in the theology of the Egyptian priests.

However, the chief preoccupation of ancient Egypt certainly was the destiny of the dead and the problem of the hereafter. The Egyptians considered the present life upon earth as only an episode of the adventure of our destiny, and believed that it was of the highest interest to obtain blessed immortality. In order to attain to this end, they relied on two great myths, those of Ra and of Osiris, both going back to the earliest Egypt, i.e., to the 4th millennium B.C.

## 2. The Myth of Osiris.

Leaving aside the variants of this myth, we present it, in summation, under its essential and most largely known form.[21] Osiris was the son of Geb, the God of the earth, and of Nout, the goddess of the starred heaven. From Ra, his grandfather, the Sun-God, Ruler of the earth, Osiris inherited the kingdom of Egypt. His older brother, Seth, an incarnation of violence, became inflamed with envy against him, and proposed to rob him of his crown. At a banquet, he presented him with a wonderfully crafted chest, and said, "This chest will belong to him who fits it exactly." Osiris, accepting the gamble without distrust, laid himself down in it, but his enemies all at once ran and closed the cover of the chest, nailed it firmly, and threw the coffin into the Nile. The Nile carried the coffin down to the sea, and the sea left it on the beach in Byblos, a colony of Egypt in Phoenicia, under a tamarisk tree.

The tree, growing, enveloped the coffin in its trunk. The king of Byblos hewed the tree and turned it into a column for his palace. But, instructed of the wonderful characteristics of the column made of this tree, Isis, the widow of Osiris, asked the king of Byblos for this column, and had him offer it to her. Inside the column, she found the coffin and the body of her husband. Bringing it back to Egypt, she hid the corpse in the marshlands of Bouto, but Seth, the usurper of the throne, who was hunting near this place, found it, and cut it into 14 pieces

---

[21] Any pruning and striving toward a clear understanding in such matters requires some systematization.

which he scattered all around. Mourning over her husband, Isis went and searched for the remnants, assisted by her son Horus, her sister Nephtis, her scribe Toth, and the jackal Anubis. She succeeded in gathering the scattered limbs, and in reconstructing, except for one part, the body of her husband. She maintained the body by putting it in a tight clothing of white wrappings. Horus proved to be the avenger of his father's death, and the court of the gods judged him right against Seth. He finally inherited his father's kingdom, whereas Seth reigned over the empire of the dead.

Osiris stands somehow in Egypt for what Jesus means for us: he was the dead and resurrected god and king. From him all the kings of Egypt, his grandsons, and, at a later epoch, all the deceased, hoped to obtain salvation and immortality.

### 3. The Myth of Ra.

The myths of Osiris and that of Ra are the basis of the Egyptian religion. Ra is the sun. Every day, Ra appears in the East, passes in his boat through the twelve regions of heaven, and finally vanishes in the West. But he continues his journey under the earth through the empire of the dead. There, he meets with Osiris, the "king with the heart that stopped beating." Then, he progresses westward through the region of Douat under the earth. He crosses the place of Amenti, where is found the palace of Osiris. Then, he crosses the region of Restau, which is full of dangerous monsters. Going from cave to cave in his boat, or sometimes on a sled, Ra gives his light successively for one hour to all the inhabitants of Hades. Finally, he rises again as in a kind of new birth from the East, in order to perform a new procession over the earth.

The boat of Ra is the conveyance for the dead, and his path is the way of the soul, the itinerary of salvation. Blessed are those who, after death, accompany Ra on his journey, for they possess the hope of enjoying together with Ra the bliss of eternal life.

### 4. The Use of the Myth of Osiris to the Advantage of the Dead.

The mysteries of Osiris were celebrated in the secrecy of the temples, like a liturgy, and were reserved to a small number of initiated. However, some of the episodes were represented outside, in popular feasts. In Bouto, for instance, a battle took place between the partisans of Horus and those of Seth. Herodotus speaks of real fights where there were wounded people.

Inside the temple, the priests played the part of the characters of the myth. The drama consisted of 24 scenes which came successively at every hour of the day and night. Isis was mourning. Clothed in a leopard's hide, a priest enacted the resurrection of Osiris, pouring libations of Nile water before his statue, raising the statue up, and performing the act of opening its mouth, nostrils, eyes and ears again, and restoring its heart to life. This daily resurrection of Osiris through liturgical rites was considered as very important for the welfare of Osiris himself, for the destiny of human souls, and for the support of life in the world. In order not to grow old and die from the "second death," that of annihilation, Osiris himself needed to be constantly given food and kept young through liturgical means.

The daily maintainance of Osiris was necessary for the welfare of the king who succeeded him on the throne of Egypt and for the salvation of the dead over whom Osiris was now reigning in the hereafter.

Osiris was also a god of fecundity: his body is usually represented painted in green, the color of growing wheat. As a frequent symbol of Osiris, we see on the paintings a pot filled with earth, where wheat has been sown and is growing. In a sense, Osiris was the land of Egypt itself, the fertility of which was as precious as it was precarious.

Mummification could be called "Osirification," for the dead became a new Osiris. In earliest times, only the Pharaoh enjoyed mummification; then, a few high officials partook of this privilege. "Osirification," reserved to kings and to great figures during the ancient Empire, was vulgarized about 2500 B.C., as a consequence of political and social changes. Afterwards, everybody was allowed to share in it.

Herodotus writes:

> As regards mourning and funerals, when a distinguished man dies, all the women of the household plaster their heads and faces with mud, then, leaving the body indoors, perambulate the town with the dead man's female relatives, their dresses fastened with a girdle and beating themselves like the women. The ceremony over, they take the body to be embalmed. Embalming is a distinct profession. The embalmers, when a body is brought to them, produce specimen models in wood, painted to resemble nature, and graded in quality; the best and most expensive kind is said to represent (Osiris); the next is somewhat inferior and cheaper, while the third is cheapest of all...The brain...then the contents of the abdomen are removed...The body sewn again is placed in natrum, covered entirely over for seventy days - never longer. When this period, which must not be exceeded, is over, the body is washed and then wrapped from head to foot in linen cut into strips and smeared on the under side with gum, which is commonly used by the Egyptians

> instead of glue. The case is then sealed up and stored in a sepulchral chamber, upright against the wall.[22]

As we observe, these funeral rites repeat the details of the myth of Osiris. The mummies, indeed, are new Osirises.

5. THE USE OF THE MYTH OF RA FOR THE ADVANTAGE OF THE DEAD.

After death, the soul - which the Egyptians call *kah*, or "copy" - is admitted onto the boat of Ra, the Sun-God, in the West. The soul passes in his company through the kingdom of Hades, and is born again together with him in the East in order to enjoy in his company a new crossing through the sky. Such is the way of immortality and deification.

This blessed immortality, however, is not easily achieved. An elaborate liturgy must be performed in order to overcome, through magical devices, every harmful power, and to secure the help of every favorable one. The experts who practiced embalming performed these rites carefully. They recited many magic formulas, and made many determined gestures. On their accurate accomplishment depended the success of the whole operation, and, consequently, the salvation of the deceased person. The *Book of the Dead* consists of this liturgy.

## THE BOOK OF THE DEAD.[23]

The *Book of the Dead* is a collection of liturgical texts recited over the deceased and often deposited in the coffin or engraved on the walls of the tombs. These texts are granted a magical power and destined to assist the soul in finding her way and in defending herself in the hereafter. The whole book consists 190 chapters. Of course, a particular tomb only contains a certain number of these chapters.

Thanks to these written formulas, the soul of the deceased one becomes the master of her destiny. She is enabled to avoid the common fate, i.e., the second death of complete annihilation. Through these rites, the soul becomes a deity.

But, for the success of this whole operation, it is important to break the first link in the chain of fate.

---

[22] Herodotus, *Histories* (Baltimore: Penguin Classics, 1965), 2:86-87.

[23] To some extent we follow the interpretation of the ritual of the dead given in his Introduction by Gregoire Kolpaktchy, *Livre des Morts des anciens Egyptiens* (Paris, 1954), pp.1-50.

1. MAKING A BODY INCORRUPTIBLE.

In order to oppose the forces of fate, which aim at the annihilation of the human being, it is necessary to preserve the body itself from corruption and destruction. For this purpose, the ancient Egyptians built "dwellings of eternity" from which the deceased would behold "billions of years." Pyramids and necropolises must not be ephemeral like the houses of the living, but indestructible.

The mummies themselves were prepared for being everlasting, and statues were added in case of destruction, carved in the hardest of rocks, black diorite or red granite, immobile, eternal, their back and head making one piece with the wall, and their limbs with the rest of the body. Without the preservation of her body, or at least of a material image representing it, how could a soul avoid the loss of her human experience, and receive the assistance expected from children and grandchildren?

2. THE MAINTENANCE OF THE LIFE OF THE SOUL IN THE HEREAFTER.

a) *Through offerings.*

After caring for the preservation of the body, it was necessary to perpetuate the soul herself. As Horus was the funeral priest for his father Osiris, the eldest son, in an Egyptian family, was the funeral priest of his father. When he was performing this office, he wore the leopard's hide over his shoulder. He brought offerings to the tomb, and performed the prescribed libations. Often the deceased had destined the income from property for that purpose. Unfortunate, indeed, was the soul deprived, for her sustenance in the hereafter, of the "copy" of the material offerings which were the symbols of a deeper reality.

The funeral priest performed upon a statue of the deceased person the Osirian rites of the opening of mouth, eyes, nostrils, ears, and the restoration of the heart. Thereby the soul became able to pursue her destiny in the hereafter.

b) *Through figurines and paintings of magical nature.*

The paintings of the Egyptian tombs which show scenes of contemporary life are actually magical paintings. Their purpose was to provide the deceased person with the pleasures of life which were lost at death, namely, food, support and happiness.

But the tombs also contain figurines of servants, of deities, etc. These figurines were deposited according to certain rites known through the rubrics of the *Book of the Dead*. They were meant to enable the deceased person to overcome enemies in the hereafter, to please favorable deities, even to evade the tiring works to which this person might be submitted in subterranean Egypt, for instance, removing sand on the borders of the Nile.

c) *Through magic formulas.*

The souls of the deceased owe their salvation to the possession of magic formulas which can be used as passports when they meets the infernal deities, and enable them to go through dangerous passageways undamaged.

Here are a few titles of these formulas: In order "to escape massacres," "to repel the crocodile-headed gods," "to cast out the snake gods," "to prevent the deceased one's head from being cut off," in order "not to die from the second death."

Some of these formulas are incantations destined to provide the deceased with power and life, and with knowledge of the path to be followed: in order "to breathe," "to obtain power over waters," "not to be scalded in drinking water in the subterranean world," "to master enemies," "to make one's way in the lower world," "to orient oneself towards Heliopolis," "to open the gates of heaven," "to permit the soul to enter her tomb."

Once made free through death from bodily limitations, and without having lost the advantage of earthly experience, the dead person somehow becomes a new-born again. As a baby, this person may in principle become everything she wishes. Let us say: a king, a pope, or a beggar! Through death, as through a new birth, is acquired the power of *metamorphosis*. One may change at will into any kind of being. Here are some titles corresponding to these metamorphoses: in order "to change one's form at will," "to change oneself into a golden hawk," "into a royal phoenix," "into a living soul," "into a serpent." There are, of course, formulas enabling the dead to accompany Ra in his journeys above and below the earth: in order "to drive a boat in the hereafter," "to voyage in the boat of Ra."

## THE NEGATIVE CONFESSION

### 1. Osiris' tribunal.

Chapter 125 is the most important in the *Book of the Dead* and deserves a special treatment. The soul has come to the region where Osiris' palace stands. Here takes place the most crucial scene of the soul's destiny. The soul is brought before a tribunal of 42 gods presided over by Osiris, in front of Maat, the goddess of justice and truth, and of Toth, the scribe-god who stands as a clerk. Anubis, the jackal-god, weighs on a scale the soul of the deceased. In case of condemnation, the soul is swallowed by the Eater, an old woman, or a dragon, seated before Osiris' throne, or she will be jailed in the region of Douat for an eternity of torments.

If, on the contrary, the soul does not encounter any dangerous obstacle, she becomes free, and, if actually she possesses the fitting magical formulas, she may journey in the boat of Ra, the Sun-god, through the heavens, the earth and the world under the earth, comfort the blessed, even grant the gods themselves the powers of a new youth, help the despairing, visit the farthest stars, turn at will into a bird, a flower, a serpent, etc., because she has become herself a god.

We find the scene of the judgment at the court of Osiris portrayed on the tympanon panels of the Last Judgment of our cathedrals, and in our popular teaching about hell.

In chapter 125 of the *Book of the Dead*, we find the most outstanding text of ancient Egyptian literature: the NEGATIVE CONFESSION, which is the address given by the soul for her defense before the tribunal of Osiris:

2. THE ADDRESS TO THE COURT.

a) *Conciliation of the judges.*

> Here is the place where, his white crown on his head, the scepter of commandment in his hand, the divine Being (Osiris) stands. Arrived before him, I stop my boat, and say: "Powerful god, lord of thirst, look at me! I have just been born, I have just been born!" He answers: "On the scaffold of punishments are revealed openly your misdeeds. You know them certainly better than anyone, but I shall remind you of them.[24]

The soul is in an uncomfortable position, but she possesses in her "bag" a prepared address, which suits the circumstances, and she reads it. In the beginning, she tries to win the favor of her judges, revealing that she is akin to each of them. For instance, she answers Osiris:

> I am Ra who makes powerful those whom he loves. I am the knot of the destiny of the world, hidden inside the beautiful sacrosanct tree. If I grow, Ra grows. Observe me carefully: my hair upon my head is the very hair of god Nout. My face is the solar disk of Ra. The strength of goddess Hathor lives in my eyes. The soul of Up-Uaut sounds in both my ears. In my nostrils lies the powers of god Kenti-Khas. My two lips are the lips of Anubis. My teeth are the teeth of goddess Serkit. My neck is the neck of Goddess Isis. My two hands are the hands of the powerful god of Djedou. It is Neith, landlady of Sais, who lives in my two arms. My back-

[24] *Book of the Dead*, ch. 42, 1-3, english tr. of G. Kolpaktchy, *Livre des Morts des Anciens Egyptiens, Nouvelle Version Française avec Introduction* (Paris 1954), p. 107. Cf. Budge, *The Book of the Dead* (N.Y. 1967), p.606-07.

> bone is that of Seth. My sexual organ is that of Osiris. My liver is that of lord Ker-Aha. My breast is that of the lord of terrors. My stomach is that of goddess Seckhmet. The forces of the eyes of Horus run in my back. My legs are the legs of Nout. My feet are the feet of Ptah. My fingers are the hooks of the Hawk, the divine one, who lives for ever. In truth, there is not a limb in my body where does not abide a deity. As for Thoth, he protects my whole body. Similar to Ra, I renew myself every day. Nobody could be able to bind my arms or catch my hands: neither the gods, nor the sanctified spirits, nor the souls of the damned, nor those of the ancestors, nor the initiated, nor the angels of heaven.[25]

b) *Affirmation of the indestructible character of the human person.*

> I am he who progresses straight ahead, whose name is a mystery. I am yesterday, today, tomorrow. My name is he who beholds billions of years... My essence is hidden in my being. I am alone, alone. I travel alone the cosmic solitudes... I have molded and shaped myself by myself, and I shall not die from the second death. A few rays of my being reach your chests, but my forms, I keep them hidden in me, for I am he whom nobody knows... A triple veil hides me... I am a being surrounded by walls, in the center of a universe surrounded by walls. I am a lonely one in the center of his loneliness.[26]

Here is obviously a wonderful proclamation of personality. The individual, incommunicable character of the soul is strongly expressed. Personality is also manifested as something eternal, indestructible, quasi-divine. Actually, in ancient Egyptian thought, a human being is not basically different from a god. All these little gods, however, do not dissolve into an impersonal pantheism. They may grow old, and perhaps someday fall into nothingness, but their individual personality is expressed in the most outstanding way ever seen. Such an affirmation is to be reckoned to the honor of Egyptian thought.

THE TEXT OF THE "NEGATIVE CONFESSION."

The most delicate part of the trial is the defense of the soul before Maat, the goddess of justice and truth:

---

[25] Ch. 42, 4-12; cf. Kolpaktchy, ibid. p. 108, and Budge, ibid. p. 607-608.

[26] Ch. 42, 13-28, Kolpaktchy, ibid. pp. 109-110; Budge, ibid., pp. 609-612.

> Hail to you, great god, Lord of Justice! I have come to you, my lord, that you may bring me so that I may see your beauty, for I know you and I know your name, and I know the names of the forty-two gods of those who are with you in this Hall of Justice, who live on those who cherish evil and who gulp down their blood on that day of the rekoning of characters in the presence of Wennefer. Behold the double son of the Songstresses; Lord of Truth is your name. Behold I have come to you, I have brought you truth, I have repelled falsehood for you. I have not done falsehood against men, I have not impoverished my associates, I have done no wrong in the Place of Truth, I have not learnt that which is not, I have done no evil. I have not daily made labour in excess of what was due to be done for me, my name has not reached the offices of those who control slaves, I have not deprived the orphan of his property, I have not done what the gods detest, I have not calumniated a servant to his master, I have not caused pain, I have not made hungry, I have not made to weep, I have not killed, I have not commanded to kill, I have not made suffering for anyone, I have not lessened the food-offerings in the temples, I have not destroyed the loaves of the gods, I have not taken away the food of the spirits, I have not copulated, I have not misbehaved, I have not lessened food-supplies, I have not diminished the arouras, I have not encroached upon the fields, I have not laid anything upon the weights of the hand-balance, I have not taken anything from the plummet of the standing-scales, I have not taken the milk from the mouth of children, I have not deprived the herds of their pastures, I have not trapped the birds from the preserves of the gods, I have not caught the fish of their marshlands, I have not diverted water at its season, I have not built a dam on flowing water, I have not quenched the fire when it is burning, I have not neglected the dates for offering choice-meats, I have not withheld cattle from the god's-offerings, I have not opposed a god in his procession. I am pure, pure, pure, pure![27]

### 3. THE BEAUTY AND WEAKNESS OF THIS PROFESSION OF INNOCENCE.

This self-examination manifests a very evolved moralism in the direction of piety, social justice, and even of charity. It is to the credit of the people which created it, and it continues to be valuable for us.

---

[27] *The Ancient Book of the Dead*, tr. R. Faulkner (British Museum Publications, 1985), Spell 125, p.29.

However, in spite of its beauty, this profession of innocence apparently does not impose on men a genuine moral effort. The *Book of the Dead* uses this profession of innocence as a trick of magic. What it suggests is that the soul should have it in her possession and pull it from her "bag" at the right moment in order to be reckoned as righteous. Justice and truth are referred to only because the soul is in the presence of Maat, the goddess of truth and justice, whose favors she needs to secure for her salvation. What does it matter if this person has actually sinned during her earthly life? The only important thing is that Goddess Maat hear a confession which may please her. Therefore, in spite of the high moral value of its contents, the "negative confession" breathes a pharisaic spirit. But what is hypocrisy worth in the presence of the God of Truth who cannot be deceived?

All these rites and texts, obviously, are of a magical nature. This entire conception of the hereafter and the remedies proposed for the injuries of fate reflect the amoralism which characterizes magic. They can be compared to the magical practices of prehistoric times and to modern sorcery. The Egyptians believed in the effectiveness of these rites, provided they be performed correctly, without taking into account the preeminent role that religious faith and inner disposition must be granted.

However, the true spiritual way is that of morality and prayer. Access to it is not forced by the performance of rites and formulas, but through caring for truth, love, justice, and genuine piety. Our Christian rites themselves, our sacraments, don't grant grace automatically, but through faith, i.e., according to their meaning or symbolism when we conform ourselves to their teaching.

The amoralism of the *Book of the Dead* certainly deserves the contempt found in the Bible, and explains the Bible's distrust of the Egyptian solution to the problem of the hereafter. Ignoring the Egyptian dream of the hereafter was better than falling into illusion and error concerning the hope for a future life. The practice of justice and charity, and trust in a reward from God for good deeds, are safer guarantees than the Egyptian tricks aimed at securing the possession of an undeserved heaven, at the cost of losing the right way.

Of course, we must distinguish the case of superior minds, able through figurative interpretation, or even through simplicity of heart, to progress in the understanding of spiritual life. The hymn of king Akenaton illustrates the genuine spiritual awareness of certain Egyptians.

## THE BIBLE AND THE HEREAFTER.

### 1. SURPRISING SILENCE OF THE BIBLE ABOUT THE HEREAFTER.

In comparison with Egypt, the Bible is astonishingly poor about the hereafter. Nearly nothing in the Pentateuch; only scraps of information in Psalms, Job, Isaiah, Jeremiah, and even Ezekiel. We must wait until the books of Maccabees and the Wisdom of Solomon before finding an explicit doctrine of the resurrection.

This quasi-silence, however, is not equivalent to a negation, and the little we possess is enough to enlighten us. Let us notice, at first, that the problem of the hereafter is not the first thing which ought to interest religion. By itself, religion is not directly in the service of humanity. It is not a philanthropic institution, but an enterprise of worship and love of God. It is not anthropocentric, but theocentric, because its center is not humanity, but God. Joan of Arc used to say, "My Lord God is first to be served!"

Therefore, we must know and do what pleases God. Religion is expected to be advantageous for us only because God is good and, in his providence, cares for his creatures. There were religions, the gods of which were cruel: the worship of such deities could not provide their worshippers with large benefits, but only with avoiding worse evil.

### 2. ISRAEL'S HOPE IN THE HEREAFTER.

Since Israel's God is almighty, just and good, his faithful ought to trust him with a complete confidence. It is this absolute and unchallengeable confidence in God which seems to have been the first step in Israel's hope. In this context of thought, it does not matter very much to ask about the destiny of the righteous after death, since they are loved by God. Nothing suggests that the hope of believers in ancient Israel was weaker than that of those in pre-historic times, even of the Egyptians.

The Israelites did not doubt; they trusted God, and were satisfied with this confidence. Such seems to be the position in Genesis. The Israelite passes away and joins his God, the "God of Abraham, of Isaac, and of Jacob," or simply "is joined together with his fathers." Abraham purchased the cave in Hebron as a place of burial where his children would join their departed relatives.

Death seems to be a very simple act in the Pentateuch. This simplicity and discretion explains why the Law of Moses forbids noisy manifestations and self-mutilation of mourners.[28] We may admire the simplicity of the death of Jacob:

---

[28] Deut. 14:1.

> When Jacob had finished giving his last charge to his sons, he drew his feet on to the bed, breathed his last, and was gathered to his father's kin.[29]

Such seems to be, even today, the death of the believer whose faith was simple and whose life was righteous.

3. THE DANGER OF EXPLAINING THE HOPE IN THE HEREAFTER.

The danger of skepticism probably came with the development of thinking. Some danger, indeed, is linked to all curiosity and intellectual inquiry, but about the hereafter more than anything else. The mere fact of inquiring about the lot of the dead, or of being willing to clear up the secret of God, involved some impiety and was a breach of total trust in God, an anxiety, a fear, a doubt. Where do the departed go? People do not know how to answer this question. The Bible refuses "to pass through the gates of Hades." And, of course, there is no appealing to the myths of Ra and Osiris!

What then is to be done for the departed? Praying for them, probably? Providing them with food, if they need it? Perhaps the Israelites did this. The Law does not speak of this usage, either in favor of it or against it, but certain Tunisian Jews still preserved this practice until recently. The Christian Monica, Augustine's mother, also did. Such a custom may presuppose that the departed are in need of food, at least of the mysterious reality symbolized by actual food, and could suffer if they are deprived of it.

Such behavior shares in the common belief in antiquity of a diminished and not enviable condition after death. The Greeks placed in Hades the souls of the dead; the Hebrews in Sheol. But both Hades and Sheol are a sorry residence. There the departed are but souls deprived of life, *shades* according to the Greeks, or *nephesh* (breath) according to the Hebrews. It is difficult to see how a soul in this condition can be considered as truly a living being, possessing a life worthy of this word.

The Bible echoes this pessimistic opinion:

> What profit in my death if I go down into the pit? Can the dust confess thee or proclaim thy truth?[30] It is not the dead who praise the Lord, not those who go down into silence; but we, the living, bless the Lord, now and for evermore.[31] Come back, O Lord; set my soul free,

---

[29] Gen. 49:33.

[30] Psalm 30:9.

[31] Ps. 115:17-18.

> deliver me for thy love's sake. None talk of thee among the dead; who praises thee in Sheol?[32]

The Bible even echoes a more radical pessimism, near to skepticism:

> I said to myself, "In dealing with men it is God's purpose to test them and to see what they truly are. For man is a creature of chance and creatures are creatures of chance, and one mischance awaits them all: death comes to both alike. They all draw the same breath. Men have no advantage over beasts; for everything is emptiness. All go the the same place: all came from the dust, and to the dust all return. Who knows whether the spirit of man goes upwards or whether the spirit of the beast goes downward to the earth?[33]

However, we should not consider Ecclesiastes as a prototype of unbelievers; he lacks the Greek doctrine of the soul; he plays the part of the pessimist and the disillusioned, but he firmly believes in God. We may consider this doubt as an excessive position, which is not shared by the whole of Israel. This doubt corresponds to a kind of trial, of temptation, which we ourselves sometimes also meet and have to overcome.

Such a temptation does not spare even great saints, as the following confession of Saint Theresa of Lisieux attests:

> When I want to release my heart full of the darkness which oppresses it, with the help of the comforting hope in a future and eternal life, my sorrow increases. It seems to me that darkness, through the voices of the impious, tell me, while mocking me, -You dream of light, of a fragrant country, you dream of possessing the Creator of these wonderful things for ever, you believe that you will come out of this fog where you languish. Go, Go!...be delighted at death which will give you, not what you hope in, but a night even deeper, the night of nothingness. (*Journal of the Soul*)

## 4. The Hope is confirmed by the belief in resurrection.

Hope fought eagerly against the temptation of despair. Two great texts in Job[34] see hope flourishing again, and

---

[32] Ps. 6:4-5.

[33] Ecclesiastes 3:18-21.

[34] Job 17:11-16; 19:25-28.

perhaps longing for resurrection. Psalms seem to sing the hope for a happy hereafter:

> I have set the Lord continually before me: with him at my right hand I cannot be shaken, Therefore my heart exults and my spirit rejoices, my body too rests unafraid; for thou wilt not abandon me to Sheol nor suffer thy faithful servant to see the pit. Thou wilt show me the fulness of joy, in thy right hand pleasures for evermore.[35] But my plea is just: I shall see thy face, and be blest with a vision of thee when I awake.[36]

The hope in resurrection, perceived through the image of the national revival of Israel in the famous vision of the dried bones (Ezekiel 37), was preached by Daniel (12:2), and taught by the book of Wisdom (3). It is granted a prominent place in many biblical and extra-biblical Apocalypses.

Resurrection was the hope of the seven brothers and their mother, the first martyrs,[37] and of the soldiers killed in the holy war against Antiochus Epiphanes, the supporter of the Greek civilization and the enemy of the law of Moses. Resurrection was the belief of the Pharisees, contrary to the position of the Sadducees, who were more earthly and skeptical, or simply more traditional. Saint Paul set Pharisees and Sadducees against each other when they gathered to attack him, in affirming his faith in resurrection (Acts 23).

Resurrection is the belief of the Gospels. In John, Martha believed that her brother Lazarus should rise again..., however only on the last day. Jesus answered her, "I am resurrection and life," and immediately raised Lazarus again. Jesus promised paradise to the penitent thief that very day. He promised the crowd the food of eternal life, "I am the living bread which has come down from heaven; if anyone eats this bread he shall live for ever. Moreover, the bread which I will give is my own flesh; I give it for the life of the world.[38] The resurrection of Jesus himself is given as the pledge of our future resurrection: never had resurrection and future life received such a guarantee before!

The Christian hope drew from the resurrection of Jesus an unchallengeable assurance. Many problems, however, still remained in suspense about the hereafter and the resurrection. We shall raise them later on when we discuss Platonic immor-

---

[35] Ps. 16:8-11.

[36] Ps. 17:15.

[37] 1 Maccabees 7:9-14 and 23-36.

[38] John 6:51.

tality, the resurrection according to Paul ( I Cor. 15), and the contemporary interpretations of the resurrection narratives.

## CONCLUSION

As a conclusion, let us say that it is not good to raise one conception of the Christian hope, v.g., the resurrection, against another, biblical also, the simple trust in God. A friend of the author, a Rabbi, lost his young wife, a survivor of Auschwitz, who was taken away in a few days by a bad flu, leaving a seven years old daughter. For him, it was a terrible blow. We met; we talked, or, better, I let him talk, and I give you his view of the hope and afterdeath. I told my daughter, he said, that her mother was in paradise, in heaven, because she needs to rely on a comforting image. As for myself, I do not even, like the Christians, share the opinions of the Pharisees, who believed in the resurrection. I would rather define myself as a Sadducee, a conservative interpreter of the Law. Moses said nothing about things after death in the five books of the Law. God has kept his secret for himself: I do not know what happened of my wife, or even whether she is still in existence. All I know is that whatever fell to her lot is the will of God, and that God is good, Blessed be He!

The answer of the rabbi was not negative, but positive: we can trust God as we can trust mother and father. Such was already the way of the patriarchs, who believed in God. It is always good, particularly in time of doubt, to remember the solution of the rabbi.

## QUESTIONNAIRE

1. How was Osiris protected against destruction, made king of the Egyptian underworld, and in some regard raised again daily in order to remain the god of fecundity and the protector of the king?

2. What was the use of the myth of Ra for the sake of the dead?

3.Explain how mummification was an assimilation of the dead to Osiris. Describe the methods of mummification, and explain how the Egyptians provided for the preservation of the body.

4. Explain the ritual performed by the funeral priest in the temple or by the eldest son in the family burial place. Explain the meaning of the paintings and figurines of Egyptian tombs. Explain the meaning of certain gestures, formulas, offerings.

5. Do you find parallels to the myths of Ra and of Osiris in Christianity? Are we "assimilated to Christ" in a way which reminds you of these rituals and myths? Are you shocked by these similarities?

6. Explain the principle of the power of metamorphosis enjoyed by the kah (soul) after death. Do you find magic in the exercise of this power in the Egyptian *Book of the Dead*? How can such a principle lead towards the theory of re-incarnations, or of the resurrection?

7. Find evidence for a judgment, for heaven, and for hell, in the Egyptian *Book of the Dead*. Compare them to the Christian notions paralleling them. Can we consider these notions in Christianity as mythical, in what sense? Do you agree with Dante?

8. Discuss the affirmation of personality found in the "negative confession." What is its purpose in this ritual? Can you make it yours? Against what influences should you affirm and maintain your personality?

9. According to the "negative confession", what are the duties of social justice? Transpose them into the realities of modern life.

10. What are, in the same text, the duties of piety towards the gods?

11. Show that the use made of the "negative confession," regardless of its beautiful moral content, is purely magical and not ethical. Can sometime our Christian sacraments or pious customs be used as if they were magical devices?

12. Does the knowledge of prehistoric magic cast some light on the practices of the Egyptian *Book of the Dead*?

13. Can we say that faith and thoughtful confidence in God is a real answer to the question of the human hope for life after death?

14. How could curiosity concerning the hereafter practically destroy confidence in God concerning our destiny after death, and generate doubt?

15. Explain how the *Book of the Dead* illustrates the danger of the tendency "to know too much" about human destiny.

16. Why do many people today, even amongst the faithful and priests, not speak, or preach, or think about death and the question of the hereafter?

17. Mention statements of Jesus in the Gospels concerning the future life. How is Jesus himself central to our hope for salvation? What seems to remain unclear to you in this matter?

## BIBLIOGRAPHY

*(The) Ancient Book of the Dead.* Ed. by C. Andrews, tr. by R. O Faulkner. New York: British Museum Publications, 1985.

BUDGE, A. Wallis. *The Egyptian Book of the Dead.* (An English translation of the Theban recension). 3 voll. Chicago: Open Court Publication Co.,1901.

HAYES, John H. *Introduction to the Bible.* Philadelphia: Westminster 1971. (Of general interest for the chapters on Scripture.)

KOLPAKTCHY, Grégoire. *Livre des Morts des anciens Egyptiens.* Paris: Omnium Littéraire, Les Editions des Champs Elysées, 1954. Introduction pp.1-50.

MAHDY, Christine el. *Mummies, Myths, and Magic in Ancient Egypt.* London: Thames & Hudson, 1989.

McKENZIE, John L. *Dictionary of the Bible.* Milwaukee: Bruce 1965. "Death," p.800. (Of general interest for the chapters on Scripture.)

_____. *The Two-Edged Sword, An Interpretation of the Old Testament.* Milwaukee: Bruce 1956 Pp.246-264.

VAUX, Roland de. *Ancient Israel.* 2 vol. New York:

# CHAPTER IV

## BABYLONIAN MYTHS AND BIBLICAL REVISIONS

In our first chapter, "Creation according to the Bible and science," we interpreted the first three chapters of Genesis in relation to science and the requirements of orthodoxy. We showed that the Christian teaching about the creation of humankind, our spiritual nature, and the sin of origin, when they are correctly presented, do not contradict the data of biology, paleontology and prehistory. In the present chapter, we interpret the same biblical texts for a second time, adding to them the narratives of the Deluge and of the Tower of Babel, but we do it from a completely different point of view: we compare them to certain ancient texts from Mesopotamia which may have inspired the biblical writers.

Narratives of the Creation and of the Deluge, which are earlier than our biblical Genesis, have been found in Mesopotamia (modern Iraq). As an event, the Deluge belongs to the history of Mesopotamia, a country which, more than once, has known devastating floods. The Tower of Babel is a Mesopotamian monument, the ruins of which are still visible today. There are about 40 such buildings in Mesopotamia, which represent in this country what cathedrals represent in Europe.

Ancient Israel, which rebuked Egypt and its culture as alien, acknowledged its kinship with Mesopotamia, the motherland of Abraham and the patriarchs. A relationship of race, language, and culture united these two peoples. Moreover, many Israelites lived for a long time in exile or as settlers in Mesopotamia. The Mesopotamian civilization was for Israel a true inheritance.

Actually, a comparison between our biblical narratives and the Mesopotamian parallel texts reveals significant similarities and differences. When the Bible does not feel obliged to doubt them, or to challenge them, or when no problem is raised about their data, it repeats its Mesopotamian "sources" nearly verbatim. Regarding these common features, the Bible does not add anything original. It treats them as commonplaces, or as the science of the time, without questioning their contents. But, on other points, the Bible makes changes, by adding or omitting, or gives a quite different interpretation of the data. Here, the Bible makes an original contribution. It judges with the light of faith, and feels it necessary to change something. These differences reveal to us the leading principles of biblical faith, the Bible's positions about surrounding culture.

The biblical narratives of the origins are neither a set of naive stories, nor the work of a school which would have cleverly borrowed and assimilated foreign literature as students would today. They represent the ripe fruit of ageless meditations of believing people and the thought of inspired authors sure of their faith. The judgments given in these texts derive from divine revelation, from the same spirit which inspired the Decalogue. Even though many of the details can be considered as obsolete today. Genesis 1-11 represents a masterly teaching on faith about God, humanity, and sin.

The order of the present chapter is as follows. The discovery of the Library of Assurbanipal, king of Nineveh (7th century B.C.), brought forth texts which significantly paralleled both the first (Gen.1) and the second narrative of Creation (Gen.2-3). This parallelism is displayed in the first section, and the way the biblical account distanced itself from the Mesopotamian model is interpreted. The second and third sections deal with the *Epic of Gilgamesh*, which, in addition to a narrative of creation comparable to Gen. 2-3, also includes a narrative of the Deluge, corresponding to Gen. 6-9. The wisdom of the Mesopotamian Epic is brought to light: it inspires pessimism and despair of the condition of the dead. The biblical story of the Tower of Babel (Gen.11:1-9), in the last section, seems to be a meditation on the grandeur and decadence of the Babylonian ziggurats.

## THE DISCOVERY OF KING ASSURBANIPAL'S LIBRARY.

In 1842, Botta, the French consul in Mossul, originated Mesopotamian archeology with his earliest excavations on the sites of Nineveh, the Assyrian metropolis, and of Korsabad, its royal residence. After the French revolution of 1848, Victor Place, Botta's successor in Mossul, took up the researches anew. But England was also on the site, and in 1853 they found and claimed possession of the wonderful bas-reliefs of Assurbanipal's hunts. There were also thousands of clay-stones engraved with cuneiform types, the importance of which was not acknowledged immediately, and which were considered as "ornamental pottery." These exhibits became the glory of the British Museum.

In 1857, the key to the language of these clay-tablets was discovered, and this "ornamental pottery" raised a great interest. The emotion was great when in England --a country so very fond of the Bible--, Smith, a young English Orientalist, published in 1872 the discovery of a Chaldean account of the Deluge. Unfortunately this narrative was incomplete because the tablets had been collected carelessly and had been damaged in transport. Smith was sent to the place, and was lucky enough to find in the refuse, after only a week, a supplement to the mutilated narrative.

The library of Assurbanipal, Assyrian king of Nineveh from 668 to 631 B.C., gave 30,000 tablets which contain texts of many kinds, including a great deal of religious literature, especially the *Epic of Gilgamesh*. This Epic can be compared with the Iliad and the Odyssey of Homer. The *Epic of Gil-*

*gamesh*, and other poems, deal with creation, the Deluge, etc., and offer surprising links with the first chapters of the Bible. They are half-religious, half-philosophical narratives, and they have strongly influenced the intellectual life of the Assyrians and Babylonians. These texts were read, learned, copied, commented upon, given as school assignments, and even publicly recited at the great religious feast of the new year.

Of course, Assurbanipal's library was not earlier than the 7th century B.C., but many of its texts were copies of much earlier sources. Actually, the *Epic of Gilgamesh* existed already in the epoch of Hammurabi, king of Babylon about 1750 B.C., who extended his empire over all of Mesopotamia during the days of Abraham. The main elements of this *Epic* have recently been discovered in the Sumerian literature which goes back before 2000 B.C. These old tales had been used as themes of meditation, with local variants, for two thousand years in Mesopotamia, and their influence was felt all around.

## THE TWO BABYLONIAN POEMS OF CREATION.

The first Babylonian poem of creation, the *Enuma Elish*, on seven tablets about 150 lines each, relates the creation of the world by Marduk, god of Babylon, and was probably used as a pattern, more or less directly, for the first biblical narrative of creation (Genesis 1).

A second narrative, the Creation of Enkidu, in the *Epic of Gilgamesh*, reminds us of our second biblical narrative of creation (Genesis 2). Whereas the first biblical narrative is closely parallel to the Babylonian text, the second only offers common images and other similarities. These features were common places, or basic materials of every literature of Semitic inspiration about the idea of creation. Therefore, it is not surprising to encounter them reappearing in the Bible. But, in the Bible, they appear in a quite different theology: a theology inspired by monotheism and ethics, no longer polytheism and magic.

### 1. THE "FIRST NARRATIVE": ENUMA ELISH.

#### a. *The beginning.*

We read on the first tablet of the Babylonian narrative of creation:

> When above, the heaven was not named yet, and below, the earth had not yet been granted a name, when the waters of Apsu ("soft-water"), the gods' first father, and of Tiamat ("salt-water") their mother, were mixed in one only thing; when the fields were not yet linked with one another, when reed-bushes had not yet appeared, when none of the gods had yet appeared, when they had not

yet been granted a name, and bound with a fate, gods were created in the depths of waters...

We may compare this text with the first two verses of Genesis 1:

> In the beginning of creation, when God made heaven and earth, the earth was without form and void, with darkness over the face of the abyss, and a mighty wind that swept the surface of the waters.
> "In the beginning, God created the heavens and the earth. The earth was without form and void, and darkness was upon the face of the deep; and the spirit of God was moving over the face of the waters."

The original chaos is a common feature to both narratives. The Bible, however, affirms the primacy of the creative act. On the other hand, the Bible deprives the elements of their identity as persons and as gods: the elements are no longer either Apsu or Tiamat, but simply "a thing without form and void." From the biblical teaching we can derive the idea that God is transcendent and that he created the universe out of nothingness.

b. *The heavenly conflict.*

According to the Babylonian narrative, after their creation, the gods multiplied, and the earliest quarrels burst forth between them. Their parents, Apsu and Tiamat, complained:

> I am tired of their behavior towards us. I am restless all day long, and I cannot sleep in the night. I shall destroy them and put an end to their behavior. Let quiet come, and we might sleep!

The gods proposed to defend their lives against Tiamat. Ea opened the conflict, but his son, Marduk, won the victory:

> In the room of destinies, in the house of the fortunes, the wise amongst the wise, the guide of the gods, Marduk was begotten. Ea, his father begat him. Lahamu, his mother, bore him. He was suckled at the divine breast. When Ea, his father, saw him, he rejoiced, full of joy. He made him perfect. He endowed him with a double divine form... Four are his eyes, four his ears. When he moves his lips, there are sparks of fire. Four times greater is his intelligence, and his eyes see everything... Clothed with the majesty of ten gods, he is supremely powerful.

At the head of the army of the gods, Marduk fought furious Tiamat, the unbridled chaos which Marduk must defeat before organizing the world. Tiamat prepared herself for war: "She begat enormous serpents... with venom instead of blood she filled their bodies. She put terror into terrible dragons. She made them like gods." As their head she appointed Kingu, the god of war, and she entrusted to him the tablets of fate.

Anshar, Ea's father and Marduk's grandfather, shivered when he saw the preparations of Tiamat: "He beat his thigh, bit his lips; his heart became restless." But he looked at Marduk who was coming. Anshar saw him, and his heart rejoiced. He kissed him, and his fear vanished. Marduk announced to him:

> I shall go, and perform the wish of your heart. Who indeed challenged you with weapons! My father, be happy and rejoice: before long you will tread Tiamat's nape of the neck under your feet!

Before the battle, an assembly of the gods invested Marduk with commandment:

> Thou art the most honored of the great gods; thy decrees are unrivaled, thy command is like that of Anu (the sky-god). From this day unchangeable shall be thy pronouncements. To raise and bring low, these shall be in thy hand... No one among the gods shall transgress thy bounds!...O Marduk, thou art indeed our avenger. We have granted thee kingship over the universe entire. When in Assembly thou sittest, thy word shall be supreme. Thy weapons shall not fail, thou shall smash thy foes! O Lord, spare the life of him who trust thee, but pour out the life of the gods who seized evil.[39]

They granted him the cloth of Palou which makes one invincible:

> "Go and end the life of Tiamat. May the winds
> bear her blood to places unclosed."

Tiamat was furious. The war went on quickly. Marduk cast the winds into Tiamat's mouth, killed her and laid hold on the tablets of fate. He tread Tiamat under foot, crushed her skull, and from her body shaped the world:

> He split her like a shell-fish into two parts; half of her he set up and ceiled it as a sky, pulled down the bar and posted guards. He bade them to allow not her waters to

---

[39] Tablet IV, tr. E. A. Speiser, *The Ancient Near East, An Anthology of Texts and Pictures*, ed. by J. Pritchard (Princeton, 1958), pp. 31-32.

> escape. He crossed the heavens and surveyed the regions. He squared Apsu's quarters, the abode of Nudimmud, as the Lord measured the dimensions of Apsu.
>
> The Great Abode, its likeness (of Apsu) he fixed as Esharra, the Great Abode, its likeness, which he made as the firmament. Anu, Enlil and Ea he made occupy their places. He constructed stations for the great gods, fixing their astral likenesses as constellations. He determined the year by designating the zones. He set up three constellations for each of the twelve months. After, he defined the days of the year... created the stars... and created mankind.[40]

c. *The heavenly conflict according to biblical and Christian faith.*

The Bible omits the episode of the heavenly war. However, some analogous conflict is presupposed by the Bible. This conflict is treated at length in the extrabiblical literature of the "pseudoepigrapha". This literature essentially belongs, in a certain manner, to Jewish-Christian faith. Here are found the sin of Lucifer, the battle of the angels, and Michael the archangel's victory over Lucifer and his angels.

Although without pressing on the detail, Christian teaching, together with Scripture, accepts the existence of angels and demons. For instance, the spirit of evil intervening under the appearance of the snake in the narrative of Adam's fall is more than a mere symbol! The idea underlying this teaching is that we must fight against an existing enemy, not simply against "something", or even against something simply missing: the absence of a required good, as philosophers concede.

Biblical faith and Christian religion have a view of evil which is more existential and more popular, more dramatic also than what philosophy can offer. According to Paul, the Christian must fight against an enemy more powerful than themselves, against evil powers from above, which are invisible, but the grace of God and the assistance of Christ are with them in this conflict in which they must win the victory.[41] Aquinas himself, the champion of essentialist theology (which teaches that evil is a "non-being," the "lack of a required good") also relies on the Christian tradition of the devil's influence. Of course, in the Bible and in Christian thought, angels are not gods, but higher creatures, faithful or unfaithful to God, rewarded or punished like humans, but whose judgment is already proclaimed. Jews

---

[40] Tablet V and beginning of VI, Pritchard, op. cit., p. 35.

[41] Eph. 6:11-20.

and Christians alike recognized demons working behind the masks of the pagan idols and the false gods. The biblical narrative of creation preserves from the Babylonian account of creation only the division between the heavens and the earth, between light and darkness, between upper and lower waters, between earth and seas.

d. *The creation of humankind.*

The fifth tablet reflects the astronomical knowledge which was the glory and pride of Chaldean astrologers. The story of the star which guided the Magi to Bethlehem where they paid homage to the Infant-God echoes their reputation as astronomers. According to the biblical narrative, on the fourth day, God created the sun, moon and stars. These are not gods, nor the abode of gods, as they were in Babylon, but merely "luminaries" that also measure time. They are creatures in the service of God, just like other creatures.

The sixth tablet relates the creation of humankind:

> Blood I will mass and cause bones to be. I will establish a savage, "man" shall be his name. Verily, savage-man I will create. He shall be charged with the service of the gods, that they might be at ease.[42]

But, from what god will Marduk take blood for man? Marduk took the blood of the god of war, of Kingu, whom Tiamat armed against the gods:

> It was Kingu who contrived the uprising, and made Tiamat rebel, and joined battle. They bound him, holding him before Ea. They imposed on him his guilt and severed his blood vessels. Out of his blood they fashioned mankind. He imposed the service and let free the gods.[43]

In the first chapter of Genesis, the creation of humankind is also the end of the divine work, and similarly humans are destined to the service of God. The man in the Bible, who received the spirit of God, was created according to the image of God, and was called to imitate God, the perfect heavenly Father! It is true also that violence and evil, which are symbolized by the blood of Kingu, are also present in the human heart from the beginning.

---

[42] Tablet VI, Pritchard, op.cit., p.36.

[43] Ibid. Pritchard, op. cit., p. 37.

## 2. THE "SECOND NARRATIVE" OF CREATION: EPIC OF GILGAMESH.

An episode of the *Epic of Gilgamesh*, the creation of Enkidu, reminds us of some aspects of our second narrative of creation in the Bible (Genesis 2 & 3). The *Epic of Gilgamesh*, however, is much earlier than the biblical narrative. Therefore, the Bible may have repeated some images of the creation of Enkidu, but teaches a different kind of wisdom.

Gilgamesh is king of Uruk, and an oppressor of his people. For this reason, goddess Arurn fashioned a rival to him, out of clay. His name is Enkidu:

> A double of Anu she conceived within her. Arurn washed her hands, pinched off clay and cast it on the steppe. On the steppe she created valiant Enkidu.[44]

All the power of Enkidu comes from his living in wild nature, in the savage world of animals, far from human society. As a consequence, he is immune from corruption and preserved from debasement and degradation. He can be compared to the "noble savage" of Rousseau, but more directly to the biblical Adam before his fall. There is also in him some similarity with Tarzan and "Superman."

Gilgamesh decided to get rid of his rival. In order to do this, he tried to take away from Enkidu his savage and pure life, and to induce him to join the civilized world. He sent a harlot, who seduced Enkidu and led him to the city. Now, Enkidu has become like any other man. He has lost his native purity which held him in kinship with the animals. Now animals run away from him because they don't trust him any longer, and this is Enkidu's first deception.

Enkidu and the harlot come through meadows and meet shepherds. Enkidu "learns how to eat and to drink in man's fashion, how to anoint his limbs with oil, to dress, to become like a man." But, near the city, the harlot calls his attention to men working hard in the fields. Surprised at the pain they take, Enkidu asks the man whom the harlot called at his request.

> The man opened his mouth, saying to Enkidu: "Into the meeting-house he has (intruded) which is set aside for the people,... for wedlock... For the king of broad-marted Uruk the drum of the people is free for nuptial choice, that with lawful wives he might mate!... By the counsel of the gods it has so been ordained. With the cutting of the

[44] Tablet I, ii, Pritchard, op. cit., p. 42.

> umbilical cord, it was decreed for him!" At the words of the man, Enkidu's face grew pale.[45]

Hard work and forced labor, for the city and the king, without even freedom in wedlock, such is the condition of humans from birth to death.

Among other similarities with the biblical text, we may note the curse of God against man after the fall: "In the sweat of your brow you shall eat bread, till you return to the dust, for out of it you were taken; you are dust, and to dust you shall return" (Gen.3:19).

a. *The anxiety of death in the Epic of Gilgamesh.*

The problem of death is already present in the mind of Enkidu, but this question does not presently trouble his new friend Gilgamesh. Like many among us, Gilgamesh needs to be struck by the death of a beloved one --here his friend Enkidu-- to become aware of the reality of death. Enkidu is disillusioned and reproaches the harlot with having deprived him of his precious happiness. He wants to escape death:

> When Shamash (the sun-god) himself heard these words of his mouth, forthwith he called down to him from heaven: Why, O Enkidu, curseth thee the harlot-lass, who made thee eat food fit for divinity, and gave thee to drink wine fit for royalty, who clothed thee with noble garments, and made thee have fair Gilgamesh for a comrade? And has not now Gilgamesh, thy bosom friend, made thee lie on a noble couch? He has made thee lie on a couch of honor, has placed thee on the seat of ease, the seat at the left, that the princes of the earth may kiss thy feet![46]

But human destiny does not cease to trouble Enkidu. Both friends have now gone together in order to fight against Humbaba, the king of the Cedar-forest. Goddess Ishtar, furious at them, sends against them the heavenly bull, which is killed by Enkidu. After their victory over Humbaba, the two friends come back to Uruk, but, in consequence of Ishtar's revenge, Enkidu dies.

Troubled in his turn by the mystery of death, Gilgamesh bewails over his friend's body:

> Enkidu, my younger friend, thou who chasedst the wild ass of the hills, the panther of the steppe!... who seized

[45] Tablet II iii, Pritchard, op. cit., pp. 48-49.

[46] Tablet VII iii, Pritchard, op. cit., p. 57.

> the Bull and slew him, brought affliction on Humbaba who dwelled in the Cedar-forest! What now is this sleep that has laid hold on thee? Thou art benighted and canst hear me! But he lifts not up his eyes; he touched his heart, but it does not beat. Then, he veiled his friend like a bride, storming over him like a lion, like a lioness deprived of her whelps.[47]

Gilgamesh is frightened by death:

> He weeps bitterly as he ranges over the steppe: "When I die, shall I be like Enkidu? Woe has entered my belly. Fearing death, I roam over the steppe,... to Utnapishtim...[48]

b. *The secret of Utnapishtim.*

Gilgamesh would like to escape death. He looks for a remedy to his evil, a way to reach immortality. He remembers that one of his ancestors, Utnapishtim, escaped the common fate. During the Deluge, with his boat, he reached the opposite border of the Ocean. From then on, he is living in a kind of Paradise and partakes of the fate of the gods. Gilgamesh takes up the long voyage which will bring him into the presence of his ancestor Utnapishtim, proposing to ask him for the secret of life everlasting. The first stage is Mount Mashu in Arabia, where he encounters scorpion-men. Then he follows westward the way of the sun, i.e., the way that the sun goes during the night before rising again in the East. Darkness reigns over his path. Fortunately, here is an oasis over which the sun shines again. Here are the trees of the gods, with branches of lapis-lazuli and wonderful fruit, and also many gems. This fabulous oasis looks somehow like the biblical Eden. Gilgamesh arrives at the house of Nymph Sidouri who does not grant him much hope:

> O Gilgamesh, there is no passageway, and nobody long ago did cross the sea. He crosses the sea, he, Shamash (the sun), the hero, but, except for Shamash, who will pass? Difficult the passage! Laborious the journey! and deep the waters of death throughout. Where, Gilgamesh, will you cross the sea? And, when you shall arrive before the waters of death, what will you do?...[49]

---

[47] Tablet VIII ii, Pritchard, op. cit., p. 61.

[48] Tablet IX i, Pritchard, op. cit., p.62.

[49] Tablet X i, Pritchard, op. cit., p. 63.

The ale-wife Sidouri teaches Gilgamesh a sane, but only earthly, form of happiness:

> Gilgamesh, whither rowest thou? The life thou pursuest thou shall not find. When the gods created mankind, death for mankind they set aside, life in their own hands retaining. Thou, Gilgamesh, let full be thy belly, make thou merry by day and night. Of each day make thou a feast of rejoicing, day and night dance thou and play! Let thy garments be sparkling fresh, thy head be washed; bathe thou in water. Pay heed to the little one that hold on thy hand, let thy spouse delight in thy bosom. For this is the task of mankind.[50]

Sidouri, however, points out to him a good guide who dwells in the forest, the same pilot who guided the ark of Utnapishtim during the Deluge. Changing continually the oar, for the hand must not touch the waters of death, they cross the dangerous passage with their boat, and Gilgamesh arrives, full of good hopes, in the presence of his ancestor.

Utnapishtim tries to persuade him to accept his mortal condition:

> Do we build a house for ever? Do we seal contracts for ever? Do brothers share for ever? Does hatred persist for ever in the land? Does the river for ever rise up and bring on flood? The dragon-fly leaves its shell, that its face might but glance at the face of the sun. Since the days of yore, there has been no permanence; the resting and the dead, how alike they are! Do they not compose a picture of their fate? The Annunaki, the great gods, foregather; Mammatum, maker of fates, with them the fates decree: death and life they determine. But of death its days are not revealed.[51]

Moved with pity, the wife of the ancestor intercedes in favor of Gilgamesh before her husband Utnapishtim, who is touched and agrees to grant Gilgamesh a wonderful secret: there is in the depth of the sea a plant which can provide you with a new youth: Go and try to get it! Fixing stones to his feet, Gilgamesh was able to reach the mysterious plant, and, with this invaluable possession, he was returning on his way home to Uruk, his city. But the plant of life is a treasure as difficult to keep as it is to get, when you are but a human being. Arriving at a fountain, Gilgamesh stops, proposing to bathe, but the Serpent,

---

[50] Tablet X iii, Pritchard, op. cit., p. 64.

[51] Tablet X vi, Pritchard, op. cit., p. 65.

using this moment of inattention, comes and steals the plant. Gilgamesh took much pain in vain!

## THE BABYLONIAN NARRATIVE OF THE DELUGE[52]

We are at Utnapishtim's, and Gilgamesh is being told how he might escape death. Utnapishtim explains to him how, taking advantage of the Deluge, he came to the country of the blissful:

> Shuruppak --a city which thou knowest, and which on Euphrates' bank is situate-- that city was ancient, as were the gods within it, when their heart led the great gods to produce the flood...
>
> Ea was also present with them; their words he repeats to the reed-hut: "Reed-hut, reed-hut! Wall, wall! Reed-hut, hearken! Wall, reflect! Man of Shuruppack, son of Ubar-Tutu, tear down this house, build a ship! Give up possessions, seek your life. Forswear worldly goods and keep the soul alive! Aboard the ship take thou the seed of all living things. The ship that thou shalt build, her dimensions shall be to measure. Equal shall be her width and her length. Like the Apsu thou shalt sail her..."
>
> With the first glow of dawn, a black cloud rose up from the horizon. Inside it Adad thunders, while Shullat and Hanish go in front, moving as heralds over hill and plain. Erragal tears out the posts; Forth comes Ninurta and causes the dikes to follow. The Annunaki lift up the torches, setting the land ablaze with their glare... No one can see his fellow, nor can the people be recognized from heaven. The gods were frightened by the Deluge, and shrinking back, they ascended to the heaven of Anu. The gods cowered like dogs crouched against the outer-wall... The Annunaki gods wept with her (Ishtar), the gods all humbled, sit and weep....
>
> Six days and six nights blows the flood wind, as the south-storm sweeps the land. When the seventh day arrived... the sea grew quiet, the tempest was still, the flood ceased. I looked at the weather: stillness had set in, and all of mankind had returned to clay. The landscape was as level as a flat roof. I opened a hatch, and light fell upon my face. Bowing low, I sat and wept, tears running down my face. I looked about for coast lines in the expanse of the sea: in each of fourteen regions there emerged a region-mountain. On Mount

[52] Tablet XI, Pritchard, op. cit., pp. 66-75.

> Nizir the ship came to a halt. Mount Nizir held the ship fast, allowing no motion... When the seventh day arrived, I sent forth and set free a dove. The dove went forth but came back; since no resting place for it was visible, she turned round. Then I sent forth and set free a swallow. The swallow went forth but came back; since no resting place was visible, she turned round. Then I sent forth and set free a raven. The raven went forth, and, seeing that the waters had diminished, he eats, circles, craws, and turns not round. Then, I let out all to the four winds.
>
> I poured out a libation on the top of the mountain. Seven and seven cult-vessels I set up, upon their pot-stands I heaped cane, cedar-wood, and myrtle. The gods smelled the savor; the gods smelled the sweet savor; the gods crowded like flies about the sacrificer...
>
> Ea opened his mouth to speak, saying to valiant Enlil: "Thou, wisest of gods, thou, hero, How couldst thou, unreasoning, bring on the Deluge? On the sinner impose his sin, on the transgressor impose his transgression! Yet be lenient, lest he be cut off, be patient, lest he be dislodged! Instead of thy bringing on the Deluge, would that a lion had risen up to diminish them!..., Would that a wolf, a famine, or pestilence!... It was not I who disclosed the secret of the great gods. I let the 'Exceedingly Wise' (the intelligent man) see a dream, and he perceived the secret of the gods. Now then take counsel in regard to him! Thereupon Enlil went aboard the ship. Holding me by the hand, he took me aboard. He took my wife aboard and made her kneel by my side. Standing between us, he touched our foreheads to bless us. Hitherto, Utnapishtim has been but human. Henceforth, Utnapishtim and his wife shall be like unto us gods. Utnapishtim shall reside far away, at the mouth of the rivers!". Thus they took me and made me reside far away, at the mouth of the rivers.

## COMPARISON WITH THE BIBLICAL ACCOUNT OF THE DELUGE (Genesis 5 to 10)

The similarity of the two narratives (Genesis 5-10 and *Epic of Gilgamesh* XI) is obvious from mere reading.

### 1. THE ARCHEOLOGICAL EVIDENCE.

The narrative of the Deluge --the biblical as well as the Babylonian-- is not a myth deprived of any historical foundation. Wooley found in the stratigraphy of his excavation in Ur a break between the civilization of Obeid and that of Sumer. This break was represented by a layer of barren deposits from two to three meters thick. Dr. Langdon observed the same phenomenon in Kish. Moreover, these floods do not correspond to one another and go back to various epochs.

Therefore, there were several deluges, more or less important in size. The narrative of the Deluge reflected a series of local floods, surviving as the memory of a terrific event which struck imagination. The Chaldean narrative is very early, since tablet XI from Nineveh repeats a former version going back to a date before 2000 B.C., therefore earlier than Abraham, and close to the flood which inspired it.

## 2. The Meaning of the Biblical Account of the Deluge.

The Bible interprets the ancient tradition of the Deluge in a quite different manner. Noah does not reach immortality, as does Utnapishtim, but only escapes death because he is righteous, and God wants to save him. The just should not, indeed, perish together with the wicked.

On the one hand, nothing, of course, is found which reflects the contemptible mediocrity of the gods who were eager to let loose the storm, who then crouched from fear like dogs, and who gathered around Utnapishtim's altar, hungry, attracted by the savor of the offering, of which they had been deprived for a long time. Moreover, in the severity of God's judgment in the Bible, we do not find, as in the Chaldean account, any allusion to disproportion and fancy in the divine punishment of humankind, but rather the idea of the judge's majesty and of the power of his justice.

On the other hand, renouncing the theme of the search for immortality, which in the Chaldean account ends in a blind alley, the Bible resolutely takes a different orientation of thought. The Deluge is, first of all, a lesson given to humans: let them observe justice! If they fail, let them fearfully expect the chastisement to come!

Another lesson also emerges, which reminds us of the narrative of the Fall of Adam. The outbreak of sin reaches everybody: God reserved only one person to prepare his work of salvation. Noah was chosen to be the father of a new people, of a just people, and was bidden, like the first man, to multiply and to fill the earth. However, his election by God was only the symbol of a future salvation, a manner of prophetic utterance, for Noah's offspring were not more righteous than the people punished in the Deluge. God seems to have acknowledged it when he blessed Noah: "I will never again curse the ground because of man, for the imagination of man's heart is evil from his youth..."[53] There shall be no other Deluge. The cause of the Deluge, sin, not the punishment which is a consequence, ought to be attacked, and this is exactly what God proposes to

[53] Genesis 8:21.

do. Although chastisement is justice, salvation is not found in punishment. Noah could only beget sinners. Therefore, Noah simply appears as a witness to the hope for salvation. His very failure to keep justice in himself and in his children points out the necessity of another Savior, whom the Christians recognized in Jesus.

The ancient Christian writers liked to speculate on the ark of Noah in which they saw a prophecy of Christ. For them, the real Noah is Jesus, the Just, the Savior, the Physician who shall heal our hearts from sin. The ark is the Church, besides which there is no salvation. Water is baptism, and drowned humankind represents sinners and unbelievers. The ark of the Church brings people back to paradise, crossing the waters of death, and giving to the faithful access to the tree of life, which is the cross of Christ. In the Church, indeed, Scripture and sacraments provide the faithful with the food of everlasting life.[54]

## CHALDEAN PESSIMISM CONCERNING HUMAN DESTINY AFTER DEATH.

### 1. Raising the shade of Enkidu.

Gilgamesh lost all hope of reaching the blessed immortality of the gods. However, his failure does not imply that people are completely annihilated at death. What then exactly is their lot in the hereafter? In order to obtain an answer to this question, Gilgamesh addresses his departed friend Enkidu in a scene of necromancy which reminds us of the raising of the shade of the prophet Samuel by king Saul in the episode of the Witch of Endor.[55] Here is the dialogue between Gilgamesh and Enkidu:

> "Tell me, my friend! Did you see the law of Hades? Let me know it!
> - All that which one has loved, turns into dust, however destinies are not similar.
> - Did you see the one who fell in battle, didn't you?
> - Yes, I saw him: his father and his mother hold up his head, and his wife leans over him.
> - Did you see the one whose body has been thrown away in the fields, didn't you?
> - Yes, I saw him: his shade does not rest in Hades.

---

[54] J. Daniélou, *From Shadows to Reality. Studies in the Biblical Typology of the Fathers* (London 1960), book II, pp. 69-112.

[55] I Sam. 28.

- Did you see that whose shade has nobody to care for it, did you?
- Yes, I saw him: he eats the left-overs of the cooking, and the refuse of the dishes thrown away in the street."

As we see, according to the wisdom of the Babylonian myths, the dead do not have an enviable lot, and death is for them, for the great as well as for the small, the worst of downfalls. Happy is he who, perchance, has a father or a mother, a wife or a son, who may comfort him with offerings. But the abandoned deceased, or those who are now forgotten, are more unfortunate than beggars on earth. One can read on the Mesopotamian tombs the impressive appeal of a deceased man asking the passerby for the alm of a glass of water to be poured as a libation over his knoll.

All these souls, who are unsatisfied because they suffered evils on earth, or because they feel neglected after death, were supposed to come back and trouble the living, and to join the army of maleficent spirits. There is nothing of the illusory optimism of the Egyptians, but, on the contrary, a radical pessimism, which deeply impressed the soul of Israel, and occasioned a temptation of despair difficult to overcome.

### 2. The myths of Adana, Adapa, Ishtar's descent to Hades.

The Mesopotamian mythology offers other narratives which attest the same pessimism. For instance, in order to steal the tablets of fate, Adana went up in the air with the help of an eagle whose friendship he had won, but he became dizzy, and crashed to earth.

Adapa did ascend unto heaven, but, once there, ill advised by a god who, however, was benevolent, refused the drink of immortality which god Ea offered him.

Ishtar, goddess of war and love, on her descent to Hades, was obliged to take off successively, at each of the seven doors of Nergal's kingdom, the magic garments in which all her powers consisted, and to appear naked under the deadly eyes of her sister Ereshktigal, Nergal's wife, who hated her. The benevolence of a god was necessary to rescue her from this misfortune.

## THE TOWER OF BABEL

Many documents inform us concerning the amazing, many-floored towers, or "ziggurats," which rose over the Mesopotamian cities, like our European cathedrals. They are represented on seal-cylinders, on vessels, pillars, and on a relief of Nineveh. The most famous of these towers was that of Babylon, named Etemenanki, the "Tower of Babylon" in the Bible (Genesis 11).

Herodotus describes it:

> The great wall I have described is, so to speak, the breast-place or chief defense of the city; but there is a second one within it, not so thick but hardly less strong. There is a fortress in the middle of each half of the city: in one the royal place surrounded by a wall of great strength, in the other the "temple of Bel," the Babylonian Zeus.
>
> The temple is a square building. two furlongs each way, with bronze gates, and was still in existence in my time; it has a solid central tower, one furlong square, with a second erected on top of it and then a third, and so on up to eight. All eight towers can be climbed by a spiral way running round the outside, and about half way up there are seats for those who make the ascent to rest on. On the summit of the topmost tower stands a great temple with a large couch in it, richly covered, and a golden table beside it... The Chaldean also say --though I do not believe them-- that the god enters the temple in person and takes his rest upon the bed.[56]

A tablet in Esagil, a nearby temple devoted to Marduk, gives information concerning the dimensions of the tower, also attested by archeological excavations in the ruins. Seven superimposed floors, set back from one another, with, on the top, the god's room, formed a quadrilateral of 300 feet X 300 feet at the base, and reached 300 feet in height. Each floor presented a different color. These colors are unknown, but can be supposed through a comparison with the nearby ziggurat of Korsabad which, from the base to the top, was successively white, black, orange, blue, scarlet, silver and gold.

Worship was celebrated there in connection with that of the nearby temple of Marduk. Ritual texts inform us of the main elements of these liturgies, which contained prayers for the salvation of the king and the fecundity of the fields.

Scholars wonder at the meaning of these ziggurats, which are as old as Mesopotamian civilization, have been the victims of many wars, were often destroyed, but always rebuilt in a more rich and grandiose fashion, till the time of King Alexander the Great. Tombs, observatories, sacred hills, they are all of these things. Rising always higher and higher, they were supposed to offer dwelling, bed, table and food to the god honored in the city. The citizens tried, through material means and magical devices, to attract one of the gods of the mountains, to keep him and, in some way, to oblige him to protect the city.

---

[56] Herodotus, *Histories* I, 181, (Baltimore: Penguin Classics, 1965).

One can suppose that the Israelites during the Babylonian captivity, or perhaps earlier during the reign of Solomon (the epoch to which this biblical narrative may go back) saw the Tower of Babel, not in its splendor, but in ruin, its more usual condition for long periods of time. Perhaps, after the example of the Babylonians themselves, he interpreted this destruction as a judgment of God and a divine curse: the impious had become too powerful, and proposed the conquest of heaven! But God was able to stop them and, for this purpose, simply confused their language.

The biblical writer was right, and the Tower of Babel is symbolically an eloquent lesson. When the wicked join the wicked, when the impious join the impious, such people cannot achieve a lasting work because their perversity contains the seeds of their failure, even if, for a while, they seem to dominate the earth and make themselves equal to heaven. Before long, their building falls down in ruin, because the impious destroy each other. The "true cathedral" is built on piety and virtue, which are the foundations of a genuine union, of a real community, of the "City of God." Then, as the psalmist says, "justice rises from the earth, and peace comes down from heaven."

## QUESTIONNAIRE

1. In the Babylonian *Enuma Elish*, or in the *Epic of Gilgamesh*, find evidence of mere repetition of data of these poems by the Bible. Why does the Bible, in that case, repeat the ancient Babylonian tradition, even since the story is unscientific?

2. In the same Mesopotamian texts, find evidence of correction by the Bible by way of addition, suppression, or change of names and of meanings. What is the importance of such alterations for the meaning and message of the biblical text?

3. Show that the Mesopotamian texts have been corrected by the people and authors of the Bible according to their own biblical faith.

4. Explain how the discovery of the Mesopotamian tablets and of their language could, and did, revolutionize the study of the Bible.

5. Explain the creation of the world and of humankind by Marduk (creation of the heavens, of the earth, of man). Explain the symbolism of the creation of men respectively after the image of God, and from the blood of Kingu? Or are the two images right?

6. Compare Adam and Enkidu (*Epic of Gilgamesh*): birth, innocence, corruption, death. What is the meaning of the story of Adam? of the story of Enkidu?

7. Show the Mesopotamian pessimism concerning the hereafter in the search of Gilgamesh for immortal life. What philosophy for the present life did Utnapishtim and Sidouri teach Gilgamesh? Do many people today think the same? Is it bad?

8. In the Biblical narrative of Adam and Eve, do you find the idea of a future life? a teaching about sin? about marriage?

9. Show similarities and differences between the Mesopotamian and the biblical narratives of the Deluge.

10. What is the meaning of the Mesopotamian story of the Deluge? Could it encourage Gilgamesh in his search for immortal life? What is the meaning of the biblical narrative of Noah? What are the conditions for salvation according to the biblical narrative of the Deluge?

11. Show from the invocation of departed Enkidu by Gilgamesh that, according to the Mesopotamian traditions, the condition of the dead was miserable. How is this pessimism about the hereafter reflected on tomb inscriptions in ancient Mesopotamia? and in the belief about unsatisfied and evil spirits?

12. Show the existence of the same pessimism about the hereafter in the myths of Ishtar, Adana, Adapa.

13. What was the meaning of the Tower of Babel and other ziggurats of Mesopotamia for the Mesopotamians themselves?

14. What deep reflections did the dilapidated condition of the Tower of Babel suggest to the Israelites?

15. What is better concerning the hereafter: the dream (a kind of science-fiction) of the ancient Egyptians? or the pessimism of the Mesopotamians?

16. Can we say that the position of simple faith and confidence in God is constructive enough regarding our hope for life after death?

# BIBLIOGRAPHY

*The Epic of Gilgamesh*, tr. N.K. Sandars. Baltimore: Penguin Classics, 1972.

HEIDEL, Alexander. *The Babylonian Genesis: the Story of Creation*. Chicago: University of Chicago Press, 1963. Includes an English translation of Enuma elish.

KRAMER, Samuel Noah. *History Begins at Sumer*. New York: Doubleday, 1959.

PRITCHARD, James B. *Ancient Near Eastern Texts Relating to the Old Testament*, 3d.ed. Princeton: Princeton University Press, 1974. Or, *The Ancient Near East: an Anthology of Texts and Pictures*. Princeton: Princeton University Press, 1958.

WESTERMANN, Claus. *Creation*, tr. J.J. Sullion. Philadelphia: Fortress Press, 1974.

_____. *Genesis 1-11. A Commentary*. Philadelphia: Fortress Press, 1984.

WOOLLEY, Sir Leonard. *Ur of the Chaldees: a revised and updated edition of Sir L. Wollley's Excavations at Ur*, by P.R.S. Moorey. Ithaca, N.Y.: Cornell, 1982.

# CHAPTER V

# PLATO'S NOTION OF IMMORTALITY AND THE BIBLICAL RESURRECTION

The Greek solution to the problem of life after death is the result of a struggle of idealism against materialism. Materialism was represented by popular opinion, Epicurean and Stoic philosophy, and idealism by Platonism. We may assume that Plato gave a valid answer. The Jewish-Christian answer was the resurrection. There is no contradiction between the Platonic immortality and the Christian resurrection. The Platonic immortality is a philosophical solution. The resurrection is more rooted in religious history and faith, but we still need the light coming from the philosophical solution.

In the context of the spiritual legacy of Homer and of the positions on death in the Greek culture of the fourth century B.C., the first part of this chapter explains the proof of Plato for the immortality of the soul according to the *Phedo*, and the contribution of dialectics and inspiration to the communication of the soul with the life-giving Forms: the Good, the Beautiful, etc. Then, after some discussion of Plato's theory, the second part presents the answer to the question of the afterlife in the last books of the Old Testament and in the New Testament, particularly in Paul: the resurrection, in the light of 1 Cor.15.

## OPINIONS CONCERNING THE AFTER-LIFE IN THE TIME OF PLATO

### 1. THE LEGACY OF HOMER.

The *Iliad* and the *Odyssey*, the famous Homeric poems, represented the sacred books and somehow the Bible of the Greeks. From Homer the Greeks drew their theology: the multiplicity, the attributes, and particularly the functions of their gods. Homer's conception of humanity and of the hereafter remained classical for the Greeks, who constantly referred to it.

First, in Homer we find remnants of prehistoric animism, e.g., the idea that the soul of the departed survives, and that it needs the offering of sacrifices for its sustenance. This conception is attested by the human sacrifices offered before the pyre of Patrocles. In addition, the custom of burning the body (the case of Patrocles again) seems to have been intended to liberate the soul more quickly. However, the notion of the soul's survival understood as real life is not frequent in Homer. The poet wrote in a time when earthly life and glory were too highly prized, especially in the Greek aristocracy. As a consequence, a more pessimistic notion of death prevails in his poems, namely, the idea that the dead enjoy only a mediocre, and joyless kind of survival. When a valiant warrior dies, night falls down upon him. He falls into darkness, and in Hades is reduced to a condition near to nothingness.

In the famous scene of necromancy in the *Odyssey* xi, Odysseus pours into a pit dug by hand the blood of a sacrifice in order to attract the souls of the dead, which gather around the pit and find a sparkle of life in this blood. With his rod, he dismisses those whom he does not need, and lets the shade of Tiresias, whom he wants to interview, drink first. He then calls the shade of Achylles, which is as pitiful as the others. He speaks with his mother, entering into a sorrowful conversation with her, since the condition of his beloved mother looks hopelessly poor.

In contrast, there are a few privileged individuals, such as Menelad, who have been taken off by the gods and placed in the Islands of the Blessed, or in the Elysian Fields. Their condition is enviable, but mostly unattainable for the majority of folk. In addition, if they enjoy a happy life, their place is too remote from ours to allow relations with them. This thin hope, however, was for the Greeks the germ of hope. If Menelad could have been taken off and led to the Islands of the Blessed, why could not I? Upon this little light of hope the Greeks built, with a greater and greater confidence, their belief in individual salvation.

## 2. The Dionysiac and Orphic spiritualism.

Coming from Thracia, the worship of Dionysos (god of wine) brought with it the idea of a real possibility of life for the soul separated from its body. The worshippers of Dionysos made use of the technique of ecstasy, relying on means often questionable, such as dancing and frenzy. But, in this experience, they found the evidence and foretaste of an ecstatic happiness in which the body becomes insensitive, but everything takes place in the soul. Would not death be such an ecstasy, and the most radical of all? Then, instead of finding in death annihilation or a poor and unhappy survival, does not the soul reach the blessed immortality of an endless ecstasy?

According to the Orphists (a group of mystics), the soul is actually a fallen god in need of being raised up, a prisoner expecting to be discharged of its corporeal fetters. The Orphists, therefore, recommended the practice of a lofty morality, and observed minute rules of purity. They even abstained from meat, because a god may live incarnated in an animal. The belief in metempsychosis is then widely spread: souls are spiritual beings, miniature gods, limited in number, who incarnate themselves again after death, according to their merit and choice, into a human, an animal, or even a plant, and who will perhaps continue to live forever. Our human life provides them with an opportunity for redemption. We must therefore emancipate these spiritual beings through ascetical practices from the bondage of matter, in order to enable them to make a better choice in their future reincarnation.

## 3. The popular and the learned materialism.

The earliest philosophers inclined towards materialism which is an easier philosophy and nearer to actual appearances and popular ideas. Heraclitus holds the soul to be a part of the general fire which burns the world. This fire is eternal, but it may go out in ourselves, and, for this reason, we cannot claim a true, individual immortality. Parmenides, considering the soul as a mixture of hot and cold, feels unable to grant it immortality.

Similarly, Philolaos holds the human nature to be a harmony of corporeal elements, obviously perishable together with the body. However, under the influence of the Orphists, he adds to this mixture an independent spiritual being, a *daimon*: the Greek, for demon, meaning a little god naturally endowed with immortality. Such were also the opinions of Pythagoras and of Empedocles. According to Empedocles, the process of thought depends on the senses, and the senses ultimately depend on the four elements: fire, water, air, earth, into which the body returns after death; but there is in the human being a divine part which does not die. Empedocles introduced himself as a fallen god who was about to return to his former status.

Nevertheless, the mass of people and the majority of the learned did not seriously believe in the immortality of the soul. What is the soul ultimately? A breath? a fume?[57] It is admitted that old folk, next to death, worry about their past behavior,[58] but the healthy and sound people do not care, and do not seriously raise the question of immortality.[59] Socrates himself is not very affirmative; he himself has nothing to fear from death, since, *if* there are gods, they will welcome him as a friend, and, *if* he is annihilated, he will not suffer in the hereafter.[60] Such were the opinions about the soul and immortality which Plato encountered, against which he had to struggle, and upon which he could build.

---

[57] *Phedo*, p.70a.

[58] *Republic*, I,p.330.

[59] *Republic* 10,p.608.

[60] *Apology*, p.171.

# PLATO'S PROOF FOR THE IMMORTALITY OF THE SOUL

## 1. THE PHILOSOPHER BEFORE DEATH.

### a. *A prejudice to be rejected.*

Books 2 and 3 of *Republic* have surprised many people by their severe judgment on poets. Homer himself is hardly spared. In the future city proposed by Plato, certain poetry has no place. Such a severity on the part of Plato is not unfounded, and the Christians used to their advantage Plato's famous diatribe against the poets and their portrayal of the gods.

In this diatribe, Plato disagrees with the poets when they disfigure death and make it ugly. Such a lie should not be part of an education suited to young people who need moral support and a trustful training. God, indeed, is one, spirit, immutable, true, good, just. On the other hand, death must not occasion fear, since it is not a bogey man.[61] On the contrary, death is good, and a philosopher both prepares for it and desires it.

### b. *Death is good.*

Death is the chief concern of a philosopher who holds that to live is learning how to die, and dying progressively. In other words, the purpose of a philosopher should be to free oneself as much as possible from the bondage of the passions and of matter.[62]

On the contrary, those who wish to avoid death at all costs, actually love their body at the cost of their own soul, and are unworthy of the name of philosopher.[63] The activity of the mind enables us to reach truth, i.e., reality, and to surpass mere appearances. On the contrary, the body is only able to provide sensory knowledge, i.e., the knowledge of appearances, which is deceiving.[64] The body stands as a screen between the soul and the reality of things.

Therefore, knowledge through the soul, without bodily cooperation, should be purer. And, since death is a separation between body and soul,[65] a philosopher should gladly welcome death, for such is the way to reach the perfection of knowledge

---

[61] *Phedo* p.77.

[62] *Phedo*, p. 64a; *Gorgias*, p. 493.

[63] *Phedo*, p. 68c.

[64] *Phedo*, p. 66.

[65] *Phedo*, p. 64c.

which represents human happiness.[66] During the present life, a philosopher only enjoys an initiation to true knowledge, but, being trained for thinking, he is purified more or less from his corporeal bondage in such a way that he may die without fear, since he is sure, after his death, to join the society of the blessed.[67]

## 2. The Platonic proof for the immortality of the soul: *Phedo*.

Plato places this proof in the time-frame of his master Socrates' last day. The imminence and the circumstances of Socrates' death give the conversation reported in *Phedo* its particularly impressive character. Socrates considers death as a personal and present affair, and, when we read *Phedo*, we feel also that we have to consider it in the same manner, i.e., as a problem which requires a solution from us, a personal problem, always present since we do not know whether we shall live tomorrow. Socrates' arguments depend on a notion of the soul which agrees with the theory of reincarnations, an hypothesis which we cannot accept. We shall therefore be obliged to reconsider the following arguments, and to find whether we can do without the hypothesis of reincarnations, or whether there is in Plato some basis which could still support a demonstration of immortality regardless of reincarnation.

### a. *The argument of the contraries.*

If, logically and actually death comes from life, and life from death, then we must admit that the dead become living again.

### b. *The argument of reminiscence.*

This argument provides us with the basis underlying the former argument which, otherwise, would be purely logical in character. When you question people correctly, they --even if they have no culture-- find out by themselves and from themselves the main principles of knowledge and, consequently, every truth. Here we refer to the famous scene where Socrates is interviewing the young slave of Meno.[68]

The lad had only forgotten these principles of knowledge, and the interrogation gave him the opportunity to remind himself of them. Since the experiment shows that he knew these

---

[66] *Phedo*, p. 68b.

[67] *Phedo*, p. 52.

[68] *Meno*, p. 81.

principles "previously," without any education, we must affirm that he had learned them in a previous life. As a consequence, the junction of both these arguments (Contraries and Reminiscence) proves the existence of a previous life and the possibility of a later life after death.

### 3. The Argument of the Kinship of the Soul with the Object of Thought.

Inclined by the body towards the object of sense, the soul is, as it were, scattered, becomes quasi-drunk, and wandering.[69] On the contrary, when the soul attaches itself to the object of thought, when it longs for the essence of things, then, it returns to the great principles, meets EQUALITY, the GOOD, BEAUTY, TRUTH. In other words, it reaches the Divine, the Immortal, the Intelligible, the Indissoluble. But it does this in the manner of a mystical experience. Here, in the very act of knowing, the soul discovers its kinship with these objects, because it can only know what is, in some regard, like itself, and to know is "to assimilate." As a consequence, the soul is immortal like these objects.

Through meditation on such objects, i.e., through intellectual activity, the soul avoids dissipation in the body; it becomes unified; it "collects itself in itself," and thereby is trained to be divided from the body, or to die.[70]

More than once, Plato describes the movement of the soul bending itself back upon itself, and thus closing the circle within itself, instead of continuously issuing roots into the field of the senses. It is inside itself that the soul then seeks truth about humanity, God, and everything. This movement is that of reflection, which is a human characteristic, and also the beginning of inner life.

Since the soul finds within itself a source of life, it does not need to seek outside. Therefore, it will not suffer any damage from the destruction of the body, but, on the contrary, death will come for the soul as a liberation.

### 4. The Objections of Simias and of Cebes.

Socrates' demonstration is interrupted by Simias and Cebes who both issue an objection. It is necessary that Socrates be successful in giving a full answer since the time of drinking the hemlock is near at hand.

If the soul --Simias says, re-asserting the theory of Philolaos--, is the harmony of our corporeal nature, then it

---

[69] *Phedo*, p. 79c.

[70] *Phedo*, p. 80e; p. 67c.

perishes together with the body, just as musical harmony vanishes together with the destruction of the lyre.

In his answer, Socrates agrees that the soul is such a harmony, but not a passive harmony which would thoroughly depend on the body. On the contrary, the soul is an active harmony, for she masters and governs the body. Therefore, the soul is essentially different from the body, and does not perish together with the body. In addition, is not the musical harmony itself something different from the lyre and its tensed strings?

If each successive life --Cebes says in his turn-- is a dress that humans take off when it is worn out in order to put another on, then humanity is not proved to be immortal. For, as one will die after one has worn out several dresses, so will one fall into nothingness after several re-incarnations.

Socrates answers that, if the bondage of matter only does harm to a person, the same is not true of our partaking of Fine, Good, Great, etc. by thought. Here is found the true activity of the soul, and the more the soul involves itself in this acquaintance with the Forms, the more it is given force and life, and the more --so to say-- it acquires immortality.

### 5. THE LAST ARGUMENT: THE ELIMINATION OF THE OPPOSITES.

The possession of these realities: the Fine, the Good, Truth, etc., as far as their possession is real, eliminates the presence of their opposites which are deprivation of such riches and a condition of the soul akin to death. Therefore, if the soul attaches itself eagerly to these objects which are the source of its life, we can say that the soul may enjoy immortality.

#### a. *A corollary to this demonstration.*

We must perform the good under all its forms in order to reach blessed immortality because there is no other way to get it. On the one hand, the immortality of the soul should depend on morality because immortality is a reward for the good. On the other hand, immortality is presupposed by Ethics, for, if the evil one is freed from sin by the mere fact of dying, then why bother doing good?

#### b. *A complement: the soul does not die from evil.*

The soul cannot die from an evil which is alien to its rational nature, for instance, a corporeal evil. But it is also true that the soul does not die from an evil which is its own, e.g., hatred, as is evidenced by experience. Therefore, the soul is immortal. Therefore the soul is indestructible as sharing in rationality which does not die.

## DIALECTICS AND INSPIRATION AS COMMUNICATION WITH HIGHER REALITIES

In Socrates' opinion, salvation is both a moral and an intellectual affair. Going to God is going both to justice and truth. However, there are two ways leading to truth: dialectics and inspiration.

### 1. DIALECTICS.

Dialectics is the favorite method of Socrates. This device relies on the assumption that everybody, if correctly questioned, is able to answer in such a way as to find a truth which one had forgotten, but which one actually possessed in the mind, having learned it in a previous life.

With the help of *dialectics*, i.e., the method of correct interrogation (hermeneutics) and of dialogue, Socrates methodically questioned his disciples, but did not fear to impose the same method on the great sophists who were puffed up with their erudition. Socrates made their ignorance and pretention manifest, a form of entertainment which pleased the young people attached to him, but did not happen without raising dangerous hostility against him.

Starting from the simplest and the most trivial comparisons, for instance, from the craft of the shoemaker, Socrates came back to the great principles, Truth, Justice, Beauty, Good, and at the same time reached a thorough knowledge of the characteristics of the mind. The Socratic dialogue is essentially an inquiry on the soul, and on the higher realities (what we call the Divine) through the soul. Plato believed in dialectics because it is the very exercise of reason. Not to believe in it, in Plato's opinion, is to be a *misologos*, i.e., an enemy to thought itself,[71] and corresponds to a complete denial of thought, which is unworthy of a human being.

However, if reason can reach truth, dialectics is a dangerous game, or better, a very serious activity. It requires much care, modesty, prudence. He who practices it must be like its object, i.e., be sincere, just and good. To do otherwise, to seek glory, to please people's opinion, to consider mere advantage or facility, would mean falling into the error of the Sophists whom Socrates criticized bitterly, and to go astray from true science. Socrates warns his disciples against this danger which is noxious both to individuals and to the city.[72] However, a true philosopher, who earnestly uses dialectics, deserves, as long as one possesses the required abilities, not only to govern

---

[71] *Phedo*, p. 89d.

[72] *Republic* 7, p. 537.

the city, but to be promoted after death to the rank of the blessed, and even to be granted a place among the gods.[73]

*The Myth of the Cave.*

Under the form of a myth, Plato explains the redemptive value of dialectics. A group of men have been from their childhood fettered in the depth of a cave. They face the back wall of the cave. Behind them, along the path which passes before the entrance of the cave, there are workers passing by and carrying their tools. A fire projects their shadows on the wall. A hill prevents the sun beams from entering the cave. The prisoners are thus able to get some knowledge of themselves and of the outer world. If one of these prisoners is set free and leaves the cave, he will at first be blinded. But, once familiarized with light, he will be able to "see" better. Then, if he walks out of the cave and reaches the top of the hill, he will know that the source of all knowledge is the sun. If he is fettered again in the cave, his knowledge will seem ridiculous to the other prisoners.

Such is the lot of a philosopher. The visible world is the cave, and we only know shadows of intelligible things. As we make ourselves free from the bondage of our body and of injustice, we arrive at the notion of the Good, source of all knowledge and of all being. The more also will we enjoy truth and happiness, even if we suffer from being dazzled every time we approach the light. And when the philosopher is returned to what humans call "reality," although he looks ridiculous to his fellows, he is actually right, and his advice is worthwhile.

The Platonic dialectics proposes to provide not only the common good of society and that of the individuals on earth, but also blessed life in heaven. Its ultimate goal is to prepare us for a kind of beatific contemplation of the deity. In spite of some difference in Plato's conception of deity, this teaching can be accepted as "Christian truth," and corresponds to the biblical ideal.

2. INSPIRATION.

The other way of knowledge is inspiration. Here knowledge does not proceed from humans, but from God himself. In *Phoedrus*,[74] Socrates acknowledges that he has spoken concerning love under the inspiration of a "god." This inspiration, granted from on high caused in him a kind of frenzy, a rapture, an enthusiasm which brought him out of himself, to a condition of ecstasy, whereby he uttered thoughts which were more divine

---

[73] *Republic* 7.

[74] *Phoedrus*, p. 243.

than human. He reached a higher mode of perception in which he was enlightened directly by God.

This notion of inspiration can be admitted without hesitation by Christians who consider it as a consequence of grace. It is linked to love. It enables us to perform the good, even heroic deeds with enthusiasm and joy.

*The Myth of the winged horse team.*

In the same book,[75] Plato, certainly under this type of inspiration, writes some of his finest pages. He sees a team of winged horses drawing a chariot which flies heavenward. The driver is the soul. The two horses are the reasonable and the unreasonable parts of the soul. The team takes off, following the gods and proposing to pass over the vault of heaven in order to run upon its outer surface. There, together with the gods, the soul will be free to contemplate the Ideas or Forms, the heavenly realities on the pattern of which earthly things have been shaped. Of course, the race is uneasy, and the horses are not equal. The driver must display much zeal and skill. Many teams fail and overturn. Some succeed.

Such is the lot of souls. Reminding themselves of heavenly realities, they endeavour to rise through contemplation and moral effort towards their heavenly ideals. Blessed they are when they reach their goal without falling down, and obtain a place in heaven.

This myth, up to this point, is worthy of the Christian teaching and has supported the meditation of many Christians for centuries. We shall see later that it requires more caution.

## EVALUATION AND ADJUSTMENT OF THE VIEW OF PLATO ON IMMORTALITY

### 1. The contribution of Plato.

Plato forgoes indulging himself in novel-making, although he uses the device of myth which is for him nothing but a parable designed to investigate the soul and deity. He discards every magical device. He does not employ material and magical forces at the cost of morality, as was the case along the borders of the Egyptian Nile.

With Plato, the search for the soul and for God, the investigation of the mysteries of the hereafter, even the accomplishment of the destiny of the soul, all these are a purely interior and spiritual affair. Plato, indeed, found out the true "key" to the human mystery: the formula "Know thyself." Actually, from Plato on, people know themselves, and this knowledge

---

[75] *Phoedrus*, p. 246.

enables them to reach the knowledge of God, and to find out the way to a blessed destiny.

Plato believes in a different destiny for the righteous and the unrighteous, and in a judgment which will reward good and punish evil after death. On account of this belief, he deserves citizenship somehow among us, because, like the Bible, he acknowledges moral practice as the only way to heaven. Often Plato alludes to a judgment after death, for instance, in the myth of Hades in *Gorgias*.[76] In his opinion also, a real philosopher deserves to be raised up to the rank of the gods.[77] And Socrates warned his disciple not to weep or mourn him after his death.[78]

2. RECONSIDERATION OF THE ARGUMENT OF REMINISCENCE.

We can see that Plato's thought is not the same as Christian thought, that we cannot agree on some of his statements, and that some of his arguments do not fit without changing our own proof for immortality. In brief, we cannot agree on his doctrine of the eternity of souls. We teach that the soul is immortal, but admit a beginning. We must, therefore, reconsider Plato's arguments to make them our own and to adapt them to our teaching.

Plato's chief argument, from which all others are derived, is certainly that of REMINISCENCE. When Socrates questions the slave of Meno,[79] the lad "reminds himself" of the idea of equality. Correctly questioned, he would be able to rediscover all the theorems of the geometry of Euclid and all truth. Does that prove that Meno's slave has really enjoyed a previous life? or that he owned these ideas when he was born? Actually, the argument of reminiscence can only prove what is sufficient in our own proof for the immortality of the soul, i.e., that we are in contact and communication with a higher Reality, with the Spirit of God, to whom we are akin since we have been created according to his image.

When we discover the enriching and beatifying reality of the deepest object of our thought: Beauty, Good, Truth, etc., we reach the knowledge of God, the only source of infinite and everlasting happiness. At the same time, we understand that we have nothing to fear from death for we know God directly through our soul, without the help of our body. Therefore, the destruction of our body should not cause that of our soul. On

---

[76] *Gorgias*, p. 253ff.

[77] *Republic* 8.

[78] *Phedo*, p. 115.

[79] *Meno*, p. 81.

the contrary, suffering itself, instead of destroying our soul, increases its power and enriches it with the value of sacrifice, lifting us to a higher degree of being and to holiness on earth. Death can make freer the faculties of our soul, and provide them with unlimited power.

The aspiration of our soul upwards does not require any necessity of a previous life. It is not a reminiscence, but only the living and true discovery of a present reality: communication with the divine, which is for us the beginning of everlasting happiness.

### 3. Reconsideration of the Conception of the Hereafter.

The idea of a previous life of the soul leads to the idea of reincarnation and metempsychosis. If we have already lived before we were born, then obviously we lived in another epoch, in another body, perhaps in an animal body, and, after our death, we shall be born again, and that indefinitely.

Plato sees in the act of reincarnation an option of the soul, which, in fact, corresponds to its merits, and to a kind of reward or punishment which the soul grants itself. The destinies, according to the myth of Er,[80] are free and left to the choice of everyone. Plato sees in this freedom in choosing a new destiny after death a chance of redemption. The soul can rediscover absolute Beauty during a later life, if, moved by inspiration, it awakens in itself the memory of its native ideals and proposes to conquer them again. Then, the soul starts again its race upwards and can reach the vision of Beauty on the outer surface of the vault of heaven. Such is the second part of the myth of the winged horse team and chariot in *Phoedrus*.

The moral elevation of Plato's view cannot be denied, but actually we must renounce the hope for a new earthly life and for a new chance of redemption. What is the ultimate reason for the impossibility of a new life? If we want an answer, we must leave Plato himself and continue beyond his own conquests. Plato is right to see in the possession of God a human goal. But why does he seem to admit that we can become tired of God, lose interest in possessing God completely, or leave God once we have discovered such a source of bliss? Can't we forever draw from the everlasting source of the greatest happiness, with all the energies of a purified soul? Or would we be unfortunate enough to despise the possession of this bliss in order to turn to lower things and fall down again into matter, to return to earthly pleasures and start a new bodily existence?

And why these perpetual new beginnings? We are in the Greek world which believed in cyclical periods of growing and destruction, before a new start. Plato stopped at this point, and refused to go further. As for us, we are left unsatisfied by the

---

[80] *Republic* p. 251.

Greek cyclical idea, and we feel that we must continue until the end of the way, without any idea of coming back, without fearing any weariness or delusion, for the one who possesses the infinite cannot foster any other desire.

4. THE REDEMPTION OF THE ENTIRE HUMAN NATURE.

The ground for this position of Plato is found in his notion of human nature. Plato places a thorough enmity between the different parts of the human being, and not just an accidental enmity, as we do in Christian doctrine. In the opinion of Plato, the soul is the enemy of the body which is its jail, the fetters preventing it from perceiving God. Moreover, for Plato, the soul itself does not reach a true unity without mutilation. The soul is a chariot with several unequal horses. In the *Republic*, these three horses are Thought (*nous*), Emotion (*thumos*), and Desire (*epithumia*). The later two unescapably come to failure, and Thought alone can reach the goal. Apparently, in the opinion of Plato,humans cannot go to God with their whole being. Only Thought can manage it, but not without losing its two companions: Emotion and Desire.

We may even add that, according to Plato, the soul does not seem to reach its perfection without losing its individual character, because, at the end, our Thought will be found exactly identical with all the other Thoughts, in the ocean of pantheism. Such seems to be the last word of Plato. It was, at least, the position of his later disciples, perhaps of Plotinus (third century A.D.),[81] and certainly of the Origenists of the 6th century A.D.

According to Paul and Christianity, this enmity between body and soul is not fundamental, or essential, but merely accidental: a consequence of sin. Body and soul are not two opposed beings, but two elements of our being, which must be reconciled in the future. If the soul is granted forgiveness, if it recovers its mastery over itself, it will eventually master the whole human being, including the material body: aren't we able to partly transfigure our body already in the present life?

---

[81] However, see Plotinus, "Of the necessary outgoing of all things from the One," *Enneads* IV, viii, 6 in E.R. Dodds, *Select Passages Illustrating Neoplatonism* (London: SPCK, 1960), pp. 29-30. See also the discussion of Jean Trouillard, *La Procession Plotinienne* (Paris: PUF, 1955), pp. 61-69. It seems that the human individuality remains at the end, according to Plotinus, but the question is debated.

# THE BIBLICAL DOCTRINE OF THE RESURRECTION ANSWERING THE HELLENISTIC MATERIALISM.

The Church followed the example of saint Paul in converting the Greco-Roman world: Paul was her inspiration and rule. He provided her with a presentation of the biblical and evangelical doctrine suited to the pagan world, particularly with a method of conversion based on the belief in the redemption: Jesus crucified and raised again for our forgiveness and our spiritual revival. This message was more powerful than abstract philosophy.

Paul adopted both the position of defense and of attack that had been used by the Jews in the Hellenistic world for a long time. The biblical Book of Wisdom of Solomon represents their thought. Written in Greek and not in Hebrew, it seems to come from the Jewish community of Alexandria. Paul relies on the Book of Wisdom, which he takes over and combines with the data of the Gospel.

## 1. The Book of the Wisdom of Solomon.

### a. *Death according to the atheist and to the believer.*

There are two positions regarding death, which beget two radically contrary conceptions of the soul. In the opinion of the atheist, or the impious, there is nothing after death because the soul is only smoke, breath, vapor, or a spark which vanishes and is scattered at death. This is the materialistic conception which denies the soul any independence from the body and any being of its own.

On the contrary, in the opinion of the believer, death is not the end nor the annihilation of the individual. In itself, death is a disorder and cannot be considered as part of God's creation. Death is the effect and the chastisement of sin. And it is the Devil, the originator of sin, who brought it into the world and into the history of humankind.

Disorder and evil, however, are not properly destruction and annihilation, and the impious are wrong when they believe that they can live with impunity in pleasure and immorality, enjoy life, as they propose, without expecting any punishment after death. On the contrary, the believers are right when they hold that there is a reward for souls which are pure from sin, a remuneration for their good deeds. But the impious, at death, are given the greatest chastisement. They see the annihilation of everything in which they placed their happiness, without being themselves annihilated, for they continue to be "an object of reprobation among the dead forever."

b. *The answer to the objection about the death of young people.*

The worst scandal for the weak is the death of a child or of young people who have not enjoyed their portion of life. The death of the just, especially premature death, is an objection against God's justice and goodness. If, according to the common view, death is a punishment, how could the just who die in their youth deserve it? Why are they deprived of the legitimate joys of life?

The Book of Wisdom answers these objections. The premature death of the just is not truly an evil, but probably a divine grace. God, who foresees and knows human weakness, granted this person the favor of calling her back earlier, upon finding her well-disposed and pure, and this in order to preserve her from future sin. We may add: fine youth equals full life. The death of the just is annihilation only in appearance because, after death, the just are granted great gifts and reach blessed immortality. They are numbered among the children of God and the saints, given a crown of glory and they enjoy life everlasting.

c. *Resurrection.*

During the present life, the soul dwells in her body as "under a clay-tent," "for a perishable body weighs down the soul, and this earthly tent burdens the thoughtful mind."[82] God, however, disposes of life and death. He can order us to come down unto the gates of Hades, or to come back from there.[83] He gives life, death, and resurrection.

d. *The Gospels.*

Jesus affirmed resurrection, promised everlasting life, granted resurrection to others, and finally raised himself from the dead. Thereby he gave the surest pledge for our hope.

He also resolved the most fallacious problem of our existence in the hereafter. He answered the objection of the Sadducees against resurrection, that of "the wife with seven husbands," saying:

> The sons of this age marry and are given in marriage; but those who are accounted worthy to attain that age and to the resurrection from the dead neither marry nor are given in marriage, for they cannot die any more, because they are equal to angels and are sons of the resurrection... The God of Abraham, of Isaac and of Jacob is not

---

[82] Wisdom 9:5-16..

[83] Wisdom 10:13.

the God of the dead, but of the living; for all live to him.[84]

In this answer, Jesus answered in principle all our problems about the form of our existence in the hereafter.

e. *Saint Paul in Thessalonians 4:13-18 and Acts 17:16-34.*

In the beginning, it seems that Paul only repeated the Book of Wisdom and affirmed resurrection. He also used the Apocalypses current in his time, which affirmed the Last Judgment, for which both living and dead had to be gathered. Paul presented Jesus' resurrection as the pledge of our own resurrection.

But the very word, "resurrection," upon which he insists because he is able to witness to the resurrection of Jesus, troubles the Greeks: Paul feels it necessary to grant resurrection a thorough study, that which we find in I Corinthians 15.

## 2. A systematic study on resurrection in I Cor. 15.

a. *Argument of fact.*

In the beginning, Paul gives an argument of fact: Jesus' resurrection, the warrant for which he presents himself, and the old testimonies which he relates, even mentioning an apparition of Jesus to 500 disciples at once, who, for the most part, are still living when he writes. If then Christ is truly resuscitated, we are able to raise again because the same Spirit of God who performed resurrection in Christ can do it as easily in us. Therefore, we shall enjoy resurrection according to Jesus' promise. On the other hand, if we should not raise again, we would be the most unfortunate of all, since we would have taken much pain vainly in order to be better than others.

b. *The "religious" or "theological" argument.*

If death is a consequence of sin, if it is the fruit and legacy of the sin of Adam, its remedy lies necessarily in forgiveness and redemption which cures the very root and cause of evil by destroying sin.

Forgiveness and redemption are actually the achievement of Jesus, our Savior. Jesus has first overcome the Devil, the chief enemy. Then he healed us from sin, obtaining our pardon and granting us supernatural forces to avoid sin in the future.

---

[84] Luke 20:34-38.

Jesus turns us away from the "works of death" and brings us to perform the "works of life."

Thirdly, when Jesus raised himself from the dead, he defeated in himself the "last enemy" resulting from sin: death, and we shall share in the same victory.

Because death is but the effect of sin, it will vanish when its cause is cleared up, and that will happen when the life of Christ will flourish in us with the gifts and the power of the Holy Spirit.

c. *The mode of resurrection.*

We must now inquire how this resurrection will be achieved under its corporeal aspect, i.e., with what body we shall rise again and live in the hereafter. This question is raised, and Paul answers it.

At first, he distinguishes between several kinds of bodies, and classifies them from the most corruptible to the most incorruptible. Then he takes the comparison of the grain of wheat, sown, buried into earth, but rising again for a new life. Sown corruptible, for it becomes rotten, it overcomes corruption, since it rises again from earth in the Spring season and finds a new youth.

Similarly, when we die, we leave to the earth a corruptible body, taken from the dust, earthly, material, unworthy to inherit incorruptibility, but, in the resurrection, we are given by God an incorruptible, heavenly, glorious, spiritual body. It is not only a matter of local change. We are called to undergo a deep transformation, i.e., a change as important as that which occurs for the sake of the deceased through death itself. This change, however, does not cause a break of our identity. We continue to be ourself, and we keep our personality. In order to affirm it, Paul borrows the comparison of the dress. It is the same person who takes off the unworthy dress of earthly flesh, and puts on the glorious dress of the spiritual body.

Following the example of Jesus, Paul fights against every kind of materialistic notion of survival, but he affirms that humans are truly living in heaven, and that we continue our existence there, but not in one part of our being (e.g., in the intellectual element) at the expense of the others.

d. *Complements in Romans 5:12-15 and Col. 3:1-4.*

Paul resumes his theological argument in his epistle to the Romans and here adds that this very work has already begun and is partly achieved on earth. We have already in ourselves put to death the "old man," and, both in principle and in practice, we have already put on the condition of a "new man." Therefore, God's Spirit works in us, and we possess the vital force which made Christ to rise again. We are living in the full sense of the term, but this life is presently hidden. It will be manifested in its fullness on the day when we shall undergo resurrection and change in our body, after the example of Christ and like him.

Obviously, Paul is aware of the fact that one of the data for the identification of the body of the resurrection is missing: we do not know the physical conditions of the future world, i.e., what our environment will be. Paul mentions an earthly, an aerial, a heavenly or glorious body. These different "environments" suggest the condition of mammalians on earth, of fish in water, of birds in the air, of demons (in antiquity: angels, or geniuses) in the upper air, of heavenly bodies (like the sun, moon and stars) in space. In any case, in order to be the proper instrument, the body has to be borrowed from the environment where it will live. If we rise again in order to dwell in a kind of "Earthly Paradise," as many ancient and modern Christians unconsciously suppose without more questioning, then we need a body of the same composition as the present one, and there is nothing wrong in such a conclusion.

But Paul does not seem to favor the idea of an earthly dwelling, even far away from our planet, and he does not even insist on the idea of a heavenly body like that of the sun, moon and stars. He seems to be disappointed by these representations which please our imagination more than the sense of the Christian faith.

Paul proposes a new notion of the body of the resurrection: the "spiritual body."[85] He does not explain this notion, perhaps because everybody understood what he meant. But this notion is not clear to us. We can think that it represents an emphasis of Paul on the internal life, in which everything is spiritual, or works for a spiritual purpose. The Fathers of the Church speak of spiritual eyes, nostrils, ears, mouth, heart, hands, blood, bowels, feet, etc., as a way to illustrate spiritual attention, spiritual works, spiritual "odor," spiritual feelings, spiritual mercy, etc. They seem to be on the right path.

However, according to ancient Jewish anthropology, we should refrain from reasoning too unilaterally in terms of (material) body versus (spiritual=intellectual) soul, which is the Greek model of a human being. For Paul, the passage from a body of sin, death and corruption to a spiritual body is the passage of our human nature (in the common, unphilosophical, sense), corrupted by sin and subjected to suffering and death, to a spiritual condition in which, by the power of the divine Spirit, our nature is restored to its integrity and shares in the incorruptibility of God in the (corporate) body of the risen Christ.

## QUESTIONNAIRE

1. Find in Homer the evidence of a pessimistic notion of death and after-life.

---

[85] 1 Cor. 15:44.

2. How did the Greek materialists (learned and popular) represent the destiny of the soul after death?

3. How could the Greeks find a hope for themselves in considering the case of Menelad in Homer? How did the ecstatic Dionysiacs (Orphists) discover a life and happiness of the soul when the soul is freed from the body?

4. What did the Pythagoreans mean by a personal *daimon* (demon)? What is the theory of the reincarnations? Do you know people who believe in reincarnations today?

5. Show that the theory of the reincarnations underlies Plato's argument of the "contraries." Show that Plato's proof for the immortality of the soul can work without the reincarnations.

6. Explain the argument of the kinship of the soul with the Forms (the Good, the Beautiful, the Truth, Equality,etc.). Explain that, by participation in these Forms (in meditation and action), the soul obtains strength, and that we can consider immortality as a possibility for the soul.

7. What is the objection of Simias? How does Socrates answer it? Show how it is the objection of materialists today as well.

8. What is the objection of Cebes? How does Socrates answer it? Is there a kind of "fountain of youth" for souls which might be exhausted by old age or wickedness, and thus deprived of "immortal" life?

9. How does Plato prove that the soul, even when deprived of moral or spiritual life, is not annihilated, but can last forever? What does Plato's definition of absolute wickedness as "endless dying" mean in this regard? What is left, according to Plato, as a remnant of existence in the soul in the worst situation?

10. What is the validity of Plato's proof for immortality?

11. What may be criticized in Plato's proof for immortality?

12. How did the Wisdom of Solomon (1st century B.C.) answer the objections from the prosperity of the impious and from the premature death of the just? Can this answer be given to people lightly (without a real faith)?

13. Does Jesus come with an answer to the problem of life after death? Among other arguments given by Jesus, do not forget the argument built on the Patriarchs and their living God.

14. What is the "argument of fact" for the resurrection in Paul's I Corinthians 15 ?

15. What is the "theological argument" in Paul's I Cor. 15? Show that there is something right with this argument, at least concerning the spiritual life. Show also that it can be contested.

16. What does it mean for a person of the time of Paul to rise again with an earthly body? an aerial body? a heavenly (or glorious) body? Is Paul pleased with these suggestions?

17. What might Paul mean by his concept of a "spiritual body"? What is the emphasis of Paul?

18. If the definition of the nature of a body is a question of environment, is it against reason to conceive of a kind of earthly paradise? What kind of body would we have in such an environment? This view, indeed, has been that of most Christians from the beginning because it is more simple. But does Paul, in I Cor. 15, recommend this solution as his own choice?

19. Compare the notion of the soul in Plato with its equivalent (the person) in Teilhard de Chardin.

20. Compare the Christian classical notion of the resurrection with Teilhard's notion of the resurrection.

## BIBLIOGRAPHY

ATHENAGORAS. *Resurrection of the Dead* (2d century), tr. J.H. Crehan. ACW 23, 1956.

CORNELIS, H., J. GUILLET, Th. CAMELOT, and M. A. GENEVOIS. *The Resurrection of the Body*, tr. M. Joselyn. Notre Dame: Fides, 1964.

MACKENZIE, John L. "Body." *Dictionary of the Bible*, pp. 100-102.

RHODE, Erwin. *Psyche.* 2 vols. New York: Harper & Row, 1966.

STENDALL, K. ed. *Immortality and Resurrection. Four Essays by O. Cullmann, H.A. Wolfson, W. Jaeger, H.J. Cadbury.* New York: Macmillan, 1965.

CUMONT, F. *Lux perpetua* Paris, 1949.

# CHAPTER VI

## ANCIENT SACRIFICIAL RITES AND THE SACRIFICE OF CHRIST

The history of sacrifice is that of the love of human beings for God. But, since this history began much earlier than the epoch when the lofty feeling of God's love was born in the human heart, it would better be called the history of the service of God. In order to grasp its beginnings, we must go back further than our Christian notion of God, further even than the Bible itself, although the Bible prescribed the sacrifice of animals, a crude practice. Actually, we must start with the earliest and the lowest representations of the deity. With such kinds of gods, sacrifice is not a matter of love, but the service of a hard master. Whether the master be a king or a god, a great or a small master, his servants are treated according to the dispositions of this master, and these dispositions are often far from being kind and noble. Humans gave themselves dreadful gods, whom they felt obliged to appease through the offering of sacrifices, even human sacrifices.

Fortunately, the notion of the deity evolved and its progress appears clearly in the development of the great civilizations, under a form particular to each of them. We observe a parallel progress in the relationship between humans and God. The service of God slowly changed for the better, and, in the time of Jesus, had reached the level of adoration in spirit. We can consider the spiritualization of the service of God as the fruit of Greek philosophy. But this ideal is due also to the influence of the Bible on worshippers and on philosophy.

With its lofty notion of God and of humanity, the Bible offered a wonderful charter of the service of God, based upon adoration in spirit, practice of morality, and love of God. This progress in the knowledge of the true service and love of God reached its highest point in Jesus himself, who crowned it when he bid us to call God OUR FATHER. From this time on, every Christian, every human, is invited to bring into their heart, and to express through words and deeds, the sentiment of pure and perfect love of God. We are engaged in doing it already while living upon earth, but we know that the perfection of our happiness is found in the perfection of our love of God, when we join Him in heaven.

The first section of this chapter deals with human sacrifices, first those offered to a king, second, to a god. The second section deals with sacrifices of animals, and attracts the attention to similarities and differences of rituel between Scythia, Egypt, Greece, and finally the Bible, and to the meaning of sacrifices: symbolism rather than explicit thought, more definite and spiritual in the Bible. It becomes thus possible to interpret the Passion of Christ as a sacrifice, and this sacrifice as the redemptive will of Christ. An appendix summarizes R. de Vaux's historical origins and development of biblical sacrifice.

## HUMAN SACRIFICES.

Before criticizing ancient human sacrifices, it would befitting to dwell upon the right of life and death that humans grant themselves over others, and which nowadays causes so many useless and unjust deaths through war or in other ways. We should also mention the modern enslavement of so many souls under the overwhelming power of materialism, and their debasement when discarded from God who is the source of inner life and of liberty. In these cases, there is certainly the matter of human sacrifices for the sake of idols under the form of power, money, and pleasure, all these being bad and deceiving masters. Now we may turn to pagan antiquity and its horrors without any sense of false superiority. Because of the vastness of the subject, only a few examples of sacrifices will be described.

### 1. THE PIT OF DEATH IN UR IN CHALDEA.

In 1927, near the Persian gulf, in Ur, the old country of Abraham, Woolley made a discovery as sensational as that of the tomb of Tut-ank-Ammon in Egypt : the tomb of king Ab-Argui and the queen, together with a complete court, more than 150 people sacrificed for the sake of their master. They were wearing their insignia, even held harps, and were adorned with their jewels. There was no sign of violence, but on the contrary a perfect order, like that of a procession, as attested by the location of the bodies. Apparently a complete court accepted, as a normal gesture, to follow their king on the great journey, and to serve him even in the hereafter. In this epoch (c. 2000 B.C.), the civilization in Ur was advanced as seen in the wealth and beauty of the ornaments. Therefore, we cannot speak of savage barbarism.

On the other hand, in such a refined civilization as that of modern India, did not widows, until recently, throw themselves upon their husband's pyre?

### 2. THE KING'S BURIAL IN SCYTHIA.

The famous Russian *tumuli* in Pazirik, which were excavated by Rudenko, are well known in the world of archaeologists. Often a layer of ice in the pit had protected the tomb and its contents, even preserved clothing. Among the Royal Scythians, as in Ur in Chaldea, the king did not leave without the Queen and an important escort of servants and stablemen.

The historian of antiquity, Herodotus, gives us a detailed account of the funeral customs of the Scythians :

> The king is carried upon a chariot through all his country so that everybody could share in the national mourning. Arriving at his burial place, he is placed in a central room that is furnished with a complete set of funeral furniture and surrounded by representatives of his own house, who are strangled and buried near him. Then everything is covered by a large hillock. Next year, fifty of his best servants are sacrificed in their turn and fixed upon bodies of horses, with the help of a wooden frame, so that they form around the hillock a funeral guard.[86]

The Scythians were not savage people. On the other hand, the Greeks themselves praised in the *Iliad* (23) the sacrifice of twelve young Trojans offered by Achilles before the pyre of his friend Patrocles.

### 3. Human sacrifices to Ares among the Scythians.

We now pass from human sacrifices offered to a dead king to human sacrifices offered to gods. Such sacrifices were performed in every country in the world, in such or such epoch.

Herodotus describes the human sacrifices offered by the Scythians in honor of Ares, the god of war:

> Ceremonies in honor of Ares are conducted this way: in every district, at the seat of the government, Ares has his temple. It is of a peculiar kind, and consists of an immense heap of brushwood, three furlongs each way and somewhat less in height. The top of the heap is leveled off square, like a platform, accessible on one side but rising sheer on the other three. Every year a hundred and fifty wagon-loads of sticks are added to the pile, to make up for the constant settling caused by rains, and on the top of it is planted an ancient iron sword, which serves for the image of Ares.
>
> Annual sacrifices of horses and other cattle are made to this sword, which, indeed, claims a greater number of victims than any other of their gods. Prisoners of war are also sacrificed to Ares, but in their case the ceremony is different from that which is used in the sacrifice of animals: one man is chosen out of every hundred; wine is poured on his head, and his throat cut over a bowl; the bowl is then carried to the platform on top of the woodpile, and the blood in it is poured out over the sword.

---

[86] HERODOTUS, *Histories* 4:71-72.

> While this goes on above, another ceremony is being enacted below, close against the pile: this consists in cutting off the right hands and arms of the prisoners who have been slaughtered, and tossing them into the air. This done, and the rest of the ceremony over, the worshippers go away. The victims' arms and hands are left to lie where they fall, separate from the trunks.[87]

Here we find a permanent altar, ritual, blood poured upon an altar, the victim thrown heavenward. In spite of the horror of murder, all of these elements already manifest a classical notion of sacrifice.

The Bible absolutely forbids the offering of human victims. Only one human sacrifice is outlined in the Bible as ordered by God, that of Isaac, offered by his father Abraham.[88] However, Isaac is returned by God to his father: God did not want the death of the child, but, before concluding a covenant with him and his descendents, he wanted proof that Abraham would be faithful and obedient.

## ANIMAL SACRIFICES

We deeply resent the practice of animal sacrifices, although we know that animals were sacrificed in the ancient religions all over the world. This practice was one of the chief acts of worship. Certainly, we must not regret the disappearance of such a cruel custom. The renouncing of these cruel rites in order to adopt more spiritual forms of worship was an advancement. However, we are not allowed to compare ourselves with our ancestors too advantageously, nor to reproach them bitterly because of these bloody practices. Actually we quite agree that animals provide us with an essential part of our food. And, if out of delicacy, we do not ourselves slaughter animals, we are very pleased that others perform this service for us. As for the animals themselves, dying, whether for human sake or for the sake of the deity, is the same!

The way animals were immolated, and the presenting of the victim to the deity, did not widely differ from one people to another. The sacrificial rites are surprisingly alike, either considered in the Scythian, the Greek, the Egyptian religion, or in the Bible itself. Only details differ. In the case of the Bible, we notice a large difference from other religions regarding sacrifices. This difference consists in the strong emphasis of the Bible on the intention of the offerer, which has priority over the external act of sacrificing. The Bible also distinguishes sacrifices

[87] HERODOTUS, *Histories* 4:62.

[88] Genesis 22.

according to their purpose: sacrifices of praise or thanksgiving, sacrifices of peace or communion, sacrifices for sin.

1. SACRIFICES AMONG THE SCYTHIANS.

Herodotus describes Scythian sacrifices:

> The method of sacrifices is everywhere and in every case the same: the victim has its front feet tied together, and the person who is performing the ceremony gives a pull on the rope from behind and throws the animal down, calling, as he does so, upon the name of the appropriate god; then he slips a noose round the victim's neck, pushes a short stick under the cord and twists it until the creature is choked. No fire is lighted; there is no offering of first-fruits, and no libation. As soon as the animal is strangled, he is skinned, and then comes the boiling of the flesh.[89]

2. SACRIFICES AMONG THE EGYPTIANS.

The same Herodotus describes Egyptian sacrifices:

> Bulls are considered the property of the god Epaphus -- or Apis-- and are therefore tested in the following way: a priest appointed for the purpose examines the animal, and if he finds even a single black hair upon it, pronounces it unclean; he goes over it with the greatest care, first making it stand up, then lie on its back, after which he pulls out its tongue to see if that, too, is clean according to the recognized marks --what those are I will explain later. He also inspects the tail to make sure the hair on it grows properly; then, if the animal passes all these tests successfully, the priest marks it with twisting round its horns a band of papyrus which he seals with wax and stamps with his signet ring. The bull is finally taken away; and the penalty is death for anybody who sacrifices an animal which has not been marked in this manner.
>
> The method of sacrificing is as follows: they take the beast (one of those marked with the seal) to the appropriate altar and light a fire; then, after pouring a libation of wine and invoking the god by name, they slaughter it, cut off its head, and flay the carcass. The head is loaded with curses and taken away --if there happen to be Greek traders in the market, it is sold to them; if not, it is thrown into the river. The curses they

---

[89] HERODOTUS, *Histories* 4:60.

pronounce take the form of a prayer that any disaster which threatens either themselves or their country may be diverted and fall upon the severed head of the beast.

Both the libation and the practice of cutting off the heads of sacrificial beasts are common to all Egyptians in all their sacrifices, and the latter explains why it is that no Egyptian will use the head of any sort of animal for food. The methods of disembowelling and burning are various, and I will describe the one which is followed in the worship of the goddess whom they consider the greatest and honor with the most important festival. In this case, when they have flayed the bull, they first pray and then take its paunch out whole, leaving the intestines and fat inside the body; next they cut off the legs, shoulders, neck, and rump, and stuff the carcass with loaves of bread, honey, raisins, figs, frankincense, myrrh, and other aromatic substances; finally they pour a quantity of oil over the carcass and burn it. They always fast before a sacrifice, and while the fire is consuming it they beat their breasts.[90]

3. Sacrifices among the Greeks.

Generally, Greek sacrifices can be described as follows. On the morning that the sacrifice is to be performed, the altar is decorated with flowers, garlands and leaves. The sacrificers wear white dresses and crowns made of leaves. The victim itself is adorned with crowns and stripes, but only in the moment of immolation. The animal, tightly kept on the leash, sometimes even carried upon the shoulders, is brought next to the altar around which the sacrificers walk counterclockwise.

They have brought a vessel full of water with which they will sprinkle both the animal and the attendants when a firebrand, taken from the altar, has been plunged into it. Cast upon the sacred flame are seeds of barley and some hairs cut from the victim's head. After a prayer has been recited, the animal's throat is opened by a stab, its head being turned backwards. The pouring blood must stain the altar, after which the hide is stripped off, the bowels examined, and the flesh distributed to the attendants.

One part of it, being set aside for the gods, is burnt upon the altar. The sacrificers bring home a large part. In certain sacrifices, for instance those offered to the Chtonian gods and the dead, the immolated victim is entirely left to the one in

---

[90] HERODOTUS, *Histories* 2:39-40.

whose honor it is offered. After the immolation, the sacrificer must always be careful to leave without looking backwards.[91]

4. SACRIFICES IN THE BIBLE.

In the Bible many elements belonging to the general ritual of sacrifice in the ancient world reappear. Sacrifices are performed in the temple of Jerusalem, though formerly they were also offered upon high places or holy places. There is an altar of holocausts, an altar for incense-offering and a table for the shew-bread which is renewed on every sabbath. A huge vessel, the bronze-sea, contains the water necessary for libations and purifications.

Certain sacrifices are prescribed for everyday in the morning and in the evening. Other sacrifices are prescribed for sabbath days only. Finally, others are offered for the great feasts or for the private intentions of those who offer them. A complete staff including the high-priest, priests, and levites, and servants and musicians, is entrusted with the cultic service.

In Israel as in Egypt, the dedicated victims are submitted to careful examination. Bulls, for instance, must not be older than three years, and turtle-doves must be grown-up and bear their feathers. Inspectors are appointed to this office to see that no victim passes without satisfying the required conditions. The doctors of the law counted 23 defects which made a victim unfit for sacrifice. Animals were divided into two classes: clean and unclean animals, and only the clean could be admitted at the altar.

The technique of immolation includes already known gestures. There is a laying on of hands on the victim. Limbs of the victim were swung before the face of God. Blood was poured upon the corners of the altar, and sometimes attendants were sprinkled with it. The victim was bled, stripped of its hide and carried to the altar, where it was consumed by fire piece by piece.[92]

In certain sacrifices, the priest, the priest's family, the offerer and his family were granted a piece of the victim and ate it. Eating a portion of the victim is a rite of communion, or table fellowship with God. Such a rite of communion is also found in pagan sacrifices. Our Eucharist includes a rite of communion in which we partake of the victim.

5. GENERAL MEANING OF SACRIFICE.

---

[91] *Dictionnaire de Mythologie* (Paris: Larousse), "Sacrifices."

[92] Exodus 29; Leviticus 8.

The meaning of sacrifice is related, on the one hand, to the exigency or needs of the divine addressee, and, on the other hand, to the convictions and reasons of the offerer. This meaning can be discovered more or less clearly through the ritual prescriptions. It can be adoration and homage, atonement for a sin, petition for a favor, or thanksgiving for a gift.

When offered to a deceased person or to a Chtonian deity (a god of the world of the dead), the sacrifice is destined to feed and calm the addressee by satisfying their needs. Food is brought to the tomb or to the temple. Sometimes, as in Cnossos and in Syria, the food is poured into the earth, into the very tomb, through a pipe dug in the altar above.

In pagan religions, the exact execution of rites and the respect of sacred traditions were more important than internal feelings.

In principle, the victim is destined to represent the offerers and to substitute for them since they cannot personally be immolated. Therefore, the offerers try to identify themselves with the victim in order to get the favor of their god. For instance, the author of the treatise *De Dea Syria* (55) informs us in this regard about the Egyptian sacrifices: "When somebody wants to journey to Heliopolis, he sacrifices a sheep and eats its flesh; then he kneels and puts the head of the animal upon his own head, while addressing a prayer to the gods."

In totemic religions, the priest wears the hide of the sacred animal as a dress or an insignia, in witness to his kinship with the animal and the deity dwelling in it. The opposite rite -- the sacrifice of an animal covered with human dress-- is found both among the Nootkas of the Northwestern U.S., and in the Greek worship of Dionysos. It is also found in the ritual used in Munchia (Greece), where a fawn, clothed with a girl's dress, was sacrificed to the goddess.

The rites of sprinkling people with the blood of the victim and of eating a portion of its flesh aim at uniting human and deity through the offered victim. When the priest, the offerer, and their families eat their portion of the victim, they share in the banquet of the god and become his guests. The Greek temples included banquet halls, where the sacrificial meals took place.

Similarly, certain sacrifices in the temple of Jerusalem included a rite of communion. If the priest would have refused the offerers their portion when the latter were entitled to it, he would have deprived them of the advantage of their offering.

## 6. THE SACRIFICE OF CHRIST.

The rite of the Eucharistic communion with the flesh and the blood of Jesus finds its meaning as a sacrificial meal of communion. According to the Synoptic Gospels (Mark, Matthew, and Luke), the Last Supper was a Passover celebration.

We read in Exodus (12:13) that the Passover was a sacrificial meal including a rite of communion, which consisted of eating the flesh of a sheep in memory of the ancient liberation of the people of Israel from servitude in Egypt. This liberation was the beginning of the growing of Israel as a nation. The "people of God" subsequently were granted a covenant, a law, and a land. It considered itself as a people adopted and protected by God in a privileged manner.

On the eve of his execution on the cross, Jesus seems to have made use of the liturgy of the Passover meal in order to explain to his disciples the meaning which he conferred upon his own suffering and death, or the purpose of his death. Like the "Suffering Servant" of Isaiah 53, he was not suffering for his own sins since he was innocent, but he offered his death for the remission of the sins of all.[93] Jesus identified himself with the lamb of the New Covenant. Taking bread, and giving thanks, he said: "My flesh, which is for you; the blood of the New Covenant, which is poured for you and for the many for the remission of sins."

Nothing could have been more significant. We can even say that, if Jesus had not expressed himself this way, it would be possible to question or doubt his actual intention and to pretend that his death was meaningless, that he was unwillingly brought to death, just like so many poor wretches who failed to escape the hands of the police. But Jesus offered his own sacrifice while he was still able, like Judas, to escape and disappear in the night, while he was still in full possession of his liberty and of his mind. Only the suffering was left for the next day; he offered his sacrifice right now, when he gave the bread and wine to his disciples as their communion with the offering of his flesh and blood.

The disciples could not doubt that they were truly partaking of their master's sacrifice. Now, indeed, Judas was gone, and the drama of the passion of Jesus had started. The tone of Jesus left no hesitation: the event, in spite of its liturgical setting, was reality. Jesus was handing to Peter, to John... what he had just called his flesh and blood. He was granting them the fruit of his sacrificial death. He was giving them the supreme pledge of his love, the gift of his life for those whom he loved. All of this was utterly true and living. The disciples may have been overcome by their emotion, owing to the surprise of the event, and left without reaction, maybe without understanding. But we can hardly imagine them arguing with Jesus that he was play-acting with them, and that the bread and wine were not the offering of his flesh and blood.

If Jesus had not performed the act of giving his flesh for eating and his blood for drinking, if he had not settled a means

---

[93] JEREMIAS, Joachim, *The Central Message of the New Testament* (Philadelphia: Fortress Press, 1965), 95p.

of communion by his flesh and blood, the disciples would not have understood that they partook of his sacrifice and benefitted of its fruit. Sacrifice and communion go together as the whole and the part.

In addition, this act was indefinitely renewable, even if Jesus would not have prescribed the repeating of it when he said, "Do this in memory of me."[94] Just as the Passover meal was essentially renewable, and celebrated yearly, the Eucharist of Christ was also renewable, although with a particular solemnity at the time of Easter. We also read in Paul,[95] that Jesus did not limit his gift to one celebration yearly, since he said, "For as often as you eat this bread and drink this cup, you proclaim the Lord's death until he comes." The early Christians understood that they could celebrate the Eucharist weekly, just as the Jews had their weekly meeting of prayer with blessings on Sabbath days. But the Christians preferred Sunday to Saturday in memory of the resurrection of Christ (the "Day of the Lord"). It was even possible to celebrate the Eucharist on weekdays, and perhaps at any meal including the recitation of blessings, as we have our blessings at meals.

During the first centuries of the Christian history, it seems that the Eucharist was celebrated on Sundays, and one, two, or three times during the week. During the persecutions in Africa, Cyprian celebrated it daily in order to prepare his Christians for an eventual trial of martyrdom. Later, in the Middle Ages, Mass was celebrated daily, and the custom (very questionable in many regards and not always praiseworthy) spread of multiplying Masses.

## APPENDIX

### ORIGINS AND DEVELOPMENT OF BIBLICAL SACRIFICE[96]

According to R. de Vaux, the earliest sacrifices in Israel were of the Passover type, i.e., the sacrificing of a young sheep or goat which has to be eaten completely on the spot, with unleavened bread baked on heated stones or on a metal sheet. The bitter herbs of the Passover ritual were the tasty herbs of the desert, and the vesture with belt and shoes suited nomads

---

[94] "Do this in memory of me" seems to mean, Do this memorial of the redemption acquired through me, and here "memory" means remembrance, gratitude, as the Paschal lamb recalled the ancient redemption from Egypt through Moses.

[95] 1 Cor. 11:26.

[96] R. de Vaux, *Ancient Israel: Its Life and Institutions* ch. ...

living in a desert. The blood applied on the door-posts has parallels in the culture of modern Bedouins when they build a house, or inaugurate a new tent, or simply the new roof of a tent. In the desert, and in ancient local practice, it was simply poured on the ground. Only when all sacrifices, including the Passover, were ordered to be offered in Jerusalem, was the blood of the Passover lambs brought to the altar by the priests.

After the Israelites were established in Canaan, and exchanged their life of shepherds for the life of farmers, the Passover became a "memorial" of the years in the desert and of the liberation from the bondage of Egypt, a tradition faithfully preserved in the sanctuary of Gilgal near the Jordan river, where Josuah and the Israelites entered the "promised land." The combination of the Passover meal, which required unleavened bread, with the feast of the *massot*, a harvest feast probably of Canaanite origin, in the Spring, on Nisan 14, conferred on the Passover the sense of a double thanksgiving.

First, thanks were given for the new crop, since the *massot* were loaves of unleavened bread made from newly grown ears. Second, thanks were given for the redemption of the people of Israel from the bondage of Egypt and for the gift of the covenant with the Decalogue on Mount Sinai. Such is the meaning and ritual of the Jewish Thanksgiving. Jesus refers to this "memorial" when we read that, *after giving thanks*, he took the bread and said... (The following was the institution of a memorial of the offering of his own flesh and blood, and of the new covenant of our salvation).

The three kinds of biblical sacrifices properly speaking (since the Passover was seen rather as a "memorial") are the sacrifice of communion (or of peace, *selamim*), the holocaust, and the sacrifice for sin (Lev. 1).

### 1. Sacrifice of Communion.

In a sacrifice of communion, the victim was divided between God, the priest, and the offerer who had promised this sacrifice probably because his prayer had been heard by God. It is a sacrifice of thanksgiving, and the sacred meal with God involves the idea that God is the host (the victim belongs to him), and the offerer and his family, together with the priest and other friends, are the guests of God. We know that friendship must be sealed by an invitation to a meal. What an honor and a joy to be invited by God!

Thanksgiving, and frienship with God, turn the sacrifice of communion into a joyful celebration, which itself finds expression in the sacrifice of praise (*todah*) with the singing of psalms and canticles, and the accompaniment of music and dancing. The portion of the victim reserved to God, and the offering of flour known as "memorial" (*azkarah*) were delivered to the flame of the altar. Wine added to the joy of the celebration.

The sacrifice of communion was the common kind of sacrifice during the whole history of the nation of Israel, and was still usual in the time of Jesus. However, in the last rewriting of the law of sacrifices, Numbers 29:12-38, the sacrifice of communion is simply mentioned at the end, and as a private form of devotion (verse 39). The reason is that the attention was attracted to the two other forms of sacrifice: the holocaust, and the sacrifice for sin.

2. HOLOCAUST.

The holocaust, or whole-burnt offering, every morning (and later also every evening) of a sheep and of flour (vegetable offering), had the meaning of a perfect sacrifice, of a pure gift to God, of an act of praise and thanksgiving for the nation, perhaps for the world (in the mind of such Jews of the *Diaspora* as Philo of Alexandria). But, because the holocaust included a ritual of blood (which the priests poured against the altar of the holocaust), this form of sacrifice acquired the meaning of expiation or atonement for sins, an idea which became more and more important after the Exile.

R. de Vaux supposes that the biblical holocausts and sacrifices of communion did not originate in Egypt nor in Mesopotamia, but were known in Canaan, where the Israelites found and adopted them. He notes, for instance, that the prophets of Baal of Queen Jezabel, and the prophets of Yahweh of prophet Elijah offered the same type of sacrifice on Mount Carmel.[97] An African (Carthage) document discovered in Marseilles, and, much more, the literature discovered at Rash-Shamrah (the ancient Ugarit), going back to the 14th century B.C., even long before the establishment of the Israelites in Palestine, provide precious information on the sacrifice of communion, and seem to know the holocaust.

De Vaux' hypothesis is that the Canaanites borrowed sacrifices of communion and holocausts from the Greeks or from a civilization earlier than Greeks and Canaanites in the Mediterranean East. The Greeks practiced the holocaust only as a sacrifice to the Chtonian deities (the gods of the dead), or to the dead, and did so seldom. But they made a large use of the sacrifice of communion, which they called *thusia*.

3. SACRIFICES FOR SIN.

The sacrifice for sin appears under two names: as *hattat* (sacrifice for sin), and as *assam* (sacrifice of reparation). It is not easy to distinguish them by the sin which makes such a sacrifice necessary. But they are different because the victim is different: a ram for an *assam*, and the consequences are dif-

---

[97] 1 Kings 18.

ferent (for an *assam*, actual restitution of damage caused to others is required, plus a compensation of a fifth).

For all sacrifices for sin, atonement is made by the priest with the blood of the victim at the altar, and the priest and his family eat their portion of the sacrifice. The grease, as usual, is burned on the altar as the share of God, and the rest of the animal is burned outside the sacred courts. The offerer of a sacrifice for sin does not eat of his own victim. The offerer is pleased enough when he sees the priest accepting his sacrifice, making the rite of atonement for his sin, and eating the flesh of his victim. It means that, as a good spiritual master, the priest recognizes his repentance and his reparation, and considers that the sacrifice presented by this now forgiven sinner is a holy sacrifice. Never would the priest eat of a sacrifice which, in his opinion, is an offense to God.

At Yom-Kippur, or the "Day of Atonement," the high priest and the whole nation practiced a liturgy including fasting, confession of sins, supplication, and several kinds of sacrifices. A bull was offered for the high priest and his family, and, for the community, two he-goats. One of them was destined by lot to be a holy sacrifice, the other to be taken to the desert and delivered to Azazel, the evil spirit. A solemn kind of atonement was performed. For this atonement, the high priest took the blood of the he-goat into the holy of holies and sprinkled the "propitiatory" (the golden cover of the Ark of the Covenant) for the purification of the sins of the people, as he had done before with the blood of the bull for his own sins.

R. de Vaux sees parallels to biblical expiatory rites among the Arabs, the Hittites, the Mesopotamians, and the Canaanites. But he does not see in these religious groups expiatory sacrifices which compare to those of the ritual of Leviticus. In his opinion, the difference consists in the deeper interiority of biblical religion and in its moralism. Instead of being dissolved by ritual and turned into magic or mere routine --which sometimes happened--, the inner religious feelings of the people of the Bible, particularly contrition and repentance, found expression and growth in the practice of liturgy and expiatory rites.

## QUESTIONNAIRE

1. How could the meaning of sacrifice and religion not necessarily be love between God and humanity? How did it become a matter of love?

2. Would the idea of animal sacrifices be conceivable today? For what reasons? Are we offering to God the equivalent of the animals sacrificed by the ancients?

3. Because we do not offer human sacrifices and animal sacrifices, are we more pure of their blood and suffering than the ancient?

4. What is particularly interesting regarding sacrifice in the discovery of the "Pit of death" at Ur in Chaldea, and in the king's burial in Scythia? Are these sacrifices offered to gods?

5. Show that, in human sacrifices to Ares, we find the chief elements of classical sacrifice.

6. Mention some interesting features of the Scythian sacrifices, of the Egyptian sacrifices, and of the Greek sacrifices, which seem to have a particular significance.

7. Mention certain features of the biblical sacrifices which remind you of what you have found in the Scythian, Egyptian, and Greek sacrifices.

8. How do some features of the ritual of ancient sacrifices, especially outside the Bible, suggest the idea of a substitution of the victim for the offerer before the deity?

9. Was there a ritual of communion in ancient sacrifices outside the Bible? in the Bible? What was the purpose of this communion?

10. In the Bible you find a ritual of communion in the Passover meal (Exodus 12), in the sacrifice of communion (Leviticus 3), in the sacrifice for sin (the communion is reserved to the priests - Leviticus 4). What seems to be the meaning of eating a portion of the victim in these cases?

11. What are the words of Isaiah 53 about the "Suffering Servant," which Jesus could ascribe to himself in his own death?

13. Without the gesture of Jesus on the bread and wine at the Last Supper, could the disciples easily understand the meaning of the death of Jesus? How did the notion of sacrifice and communion make it clear for them?

14. Could the disciples raise the question of the "real presence" of Jesus in the bread and wine? Can we answer this question?

## BIBLIOGRAPHY

HERODOTUS. *The Histories.* Baltimore: Penguin Classics.

JEREMIAS, Joachim. *The Central Message of Jesus in the New Testament.* Philadelphia: Fortress 1965.

_____. *The Eucharistic Words of Jesus.* New York: Scribners, 1966.

VAUX, R. de. "Religious Value of "Sacrifice." *Ancient Israel; Studies in Old Testament Sacrifice.* Cardiff: Univ. of Wales Press, 1964.

YERKES, R. K. *Sacrifice: In Greek and Roman Religions and Early Judaism.* London: A. & Ch. Black, 1953.

YOUNG, Frances. *Sacrifice and the Death of Christ.* London: SCM Press, 1983 (1975).

# CHAPTER VII

## THE PROBLEM OF EVIL

Like other great problems, the problem of evil is all-inclusive, and offers different aspects on every level of consideration. Before all else, the problem of evil is a concrete problem, and must be coped with as such. Only on a second level does it become a philosophical problem, requiring abstraction. As a concrete problem, we are part of it, either as the victim or the comforter, and we must adjust our feelings and our attitude to a concrete reality. Our reaction must come from our whole self, not from mere reasoning or, on the contrary, from blind sympathy or antipathy. Our reaction must also be a Christian one, full of respect for God (piety), and for those who suffer (charity). Only later, on another level are we expected to consider and analyze, to use scientific and philosophical or theological distinctions, to display concepts and reasonings. Beginning with evil as an abstraction would be to miss the most essential aspects of the case, and, also, to lack compassion.

For these reasons, it is better for us to begin with a few cases, and to become acquainted through reflection on them with the essential components of the problem of evil. After this initiation to the problem of evil through cases taken from modern life, it will be easier for us to discover and value the relevance of the biblical materials related to evil. Psalms in particular offer a very concrete approach to suffering and evil, with an amazing strength and depth of feeling and expression. Then, in the Bible again, we come to the theoreticians of the problem of evil: the biblical book of Job and Ecclesiastes, and the poems of the Suffering Servant, whom Jesus used as a model in his own suffering. Finally, we shall deal with the philosophical approach to the problem of evil found here and there in Plato and Aristotle, and in the Stoic tradition of philosophy and ethics, which have been the inheritance of the Christian world.

### THE DEATH OF A CATECHISM-TEACHER.

A catechist, fully devoted to her family and her parish, died by drowning. She suffered from a nervous break-down. This disease is so overwhelming that, in spite of everything, especially of her outstanding Christian faith, she surrendered to it. The author proposes this case as a concrete start in our inquiry into the problem of evil because it is a real case, not a story. Here are extracts of the two letters written by her husband and her teenage her son, who was preparing to enter seminary.

*The letter of the husband.*

> ... You can imagine our anguish when that night she had not yet returned. For three days we expected the worst. Why did she do that, she who was such a believer? Why did God allow it? What a terrible disease which brings to such an extreme a mother who loved her children so much? But she left us without one single word, without any farewell. She had to have been in the utmost despair to come to this end. Religion was not a social convention for her, nor a routine, but her deepest conviction, for she truly believed. She devoted herself to everything heartily, and was conscientious to the point of scruple. Those who lived close to her knew how straightforward her life was. What then was the extent of her suffering, which disease made insurmountable? Mystery!
>
> What a pain for us, her husband, her old mother whom she leaves with such a heavy task: this unfortunate six year old daughter! God manages it well, for she does not realize it presently... A. (the seminarian) was well supported by the priests in the seminary. We shall accept every sacrifice so that, if God wills, he might continue in the way his dear mother liked so much to see him engaged. We ask you to pray for our beloved departed, and also remember us. Pray that the Lord grant us his grace in proportion to the sacrifice he asked us for.

*From the letter of the young seminarian* (13 years old).

> You have heard of my sorrow, and I hurry to ask you for your help which I need very much. Here, however, I am very well comforted by all. The very evening when I heard of it, I spent a part of the night at Father V.'s. We reflected together, and certainly when I left, I was no longer the same. Owing to the discoveries which we made, I was full of courage.
>
> At the burial, I tried to "witness" (to show my faith as a Christian) as I could, retaining my tears... I'll try to be as courageous as possible and to bring joy to the others. Sometimes I shall have to struggle against despair. For instance, I expect it to be hard at Christmas. Fortunately, God is here to help us. Now, more than ever, I pray to Him, and also to Mother, because, after an exemplary life, I am sure that she is with God. Now that Mother is in heaven, she is with me even more than before. And she guides my hand, and I can make her happy if I am firm, but if she sees that I am not firm, she shall not be happy.

> With Father V., I realized that this suffering sent by God is His smile to me. It may be a way to have me pay for all the qualities with which He endowed me. May it be a test to try my trust, for He sees that, even in suffering, I have faith, and He will love me even more. Perhaps it is His way to assimilate me more to His Son on the Cross. And it is an honor for me to imitate Christ.

Answering the widower, the addressee manifested his sympathy, then praised the departed one: her devotion to her family and to the service of God. And he expressed his conviction that God welcomed her with mercy and love as His good servant. To the child, he repeated his love for him and especially tried to give him the most beautiful image of his mother's soul, a praise which she fully deserved, considering that his sorrow could be tempered if he could partly forget the sadness of what surrounds death, and foster instead in his imagination a comforting image of her.

These people were too good as Christians to have turned to bitterness, despair, impiety. However, their behavior in suffering, keeping faith, courage, charity, truly is a wonder, an achievement and a perfection beyond the normal human reach. Especially in the husband's letter, there is no sophistication, but he expresses his sorrow, utters his Why? and also his willingness to accept any kind of sacrifice necessary to support his son on the way of his call. God asked him for a very great sacrifice, his answer was: May God grant grace in proportion! These thoughts and feelings, plainly stated by a simple employee in an institution, are very direct and reflect a genuine faith, a genuinely Christian reaction. How can one compare this with the writings of the theoreticians of the problem of suffering? But here there is love, and concrete reality is better than fiction and artificial expression, even according to the patterns of theology.

The child's letter shows the same qualities. Perhaps was the priest too lofty in his considerations, and daring: this trial presented as a smile of God! The addressee would have omitted these views in order not to foster in the child's soul something artificial, i.e., something which he could hardly foster in his own soul. But a child, is more idealistic than a grown up, and Fr. V. was a young priest, very idealistic, perhaps too idealistic: he was very close to the child, and proved to be a good comforter for him. But what a believer who retains his tears at his mother's burial! The addresse wrote to him that he wept with him, because he felt it is natural for a child to weep, and nature prevails anyway. If nature as such is good, tears are good too; only sin is evil. The poor lad fell behind one or two grades at school, and had the jaundice at Easter.

*Condolence: a way we answer the problem of evil.*

Condolence is the most delicate thing to perform, and many prove to be very poor at it. They simply don't know what to say because they are not truly involved and have only poor feelings. The best would be to say nothing, or a very simple formula, to shake hands, to bow, to smile kindly in order to manifest sympathy, if we cannot do better.

Many condolence letters or talks are very poor. Observe only for a while the sayings of those who visit mourners, and you will be struck by the triviality, or even by the offensive character of condolences. For instance: "Oh, now he does not suffer any longer; now you are free from this burden; how quiet he looks now; he enjoyed his share of life; God should not permit such a suffering, or such an early or violent death, etc." We should not condemn these poor comforters since they are people of good will and their intention is good. They sincerely try to comfort, but they don't manage to resolve the problem of evil in the present circumstances.

Much better was a simple worker who spent his entire day with a friend who was mourning his wife's death very bitterly. Feeling that his friend needed his presence, he remained there with him, but they hardly exchanged a word all day long. Only in the evening, before leaving, the comforter invited the mourner to come and have a glass of wine in a nearby pub. Probably this glass of wine was what the mourner needed the most, and it was a sign of friendship. His silent presence and this glass of wine were more meaningful than a flood of words, or even of theology.

## BIBLICAL APPROACHES TO THE PROBLEM OF EVIL: AN ANALYSIS OF BIBLICAL PRINCIPLES AND CASES

As posed to all religions, philosophies and individual minds, the problem of evil is given many answers on account of the diversity of perspectives. These various answers can be compared to one hundred doors giving access to the same place, but each has its own key. It is hopeless to try to open a door with the wrong key, and meaningless to complain at failing to do so. The problem of evil is posed and resolved in a different way by a believer, a Marxist, a Buddhist, etc. The same answer cannot agree with all of them, but actually all the answers joined together contribute to an answer that everyone needs.

As the book of the living who cope with life and converse with the living God, the Bible provides us with a very valuable approach to the problem of evil. The way the Bible raises this problem seems to correspond to the very way we raise it in our own life as believers, and the way the Bible resolves it casts a precious light on the attitude we are expected to adopt when we cope with our own personal evil. The answers of philosophers provide us with another kind of insight, but cannot eliminate, or substitute for, the biblical answer.

1. *A basic principle: virtue provides well-being and pleases God.*

We must begin with an average and plain observation of life, and define the proper background on which we can rely for further developments: generally the person of worth is successful while the unworthy one fails. Such is the common truth which parents have in mind when they tell their children: "Study hard, and you will have good marks; you will succeed in your examinations and get a good job if you deserve it, etc." Similarly a boss tells employees: "If you are trustworthy, I shall promote you; but if you deceive me, or if your work is poor, I shall fire you."

Such is the fundamental certitude, the normal case, the principle which we should not forget when we come to exceptional cases: namely, that material success, fame, harmony, peace at home, good esteem, or whatever we commonly call "happiness", is the fruit of virtue. We find this affirmation in Psalm 1:

> Happy is the worthy one... He is like a tree planted beside a watercourse, which yields its fruit in season and its leaf never withers; in all that he does he prospers. Wicked men are not like this; they are like chaff driven by the wind. So when judgment comes the wicked shall not stand firm, nor shall sinners stand in the assembly of the righteous. The Lord watches over the way of the rigtheous, but the way of the wicked is doomed.

However, nothing is simply trivial in life, for we are subject to God who governs and judges, rewards or punishes. To do good and reject evil is to obey God, to please Him, to deserve His friendship and protection. To misbehave is to offend God, whose judgment nobody can escape. And to return to goodness and do obedience to God is to recover His friendship and protection. Even His reprobation is but a dimension of His love.

God's commandments cover all our life, and are the basis for our "covenant" with God. We must observe this covenant as we do a contract. Actually, we may observe this contract, or denounce it, or decide to follow it again. Since it is a contract with the highest of partners, we may expect from its fulfillment the best reward, and from its failure the worst consequences. With God, our covenant implies fear, but it is also, and more properly, a matter of love. Psalm 119, the longest psalm, sings the delights of the law of God, a law dear to the soul since it is a dialogue of friendship with God.

The idea that life is obedience or disobedience to the commandments of God regarding justice towards our fellow human beings clearly appears in Isaiah 1[98]: God rejects sacrific-

[98] Cf. Isaiah 1:11-20, ch.2 above, p.ooo.

es and prayers from those who practice social injustice, but he is willing to forgive them if they comply to these duties, particularly regarding widows and orphans.

2. *Exceptions: Two objections and their answer.*

*The prosperity of the impious.* Are the impious who are "successful" in life enviable? Are they really blessed as they seem to be? Certainly not according to Psalms 49 and 37, for the impious, when they die, lose all that made them happy, while the just expect redemption from God even on the threshold of death.

*The suffering of the just.* When the just suffer, there is a problem: why do they suffer, since they are just? and what are they expected to do? The Bible invites us to avoid a superficial answer, and to find a deeper explanation.

The story of Joseph in Genesis 37-50 is a good illustration of this problem. Joseph had not done anything wrong when he was sold by his brothers who even planed to kill him. However, he kept his faith in God, and carried on doing justice. As a consequence, he became the attendant of Potiphar, his master: virtue pays! But, because of his honesty toward Potiphar when he resisted the solicitations of his master's wife, he was cast into jail: a truly undeserved reward for virtue! Should he, then, like many prisoners, reject his faith and good behavior, renounce everything and resort to despair? Joseph kept on being just in jail, and was trusted by the jailer; later on, Pharaoh took him out of jail and introduced him into the palace as his first minister. Joseph suffered unjustly for he was violently deprived of his father, sold as a slave, cast into jail, etc. He suffered because of the envy of his brothers, because of Potiphar's lack of discernment.

We too suffer from the facts of life, for instance from disease, and from the sins of others. When individuals are beaten, they suffer from the blows inflicted on them. Such explanations are enough to account for the suffering of both the just and the unjust. However, a religious soul resents the triviality of these explanations, and expects from God another motive.

In the present, when we endure evil, God's answer does not appear clearly, since we do not see the consequence of events. Therefore, we must trust God without understanding his plan. Such is what Joseph did when, in spite of God's apparent failure to treat him fairly, he carried on his faith and trust in God and his faithfulness to virtue. However, later on, in retrospect, everything became clear. Joseph wondered why he had undergone such undeserved misfortunes, but he then suddenly enjoyed a prosperity undeserved, and humanly inexplicable. His conclusion was that only God can, on the same day, cause a prisoner to settle in a palace, a servant of a jailer to turn into a minister of the king, and a shameful wretch to enjoy the highest honor.

The reason was that God wanted to save the race of Israel from starvation. Joseph did not so much accuse his brothers of sin as much as he ascribed the whole affair to divine mercy and providence. He realized the existence of divine providence with its long range plans, which can make use even of sin, although, of course, providence mainly relies on the faithfulness of the just. Like Joseph, we must keep on being faithful to God in our misfortunes in order to correctly minister to the plan of God who needs our cooperation.

3. *Aspects of the problem of evil suggested by a series of biblical characters.*

*The case of Adam (Genesis 3).* The question is, Why was Adam sentenced to suffering and death? The answer follows: because he sinned, and he was not allowed to use as an acceptable excuse the temptation by the serpent, or even Eve's solicitation. To accuse the devil, or others, is no excuse for sin. Since the case of Adam can be applied to every sinner, we may conclude that our sin also deserves condemnation.

*The case of Cain (Genesis 4).* Cain is the typical sinner, unwilling to overcome his bad feelings against his brother in spite of God's warning, who becomes a victim of his own hatred and actually kills his brother. Although his free will is diminished on the very day of his crime, his responsibility remains complete. Moreover, in order to escape death, Cain asks for a mark, a kind of pass-word, and runs away. Cain should rather come back to God and ask for pardon. Is not the utmost misfortune of sinners, and their chief chastisement, that which they impose on themselves, to run away from God for ever, instead of coming back to themselves and to God?

*The case of Noah (Genesis 5-10).* Suffering and death in the Flood appear to be a chastisement for sin. In the present case, the matter is with general sin (not directly the "original sin"), which calls for general chastisement. God's mercy is tired of human wickedness, and His justice takes over: justice must have the last word, or there is no justice at all! In return, God saves from the flood the only just ones found upon earth: Noah and his family. It is necessary that the just should be saved, as it is necessary also that the guilty should perish.

However, Noah did not, more than Adam, fill the earth with a posterity of just people, since he himself and his sons sinned after the flood. Concluding the story, God promised He would not again try to destroy humankind because of their sins, or send a flood again. On the contrary, He will send a Savior, a just one like Noah and better than Noah, a second Adam, who will renew humankind and re-establish the Kingdom of God.

*The case of David (2 Samuel 11 & 12 and Psalm 51).*[99] David, the king according to the heart of God, suddenly realized that actually he had become a great sinner: he killed his lieutenant Uriah in order to take his wife. God could not be deluded by his "perfect crime." Troubled throughout, David defended his cause before God: Sinner, he said, indeed, I am, and I deserve chastisement. But how did I come to that extreme of wickedness without noticing it? When did am I become a sinner? Little by little one advances to grievous sins. Although they come as a surprise, we are fully responsible for them, for they are the result of a thousand little surrenders, of a thousand unrefrained desires.

David goes further on in his reflection about the origin of his sin. Actually David shares in the common lot: "I have been born in sin; my mother bore me as a sinner," he says. With these words, David gave expression to the doctrine of the original sin. He discovered the sinfulness of the human condition in his own experience. We can make the same observation without necessarily referring to Adam.

*Ezekiel's preaching on individual responsibility for sin (Ezekiel 18).* Ezekiel argues with those who give as an excuse for their sins and neglect that they cannot escape the divine chastisement of suffering since they must atone for the sins of their parents. They quote the proverb: "The fathers have eaten sour grapes, and the children's teeth are set on edge." This proverb contains some truth, but Ezekiel strongly affirms the principle of individual responsibility for sin:

> Why is not the son punished for his father's iniquity? Because he has always done what is just and right and has been careful to obey all my laws, therefore he shall live. It is the soul that sins, and no other, that shall die; a son shall not share a father's guilt, nor a father his son's. The righteous man shall reap the fruit of his own righteousness, and the wicked man the fruit of his own wickedness. It mat be that a wicked man gives up his sinful ways and keeps all my laws, doing what is just and right. That man shall live; he shall not die. None of the offences he has committed shall be remembered against him; he shall live because of his righteous deeds. Have I any desire, says the Lord God, for the death of a wicked man? Would I not rather that he should mend his ways and live.[100]

---

[99] The fact that this psalm is traditionally put in the mouth of David, although of a later period than David, proves that creative meditation on biblical characters is a biblical tradition.

[100] Ezekiel 18:19-23.

*The case of Job (Book of Job).* The book of Job is entirely devoted to the problem of evil considered under its religious aspect. This book is not written in the way of a systematic exposition, or of a philosophical treatise, abstract and cold, but is presented as a personal drama which brings its hero to speak with the truest expression. This gives the book of Job a strongly human and poetic density, and increases its educative value for faith.

Everyone, more or less, lives the case of Job. This book is a wonderful guide in suffering, since it describes a man who undergoes the trial of suffering through all the turnings of his spiritual struggle, and enlightens him only little by little, in a way which is true and not artificial, like a personal discovery. It is even true that Job does not find the complete light, and does not need it. As soon as he adopts the right spiritual attitude and surrenders to the mysterious will of God, his problem is resolved. It belongs to others to find out additional, even better, solutions, since there are only personal solutions to the problem of evil. The rest is abstraction, and left to philosophers and theologians.

The drama of Job is played out on two platforms: in heaven and on earth. A challenge is proposed by Satan to God: "Touch his possessions! his flesh! and I bet that he will curse you bluntly!" On trial, Job behaves perfectly, with an impressive piety which justifies God against Satan. Job is righteous in misfortune as well as in good fortune. Why should he suffer any longer? He deserves his reward, and God returns Job to earthly prosperity.

On earth, or, better, in the heart of Job, things are less simple, and Job is engaged in a difficult struggle. He does not know why he is suffering, since he is righteous. His friends visit him, but all they can do is twist the sword in every direction through his wounded soul, seeking the sin which would explain everything. At last, Job understands that one must not argue with God, but surrender to His mysterious will, since one is not expected to give lessons to God. As a consequence of his submission to God's will, Job recovers his inner peace and the loving presence of God. He does not need anything more.

*After Job, the Suffering Servant (Isaiah 53).* The book of Job does not properly resolve the problem of evil. Job stops his discussion when he returns to piety and thereby recovers his inner peace, and everyone does the same. Going further would be idle words. However, some have gone beyond Job: let us follow them.

For instance. the Suffering Servant in Isaiah 52 & 53, who has not sinned, is suffering in atonement for the sins of others. His personal sacrifice, hard and pure, full of love for humanity and for God, possesses a redemptive value, becomes relevant, useful:

> He was despised, he shrank from the sight of men, tormented and humbled by suffering; we despised him, we held him of no account, a thing from which men turn away their eyes. Yet on himself he bore our sufferings, our torments he endured, while we counted him smitten by God, struck down by disease and misery; but he was pierced for our transgressions, tortured for our iniquities; the chastisement he bore is health for us and by his scourgings we are healed. We had all strayed like sheep, each of us gone his own way; but the Lord laid upon him the guilt of us all. He was afflicted, he submitted to be struck down and did not open his mouth; he was led like a sheep to the slaughter, like a ewe that is dumb before the shearers...
>
> Yet the Lord took thought for his tortured servant and healed him who had made himself a sacrifice for sin; so shall he enjoy long life and see his children's children, and in his hand the Lord's cause shall prosper. After all his pains he shall be bathed in light, after his disgrace he shall be fully vindicated; so shall he, my servant, vindicate many, himself bearing the penalty of their guilt... He exposed himself to face death and was rekoned among transgressors; he bore the sin of many and interceded for their transgressions.[101]

Psalm 22 repeats the same dramatic theme and sings the suffering and hope of the just. According to the Gospels,[102] Jesus uttered this psalm upon the cross: "My God, my God, why hast Thou forsaken me?" These words should not let us the impression of a confession of despair from Jesus, since the whole Psalm 22 reflects the prayer of the Suffering Servant.

*Jesus as the Suffering Servant.* It seems that Jesus adopted the attitude of the Suffering Servant in own suffering. He offered his suffering and his death as a sacrifice for the remission of the sins of humankind.[103]

Jesus'positive attitude in regard to suffering turned evil into love for God and for humanity, as well as into a redemptive sacrifice. Why not use suffering for the same purpose? Why not follow the Suffering Servant of the Bible? Why not follow Jesus? Such an attitude is no longer passivity in regard to suffering, since we are making something good out of suffering, which by itself is ugly and morally indifferent.

---

[101] Isaiah 53:3-12.

[102] Mark 15:34; Mat. 27:46.

[103] Matt. 26:28.

As for Jesus, the time of his suffering proved also to be the very time of his victory, of his purest and greatest victory: the Cross is the moral and religious apogee of humankind! Actually Jesus was right when he prophetically said, "When I shall be lifted up above the earth (on the cross), I shall then draw everyone to myself."[104]

## THE STOICS AND THE PROBLEM OF EVIL

The answer of the ancient philosophers to the problem of evil is more theoretical and less human than that of the Bible and of Christianity, which consider the problem of evil with a more existential approach. Plato's distinguished between physical and moral evil. Physical evil derives from an error of perspective when the good of the part is considered before that of the whole, on which it depends. Moral evil is simply the denial of our own responsibility for sins. In Aristotle, the problem of evil does not involve divine providence, which is non-existent. Therefore, evil is only an "ontological" and a moral problem, not a theological problem, at least in so far as the Prime Mover is concerned.

Later on, the discussion of the problem of evil focussed on divine providence. The Stoics, although materialist and pantheist, believed in providence, whereas the Epicureans, Cynics, and Skeptics denied providence. This discussion is echoed in Cicero, Philo, Plutarch, Porphyry, etc., and the Fathers of the Church.

Much more interesting than this discussion on divine providence, where not many new elements were added, and which continued unconvincing and sterile, is the attitude defined by the Stoics regarding evil, especially by later Stoics such as Epictetus, Marcus Aurelius, and Seneca, who developed a very lofty morality. Their belief in a form of fate permeated their thought with a sense of noble resignation which makes their positions even more impressive. We summarize their positions and give a few suggestive texts.

According to Stoic ethics, we must adjust our judgment to reality, and act conformably with nature. If we pass a right judgment on the nature of things, and make a fair analysis of the situation, we are in a good position to accomplish what depends on us and which is our duty. It is better to accept without bitterness what does not depend on us, since there is no obligation to do the impossible. Moreover, a good, clear, and realistic judgment is a source of peace, since it cuts down much of the trouble and unneccesary emotion due to the concern for things which do not depend on us or are not good for us. The struggle against the passions (uncontrolled inclinations) leads toward the ideal of "impassibility" (*apatheia* in Greek). Impassibility is not

---

[104] John 8:28.

just indifference, or resignation, but a form of renunciation and an act of realism. It enable us to do what can and must be done more efficiently and reasonably.

*What is, or is not, in our power to do?*

> EPICTETUS: Of all existing things some are in our power, and others are not in our power. In our power are thought, impulse, will to get and will to avoid, and, in a word, everything which is our own doing. Things not in our power include the body, property, reputation, office, and, in a word, everything which is not our own doing. Things in our power are by nature free, unhindered, untrammeled; things not in our power are weak, servile, subject to hindrance, dependent on others. Remember then that if you imagine that what is naturally slavish is free, and what is naturally another's is your own, you will be hampered, you will mourn, you will be put to confusion, you will blame gods and men; but if you think that only your own belongs to you, and that what is another's is indeed another's, no one will ever put compulsion or hindrance on you, you will blame none, you will accuse none, you will do nothing against your will, no one will harm you, you will have no ennemy, for no harm can touch you... Therefore let your will to avoid have no concern with what is not in man's power; direct it only to things in man's power that are not contrary to nature.[105]

*In the divine providence, humans have no priority over the whole.*

> MARCUS AURELIUS: All that is from the gods is full of providence. That which is from fortune is not separated from nature or without an interweaving and involution with the things which are ordered by providence. From thence all things flow; and there is besides necessity, and that which is for the advantage of the whole universe, of which thou art a part. But that is good for every part of nature which the nature of the whole brings, and what serves to maintain this nature. Now the universe is preserved, as by the changes of the elements so by the changes of things compounded of the elements.[106]

---

[105] Epictetus, *The Manual* (The Modern Library), 1,2 & 13, pp. 468-69.

[106] Marcus Aurelius, *Meditations* (Modern Library) 11:3, p. 497.

*There is no good reason to accuse God's Providence or other people.*

> MARCUS AURELIUS: Whatever of the things that are not within thy power thou shalt suppose to be good for thee or evil, it must of necessity be that, if such a bad thing befall thee or the loss of such a good thing, thou wilt blame the gods, and hate men, those who are the cause of the misfortune or the loss, or those who are suspected of being likely to be the cause; and indeed we do much injustice, because we make a difference between these things. But if we judge those things only which are in our power to be good or bad, there remains no reason either for finding fault with God or standing in a hostile attitude to man.[107]

*At the death-bed of a child.*

> MARCUS AURELIUS: When a man kisses his child, said Epictetus, he should whisper to himself, - Tomorrow perchance thou wilt die. - But those are the words of bad omen? - No word is a word of bad omen, said Epictetus, which expresses any work of nature; or if it is so, it is also a word of bad omen to speak of the ears of wheat being reaped.[108]

*Death is a natural process, not evil.*

> MARCUS AURELIUS: Do not despise death, but be well content with it, since this too is one of those things which nature wills. For such as it is to be young and to grow old, and to increase and to reach maturity, and to have teeth and grey hairs, and to beget, and to be pregnant and to bring forth, and all the other natural operations which the seasons of thy life bring, such also is dissolution. This, then, is consistent with the character of a reflecting man, to be neither careless nor impatient nor contemptuous with respect to death, but to await it as one of the operations of nature. As thou now waitest for the time when the child shall come out of thy wife's womb, so be ready for the time when thy soul shall fall out of this envelope.[109]

*Readiness for passing away with thanksgiving.*

---

[107] Ibid. p. 532; cf. Epictetus, *Manual* 1.

[108] Ibid. 11:34, p. 578.

[109] Ibid. 9:3, p. 554.

> MARCUS AURELIUS: Think continually how many physicians are dead after contracting their eyebrows over the sick; and how many astrologers after predicting with great pretensions the deaths of others; and how many philosophers after endless discourses on death or immortality; how many heroes after killing thousands; and how many tyrants who have used their power over men's lives with terrible insolence as if they were immortal; and how many cities are entirely dead, so to speak, Helice and Pompei and Herculanum, and others innumerable. Add to the reckoning all whom thou hast known, one after another. One man after burying another has been laid out dead, and another buries him: and all of this in a short time. To conclude, always observe how ephemeral and worthless human things are, and what was yesterday a little mucus will be a mummy or ashes. Pass then through this little space of time conformably to nature, and end thy journey in content, just as an olive falls off when it is ripe, blessing nature who produced it, and thanking the tree on which it grew.[110] (MARCUS AURELIUS, *Meditations* 4:48)

*Show no bitterness if life is shortened.*

> MARCUS AURELIUS: Man, thou hast been a citizen in this great state (the world); what difference does it make to thee whether for five years or three? For that which is conformable to the laws is just for all. Where is the hardship then, if no tyrant nor yet an unjust judge sends thee away from the state, but nature who brought thee into it? The same as if a praetor who has employed an actor dismisses him from the stage. - But I have not finished the five acts, but only three of them! - Thou sayest well, but in life the three acts are the whole drama; for what shall be a complete drama is determined by him who was at once the cause of its composition, and now of its dissolution: but thou art the cause of neither. Depart then satisfied, for he also who releases thee is satisfied.[111]

*Suffering is surmountable.*

> MARCUS AURELIUS: Nothing can happen to any man which is not a human accident, not to an ox which is not according to the nature of an ox, not to a vine which is

---

[110] Ibid. 4:48, p. 515.

[111] Ibid. 12:36, p. 584.

not according to the nature of a vine, nor to a stone which is not proper to a stone. If then there happens to each thing both what is usual and natural, why shouldst thou complain? For the common nature brings nothing which may not be borne by thee.[112]

*Indulgence toward offenders.*

MARCUS AURELIUS: When a man has done thee any wrong, immediately consider with what opinion about good he has done wrong. For when thou hast seen this, thou wilt pity him, and wilt neither wonder nor be angry. For either thou thyself thinkest the same thing to be good that he does or another thing of the same kind. It is thy duty then to pardon him. But if thou dost not think such things to be good or evil, thou wilt more easily be well disposed to him who is in error.[113]

*Too hard? Change your jugdment, or leave!*

MARCUS AURELIUS :If thou art pained by any external thing, it is not this thing that disturbs thee, but thy own judgment about it. And it is in thy power to wipe out this judgment now. But if anything in thy own disposition gives thee pain, who hinders thee from correcting thy opinion? And even if thou art pained because thou art not doing some particular thing which seems to thee to be right, why dost thou not rather act than complain? But some insuperable obstacle is in the way? Do not be grieved then, for the cause of its not being done depends not on thee. But it is not worth while to live, if this cannot be done. Take thy departure then from life contentedly, just as he dies who is in full activity, and well pleased with the things which are obstacles.[114]

The Stoic attitude toward evil aims at a sane ethical realism. A Stoic should first be careful to judge correctly, because error of judgment, not things in themselves, is the origin of our trouble. And he must judge others according to their intentions, not hating, but pitying them if they are wicked. He must accept the death of his dearest ones and the idea of his own death without revolt and even with thankfulness for the good enjoyed. There is no reason for complaining, since suffering is not above the capacity of an ordinary human being.

---

[112] Ibid. 8:46, p. 551.

[113] Ibid. 7:26, p. 538.

[114] Ibid. 8:47, p. 550.

The Stoic struggle aims at eliminating the disorder of the passions (passions are disorderly feelings and behavior), and at reaching the ideal of "impassibility." By do doing, the Stoic obeys the will of nature or of the gods, playing the role which is ascribed to him by the convergence of the universe with its many implications in human life.

This attitude regarding evil may seem hard, apparently heartless, but it is noble and relevant. The Christian attitude may be better sometimes, but it always supposes the presence of the Stoic attitude as a reasonable basis. Modern ethicists, often unconsciously, rely on Stoicism when they refer to the law of nature (or on practical sociological equivalents), and sometimes too systematically derive conclusions from it on practical issues. They should remember how, with the same kind of reasoning, Tertullian (second cent. A.D.) condemned as immoral, because it did not conform to nature, the use of make-up by women!.

However, only Jesus and Christianity developed the idea of the biblical Suffering Servant that suffering can become a sacrifice: evil liberated from itself and turned into love of God and of brethren. Antiquity did not know this key to the problem of evil.

## CONCLUSION

We would be fools if we thought we have resolved the problem of evil. Its solution is more an existential one than a theoretical one. The problem of evil is that of our own attitude regarding evil. It does not consist in accusing God or nature, or even society.

Moreover, the matter lies rather in raising instead of answering the problem of evil, for the question is included in the answer and the answer in the question. In other words, like all existential problems, it belongs, together with its answer, to every different contextual situation, and must be resolved on that particular level. Mixing data from different contexts only creates false problems and generates nonsense. It seems to add a dramatic note to the purely theoretical approach, but the difficulty is only one of confusion, and is cleared up when we return to the appropriate distinctions and to a good analysis. Our times seem to favor this confusion and to almost hopelessly mix the theoretical and the existential lines.

We may speak of evil as a being, or only as a lack of being. We may introduce evil as a metaphysical principle, a kind of anti-God. We may look for a supernatural cause of evil, accuse Providence, the divine predestination, or the divine grace itself. We may consider the external or the internal conditions for the exercise of the free will. We may refer to the original sin, to actual sin, to differences in the evaluation of good and evil according to our progress in spiritual intelligence and in virtue. All these questions and many others have been raised and, on their particular level, resolved in the past. But evil is always present and waiting for an answer from us.

We may also consider that, whenever we cope with evil, a solution is ready at hand. We can yield to evil, or be the accomplice of the forces of evil which cannot lay hold on us without some complacency on our part. But we can also behave in such a way that, with the help of God, even evil turns into grace.

## QUESTIONNAIRE

1. Concerning the death of the lady-catechist, what do you think of the answer of Fr. V.?

2 What is the similarity --the difference also-- between his answer and the answer of a Stoic (for instance, Epictetus or Marcus Aurelius)? and the result (no tears of the child)?

3. In your own experience of a beloved one, or in the experience of your parents, or of a friend, in the presence of death, what do you observe in people: sorrow and manifestations of sorrow? of despair? of hope? of love? permanence or vanishing of the beloved one in their feelings? What is the best behavior in such a circumstance?

4. What could you say as a form of condolence to mourners? Have you heard poor condolences in such circumstances?

5. Have your parents often told you that virtue, or effort, pays? Is it the rule or the exception?

6. Is there a meaning in Teilhard de Chardin's saying : "Nothing is profane in human endeavour," even the most ordinary acts, and our ordinary work? ("profane" means le contrary of "religious")

7. Explain the story of Joseph: 1) with the idea that things have their cause on earth in nature or humans; 2) with the idea that God provides for us through events. What was the conclusion of Joseph? Could Joseph be sure of God's providence on the spot? or in the consideration of the past?

8. Derive one good idea about sin and repentance from biblical cases: Adam, Cain, Noah, David, Ezekiel.

9. In the story of Job, what happened in heaven? on earth? How was the principle, "Virtue is rewarding," challenged in this story? What was the spiritual struggle of Job? Are people (whom you know) challenged by "unjust suffering" in their religious life?

10. What did the "Suffering Servant" of Isaiah 53 add to the solution of Job in his own answer concerning "unjust suffering"?

11. What did Jesus seem to borrow from Job? from the "Suffering Servant"? in his motivation when he accepted to die an unjust death?

12. How did the Book of Wisdom of Solomon resolve the problem of the premature death of the just, and that of the death of a young person?

13. What is Plato's solution to the problem of physical evil? of moral evil or vice?

14. What is the answer of Aristotle? For him, is God involved in our business with evil?

15. What is the answer of Epictetus or of Marcus Aurelius in the case of the death of a beloved one, or in the case of disease and the proximity of death? What should we do? What should we not do in such a case?

16. Are the Stoics right when they advise not to grieve? What is their teaching about emotion and the analysis of events? Are they too indifferent regarding suffering?

17. What advice do the Stoics derive from the idea that, as being the part, we serve the whole (of the Universe), and not conversely? Can we resolve many of our problems with this consideration?

18. Mention things which, according to the Stoics, are (morally) good, (morally) wicked), and (morally) indifferent. What attitude should a Stoic adopt regarding each of them? Give examples.

19. In case of hardship in your own life (death of a dear one, disease, failure in a project, etc.), would you adopt the Stoic attitude?

20. What do the Stoics mean (if the painful event cannot be removed) by their formula: "Change your judgment"?

21. Show that the Stoic principle of the morally good as doing what conforms to nature is underlying modern Christian ethics. Give examples. In certain cases, is not this reasoning too superficial, and the conclusion wrong?

22. What do you think of Marcus Aurelius' reflections concerning the acceptance of death? Is it better than "to forget" about death? Does the idea of death as offered up to God as atonement for sins, or as paying off the debt of sin, or as love, make useless the Stoic consideration of death as a duty of nature?

## BIBLIOGRAPHY

BLENKINSOPP, Joseph. *Wisdom and Law in the Old Testament: The Ordering of Life in Israel and Early Judaism.* New York: Oxford University Press, 1983. (Job, pp.52-73)

JEREMIAS, Joachim. *The Central Message of the New Testament.* Philadelphia: Fortress Press, 1981. Ch. 2.

MURPHY, Roland E. *The Tree of Life. An Exploration of Biblical Wisdom Literature.* The Anchor Bible Reference Library. New York: Doubleday, 1990. Ch.3, "Job the Steadfast" pp. 33-48.

*The Stoic and Epicurean Philosophers.* Tr. W. J. Oates. The Modern Library. New York: Random House, 1957.

# CHAPTER VIII

## THE EVIDENCE OF GOD IN EXPERIENCE AND ANCIENT PHILOSOPHY

In this chapter we shall first consider the evidence of God in experience, with the presentation and discussion of several cases, and see what we can derive from them concerning the existence of God, his presence to us, and his providence for us. Then we shall turn to the evidence of God according to ancient and classical philosophy. The Bible is par excellence the book of the experience of God, an experience lived on various levels by common people and prophets. But the Bible does not offer a proof for the existence of God: such a proof is not required by believers. For this reason, the reader is left on the threshold of the Bible with the promise of a rich discovery of God in it, but only offered the preamble of religious experience and of philosophy. Similarly, before opening the Bible, Augustine asked the future catechumens for the events which motivated their coming to church, anf for their past readings.

*A natural belief in God? The story of Lacordaire.*

Lacordaire (1802-61), the great preacher of the last century at Notre Dame de Paris, emphatically refused in a sermon to give a demonstration of the existence of God, under the pretext that it would be an offense to the congregation. Just as it would be offensive to question the identity of one's father, any doubt concerning the existence of our Father in heaven is something shameful, for our belief in God, Lacordaire said, is a natural belief in our heart. Lacordaire gave, as an impressive illustration of this so-called "natural belief," an event which took place during the revolution of 1848 which overthrew the French monarchy.[115] When the royal palace was laid waste, some revolutionaries, in a kind of extemporaneous procession, respectfully carried the cross of the royal chapel to a church in the neighborhood. Joining their procession, the crowd shared in their act of piety with respectful attitude. Obviously, these people cast out their king but paid homage to their God. Lacordaire considered their spontaneous gesture as evidence of the depth of belief in God within human nature, even among the populace. Of course, after this demonstrative preamble, then Lacordaire actually presented the classical arguments of the proof for the existence of God.

---

[115] Lacordaire, *45th Conférence à Notre Dame* (Paris: Poussielgue), t. 2, p. 265.

Lacordaire was echoing Tertullian who, in the second century A.D., had said :

> Would you have the proof from the work of his (God's) hands, so numerous and so great, which both contain and sustain you, which minister at once to your enjoyment, and strike you with awe; or would you rather have it from the TESTIMONY OF THE SOUL itself? Though under the oppressive bondage of the body, though led astray by depraving customs, though enervated by lust and passions, though in slavery to false gods, yet, whenever the soul comes to itself, as out of a surfeit or a sleep, or a sickness and attain something of its natural soundness, it speaks of God, using no other words, because this is the peculiar name of the true God. "Great God!", "Good God!", "Which may God give!" are the words on every lip. It bears witness, too, that God is judge, exclaiming, "God sees!", and "I commend myself to God", and "God will repay me". O noble testimony of the soul by its very nature Christian![116]

Lacordaire was a convert. He lost his faith about the time of his first Communion when he was a student in high school in Dijon, a change due to the influence of his milieu rather than to any positive attack against religion. Here a life of faith would have been an exception and could hardly flourish. But, since the young Lacordaire was a lofty and friendly soul, he found satisfaction in study and companionship until the moment when, after his degrees, he went to Paris to study for the law. There, deprived of his friends, he felt very much alone. In Paris, on account of his advanced opinions he did not feel at home in the royalist circles of Catholic young people. He suffered from solitude, visited churches, then wept and surrendered to faith. A few weeks later, in the eagerness of his youth, he confessed to his mother that he wanted to become a priest. Why this evolution of the young Lacordaire, and even his conversion to faith and vocation to the priesthood? Because he needed God, and, after friendship had filled the need of God for a while, he realized the gulf and found the presence of Him who, according to Augustine, is "*intimior intimo meo et superior summo meo*", "Greater than I and more intimate than I to myself."

*A proud seminarian found how simple people may deeply know God from experience.*

Once, a seminarian proud of his newly acquired theology, out of curiosity, asked an old and simple devout person how she could prove the existence of God. Amazed by this question,

---

[116] TERTULLIAN, *Apologeticum* 17:4-6.

scandalized, she answered, "Don't you, a seminarian, believe in God? Why then do you propose to become a priest? As for me, how could I doubt God's existence when I see Him daily? Ashamed, the seminarian stopped displaying his theology, and, pondering on the case, realized that belief in God relies more upon spiritual experience than demonstration. It would even be dangerous and unfair to ask people for explanations of faith because they would feel obliged, and maybe unable, to express themselves fittingly on philosophical questions. In absence of any rational evidence, they might themselves conclude that belief is groundless. Therefore, it is much better to assume this belief, even implicit, in them, and to nurture it with pastoral care, intelligently and with love. Interfering in matters of spiritual experience is always delicate. A description of the experience of God can only be an account of individual experience. It is impossible to give an adequate account of it because individual experience is manifold, original as it is in everybody.

*God found in charity to neighbor.*

A youngster who saved a little money for candy and delighted in the hope of gluttony was asked by God to give this money to some passing Sisters who were begging. A hard discussion with God followed, -"Your candy? Don't you know what I think of your eating them alone greedily?... You must give up your money!" And the money was wet with perspiration in the boy's hand before he made up his mind. Running to the Sisters who were already on their way, he left the coins in their hand and, unable to speak, returned to his place, his heart full of joy, and God delighted together with him for three entire days: "How to compare, he admitted, the despicable pleasure from the candy with such a lasting joy of the presence of God!"

Here we find God arguing about candy in a boy's heart, i.e., a God near to us, interested in our affairs, and not some philosophical entity confined in abstraction, feelingless and voiceless. But perhaps you do not believe that God talks with young children about candy!

Another case concerns a young priest who refused some money to a poor woman in Jericho, Palestine. Later, troubled by the impression of her distress, and in order to recover his spirits when she was gone away, he opened his Gospel and realized that he was the priest of the parable of the Good Samaritan, the priest of whom Jesus speaks! Caught red-handed, he felt very ashamed and guilty, and he heard the voice of the Lord with much emotion in his heart. However, in his sorrow at being reproached with his hardness of heart (his unfortunate prudence, since almsgiving attracts beggars), he experienced the presence of the Lord and loved this voice of the Lord which mercifully corrected him as "a father corrects his beloved son."

Truly, in sin itself it is possible for a religious soul to experience God. In good deeds and sins, through the moral conscience, people enjoy God's presence. It is when they don't listen to God any longer, and come to forget Him in disbelief, that their spiritual disease is very dangerous, even hopeless.

The experience of God in prayer may be rare if prayer is too sophisticated and formal: theologians often address speeches to God, almost dissertations! This prevents a true conversation with God. On the contrary, "the poor in spirit are granted the kingdom of heaven".[117] It is wonderful to train little children in prayer because they are simple, and their discovery of God's presence is new.

## REFLECTION ON CASES OF EXPERIENCE OF THE PRESENCE OF GOD.

Now we can reflect upon these few cases. The deity which is found is a God who lives, speaks, answers, feels, congratulates, reproaches and advises. It is a God who loves us and whose presence, even in rebuke, fills us with joy. Usually there is no fear and shivering in a true experience of God, but a feeling of piety, i.e., both of respect and of love.

We realize that God is a living Person, and not a cloud made of echoes of our education and of social pressure. He is our Master to Whom we listen and Whom we obey. He is at the same time the Master of all, because we are sure from our own experience that the same God speaks to other people as he speaks to us, because we are made of the same stuff. We also feel that nothing nor anyone can be nearer to us or communicate with us more directly. None also can be higher than God is, and we immediately conclude that He is the Supreme Being, the Sovereign and Creator of the universe.

Actually, every doctrine of God, every theological development basically relies upon an analysis of our spiritual experience of God. That does not deprive philosophical study and demonstration of God of its specific interest, but spiritual experience was, is, and will ever be the living basis of belief in God. On the other hand, we must not despise the philosophical approach to God because there are people who have come to God through this way. If this door had not been open to them, they probably would never have entered the palace of faith and met the Lord. Out of prejudice, or out of a particularly rationalistic type of mind, these people needed to be led to God by reasoning.

*A knowledge by induction.* What is the value of the individual experience of God as evidence? Experience is a form of science, in which the mind proceeds by induction, instead of

---

[117] Matt. 5:3.

deriving conclusions from a principle as it does in reasoning by deduction. Actually, modern science relies on induction and on experience, a device more fruitful than the deductions and syllogisms of the ancients. Spiritual experience is a knowledge of God by induction, which, as such, must follow the rules of this form of knowledge. We must, first, welcome spiritual experience as a method of knowledge, and reject every prejudice against its reliability.

The use of this method in spiritual things is not condoned easily. People trained in physical science are not ready to accept the reliability of an experience in the spiritual life. They are so careful to avoid confusion in their own research that they can hardly imagine scientists taking for their special object the spirit itself. But, once the originality and the reliability of spiritual experience are accepted, we must consider the success of such an experience, correctly observed, as a scientific achievement, valuable and worthy to be extended to similar cases in the way of a general rule or law. One experience, properly observed, can be indefinitely repeated with the same result. Repetition confirms the rule and leads to a better observation of the essential elements of the phenomenon, although without truly adding to the value of the first experience. It is useful to repeat it in order to convince others. And perhaps others can improve the method and results through their own experiences.

The same remark applies to spiritual experience: if somebody has discovered the existence of God, his or her experience is absolute. But there are so many possibilities of fear and delusion in such an area that we are tempted to doubt ourselves, especially after the experience itself, when the divine presence has vanished and we vainly try to bring it back by memory, imagination or abstraction. Therefore, it is important to know that many people undergo the same experience; that they undergo it in many ways, and that all come to the same general result: the presence of God. Billions and billions of experiences have occurred in the past and the present, everywhere, to every kind of people, young and old, women and men, poor and rich, cultured and uncultured, under all aspects of the spiritual life. Such a quantity and quality of experience is determinant, and we can conclude the existence of God with some certitude.

However, there is also the experience of God's inexistence. Some people, not very many, after true inquiry, conclude that there is no God. Are we to be troubled by their result? We might first observe that their experience most probably was not correctly performed.

There was once an old schoolmaster who sometimes endeavoured to perform some experiments in the classroom. He was nervous from the first moment, and the children enjoyed a long recreation while he was preparing test-tubes, chemical products, heaters, connections. A stench immediately choked the children when they entered. Solemnly he foretold the result, which could not fail because of the laws of science. Unfortunately, the expected result was rarely attained, and the schoolmaster, in order to restore their belief in science, used to pour vinegar upon a piece of natural chalk and produce some carbonic gas, or he would drop a piece of cloth into litmus solution and then into an acid and into a base, and the cloth became red, then blue at will! Something was wrong in the former experiment, certainly! There was some mistake somewhere.

The same mistake can be made in the interpretation of spiritual experience. Perhaps people who have not concluded to the existence of God have walked on a wrong way, used wrong means, or failed out of prejudice to observe it correctly. Those who want to observe the fact of spiritual experience must, first, admit the possibility of a positive result. In philosophy, they must admit the principle of causation if they want to find a cause of the world. They must be silent and pray if they wish to hear the voice of God, and speak to Him if they want an answer. They must distinguish between good and evil, and recognize the authority of their moral conscience if they wish to discover the Divine Adviser and Judge. If they distort the judgment of their conscience or show contempt for its authority, they lead themselves astray. Finally, they must use the right terms. We call God that One whom we find present within us in our prayer and conscience as well as the One whom we acknowledge as the source of everything. But people can reach the same substantial belief and refuse the name of God, or express it in such a display of concepts that their own discovery is misrepresented and hardly recognizable. Therefore, the failure of their experience stands for an additional proof of the existence of God because in such conditions they could not succeed!

## THE OBJECTIVITY OF GOD

The question is whether the OTHER abiding within us, Whom we respect, obey and love, is some temporary vanishing figure, existing from time to time and vanishing into oblivion, and finally dying together with us for ever. In brief, is it some "idealistic superstructure" belonging to the individual and not surviving us? We can answer this objection by insisting on the OBJECTIVITY of the presence of God in us. Such an experience surpasses the boundaries of mere SUBJECTIVITY and individual observation because it is performed by many with the same result.

I take as an illustration a very trivial one, indeed. If only one person in a village has seen a bear, the testimony of this person can be contested. But if many have not only heard of its presence, but also have seen the bear itself, then it is true that this bear exists and is wandering in the country around. The illustration above is trivial, but clear, and we can use it for our purpose. If many, indeed, have "seen God," then God is no longer a mere individual and subjective entity, but must be granted an objective existence. Nothing more is required concerning objectivity in other areas. Modern science does not work with the tools of ancient or medieval metaphysics, but only with observation and numbers.

Moreover, there is progress in our enjoyment of God. We observe this progress in the life of the saints, whose achievements are made known on a wide scale, and also in our own life, at least enough to conclude that, under the influence of God and in his friendship, there is a possibility of improvement for us unto perfection, and a source of joy, inexhaustible and infinite. Is that all about to vanish at the time of our death? We may observe, first, that God is not a purely individual possession. Therefore, the fact that God "continues" as an experience for others, means for Him a form of eternity. Secondly, why should such a rich and fulfilling experience of God necessarily come to an end for an individual at the hour of death, when it might actually reach its maximum power of life?

The diagram of our corporeal development is not parallel to that of our soul. For both, there is the same beginning and first steps of growing, but afterwards each of the two lines follows its own path, with ups and downs. The body, after a decided increase until the adult period where it reaches its climax, makes a plateau and then descends, step by step. Ineluctably it comes to a critical point where it is no longer a fitting instrument: like an old car, it is discarded as refuse, i.e., it returns to the earth. On the contrary, the soul continues her own way up, more and more trained to intellectual and moral activity, and rises again and again. Even the failures of the body, its inactivity, disease and suffering, provide the soul with opportunities of meditation, patience, courage and sacrifice. At the time of death, when the body is near to dissolution, the soul may be more alive, healthy and powerful than ever. Therefore, instead of following the body in its dissolution, the soul probably continues her own adventure, as being self-centered and, according to a word of Plato, "the cause of its own motion." In that case, since the soul becomes completely independent and free after death, we can imagine that her power may increase, and that, instead of vanishing into nothingness, she may progress towards perfection and union with God.

An interesting testimony of an experience of God near the time of death is found in Augustine's *Confessions*, the famous "Vision in Ostia," where Augustine acknowledges having enjoyed, together with his mother Monica who was close to her death, a brief moment of union with God and of perfect happiness. This moment of heavenly life soon vanished because of their present inability to cast out for a long time the activity of their senses and because the usual method of thought by abstraction ultimately relies on the data of the senses. However, their moment of bliss can be conceived of as a glimpse on the beatitude found in the future and everlasting life. Through this window just opened and soon closed, an eternity of blessed union with God was discovered. This short experience of the presence of God gave Augustine both the sense of the immortal life of the soul with God and the sense of the eternity of God.[118]

## THE EXPERIENCE OF DIVINE PROVIDENCE

The idea of a divine providence means that God is exercising some activity within us and around us. Is it possible to be sure of this divine activity, and to identify its divine author with some certitude?

Somehow the question of divine providence is akin to the question of miracle. There is a general providence evident in nature, and there is a particular providence in certain special events of our life.

I set apart here the question of miracle in the full sense of its modern definition: an event so striking and so unexpected according to the laws of nature, and so openly the consequence of prayer, that its divine origin cannot reasonably be doubted. Such an event, of course, is by itself a proof of God, and our faith in God can rely on it, even if our evidence for it is indirect, i.e., when it comes to us through other witnesses or historical testimony. If we believe in God, we must admit, at least in principle, the possibility of miracle, even if we may doubt many stories of miracles. There are miracles in the Bible, in the Gospels, in the life of the saints. There are miracles even in our times, which are especially important for us on account of their proximity, their more objective observation, and their easier historical proof. We may mention the miracles recorded in the life of the Curé of Ars and those of Lourdes. Miracles are good evidence for the existence of God. But they are not frequent under the modern definition, and usually come from indirect testimony. Moreover, they are presented in the way of a challenge to science, which can offend scientists and rebuke them.

For the present purpose, I prefer to consider such miracles as those which can easily be explained by the laws of nature. Since God is the author of the laws of nature, we can assume that, usually at least, He operates through these laws. But, in these conditions, how can we be sure of God's intervention at all? Such interventions will always be questionable, since we come across events which we can ascribe to nature, but nothing proves that they are performed with a special intention of God. Often, even we are inclined to deny any will of God operative in an event, when, for instance, we endure evil, suffering, delusion, damage, sorrow, etc. Are all these natural events, however, indifferent and deprived of any divine purpose? In the present --at the time we are coping with them-- it is nearly impossible to be certain of the divine intention attached to them.

[118] Augustine, *Confessions* IX 11.

But the same is not true if we consider past events. The purpose of God can become evident from a succession of events, and even something which looked wrong when happening is proved to be right in its consequences. I give an illustration: when a child is enduring some correction from his mother, he may be tempted to doubt her love for him, nevertheless... The same is true with God: some disease, even some sin which was held to be harmful, proved to be to our profit because it provided us with an opportunity for reflection or correction. If God is not a distant monarch, indifferent to earthly things or only interested in the general government of the world, and if He is truly a close adviser to us, we can assume that he uses the opportunities of many events in our life to influence us, proportioning everything to our good and to our capacity.

Certain spiritual guides in the 17th century had their retreatants write down in a notebook the noticeable graces of their past, i.e., that which turned good for their spiritual advantage, or could have done so had they obeyed the will of God. They were also to record events close to miraculous which they had observed. The result was usually conclusive: they were amazed to observe the evidence of the divine guidance over them, and they came to regard this manifestation of divine providence as their most intimate proof of the existence of God. If we ourselves notice the few obvious graces we enjoy everyday, before long we shall believe in providence and in the guidance of God with renewed conviction. Our best evidence for the existence of God is likely to be found in our everyday life.

Are we able to perceive God operating in nature: plants, animals, even in our body? We do conclude to His action in this area, but we do not experience it. On the contrary, in every event of our moral life we hear the advice of God in our conscience, we perceive His power enabling us to lift ourselves above ourselves, and His judgment is communicated to us immediately. Only in our moral life, do we cooperate consciously with God. Nowhere else is His divine providence --and existence-- more obvious.

## THE PHILOSOPHICAL APPROACH TO GOD

In the present section we simply propose to make a few inquiries into the way God was understood by the two most influential philosophers in antiquity: Plato and Aristotle, and to check the doctrine of God in a few representatives of its later development, for these also deeply influenced Christianity.

1. PLATO IN *TIMAEUS*.[119]

*Timaeus* gives a description of the origin of the "macrocosm" (the world) and of the "microcosm" (humanity). Plato starts with the assumption that the world has not always existed because it undergoes change and becoming, as being visible and corporeal. There is, Plato says, a beginning and an end of the world, but "to discover the Maker and Father of this universe is indeed a hard task, and having found Him, it would be impossible to tell everyone about Him" (28).

> The Framer was good and, owing to His goodness, wished all things to be as much like Himself as possible. Therefore, finding the visible universe not in a state of rest but of disharmonious motion, He reduced it to order from disorder. But, in fashioning the universe, He implanted reason in soul and soul in body (the universe) and so ensured that His work should be by nature highest and best. And so, through His providence, the world came to be a living being with soul and intelligence.(30)
>
> However, because He used the highest model, there is one universe only, and not a plurality of them, and it will continue to be the only existing one. (30-31) The Framer disposed two circles in X, that of the same, the outer one, which was destined to become the sphere of the fixed stars, and the circle of the different, the inner one, which would be later divided into six concentric spheres corresponding to each planet. The earth stands at the center of this universe. (36)
>
> All these stars share in the Soul of the universe, the fixed ones enjoying only two motions, one uniform in the same place and the other forward, but the other beings, as less perfect, are affected by the other five kinds of motions, e.g., the planets and the earthly beings. (40)
>
> Now He turned again the bowl in which He had mixed the Soul of the universe, and poured into it what was left of the former ingredients, mixing them in much the same fashion, only not quite so pure, and divided it into as many souls as there are stars, and alloted each soul to a star. And mounting them on their stars, as if on chariots, He showed them the nature of the universe and

---

[119] The modern reader should always remember that, if *Timaeus* looks like a real, although antiquated, cosmogony and cosmology with their anthropological counterpart, actually Plato is using myth in order to explore and express through symbolism the secrets of the inner life. Myth is a philosophical tool.

> told them the laws of their destiny. The first incarnation would be one and the same for all, and the souls would be born as the most god-fearing of living things. Later on, these souls will become men and women, endowed with a body subject to gain and loss, and with the faculty of sensation which depends on external stimulation, and with desire and its mixture of pain and pleasure, and fear and anger...
>
> Mastery of these would lead to a good life, subjection to them to a wicked life. And anyone who lived well for his appointed time would return home to his native star and live an appropriate happy life; but everyone who failed to do so would be changed into a woman at his second birth. And if he still did not refrain from wrong, he would be changed into some animal suitable for his particular shape of wrongdoing, and would have no respite from change and suffering until he allowed the motion of the Same and uniform in himself to subdue all that multitude of riotous and irrational feelings which have clung to it since its association with fire, water, air and earth, and with reason thus in control returned once more to his first and best form. Some of these souls He sowed in the earth, some in the moon and some in all the other instruments of time.(41-42)

According to Plato in *Timaeus*, the "way of redemption" for humans, therefore, is their return to their understanding and imitation in deeds and thoughts of the order of the universe, i.e., philosophy. This knowledge is recovered at first through the best of our senses: sight, the best gift of the deity to humanity, because it is the source of philosophy.

We may now draw the main conclusions: there is a "Maker of the world," whose work consisted in reducing things to order. As we can see, Plato does not teach the theory of creation out of nothing, and, for him, only order --not matter-- is worthy of the consideration of God and object of His work. With this reservation, according to Plato, the world has not always existed, but has had a beginning.

Plato affirms the existence of a "Soul of the world," which seems to be a god. There are similar gods in the stars. Humans also own a soul, which is not different in nature from the Soul of the world and from the higher gods, but only not so pure. These human souls are offered a special destiny: being born in stars, they incarnate, and finally return home either directly, or through a descent to a condition in which ultimately they will be straightened out by the native basic goodness of the simplest beings, and, from there, will resume their progressive ascent to heaven. Very important for the fallen souls is their rediscovery of the notion of order through the sense of sight and the contemplation of the universe, for it represents a way of redemption from sin to righteousness, both morally and intellectually. It is essentially a recovery of knowledge, which Plato considers as a reminiscence.

Although the order of the universe leads us to acknowledge its Author, Plato confesses that it is a hard task to discover the Maker and Father, and even more to declare it to people. Why such a difficulty? It seems that it is due to the fact that our soul is more adjusted to the intelligence of the material world than to metaphysics. Actually, after stating the existence of a Creator, Plato seems to forget this notion, and usually applies the term God to the Soul of the Universe or to the souls of the heavenly bodies. In a certain sense, he regards human souls as miniature gods. Concerning the gods of Greek mythology, he refers to the "children of the gods" (probably the poets) without paying attention to their stories.

## 2. Plato in Laws X: Proof for the existence of God and for divine providence.

*The existence of God.*

Plato discusses the necessity of having the gods believed in and honored in the city, especially of persuading the young people to do so. Actually many people despised the beliefs in which their parents trained them (881b). Plato felt obliged to be apologetic, and to support faith with evidence. He supported the gods of the city, but, since his ideal city was an image of the world, the gods that were to be honored seem to be the souls of the heavenly bodies (which govern the world with order), rather than those of Homer and of popular religion (objects of superstition). His apologetic stresses the importance of belief among the young, but this belief has to be correct:

> Nobody believing in the existence of the gods according to the laws has ever committed any impious deed or indulged himself in any criminal utterance; only one of the three following opinions could induce him to do so: either they don't exist at all, or they exist but don't care for men, or they are easily swayed and agree to change their mind under the influence of prayers and sacrifices. (885b)

Plato carries on his efforts at persuasion by answering objections. The first objection reads:

> When we affirm that the sun, moon, stars and earth are gods, we are answered that they are only earth and stones, unable to think of human affairs. (886a, 889c)

According to the second objection, the primary cause of all generation and destruction is chance. In these two objections, we recognize the theses of materialism, and the second is close to modern Marxism: the deity, or the metaphysics which replaces it, are pure idealistic superstructures, the product and not the cause of the development of the world. (891c)

In order to answer these objections, Plato first tries to prove the existence of the Soul of the world. There is motion in the world, but everything which is moved needs a mover, and, in the beginning, a mover which is the cause of its own motion; otherwise there would not exist any motion at all (994-995). This Prime Mover is identical to the Soul of the world.

Now, there are three places where the Soul of the universe can dwell: either inside the sphere of the world, or outside moving it by impulsion, or again outside, but independently from the universe, free from all bodily influence, and moving the universe in the way of a Guide, because of its perfection, i.e., through imitation. (999a) Plato proposes these three solutions without expressing his favor for the third, this choice not being necessary for his present demonstration, but the mere fact that he proposes the three proves that he realized the importance of the "Final Cause" which his disciple Aristotle and later on Aquinas will explain at length, and which is more suitable to God.

*Divine providence.*

Now Plato takes up his second demonstration: the gods care for human affairs, i.e., there is a divine providence. Plato must answer an objection: the success of unjust people and the abundance of evil on earth are a scandal and seem to destroy the thesis of divine providence.

First, Plato answers that the gods are surely good, and certainly not lazy; therefore they care for people (900); they even care for small things and detail, because there must not be neglect in them (901a). Even a crafter corrects the small defects, out of love of the craft and of personal dignity.

However, there is evil. Evil becomes a problem because, Plato notes, we take a wrong view of things, and are mistaken about them. But the Maker disposed every part of the world for the common good, and proportioned it to the perfection of the whole. The whole is not made for the part, or proportioned to the blind advantage of the part (903b).

The specific problem of moral evil remains to be resolved. Plato observes that, in His planning of the whole, the deity entrusted the development of virtue to the responsibility of the individual will. Therefore, since our souls have been created out of the same stuff as the gods, instead of neglecting our task, we should better imitate the gods, i.e., imitate the virtues of the souls of the heavenly bodies which perform their duties perfectly (904-905).

*The question of worship.*

There is one question left, that of worship. We must not imagine that the gods, Plato says, are corruptible and can be bent by prayers and sacrifices (905a).

Here, Plato actually refers to superstitions and magical practices. Since women particularly liked this style of religion, Plato proposes to destroy all the private sanctuaries where these superstitions were entertained and these sacrifices performed. Only public sanctuaries are to be maintained, and worship here to be attended, because here only is worship performed according to law by magistrates, and everything is managed correctly (909-910). Plato does not describe the rites of his religion, but he says in *Epinomis* 980, that the purpose of the laws is to praise the gods in hymns and speeches, a pure life, a good end, paying attention to the example given by the better and to the study of the science of numbers and of astronomy.

Concerning demonology, *Epinomis* 984 mentions the existence of demons of the air and of the ether, that of intermediary places and natures of bodies, teachings which reappear in later philosophy and in Judaism.

3. THE THREE WAYS OF PLATO.

When we deal with Plato's notion of the deity, we must resist the temptation of combining "Maker," "gods," and "Forms" into one notion of God in the way of later Greek philosophy or of modern theology. Such a synthesis was achieved by Philo and the Christian Apologists of the second century A.D.

There is no such synthesis in Plato. Is it a weakness? No, but Plato opens three ways of research, three original ways which lead to what we now call God, and he does not confuse these ways. It belongs to people who start from a dogmatic position on God to forget the relevance of the three Platonic ways.

The three Platonic ways to the notion of God are: 1) the notion of causation which leads to affirm the Cause of the world, or the "Father and Maker;" 2) the notion of rational beings which leads to consider the existence of the "gods" properly speaking, i.e., the souls of heavenly bodies; 3) and the notion of the "Forms," which leads to acknowledge the existence of higher spiritual realities, the authority and influence of which we experience in our intellectual and moral judgments, and which are the source of our spiritual life now and its guarrantee in immortality.

Among the Forms, the Good stands as a queen and transcends the other Forms.[120] The Good is the object of the highest knowledge. And Justice, like all other virtues, depends

[120] Plato, the "Myth of the Cave," *Republic* 6 & 7.

on the Good for its relevance and profit. The Good works as the sun of our mind, and transcends the other virtues. The philosopher who acknowledges absolute priority for the Forms is the most realistic, even if the cartoon represents him as lost in contemplation and falling into a pit. Popular opinion does not understand him, but praises earthly powers and commerce. Such is the message of the Myth of the Cave.

What are ultimately the Forms for Plato? They are not persons; they are not gods in the sense of a Soul of the world; they are life-giving principles which, because of their dynamic influence, are rightly granted an existence of their own. Who can doubt the existence of an influence which is an object of experience, even when its source remains invisible? Would we doubt the existence of a wind, which is invisible, but able to carry leaves away?

### 4. ARISTOTLE'S NOTION OF GOD.

As it happens with the best disciples, Aristotle came to support a position, concerning the Forms, that was quite contrary to that of his master Plato. During his life, Aristotle moved from Platonism (even a mystical and religious Platonism with a belief in divine providence) toward a more rationalistic position.

In *Metaphysics* Book II, God is a requirement of the universe which needs a Cause. But this Cause is a mere transcendent Cause, the "Prime Mover" outside the Universe, working as a "final cause" only (cf. the third hypothesis for the place of the Soul of the world in Plato's *Laws* X). The Prime Mover deserves the title of cause because the world "moves" towards it as a goal, or imitates the Prime Mover in perfection as much as possible. But the Prime Mover itself is unmoved by creation, indifferent, unaffected. According to this theory, God is the transcendent Cause without any commitment, care, or providence for creatures. To God can be ascribed only intuitive activity and self-interest: He is himself the only object of His thought.[121]

But we are far from our notion of the living God. Aristotle's notion of the Prime Mover has much in common with the "Maker" of Plato's *Timaeus* and the "Final Cause" of the universe of *Laws* X, but Aristotle is more radical, and we find in him only one part of the Platonic tryptic: only the notion of the "Prime Mover," but nothing of the "Forms" enlightening our minds, nor of the "gods" who, in Plato, performed the works of providence and conferred some philanthropy on the deity.

---

[121] Aristotle, *Metaphysics* XII, 6-10; cf. Werner Jaeger, *Aristotle* (New York: Oxford University Press, 1948), ch.14, "The Revision of the Theory of the Prime Mover," pp.352-367.

5. God in Later Philosophy.

Toward the beginning of the Christian era, philosophy became more and more religious. The three apparently irreducible parts of the deity in Platonism: the "Maker," the "Forms," and the "gods," tended to gather and be combined into one Being, and probably the Bible here worked in the way of a catalytic agent. The God of the Bible indeed was the Creator of the universe, the Adviser dwelling in human hearts, and the Providence whose activity and gifts were seen everywhere and asked for in prayer.

This synthesis is achieved already in the pseudo-Aristotelian treatise *De mundo* which Justin ascribed to Aristotle and which, together with *Timaeus*, was very influential on Christian thought. Justin observed that, in *De mundo*, the influence of God did not extend to us, completed as it was by the action of the lower gods, His ministers, which *De mundo* compared to the satraps and messengers of the great Persian king.

In the third century, Plotinus developed a philosophy of the unity of God which integrated the purifying and enlightening power of the "Forms." Aquinas,[122] in the thirteenth century, gave full development to the Aristotelian theory of the "Prime Mover," which he completed with mystical aspects borrowed from Neo-Platonism (Plotinus) and Pseudo-Dionysius, a Christian neo-Platonist of the fifth century whom he thought was Dionysius, disciple of Paul in Athens.

CONCLUSION

The philosophical achievement of a doctrine of God was an unquestionable gain, and as such belongs to the Christian tradition of teaching. However, even in the best philosophers, this teaching is not without some danger.

In Plato we noticed the use of myth --a questionable mode of reasoning and expression-- and the absence of a synthesis of the three aspects of the deity: the "Creator," the "Forms," and the "gods." In Aristotle we observed that the exclusive consideration of the "Prime Mover" led him to a conception of a God empty of any kind of philanthropy.

Actually, God could not be contained in only one of these conceptions, and none of them could exhaust the wealth of an analysis of our experience of God. Their danger was a distortion and impoverishment of the notion of God, consequently, an increased difficulty with some problems, for instance that of evil.

Moreover, even if we take for granted the ancient speculations on the "Logos," or Creative Thought of God, philosophy can hardly lead people to the Christian Trinity: the Father, whose children we are in His beloved Son, enjoying the

[122] Aquinas, *Summa Theologica* Ia Q2 A3..

inspiration and gift of the divine life through the Holy Spirit. Such a revelation is a concrete thing, a gift of God through the Bible and the New Testament, and cannot be derived from mere philosophy. In addition, philosophy leads us to unconsciously accept its own theology as a basis, and to consider the theology founded upon revelation as a complement. Such a shift causes an indirect distortion of the right meaning of God. There is also the danger of reaching a notion of God which would be pure abstraction, and would apparently preserve nothing of concrete existence.

However, as a conclusion, we must stress the usefulness of the philosophical achievements in theology, although at the same time the necessity not to rely only on them. We must return to our living experience of God in our daily life and in the life of our friends.

More particularly, we should read Psalms, and use them in our meditation and prayer. These wonderful hymns are the fruit and the expression of piety and life. They are neither philosophy nor theology. If some theologian or priest had written them, he would probably have corrected many "imperfections" in them as suggestive of blasphemy! But, whether in suffering, or in joy, our prayer unconsciously joins that of the Psalms. A right analysis of religious experience can certainly rely on a study of Psalms, and, in return, acquaintance with, and use of, Psalms is the best way to open our souls to the presence of God.

An inquiry into the records of conversions would complete our analysis of the discovery and analysis of God. Among others, the conversion of Claudel, of Augustine, Justin, Pascal, even of Socrates, is particularly instructive. People go to God through beauty and art, through the dizziness of metaphysical experience, through philosophy and wisdom, through the influence of the Bible, the Gospels, the writings of the early Christians, the life of the saints, through the practice of devotion and charity, under the influence of solitude, etc.

The tradition of classical philosophy and theology with Plato, Aristotle and Aquinas, as seen above, provides a comfortable proof for the existence of God in his perfections and as creator of the world and of humankind. Theologically the Creator must remain the transcendent God, and all cheap or popular notions of the work of God and of the creator are liable to meet with destructive criticism. The image of a carpenter making a table can be useful pedagogically on a low level of understanding. The image of the architect, as a cause invisible and effective on a larger scale, may also be useful as more suggestive of the divine transcendence. A proof for the existence of God relying on his works requires a good analysis of causality and the sense of analogy. The Final cause of the universe is also the Prime Mover unmoved, the cause of causes. And every good observed in created things points toward the absolute and perfection.

Can we say that there is an experience of God in the contemplation of the creation? How can we deny it of Francis of Assisi (*The Little Flowers*), who was both a mystic and a poet. Both mysticism and poetry are experiential. But we may ask whether we perceive God as a creator when we look at things. It seems that generally we rely on a reasoning, at least implicitly. But we only perceive the living action of God when we listen to the divine word in the secrecy of our soul and cooperate with it. The Bible, and particularly Psalms, make a large use of popular language and images about the creator. Thank God! The Bible is not a manual of speculative theology. And popular language and images are the style of prayer.

## QUESTIONNAIRE

1. What kind of feeling of the existence of God did Lacordaire recognize in his audience only a few days after the event of the spontaneous carrying of a cross by the populace to a church? In his opinion, what is the meaning of such a "natural belief"? Is it philosophy? superstition? routine? social conditioning? How would you regard it?

2. Do you think, like Tertullian, that the soul left to herself would soon affirm God? Have you observed such a disposition in yourself, in others? Do people easily turn to God? How would you interpret the "conversion" of the young Lacordaire?

3. From the conversation of the seminarian with the old devoted woman, can we conclude that it is always better to leave people with their unsophisticated forms of faith?

4. Criticize positively, negatively, the riddle, "How not to believe that God talks with children about candy?"

5. In your opinion, did Jesus really talk to the young priest who refused money to the poor woman of Jericho? Why was he happy in spite of, or because of, this sin?

6. Do you think that people often experience the presence and voice of God in prayer? Is not prayer sometimes illusory and deceptive? Why?

7. How can we say that a well observed analysis of an experience of God is an absolute proof for God's existence, and, at the same time, that it is not enough?

8. How can the experience of the non-existence of God often be invalidated for reasons of method? Are there conditions for the perception of God?

9. Do you think that these spiritual guides of the 17th century were wise when they invited their retreatants to consider the providence of God in their past life? What kind of certitude can the past provide which the present could not, about the divine guidance of our soul?

10. Have you seen, or heard of, events close to being miraculous? Can you still interpret them as a warning of God, even if you can explain them naturally or scientifically?

11. How did Plato explain the creation of the world and of humanity in *Timaeus*?

12. What is the religion which Plato dreams of introducing in his ideal city? What kinds of religion does he reject, which seem to lead the young people to unbelief? Does Plato consider a "religion of science"?

13. Does the Soul of the world in Plato's *Laws* X suggest the notion of the "Creator," of a "god," of the "Form of the Good"? What does it mean if it is located inside? on the circle? outside the sphere of the world?

14. Did Plato consider the Forms as persons? If not, what kind of existence was he granting them?

15. How can Aristotle say that, as a "Final Cause" (a goal), God is existing, and moves (transforms) the world without doing anything in it?

16. Show that we now consider that God is at the same time "Maker," "Soul of the world" (transcendent to the world), and "Form of the Good," -the three aspects of the deity analyzed by Plato? With what words do people pray to God under these three aspects?

17. Does philosophy give the right notion of God in every regard? How should we complete it? Is philosophizing advantageous for faith?

## BIBLIOGRAPHY

ARISTOTLE. *Metaphysics*, Book 12, 6-10 (1071-1076). English translation in *The Basic Works of Aristotle*. New York: Random House, 1941. Pp. 875-888.

*Select Passages illlustrating Neoplatonism*. Translated by E.R. DODDS. London: SPCK, 1960.

DIES, A. *Autour de Platon. Essai de critique et d'histoire.* 2 vol. Paris: Beauchesne, 1927. Ch. 3, "Le Dieu de Platon;" ch. 4, "La religion de Platon," pp.523-603.

JAMES, William. *The Varieties of Religious Experience.* New York: Image Books, 1978.

PLATO. *Timaeus. Laws.* English tr. in *The Collected Dialogues of Plato.* E. Hamilton & H. Cairns ed. New York: Bollingen Foundation, 1963.

# CHAPTER IX

# HISTORICAL JESUS

Diversity in the understanding of Jesus existed from the beginning. First, there are four Gospels instead of one. Moreover, in many places, the text itself reflects the apostles's preaching on Jesus, after Easter, and not simply the preaching of Jesus himself. Actually it is often very difficult to ascertain the very words of Jesus. Modern scholars have worked at it carefully with better and better methods of textual criticism. The purpose of this chapter is to initiate the reader to the work (methods and results) of modern exegesis (interpretation) of the gospels.

After a preamble about the problems and methods of criticism in the area of the Gospels, we present the book of J. Jeremias on the parables of Jesus, and explain his views on the core of the gospel: the kingdom of heaven is open for the poor and sinners. Then, we turn to Sanders's version of the causes of the death of Jesus, which were political reasons. For the motive of the death of Jesus, i.e., for the meaning confered by Jesus on his own suffering, Jeremias seems to have the right answer: the intention of the Suffering Servant. Finally, we deal with the narratives of the resurrection, according to Jeremias and especially N. Perrin.

## PROBLEMS AND METHOD OF TEXTUAL AND HISTORICAL CRITICISM

The first concern of New Testament exegesis is the establishment of a critical text on the basis of the best and earliest manuscripts, and also of literary sources (for instance, quotes of the Gospels in early Christian writings). The second concern is the identification of all editorial and exhortatory additions made by the evangelists themselves to the words of Jesus. For instance, short references to time, place, and circumstances, the mentioning of partners in dialogues, etc. are often artificial and attributable to the author of the narrative. Often it also happens that a parable is given a new meaning.[123]

---

[123] For instance, the story of the Pharisee and the Pulican ends (Luke 18:14) with an exhortation to humility, "for everyone who exalts himself will be humbled..." which hardly reflects the heat of the controversy in which a tax-collector was justified by God, while Pharisees were refused justice for their merits because of theif self-righteousness before God.

Another difficulty comes from the existence of four gospels. Among them, the Gospel of John is more a "theological meditation" than a biography properly speaking. The gospels of Mark, Luke and Matthew, because they contain important sections in common, and can be read in parallel columns --the reason why they are called Synoptics-- raise a problem of sources. Today Mark is considered as the earliest of the three, and widely used by Matthew and Luke. Exegetes also identify another source for the Synoptics, which they call *Q*, from the German word *Quelle* (source). This source seems to have contained materials concerning the preaching of John the Baptist, multiple sayings attributed to Jesus, and some stories about Jesus focussing on his controversies and miracles. Finally, there are valuable materials concerning the sayings of Jesus in the recently discovered *Gospel of Thomas*, of Gnostic origin. All these sources, along with what we know of the literature and life of first century Palestine, make possible an analysis of the gospels which surpasses all previous efforts.

But the existence of four gospels also involves differences of meaning, not simply textual criticism. Before the work of modern scholars, it was common practice to add and combine the data of the four gospels in such a way as to obtain a unique and complete picture of Jesus. Most of our biographies of Jesus are composed this way. But these compositions are mediocre and objectionable. They may be compared to the silly attempt of reducing the portraits of the same person painted by 4 different artists into one painting, when it is obvious that each artist had his own perception and understanding of the model. Actually, we have four images of Christ, and each author had his own theological view of Jesus. This view depended on the written or oral traditions at his disposal, on his personal reflection on Jesus, and on his own purpose, i.e., on the way he found it pertinent through this new gospel to resolve the problems raised in his community, for instance the acceptance of Gentiles without circumcision and other legal prescriptions of the Law of Moses. The difficulty could also be the delay of the *parousia* (the end of the world and divine judgment). In that case, the implications could affect the understanding of the resurrection of Christ and of the kingdom of God.

The task of ascertaining the very words of Jesus is further complicated by the new understanding of his teaching by the disciples after the resurrection. N. Perrin (1920-76) puts it this way:

> The disciples completely identified the risen Lord of their experience with the earthly Jesus of Nazareth. They made no attempt to distinguish between the words the earthly Jesus had spoken and those spoken by the risen Lord through a prophet in the community, nor between the original teachings of Jesus and the new understanding and reformulation of that teaching

> reached in the catechesis of parenesis (moral exhortation) of the church under the guidance of the Lord of the church. This is the reason for our major problem in reconstructing the teaching of Jesus. We are not hearing the voice of the earthly Jesus addressing Galilean disciples in a Palestinian situation, but that of the risen Lord addressing Christian missionaries in a Hellenistic world[124]

The criterion of "double dissimilarity" seems to be reliable for the ascertainment of the very words of Jesus. This criterion consists of discarding as uncertain, every item which can be ascribed to traditional Jewish material of the time of Jesus, or to early Christianity. For instance, Jesus' behavior towards sinners is certainly historical, but Sanders challenges sayings about the "Son of Man" as a later justification of Jesus' dignity and mission derived from Daniel 7 and other sources. But the criterion of double dissimilarity can also be destructive, and unfairly discards a legitimate use by Jesus of his own Jewish tradition. Ultimately, no word of Jesus may be received as certain. Moreover, by focussing on one only aspect of Jesus considered as historical, it can distort the whole view of the historical Jesus, as we see in the book of Sanders, in which the political prevails over the spiritual. However, the general result of modern textual criticism as applied to the gospels is positive, and leads to a more accurate knowledge of Jesus.

A last obstacle to an objective analysis of the gospels is found in the prejudice of the exegete himself. For instance, A. Harnack (1851-1930) speaks well of the preaching of the kingdom, a purely spiritual message of pious love, with a complete freedom from the Jewish establishment, but, going too far in that direction, he sees the church as a betrayal of the message of Jesus. For Harnack, the church implies a hierarchical organization recognizing human power rather than God's authority, and relies on both a moral conversion to philosophical ethics, and on a ceremonial system, which for him respectively mean rationalist teaching and irrational magic.[125] However, how can Harnack reconcile his understanding of Jesus' teaching with Jesus' faithfulness to synagogal service?

Albert Schweitzer (1875-1965) reminded scholars of the importance of eschatology (the imminent coming of the end and

---

[124] N. Perrin. *Rediscovering the Teaching of Jesus*, (New York: Harper & Row, 1967), pp.15-16.

[125] A. von Harnack. *History of Dogma*, tr. N. Buchanan (New York: Dover Publications, 1961), vol.I, *passim*.

judgment) in the time and thought of Jesus.[126] Schweitzer was right, but, because of his emphasis on the imminence of the end, he too could not see the relevance of a church as an institution.

E.P. Sanders criticized Joachim Jeremias who may have exaggerated the presence of the theme of the Suffering Servant in the thought of Jesus from baptism to the cross, but, carrying his criticism too far, he fails to find an adequate motivation of Jesus in his death.[127]

J. Jeremias and Norman Perrin seem to remain two major figures of present scholarship concerning Jesus and his message, and Sanders provides a useful discussion of the events of the life and death of Jesus.

## THE MIRACLES OF JESUS

Jesus was a faith healer and a wonderworker. This aspect of Jesus stands as a first challenge, a kind of test for the interpreter. Miracles can just be disregarded by scholars, or be reduced to a "minimum," or misinterpreted as magic, or seen as automatically connected with the great intervention of God. Many miracles may have been amplified and distorted.

Sanders criticizes the idea that Jesus' miracles are just the enactment and confirmation of Isaiah 35: the Messiah is prophesied as healing the lame, the dumb and the blind - the sign given by Jesus of the coming of the Kingdom. Without denying this implication, Sanders says that Jesus simply performed miracles that were called for by circumstances and needs.[128]

For Morton Smith, Jesus' miracles bear some mark of magic, and Jesus was a magician who moved upward to the status of holy man and god on the strength of his ability to work wonders. The miracles attracted the crowds, to whom Jesus proclaimed the good news of salvation for sinners. Jesus found that he could heal; that he attracted crowds and special followers. Jesus not only healed the needy in Galilee but also promised the kingdom to the poor and the outcasts.

While G. Vermes maintains that Jesus fits the type of a Galilean charismatic such as Honi (a first century holy man, prophet, exorcist, and wondermaker), Sanders prefers to compare him to Theudas and other prophets or "messiahs" of the

---

[126] Albert Schweitzer (1875-1965), *The Quest of the Historical Jesus; A Critical Study of its progress from Reimarus to Wrede* (New York: Macmillan, 1956).

[127] E.P. Sanders, *Jesus and Judaism* (Philadelphia: Fortress Press, 1985), *passim*; see p. 332.

[128] Sanders, p. 163.

same period, who were all sentenced to death by the Romans.[129]

For Jeremias, the baptism of Jesus is the communication of the divine spirit for the fulfilment of his mission as a Savior. In the desert, Jesus confirms his mission, winning the victory over the temptation to political power suggested to him by the evil spirit. The first and most obvious manifestation of this divine spirit and mission are the miracles.

However, when the question of the quantity and quality of these miracles is raised, Jeremias reduces as much as possible the phenomenon itself of gospel miracles. He discards duplicates and borrowings, explains away Jesus' walking on the waters, the "legion" of the devils in the demoniac of Gadara, the curse on the fig tree, the coin found in the mouth of a fish, etc. He distinguishes a Hellenistic miracle tradition, more verbose, descriptive and moralizing, from an earlier Palestinian miracle tradition which was more briefly stated. The miracles which survive his criticism are chiefly exorcisms and faith-healings, both "shock therapy" in the modern sense.[130]

Jeremias is probably right. Diseases, even leprosy, were not well identified in the time of Jesus. However, his anxiety to reduce the importance of miracle in the gospels seems to be too negative. The idea of faith-healing is more the affirmation of the power of faith as surrender to, and total confidence in, God's will. It teaches the power of the prayer of petition addressed to a living God, who is not just the equivalent of the laws of the cosmos.

## THE PARABLES OF JESUS[131]

The parables represent the essential core of the "teaching" of Jesus. They relate to 1) the good news of salvation, with God's mercy for sinners, and confidence in God's ways; 2) the imminence of the end, with a foretaste of the grace of God; 3) and the suffering and exaltation of the Son of Man.

### 1. NOW IS THE DAY OF SALVATION!

The *sign* given by Jesus to John the Baptist concerning the divine authenticity of his own mission is taken from

---

[129] For Smith and Vermes, see Sanders, ch. 5, "Miracles and Crowds," pp. 157-173.

[130] Joachim Jeremias, *New Testament Theology* (New York: Scribner 1971), ch. 3.

[131] Joachim Jeremias, *The Parables of Jesus* (New York: Scribner 1963).

Isaiah,[132] and describes the style of the Kingdom of God preached by Jesus: "Blind see; lame walk; lepers are cleansed; deaf hear; dead are raised; poor have the Gospel preached to them."

It is the joyful time of wedding: "Can the bridal guests mourn during the bridal celebrations?"[133] i.e., while Jesus is among his disciples. Something new has happened, which causes a break with the religious routine of the past: one does not put new wine into a worn-out skin; nor a new piece of cloth on an old garment.[134]

The day of salvation has come! Jesus has resisted temptation in the desert, defeated Satan, and potentially delivered humankind from the servitude of the devil. When the "strong one" (the devil) is bound by a "stronger one" (Jesus), his plunder (humankind) is wrested from him.

a. *God's mercy for sinners.*

J. Jeremias notes that the parables of the Lost Sheep and the Lost Coin of Money are addressed to murmuring scribes and Pharisees;[135] the parable of the Two Debtors is spoken to Simon the Pharisee;[136] the parable of the Pharisee and the Publican is likewise addressed to the Pharisees;[137] the parable of the Two Sons is spoken to members of the Sanhedrin.[138] These parables are addressed, not to the crowd, but to opponents. Their main object is the defense and vindication of the gospel: they are controversial weapons against the critics and foes of the gospel who are indignant that Jesus should declare that God cares about sinners, and whose special attack is directed against Jesus' practice of eating with despised people.

According to the parable of the Prodigal Son,[139] just as the father kissed and returned to his previous dignity a son who had taken away his share of inheritance, defiled himself with harlots, and shared the food of pigs (certainly a levitical im-

---

[132] Isaiah 35:5-6.

[133] Mark 2:19.

[134] Mark 2:21.

[135] Luke 15:2.

[136] Luke 7:40.

[137] Luke 18:9.

[138] Matt. 21:23.

[139] Luke 15:11-32.

purity), Jesus accepts to eat with sinners who repent from their sins, and even actively looks for their conversion. This behavior of Jesus is not understood by his enemies, i.e., by good Jews who were in this regard the prisoners of their own righteousness.

The parable of the Good Employer,[140] who gives the full wages to those who have worked only one hour, criticizes those who murmur against God's goodness for repenting sinners because they themselves have worked so hard on fulfilling their duties toward God and his law. The parable of the Two Debtors[141] even condemns the righteous who refuse to forgive those who have offended them: God had forgiven these righteous men more than what their brethren may owe to them.

b. *Confidence in God's ways.*

The parables of the Mustard Seed, and the parable of the Leaven[142] show that, out of the most insignificant beginnings, invisible to the human eye, God creates his mighty Kingdom, which embraces all the peoples of the world. The parable of the Sower,[143] with the seed being spoiled in most circumstances, shows to those who doubt because of the apparent failure of Jesus' preaching, that, in spite of poor results, hostility, and increasing desertions, the disciples must maintain their faith in him.

The parable of the Seed growing secretly[144] shows that we must patiently wait, and not anticipate God's will, but in full confidence leave everything to him. The insignificance of the beginning prepares the triumph of the end: such is the work of God in the secrecy of the hearts. The parable of the Unjust Judge,[145] in which a poor widow obtains justice from a lazy judge because of her insistence, shows that "God also will hasten to the rescue of his elect, who cry to him day and night, even if he puts their patience to the test."

2. THE IMMINENCE OF THE END.

The message of Jesus is not only the proclamation of salvation, but also the announcement of judgment, a cry of warn-

---

[140] Matt. 20:1-15.

[141] Luke 7.

[142] Mark 4:30-32; Matt. 13:33.

[143] Mark 4:3-8.

[144] Mark 4:26-29.

[145] Luke 18:2-8.

ing, and a call to repentance in view of the terrible urgency of the crisis. The first century in Palestine was an adventist era in which the end of the world was common teaching.

The parable of the Children in the Market-Place,[146] a street-scene in which children who are themselves too lazy to move, criticize other children for not doing their part in the game (marriage and burial were their favorite games), is a warning against neglect and is a strong invitation to active repentance instead of just "criticizing the preacher."

The parables of the fig-tree (the tree that did not bear fruit will be cut down[147]), of the traveller in trouble because of the coming of night,[148] of the householder who lay fast asleep while his house was broken into,[149] of the Rich Fool[150] who, after a rich harvest, makes his preparations for a still heavier one, and whose security God shatters in the same night - all these parables teach the coming of the end of the world and of the judgment. The parable of the Ten Virgins[151] shows that, just as those who are not waiting for the late but sudden arrival of the procession of the bridegroom will not enter the place of the wedding-party, many will be caught unprepared by the coming of the end.

The parable of the Great Supper,[152] in which beggars are invited as substitutes for ill-disposed guests, illustrates the unwillingness of the righteous to sit along with tax-gatherers and other repenting public sinners in the banquet of the Kingdom. When the hall of the banquet is completely occupied, there is no place for further comers: it is too late! So is it with the Kingdom. The parable of the Choice of Places at the Table[153] teaches humility to the righteous who consider as their right to take the first place, while some more important guest --perhaps a repented publican or a harlot-- is entitled to it.

Jesus warns his disciples "to become again like little children",[154] i.e., to speak to the Father in a childlike, trustful,

---

[146] Matt. 11:16f.

[147] Matt. 7:19.

[148] John 12:35.

[149] Matt. 24:43f.

[150] Luke 12:16-20.

[151] Matt. 25:1-12.

[152] Matt. 22:1-10.

[153] Luke 14:7-11.

[154] Matt. 18:3-4.

and intimate way as a little child to its father. It involves the confession of guilt, humiliation, self-abasement, and becoming little again before God.

The eschatological crisis demands a complete break with the past, even, if necessary, from one's nearest relations.[155] Jesus assumes on the part of his followers a readiness to make a complete surrender: the ploughman must only look straight ahead of him.[156] The renunciation is particularly difficult for the rich, since "it is easier for a camel to go through the eye of a needle than for a rich man to enter the Kingdom of God."[157]

a. *Foretaste of divine grace.*

The parable of the Treasure in the Field and that of the Pearl[158] manifest the outburst of joy accompanying the discovery of a hidden treasure or the opportunity of an unexpected good bargain: thus it is with the Kingdom of God!

The parable of the Good Samaritan[159] is addressed to a scribe who has correctly expressed the double command of love for God and for neighbor, but who asked, "Who is my neighbor?" Probably the priest and the levite were prevented from helping the wounded (apparently dead) man by considerations of levitical purity. Against such restrictions, Jesus insisted on the boundless nature of love, at which a Samaritan (considered as a sinner) proves to be more successful.

The sentence pronounced at the Last Judgment[160] teaches that the guilt of the rebuked does not lie in the commission of gross sins, but in the omission of good deeds, particularly deeds of mercy. The parable of the Unmerciful Servant[161] who, after being remitted his debt, sues his friend who owes to him a much smaller amount of money, insists on the duty of forgiveness. We must know that compassion, assistance, and forgiveness granted to our brethren will obtain the same for ourselves from the divine judge.

---

[155] Luke 14:26f.

[156] Matt. 8:21f.

[157] Mark 10:25.

[158] Matt. 13:44-45.

[159] Luke 10:25-37.

[160] Matt. 25:31-46.

[161] Matt. 18:23-35.

3. THE WAY OF SUFFERING AND THE EXALTATION OF THE SON OF MAN.

From Caesarea Philippi onwards, the imminence of the Passion is fully disclosed to the disciples. Jesus spoke of the cup he must drink and of the baptism he must undergo,[162] for the shepherd must lay down his life for the sheep.[163]

Already on the right hand of the throne of God the Son of Man is sitting;[164] the sinful world has passed away, the judgment of the dead and the living has taken place; Satan has been cast out of heaven.

The parable of the Tares among the Wheat,[165] in which the father postpones the removal of the tares to harvesting time, speaks against the idea of a Church of the pure which would exclude sinners. The parable of the Net[166] also insists on the necessity to postpone the separation of good and bad fish until the net is brought to the beach. The judgment belongs to God, not to humans, who cannot discern the secrets of the heart.

GOOD NEWS FOR THE POOR AND SINNERS

The interest of Jesus in "publicans (tax-collectors hired by the Roman treasury) and sinners" is the most delicate problem of the gospel.

For Jeremias, "publicans and sinners" refer to people employed in questionable activities. He also thinks that the enemies of Jesus considered as "sinners" the poor, i.e., "the small and simple" who lived under the burden of hardship. The problem, Jeremias continues, is that "sinners" were Jesus' ordinary table-companions. The inclusion of sinners in the community of salvation was for Jesus the best expression of the redeeming love of God. In addition to such banquets, Jesus visited Zachaeus, the head of the publicans of Jericho: "he came to call, not the just, but sinners!" "Publicans and harlots," Jesus insisted, "will precede pious people in the kingdom of God." Here we observe a reversal of situations, an ancient eschatological theme: the ways of God are different from human ways. But Pharisaic society strongly opposed this message. Judaism considered it a religious duty to shun sinners: they first needed to convert and become righteous. Jesus was overthrowing the basis of religion: the religious relevance of

---

[162] Mark 10:38.

[163] Mark 14:27.

[164] Mark 14:62

[165] Matt. 13:24-30.

[166] Matt. 13:47f.

ethics. Jesus' message of the forgiveness granted to sinners and of their vocation is unique in Judaism, and takes place before his death.

Sanders gives an interesting criticism of the thesis of Jeremias concerning "the poor and sinners"[167] First, he shows that the poor, or *amme haarets*, "common people," were not considered as sinners by Jewish society: it is an opinion of later Pharisees, but not the situation in the time of Jesus. "Common people" were not subjected to priestly purities, but they worshipped and sacrificed in the temple, and were considered as good Israelites. Therefore, Jesus' appeal to sinners and outcasts cannot be understood as an appeal to the "common people." Sanders' conclusion is that Jesus may have offered sinners inclusion in the kingdom not only while they were still sinners, but also without requiring repentance as normally understood, and therefore he could have been accused of being a friend of people who indefinitely remained sinners. Jesus, persuaded that the end was at hand, proclaimed the inclusion of the wicked who followed him. For instance, he did not impose on the tax-collectors and other sinners the ritual obligation which he imposed on the leper (to go to the temple and offer the sacrifice for sin prescribed by the law).

Sanders contributes welcome corrections to the thesis of Jeremias when he says that Jesus is granting forgiveness for real sinners without requiring the usual forms of repentance and conversion. Such sinners, among Israelites, were considered as beyond the hope of salvation, and treated like Gentiles, who were commonly seen in Judaism as absolute sinners. However, as long as death had not put an end to the delay granted by God for repentance, conversion remained possible, and the repenting sinner could offer a sacrifice for sin, or benefit from the general forgiveness granted on the Day of Atonement.

Jeremias shows that Jesus' gratuitous offer of forgiveness to sinners is typical of the ways of God, and a sign of God's immense love for all, particularly for the lost sheep, who are his, and in deeper need of love. Actually, love wins hardened hearts which remain unmoved by fear and threats. Jeremias writes:

> Such communities as Qumran excluded crippled people as well as sinners. On the contrary, Jesus offers salvation to sinners even before they do penance. Grace is offered without limits and without conditions: God is the Father of the humble and of those lost. Jesus opened the gates, and called all without exception. It is not his fault if only few enter! The separation of the good from the

[167] E. P. Sanders, op.cit. pp.188-209.

> wicked is the job of God at the end, but the hour has not come for judgment.[168]

According to Jeremias, the opponents of Jesus, who opposed Jesus' welcoming sinners, did not join Jesus' following. Their righteousness kept them away from Jesus as it did from John the Baptist. Because of their merit, they did not feel the need of being saved by grace. Sinners were more inclined to perceive the saving grace and love of God granted through Jesus.

Sanders notes that, regarding the vocation of sinners, the early church did not follow the way of Jesus. He writes:

> What survived after Jesus' death and resurrection was a movement which followed more-or-less traditional expectations about the end. The end was at hand. It was therefore also time to start admitting Gentiles - on some condition or other. The most distinctive aspect of Jesus' own message - the admission of sinners without requiring formal restoration of status within the covenant - seems to have been dropped. The church of Jerusalem, apparently dominated by James and influenced by people whom Paul called "false brethren," was no more enthusiastic about counting among its membership the wicked of Israel than it was about admitting Gentiles while they were still "sinners," that is, non-observers of the law. The early church was not just a continuation of Jesus' own work. It lacked fellowship with sinners. Sinners should repent and adapt their lives to the requirements of the law.[169]

Sanders' criticism is interesting, but reflects his systematization of Jesus' message more than the complex reality of the gospel. Conversion, even today, is a time of grace and of love, particularly when God is calling a great sinner to repentance and Christian fellowship. But one does not remain a great sinner forever, and a life fed on grace and love can survive in the community of the faithful and in the institution of the church. The Beatitudes are offered to these previous sinners now called to perfection. Moreover, the urgency of the *parousia* (the end of the world), which was a feature of the first century, made room for the idea of a delay granted by God for the sake of conversion, while the idea of a "personal judgment" at death brought about the idea of an individual *parousia*.

## THE DEATH OF JESUS: CAUSES AND MOTIVATION

---

[168] Jeremias, *Theology of the New Testament*, ch.5.

[169] Sanders, p. 323.

The cause of the death of Jesus is well analyzed by Sanders.[170] Jesus was not put to death because of a definite violation of the law of Moses, although sometimes his behavior may have been perceived as very offensive. Being associated with Beelzebub as a "false exorcist," with tax-collectors and sinners because of table-fellowship with them, forgiving sins, and speaking in the name of God, even promising forgiveness without repentance and restitution or ritual sacrifice, all these grievances, according to Sanders, do not adequately explain the condemnation of Jesus to death.

> What, then, could have been the immediate cause of Jesus' death, which could be presented to the Procurator, Pontius Pilate, as meriting death? The temple scene is the last public event in Jesus' life. This means that we should make a connection between the prediction of the destruction, and the gesture against the temple. The gesture could readily have led the Romans to think that Jesus was a threat to public order. According to the Jewish historian, Josephus, Herod acted quickly to execute John the Baptist because his preaching excited the populace. The cases of Theudas and of the Egyptian lead to the same observation.[171] There were enough followers to make it expedient to kill Jesus, rather than simply flog him as a nuisance and release him. It was the combination of a physical action with a noticeable following (Paul alludes to five hundred as the number of Jesus' followers), which accounts for and led immediately to Jesus' death. The Jewish leaders could then reasonably and persuasively propose to Pilate that Jesus should be executed, and Pilate agreed. Caiphas' saying, "It is expedient that one man should die for the people, and that the whole nation should not perish" comes true.[172]
>
> Why, now, was Jesus executed as a king? The reference is to the entry into Jerusaslem, and to the exclamation, "Hosanna Son of David, king of Israel!" Is the story true? Perhaps it is. Jesus was executed as one who claimed to be king of the Jews. In a last symbolic act, Jesus entered Jerusalem as king, demonstrated the destruction of the present temple, and had a meal with his disciples which symbolized the future banquet. Jesus gave himself and his disciples a role in the kingdom. This may have led to discussions of him as Messiah in his

---

[170] Ibid., pp.245-317.

[171] Acts 5:33-39; 21:38.

[172] Sanders, p.301.

lifetime (possible), but in any case this is the title which was given him after the resurrection (certain).[173]

What was the kingdom expected by Jesus, which challenged worldly powers? According to Sanders again,

> It is like the present world - it has a king, leaders, a temple, and twelve tribes - but it is not just a rearrangement of the present world. God must step in and provide a new temple, a restored people of Israel, and presumably a renewed social order, one in which "sinners" will have a place. This view explains many questions, for instance, the development of the idea of Messiah from a political leader to an eschatological figure at the end of time. Theudas as well as others unnamed expected an eschatological miracle. The Egyptian promised a miracle, and expected it to be followed by a military defeat of Rome. Jesus did not make great gestures or promise grand events which were designed to convince all. By riding on an ass he demonstrated his claim to a special role in God's kingdom by one who was meek and lowly, and the servant of all. Like Theudas and the Egyptian, Jesus believed that God would bring in the kingdom miraculously. This explains that Jesus did not have a plan which included a practical strategy. He did not need one, since he looked to God for the vindication of his message and his claim. He performed prophetic actions, and they were understood.[174]

### 1. The Motive of the Death of Jesus.

The motivation of Jesus' death is another question. Sanders has no answer to the question whether Jesus identified himself with the Suffering Servant of Isaiah 53.[175] He seems to incline to the negative when he says that the act of Jesus calling the wicked was transformed into the belief that he died to save sinners from sin and make them upright.[176]

Regarding the motivation of Jesus at his death, I follow Jeremias,[177] who thinks that Jesus saw himself in the image of

---

[173] Ibid., p. 306.

[174] Ibid., p. 226.

[175] Ibid., p. 324.

[176] Ibid., p. 322.

[177] Jeremias, *The Central Message of the New Testament* (Philadelphia: Fortress Press, 1977), ch.3.

the Suffering Servant. The texts concerning the Suffering Servant are Isaiah 42, 49, 50, 53, and Psalm 22 which the evangelists put in the mouth of Jesus on the cross. If Jeremias is right, the death of Jesus does not appear as a failure because of the absence of a divine miracle which would have brought about the kingdom with a new temple, an era of renewed innocence, and the return to the political system of the twelve tribes now under the authority of Jesus and the apostles. Also the interpretation of the death of Jesus as atonement for sin does not appear as an answer to an objection based on his failure and death. But the image of the Suffering Servant of Isaiah 53 appears as the real motivation of Jesus in his death. Jesus' obedience to the mysterious will of God is the most important contribution of Jesus to our redemption. After all, every sensible and mature person, who is not caught unaware by death, wants the best death, and the most profitable, particularly on the spiritual level. For this reason people on their deathbed repent from their sins and forgive their enemies. Jesus must have prepared for his own death which he had more and more reason to expect would be the violent death of a martyr.

Jeremias proves that, before his death, Jesus had in mind the image of the Suffering Servant, accepting and offering his condemnation and death as a sacrifice for the remission of the sins of others. The Letter to the Hebrews presented Jesus as the high priest of the new covenant offering his own blood for the remission of sins on the heavenly altar. The Letter of I Peter compared Jesus to the Suffering Servant. Paul himself, in the earliest Christian documents, applied to Jesus the motivation of the Suffering Servant. Jesus, shamefully crucified and apparently cursed by God as "the man hanging on the tree",[178] was "cursed for us,"[179] and redeemed us through his blood offered up to God as expiation for our sins.[180] Jesus paid the ransom of our redemption at the expense of his blood, thereby nailing to the cross the bond which stood against us as debtors before God.[181] Through baptism we are buried and raised together with Christ: the "old man" (the sinner) in ourselves is put to death, and the "new man" modelled on Christ is born, who shows obedience to God.[182]

But Paul himself did not invent the motivation of Christ in his death as the Suffering Servant of Isaiah 53. As early as I Corinthians 11:23, i.e., less than 20 years after the death of

---

[178] Deut. 21:23.

[179] Gal. 3:13.

[180] Rom. 3:23-25.

[181] 1 Cor. 6:20.

[182] Rom. 5:18-21.

Jesus, Paul acknowledged he had received a tradition concerning the Last Supper and the words pronounced by Jesus on the bread and wine, which confirmed the offering of his flesh and blood for the remission of the sins of the multitude. Therewith Jesus identified himself with the Suffering Servant.

But is it possible to go further back, and to find in the mouth of Jesus himself during his earthly ministry the idea that he was the Suffering Servant? According to J. Jeremias, the voice of God at Jesus' baptism[183] combines Ps. 2:7 ("Today I have begotten you") and Is. 42:1 ("Behold my Servant, my Elect, in him my soul rejoices"). Since the terms "son" ( or "servant") and "elect" were the earliest messianic titles for Jesus (later on forgotten), and since Is. 42 is one of the poems of the Servant, the identification of Jesus as the Servant is obvious. Moreover, when Jesus rejects the temptation of political power, he accepts the idea of the Servant suffering at the hands of his enemies.

More and more Jesus was aware of the imminence of his death, and began to see himself in the manner of the prophets who, he noted, all died as martyrs, a belief which was common in his time. The recent death of the last of them, John the Baptist, could only convince him that he himself would die as a martyr. In Palestinian Judaism, the death of martyrs hastens the coming of the end, opens to the martyr the gates of the world to come, makes him an intercessor, makes converts, and atones for the sins of Israel.

Jesus, while keeping it secret to the crowd, revealed to his disciples the violent death to which he would be condemned by the elders, priests and scribes, and rebuked Peter as a Satan because he opposed this pessimistic view of the future. Jesus repeated the prediction of his passion.[184] Even if we disregard as historically questionable the scene before Caiphas and the recitation of Psalm 22 by Jesus on the cross, evidence remains for the fact that Jesus died with the motivation of the Suffering Servant, offering his passion as atonement for our sins. According to Jeremias, Jesus even expected that his disciples would be subjected to the same persecution, and should face it with courage[185]

---

[183] John 1:34.

[184] Mark 9:43; 10:33; 12:1-12, the parable of the Vineyard; 14:8, the woman anointing him for his burial.

[185] Jeremias, *Central Message*, p.44.

## THE RESURRECTION[186]

How do leading biblical scholars today interpret the narratives of the resurrection of Jesus? I will refer to N. Perrin, J. Jeremias, and R. Brown.

N. Perrin accepts the fact of the resurrection of Jesus, but he is particularly interested in its meaning in each one of the three synoptic gospels: Mark, Luke, and Matthew. These gospels were composed during the last third of the first century, i.e., two generations after Jesus, and one generation after the apostles and disciples who had known Jesus. The attributing of the gospels to direct disciples of Jesus was a way of identifying their respective traditions and of confirming their authority. But the evangelists were not just eye-witnesses and compilers: they wrote literary masterpieces, and their compositions attempt to distill how Jesus might have responded to the needs of their communities in their own time.

Mark understands the resurrection of Jesus as God having vindicated Jesus from his death by taking him "up" into heaven to be with him until the time of Jesus' return to earth as Son of Man, to judge and to redeem the world. Mark does not describe (if we agree that his gospel ends with 16:8) the appearances of Jesus to the women or to the disciples. He portrays the disciples as having failed to understand Jesus and his passion. Now they must assume that Jesus in his resurrection enjoys the condition which is symbolized by the story of the transfiguration, a condition which Moses and Elijah also enjoy, who are already with God in heaven.

Matthew's resurrection narrative includes two wholly new elements: the story of the guard at the tomb, and the commissioning of the disciples in Galilee - and attaches great significance to the latter. Jesus is considered as present in the church, "I am with you always." The *parousia* is not forgotten, but Matthew sees the resurrection of Jesus as inaugurating a new age in history: the age of the church.

Luke adds three new elements to the Markan narrative of the resurrection: an appearance of the risen Jesus to two disciples on the road to Emmaus; an appearance to the disciples as a group in Jerusalem; and the ascension of Jesus into heaven. Luke is the first Christian writer to understand the ascension as an event distinct from the resurrection itself. Luke locates the appearances of the risen Christ to the disciples as a group in Jerusalem.[187] The reason for this departure from Mark and Matthew who both place it in Galilee seems to be the idea that the Christian movement, which started from Jerusalem as the

---

[186] N. Perrin, *The Resurrection according to Matthew, Mark, and Luke* (Philadelphia: Fortress Press, 1977).

[187] Luke 24:36-49.

center of Israel, is progressing to the symbolic center of the world, to Rome.[188]

1. THE EXPERIENCE OF THE RESURRECTION OF JESUS.

To ascertain the facts and identify witnesses of the resurrection is one thing, but another, more delicate problem is to describe the experience itself of the resurrection of Christ by the witnesses. A passage of Jeremias[189] is puzzling in this regard, and prompts us to make a few distinctions.

> Christophanies (Christ appearances) may have lasted for years, but tradition limited them to 40 days. A purpose of apologetic led to add complements (guards at the tomb; Jesus showing his wounds; inclination to materialize the bodily nature of the raised Christ as far as conceivable). The earliest layer of Easter traditions are characterized by the transcendent, enigmatic, mysterious aspect of events: eyes are opened at the breaking of the bread; a ray of heavenly light; a human shape at dawn on the lakeshore; the unexpected appearance in a locked room; the speaking in tongues at Pentecost; and the sudden disappearance. Sometimes the witnesses do not recognize the raised Jesus; sometimes they are blinded by the heavenly light; sometimes they believe they are seeing a ghost.
>
> The date is Sunday. Mary of Magdala is the first witness, but no disciple believes the women. The decisive event is the appearance of the Lord to Peter, attested by Paul and the whole tradition, but never described. The appearance to 500 disciples together in I Cor. 15:6 seems to correspond to Pentecost in Acts 2:1-13, and refers to the same event. The appearance to Paul on the way to Damascus as heavenly light attests to the charismatic character of christophanies, and can be considered as typical of all christophanies. The resurrection to the glory is an eschatological event. The session at the right hand is an enthronement, and refers to Daniel 7:14, the "all power is given him on earth and heaven." The disciples have seen Jesus in a display of light, and witnessed to the event of his kingdom. In this sense, they have lived the *parousia*.

Is that all there is in the experience of the resurrection by the witnesses, or is Jeremias only describing external features

---

[188] Perrin, *The Resurrection*, p.69.

[189] Jeremias, *New Testament Theology*, ch.7.

of the appearances of Jesus (a kind of "supernatural"), but not the contents of the appearances in terms of real visitation and conversation? Did they truly experience the miracle of the resurrection of Jesus?

The text of the respective gospels suggest further consideration. For Mark and Matthew, the realism of the resurrection of Jesus is part of the general belief of first century Judaism in what we call "apocalyptic". Apocalyptic is a representation of the world and of humanity in which the earthly is part of the heavenly. It is reflected in the biblical books of Ezekiel and of Daniel, in the apocryphal *Books of Enoch*, in the *Ascension of Isaiah*, in the *Testaments of the Patriarchs*, etc. It is also represented in the New Testament: the gospels, Paul, and particularly Revelation. According to this view of the world, the account of the transfiguration was the best suggestion of the resurrection, and does not require a particular emphasis on the earthly aspect of the body. Jesus is alive in heaven just as Moses, Elijah, and Enoch, who were "carried away" to heaven according to biblical tradition, and the Patriarchs are alive who are the friends of the living God, who is the God of the living, not of the dead. Jesus is sitting on the right hand of the Father in the divine glory, and has really manifested himself to his disciples in a series of appearances.

On the contrary, when we read in Luke, and to some extent also in John, the narratives of the appearances of Christ to his disciples after Easter, we get the feeling of the importance of the affirmation of the body in its concrete material existence. Jesus was not only seen, but also touched, and even ate fish before the eyes of the disciples after the resurrection, thereby proving that he was not a ghost, but a real body. Although there is no reason to deny the traditions which transmitted these data, we might suggest that they translated the understanding of the resurrection of Christ by, and for, people who were more "carnally" oriented in their thinking (the doubting Thomas of John 20:24-29). The materialistic reaction is found in some of the disciples, and much more among the believers converted from the Gentiles, who strongly insisted on the duality of soul-body. The same anxiety concerning the destiny of the body of Jesus is rooted in our our scientific culture.

For us, as well as for them, the spiritual experience needs to be completed by the experience of the bodily senses. We may confess that we don't believe in the resurrection if we believe in the spiritual reality of Christ's life in heaven without referring to his individual body. For us, the appearance of Jesus to Thomas makes much sense. Thomas, who needed such an experience in order to believe, was probably provided with this grace. However, carnal as it was, this experience of the risen Christ led Thomas to the apocalyptic understanding explained above, which is the direct object of faith and revelation. Like Thomas, the Christians are invited to raise their hearts to heaven, and confess Christ in the divine glory. According to the so-called Creed of the Apostles, Jesus descended and was incarnate, suffered, died, was buried, and rose again, and now sits on the right hand of the Father until he comes again for the judgment of the living and the dead.

We must admit that the world of apocalyptic as reflected in the aforementioned literature sometimes defies our reason, and falls into the categories of fancy, and the many references to divine revelation destroy rather than confirm the credibility of the contents. But we have noted above, at least in relation to the Egyptian "dream" of the hereafter, that, in such matters, discretion is a safe position, and the abuse of detail is vain imagination and weakness. Therefore, simplicity of faith, and a limited reliance on traditional apocalyptic in so far as it is the expression of our faith, represent the best approach to the mystery of the living Christ who welcomes us in the love of the Father.

Finally, does it make sense to ask why Mark ends his gospel with the death of Jesus on the Cross, whereas the other gospels offer narratives of the appearances of the raised Lord. There seems to be a shift of emphasis from Good Friday to the Sunday of Easter. Luke even introduces the Ascension and Pentecost as separate events. However, it seems that the essence of the Paschal mystery is the death of Christ on the Cross, which Mark[190] and John associate with his glorification by the Father, a glorification which potentially included that of his disciples. With many good reasons, and on the basis of his own experience, It seems that Paul preferred to focus his preaching on the resurrection of Christ, which was clearer and of more significance for the Gentiles than the Jewish apocalyptic notion of the "glory." We can be thankful to him.

However, an earliest Christian tradition, represented by the Gospel of John, and still supported by Irenaeus at the end of the second century,[191] existed in Asia Minor, which maintained the "quatuordeciman" custom of celebrating the Pasch on the 14th of Nisan, date of the Passion, not on the following Sunday as in all other Churches. Polycarp, the bishop martyr of Smyrna, was a "quatuordeciman", and so was Melito, the holy bishop of Sardis. In his recently discovered *Homily on the Pasch*, Melito celebrates the victory of Christ on the Cross as including the resurrection of Christ and our salvation:

> But he arose from the dead to the heights of the heavens, God who put on man, and suffered for the sufferer, and was bound for him who was bound, and judged for him

---

[190] Mark 15:37-39, and John 12.

[191] Eusebius, *Ecclesiastical History* V, 23-24.

> who was condemned, and buried for him who was buried. And he arose from the dead and cries thus (to you): "Who is he that contendeth against me? Let him stand before me. I freed the condemned, I made the dead to live again, I raise him who was buried. Who is he who raises his voice against me? I, "he says," *am* the Christ, I *am* he who put down death, and triumphed over the enemy, and trod upon Hades, and bound the strong one, and brought man safely home to the heights of the heavens; I", he says," Christ."
>
> Therefore, *come* hither all ye families of men, who are sullied with sins, and receive remission of sins. For I am your remission. I *am* the Passover of salvation, the Lamb that was sacrificed for you, I *am* your ransom, I *am* your light, I am your Savior, I *am* the resurrection, I am your king, I lead you up to the heights of the heavens, I will show you the Father *who is* from the ages, I will raise you up by my right hand."[192]

## QUESTIONNAIRE

1. What questions does scholarly criticism of the text of the Gospels raise in your mind? Do you --or other people you know-- incline to consider such criticism as manipulation of the word of God and blasphemy? Discuss this position.

2. Give some ideas of the problems and methods of the modern criticism of the Gospels, and some examples of an interesting result.

3. What is the criterion of double dissimilarity? Discuss its application to Jesus' identifying himself to the Son of Man, and to the Suffering Servant?

4. What are the Synoptic Gospels? Which one of them was written first? What are the sources of the other Gospels? Is the Gospel of John one of the Synoptics? How would you characterize the Gospel of John?

5. Can we seriously assimilate the miracles of Jesus in the Gospels to the "miracles" claimed by today's "faith-healing"?

6. According to the book of J. Jeremias on parables, under the headline, "Now is the Day of Salvation," explain two parables which mean that the Savior has come, and we can rejoice.

---

[192] Translated by Campbell Bonner, *Studies and Documents* 1940, p.17.

7. According to the same book, under the headline, "God's Mercy for Sinners," explain why righteous Pharisees and Scribes were indignant at Jesus' style of life and preaching.

8. Under the same headline, according to the parable of the Prodigal Son, how is the title of God as "Our Father" more appropriate than the title of King?

9. According to the same book, under headline, "Confidence in God's Ways," show how the disciples may have been discouraged by the poor results of the preaching of Jesus, and how Jesus re-assured them. How were the parables of the seed and the Unjust Judge appropriate for that purpose?

10. According to the same book, under the headline, "The Imminence of the End," show how Jesus tried to communicate to his audience the sense that it was not a time for playing or for endlessly criticizing, but the time for serious consideration and action regarding entry to the Kingdom.

11. According to the same book, and your own reflection, what does Jesus warning "to become again like little children" mean, and not mean?

12. According to the same book of Jeremias, under the headline, "Foretaste of divine grace, it seems that the parable of the Good Samaritan was less a sermon about charity than about obstacles to charity, or restrictions found in the Law of Moses. Explain this idea.

13. Can we say with Sanders that Jesus just forgave sinners and welcomed them in the Kingdom without requiring from them moral conversion and sacrificial rites of purification?

14. What was, according to Sanders, the cause of the condemnation of Jesus?

15. How, according to Sanders, did the events of the Passion destroy the dreams of Jesus and of his followers, leaving Jesus with the only perspective of martyrdom?

16. What was Jesus' motivation in his suffering and death? How, according to his words at Caesarea Philippi, at the Last Supper, at Gethsemani, and perhaps on the cross, did Jesus interpret his own suffering and death?

17. According to the book of N. Perrin, what is the way Mark conceives of the resurrection of Jesus?

18. How do Matthew and Luke see the continuity of the action of Jesus and the mission of the church after the resurrection?

19. How do Mark and Matthew, as contrasted with Luke and John, represent the realism of the resurrection of Jesus?

## BIBLIOGRAPHY

BROWN, R. E. *The Community of the Beloved Disciple.* Paramus: Paulist Press, 1979.

_____. *The Church, the Apostles Left Behind.* New York: Paulist Press, 1984.

_____. *The Virginal Conception and the Bodily Resurrection of Jesus.* New York: Paulist Press, 1973.

BROWN, R.E. & J.P. MEIER. *Antioch and Rome, New Testament Cradles of Catholic Christianity.* New York: Paulist Press, 1982.

COLLINS, J.J. *Daniel, First Maccabees, Second Maccabees, with an excursus on the Apocalyptic Genre,* Wilmington: Glazier, 1981. ("The Son of Man.")

COLLINS, Thomas P. *The Risen Christ in the Fathers of the Church.* Glen Rock: Paulist Press, 1967.

EPP, Eldon Jay & G.W. NacRae ed. *The New Testanent and its Modern Interpreters.* Atlanta: Scholars Press, 1989. (General.)

FITZMYER, J.A., *A Christological Catechism. New Testament Answers.* New York: Paulist Press, 1982.

JEREMIAS, J. *The Parables of Jesus.* New York: Scribner, 1963.

_____. *New Testament Theology.* New York: Scribner, 1971.

_____. *The Central Message of the New Testament.* Philadelphia: Fortress Press, 1981.

PERRIN, N , *Rediscovering the Teaching of Jesus.* London and New York: Harper & Row, 1967.

_____. *The Resurrection according to Matthew, Mark, and Luke.* Philadelphia: Fortress, 1977.

SANDERS, E. P. *Jesus and Judaism.* Philadelphia: Fortress Press, 1985.

VERMES, Géza. *Jesus the Jew.* London: Collins, 1973.

## CHAPTER X

## GENESIS OF THE CREED: GOD AND CHRIST

Since early Christianity produced the CREED, it also belongs to early Christianity to explain the CREED, its development and its meaning. The christology --the study of Christ-- of early Christianity remains a bridge between the later developments, which faced problems of their own (philosophy or heresy), and Christian sources, which offer the most genuine approach to the Christian mystery for those who are familiar with them. Modern problems of christology can be seriously discussed only by those who have a good grasp of the genesis of the Creed, and who know the reasons for which each of the articles of the Creed have been included in it.

After a preamble about God and the divine Word in the Old Testament, a first section deals with faith in Christ in the New Testament as faith in the divine Word speaking with a human nature. He died and raised again for our salvation, and now sits in the glory of the Father, ready to come again as our judge. A second section deals with Christ in the faith of early Christianity before the council of Nicaea: early heretics, the apologists of the 2d century (Justin, Athenagoras), Origen in the third century. A third section deals with the fourth century: the councils of Nicaea and of Constantinople (325, 381 A.D.). Athanasius opposed Arius who denied the divine nature of Christ. Later on, the Cappadocian Fathers (Basil of Caesarea, Gregory of Nyssa, Gregory Nazianzen) defended against the second generation of Arianism the deity of the Holy Spirit, which completes the divine Trinity. A fourth section deals with the controversies of the fifth century, called "christological" because they were limited to Christ. They focussed on the unity of Christ and his integrity as human. The conflict, which started between Nestorius and Cyrille of Alexandria, required two important councils: Ephesus and Chalcedon (431, 451 A.D.).

### THE OLD TESTAMENT TEACHES US ABOUT GOD

The Old Testament teaches us concerning God, as we see in the narratives of creation, in Psalms, etc. Psalms 95-96 fittingly express what God is for us and for the world:

> Come! Let us raise a joyful song to the Lord, a shout of triumph to the Rock of our salvation. Let us come into his presence with thanksgiving, and sing him psalms of triumph. For the Lord is a great God, a great king over all gods; the farthest places of the earth are his; the sea

is his, he made it; the dry land fashioned by his land is his.

Come! Let us throw ourselves at his feet in hommage, let us kneel before the Lord who made us; for he is our God, we are his people, we the flock he shepherds.

You shall know his power today if you will listen to his voice. Do not grow stubborn, as you were at Meribah, as at the time of Massah in the wilderness, when your forefathers challenged me, tested me and saw for themselves all that I did. For forty years I was indignant with that generation, and I said: They are a people whose hearts are astray, and they will not discern my ways. And I swore in my anger: They shall never enter my rest.

Sing a new song to the Lord; sing to the Lord, all men on earth. Sing to the Lord and bless his name, proclaim his triumph day by day. Declare his glory among the nations, his marvellous deeds among all peoples. Great is the Lord and worthy of all praise; he is more to be feared than all gods. For the gods of the nations are idols every one; but the Lord made the heavens. Majesty and splendour attend him, might and beauty are in his sanctuary.

Ascribe to the Lord, you families of nations, ascribe to the Lord glory and might; ascribe to the Lord the glory due to his name, bring a gift and come into his courts. Bow down to the Lord in the splendour of holiness, and dance in his honour, all men on earth. Declare among the nations, "The Lord is king. He has fixed the earth firm, immovable; he will judge the peoples justly." Let the heavens rejoice and the earth exult, let the sea roar and all the creatures in it, let the fields exult and all that is in them; then let all the trees of the forest shout for joy before the Lord when he comes to judge the earth. He will judge the earth with righteousness and the peoples in good faith.

The two psalms teach that God is the Creator of the universe and the God of all. He is the King of heaven and earth. Believers worship him, and bring offerings to his temple (the temple of Jerusalem, or in a deeper sense, the temple of the universe). Finally, God is the judge of all the nations and of every human being. Accordingly, in the CREED, we too *believe in one God, almighty, creator of heaven and earth, who will judge all humans at the end.*

All those among us who can sincerely say, *my God*, because they have some experience of God in their spiritual life, know very well that God is above them, above all. They also know that God who is closest to them is, at the same time, the "Highest" who is above the world, the Creator of the world, and the God who provides for them and for all. The Bible witnesses to this experience of God, and attacks the vanity of polytheism and idolatry.

The religion of the Bible also extols as a manner of extension of God his *WISDOM*, his *WORD*, his *LAW*, his *JUSTICE*, his *MERCY* and *LOVE*, his *FAITHFULNESS*, etc.

In the Bible, WORD and WISDOM are sometimes personified, but do not appear to be properly speaking persons. Texts containing these expressions will be used as the basis of later speculations on the deity of Christ. For instance, Proverbs 8:22-36 provides a beautiful speculation on the eternity of WISDOM:

> The Lord created me (WISDOM) the beginning of his works, before all else that he made, long ago. Alone, I was fashioned in times long past, at the beginning, long before the earth itself. When there was yet no ocean I was born, no springs brimming with water. Before the mountains were settled in their place, long before the hills I was born, when as yet he had made neither land nor lake nor the first clod of earth. When he set the heavens in their place I was there, when he girdled the ocean with the horizon, when he fixed the canopy of clouds overhead and set the springs of ocean firm in their place, when he prescribed its limits for the sea and knit together earth's foundation. Then I was at his side each day, his darling and delight, playing in his presence continually, playing on the earth, when he had finished it, while my delight was in mankind.
>
> Now, my sons, listen to me, listen to instruction and grow wise, do not reject it. Happy is the man who keeps to my ways, happy the man who listen to me, watching daily at my threshold with his eyes on the doorway; for he who finds me finds life and wins favour with the Lord, while he who finds me not, hurts himself, and all who hate me are in love with death.

Just like the divine WISDOM, the WORD of God is living and active in the world and in human hearts, as Isaiah 55:10-11 says,

> For as the rain and the snow come down from heaven and do not return until they have watered the earth, making it blossom and bear fruit, and give seed for sowing and bread to eat, so shall the WORD which comes from my mouth prevail; it shall not return to me

> fruitless without accomplishing my purpose or succeeding in the task I gave it.

Like the divine WISDOM again, the WORD of God is eternal, and, as we see in the narrative of Creation (Genesis 1), God created the world and each of its parts by his WORD. At the other end of the sacred Scriptures, in the *Prologue* to his Gospel, John repeats this idea, and explains that the WORD of God has been made flesh in Jesus, in order to live among us, to teach, exhort, and save us.

## FAITH IN CHRIST IN THE NEW TESTAMENT

On the one hand, Jesus preached the Kingdom of God, a Kingdom in the hearts of the faithful, a Kingdom which is "not of this world", i.e., not a matter of civil government and military power. On the other hand, the apostles preached about Christ himself as a key figure in this Kingdom of God, and who is now sitting on the right hand of the Father in heaven. He will come again for the judgment at the end of the world. Such is the belief of the disciples after the resurrection who refer to Jesus' confession in front of Caiphas the high-priest. In this confession, Jesus identified himself with the SON OF MAN of the prophecy of Daniel, which reads:[193]

> I saw one like a man (the "son of man") coming with the clouds of heaven; he approached the Ancient in Years and was presented to him. Sovereignty and glory and kingly power were given to him, so that all people and nations of every language should serve him; his sovereignty was to be an everlasting sovereignty which should not pass away, and his kingly power such as should never be impaired.

The Confession of Jesus before the high-priest, which adds to the prophecy of Daniel quoted above the eschatological return of the Son of Man as a judge, was a strong christological statement, an early form of Christian faith in Christ.[194]

This faith in a Christ exercising a function more than human, and supposing the possession of divine power and dignity, is not only explicit, but clearly stated and theologically elaborated in John (his Gospel, *passim*, particularly "Prologue," and in Revelation). And the same can be said of Paul (prefaces about the Redemption in the Pauline epistles, and, *passim*, the epistles of the captivity: Ephesians, Colossians, Philippians), and of Hebrews. Christ is the Son and the Word of God. The title

---

[193] Daniel 7:13-14.

[194] Mark 14:62; Luke 22:69-70; Matt. 26:64.

Son of God seems to be rooted in the prayer of Jesus. But the title WORD OF GOD is so early (Paul) and so deeply rooted in the Christian faith (John's Prologue, the Fathers of the Church and theological tradition), that it cannot be explained by philosophical influences. An inquiry into the scholarly aspect of this question is out of the scope of this book. Perhaps is there a suitable and simple way to introduce the modern reader to it.[195]

How, then, could illiterate Christians in the time of Paul and John accept this notion as the expression of their faith in Christ? How can the modern average Christian think in terms of the divine Word? Jesus was a preacher: the example of a good preacher can facilitate our understanding. Even today, those who listen to a preacher, a good preacher, may get a sense of the word of God as a dynamic reality from above, which eventually deeply influences our thought and life. It seems to me that those who listened to Jesus with faith recognized that the word which was coming to them was the living word of God, strong, illuminating, dynamic, more genuine than the word of God delivered by any other preacher.

The spoken word of Jesus could be compared to the word of God found in Scripture. Scripture, indeed, is not simply a written book, "dead speech," but the "living word of the living God," the "Word of God speaking to us through Moses and the prophets," a "word of power," as Justin noted in the second century, which can overturn the dispositions of the soul.[196] In the opinion of Jesus' listeners in faith, the same living Word of God appeared to be at work again in Jesus. The "Divine Word" was now speaking through the lips of Jesus. As a consequence, in their opinion, Jesus was more than an average human being, even more than one of the prophets: he was "the Divine Word made flesh," speaking to us in person through these lips. The mysterious EGO of Jesus was understood as the "Divine and living Word," the "Word of God," the "Wisdom of God." More than King David himself, he was the "Son of God," the Son of this God whom he addressed as his Father in a privileged manner.

---

[195] Concerning the exegesis of texts traditionally brought forth as evidence for the deity of Christ, modern interpreters should be consulted. See *The New Testament and its Modern Interpreters*, E.J. Epp & G.W. MacRae ed. (Atlanta, Ga.: Scholars Press, 1989), "The Christological Titles," pp.509-514. Once isolated from their historical and textual context, certain expressions have taken up a theological meaning different and far more absolute. As such, however, these expressions have been used as valid tools of theological reasoning.

[196] Justin, *Dialogue with Trypho*, 8.

For the unbeliever, Jesus was simply that kind of "son of man" which has nothing in common with the SON OF MAN of the prophecy of Daniel: he was simply a human preacher like many others. But for the crowd, Jesus was a wonderful preacher and a healer of their sick and of the victims of evil spirits. For theJerusalem leaders, he was a political danger, without further consideration. For many sinners, he may have been a cause of more hardening of their heart, as happens when sinners meet with warning.

For his disciples, he was a Master, a "Rabbi," and they placed in him many of their hopes, not all purely spiritual. But a perfect faith needs a long time to evolve, and probably also needs the trials of life. In their case, long meditations on the message of Jesus and on his passion and resurrection, in the light of Scripture ( what they called "prophecy"), contributed to bringing their faith to maturity. Through this maturation of faith, the message of Jesus, his very words, attained in their minds the full depth of its meaning. But, to learn is not simply to repeat like a parrot what we have heard from a master or read in a book. It is a re-enactment of an event in our mind. It is an internal and personal new creation of meaning within ourself. This explains how the different forms and different scriptural images, even discrepancies in the text, as they appear in the various documents of the New Testament, reflect the same basic faith in Christ as sent to us from God.

The fact of the resurrection of Christ confirmed the Apostles in their faith in Christ. It is basic to their faith and the Christian faith of all generations. At the same time, it strongly contributed to their understanding of Christ. At that point, it was more than a fact and its comforting effect for the faith of the disciples, since it was the consecration of the christology derived from the prophecy of Daniel on the Son of man. They believed in him as living in heaven and as having reached his glory. He is now sitting on the right hand of the Father, and ready to come again and to act as a judge.

The faithful should rather insist on this basic belief in the resurrection of Christ than derive from the narratives of the resurrection, or other scripture, clues for a detailed knowledge of things in the hereafter --even concerning the status of the body of Jesus himself--, which is not the purpose of these texts. It is particularly wrong if we "materialize" these details as we do for everything else today. Augustine tried to derive from these texts a detailed knowledge concerning our bodily condition and life in heaven, but, in my opinion, he failed in his inquiry.[197] Instead of taking these narratives as models for his description of the body of the resurrection, Augustine should have followed I Corinthians 15, Paul's treatise on the Resurrection.

---

[197] Augustine, *City of God*, Book 22.

## CHRIST IN THE FAITH OF EARLY CHRISTIANITY

The development of faith in Christ in early Christianity is not --in spite of certain scholars-- essentially the consequence of heresy, or the inspiration of philosophy. Essentially, early christology found meaning and expression in the many "titles," or "attributes" of Jesus in the New Testament. These images of Christ had been picked by Jesus, or by the disciples, from the Old Testament. We can mention the titles of PROPHET, MASTER, SON OF MAN, SON OF DAVID, SON OF GOD, MESSIAH, GOOD SHEPHERD, REDEEMER, SAVIOR, WORD OF GOD, WORD INCARNATE, LIFE, LIGHT, WAY, LAMB OF GOD, HIGH-PRIEST, etc. Since these images were used by the first Christian generations in their representation of Jesus, they reveal important aspects of faith in Jesus. Early Christian writers, such as Justin, Irenaeus, and Origen, continued to list these titles and comment on them. These titles were often commented upon from the pulpit.

However, theologians tended to emphasize the "more divine titles," as Origen noted in his *Principles*, particularly the titles SON of God and WORD of God, which were more often challenged by heretics.[198]

The EBIONITES represented an early tendency in Jewish-Christian communities to see Jesus as a mere human being, a prophet, a servant of God. They denied his divinity as being a blasphemy against the Jewish belief in the unity of God. Against the Ebionites, the Church maintained both the principle of the unity of God, and faith in the divine nature of Christ.

The DOCETISTS (all "Gnostics" were Docetists) saw in Jesus a supernatural being, a divine "Aeon", but denied that such a noble being could really take on the flesh, which they considered as a cause of defilement. For them, the flesh of Christ was a mere appearance. The Docetists may have been inspired by Platonism which considered the body as a jail for the soul, or by the widely-held idea of defilement by the flesh. Against the Docetists, the Church insisted on the realism of the Incarnation.

The MONARCHIANS confined themselves to the Christ of the "Economy," or of the "Mission." The mission of Christ was to establish the Kingdom of God, and the period of time corresponding to the completion of the Kingdom began with the birth of Christ, and should end when Christ surrenders the Kingdom to the Father, at the end of the world. As a consequence, the Monarchians refused to consider the question of a

---

[198] Origen, *Commentary on John*, I, 125 (SC 120, p. 126), on John 1:1. The whole section, book 1 and 2:1-72 deals with the titles of Christ (ibid. pp. 126-252). The titles of Christ are discussed also in *De principiis* Book 1, ch.2. See Origen, *On First Principles*, tr. Butterworth (New York: Harper & Row, 1966), pp.15-28.

pre-existing Christ, or of the relevance of Christ after the end. Since they refused to acknowledge the eternity of Christ, and since they only accepted to see in Christ a temporary form of divine manifestation and action, the Church thought it necessary to affirm that, in his divine nature, Christ is eternal, and that he is *other* (as a "person") than the Father.[199]

## THE APOLOGISTS OF THE SECOND CENTURY

The apologists of the second century (Justin, Athenagoras, Theophilus of Antioch, Tatian, Tertullian, etc.) were cultured converts who wrote in order to defend their fellow Christians during the persecutions. Because of their knowledge of Greek philosophy, they were also able to express the foundations of the Christian faith with concepts and terms which could be understood by the Hellenistic world.

They insisted on the two sides of Christ, as human, and as divine. Christ is THE WORD OF GOD INCARNATE. But they developed a theology of the WORD (or LOGOS, in Greek). According to the apologists, the divine WORD is not only personified, as it was in the Bible before Jesus, but it also properly a divine Person, with a divine EGO, an affirmation which is suggested by the duality of Father-Son in the gospels.

The apologists also took advantage of the idea of the LOGOS found everywhere in Greek philosophy, particularly in Stoicism. The Stoic LOGOS is a principle of the universe, present in every rational being. It is, as it were, a Soul of the world. The apologists accepted this theory, but specified that the Logos was the Logos of God, of a God transcendent to the world and not just Soul of the world.

We give a few quotes of the Apologists concerning the divinity of Christ and the Trinity:

### JUSTIN

> We reasonably worship Christ, having learned that he is the Son of the true God himself, and holding him in the second place, and the Holy Spirit in the third.[200]
>
> In these books of the prophets we found Jesus Christ foretold as coming. born of a virgin, growing up to man's estate, and healing every disease and every sickness, and raising the dead, and being hated, and unrecognized, and crucified, and dying, and rising again, and ascending into heaven, and being, and being called, the Son of God. We find also predicted that certain persons should be sent by

---

[199] Origen, *Dialogue with Heraclitus*, LCC vol.3.

[200] Justin, 1 *Apology* 3, ANF 3.

him into every nation to publish these things, and that rather among the Gentiles than among the Jews men should believe in him (31).

We believe of a crucified man that he is the first-born of the unbegotten God, and that he himself will pass judgment on the whole human race, because we have found testimonies concerning him published before he came and was born as man (53).[201]

ATHENAGORAS

The Christians are not atheists, since they acknowledge one God uncreated, eternal, invisible, incomprehensible, unlimitable, who is apprehended by the understanding only and the reason, who is encompassed by light, and beauty, and spirit, and power ineffable, by whom the universe has been created through his LOGOS, and set in order, and is kept in being...

It is not ridiculous that God should have a Son... But the Son of God is the Logos of the Father, in idea and in operation; for after the pattern of him and by him were all things made, the Father and the Son being one. And the Son being in the Father and the Father in the Son, in oneness and power of spirit, the understanding and reason (*nous kai logos*) of the Father is the Son of God... He is the first product of the Father, not as having been brought into existence, since, from the beginning, God had the Logos in himself, being from eternity permeated with Logos (*logikos*).

The Holy Spirit himself also, which operates in the prophets, we assert to be an effluence of God, flowing from him, and returning back again like a beam of the sun.

Who, then, would not be astonished to hear men who speak of God the Father, and of God the Son, and of the Holy Spirit, and who declare both their power in union and their distinction in order, called atheists?

We also recognize a multitude of angels and ministers whom God the Maker and Framer of the world distributed and appointed to their several posts by his Logos, to occupy themselves about the elements, and the

---

[201] Ibid. respectively 31 and 53.

heavens, and the world, and the things in it, and the godly ordering of them all.[202]

They know God and his Logos, what is the oneness of the Son with the Father, what is the communion of the Father with the Son, what is the Spirit, the Son, the Father, and their distinction in unity.[203]

For, as we acknowledge a God, and a Son his Logos, and a Holy Spirit, united in essence, --the Father, the Son, the Spirit, because the Son is the Intelligence, Reason, Wisdom of the Father, and the Spirit an effluence as of light from fire; so also do we apprehend the existence of other powers (angels), which exercise dominion about matter.[204]

As we see, the apologists recognize the unity of God, and the divinity of the Persons --particularly Father and Son-- in their distinction from each other. The Father is both the principle of the Son and Spirit, and the Creator of the world. The Son or Logos is identified with the intelligence and thought of God, and the Holy Spirit with divine energy.

## ORIGEN

Origen, in the third century, is probably the greatest theologian of all times. Among many other topics, he developed a theology of the WORD of God, and of the titles of Christ found in Scripture. Through all these titles or attributes, which correspond to every aspect of our faith, *Christ adjusts to the spiritual capacity and needs of everyone of us.* Thereby Origen was expanding a view of Paul, who distinguished between the "milk of doctrine" for beginners (the cross of Christ), and the "solid food" for the perfect (heavenly things). Many titles suit beginners in spiritual life, for instance, those of Judge, Redeemer, Lamb, Shepherd, King, etc., whereas others become useful on a higher level of faith and understanding, for instance, those of High-Priest (mediator of prayer), of Light, Life, Way, Wisdom, Word and Son of God.

In his controversies with his opponents the Monarchians, in order to have them acknowledge that Christ is God, and that he is other (as a Person) than the Father, Origen obliged them

---

[202] Athenagoras, *A Plea for the Christians* 10, ANF 2.

[203] Athenagoras, Ibid. 12.

[204] Athenagoras, ibid. 24; cf. also Tatian, *Address to the Greeks* 5, ANF 2.

to accept the challengeable formula: "Christ is a second God."[205] There was a difficulty, an apparent contradiction: God is one, and yet the Father is God and the Son is God. The contradiction must be resolved in the "mystery," i.e., in the transcendent secret of God, not in our reason.

Origen was not the type of person who turned away from difficulties, but frankly coped with them. For instance, Christ is said to be "the first-born of all creatures." One could say that, if Christ is a creature, or "made," then he is not properly the Son of God. There is a difference between "made", and "born", between "creature" and "Son" of God, and it is all this: a son is begotten, but a table is made. However, in Scripture, this difference does not appear clearly, and often "made" means "born," and "born" means "made." During the Arian controversy of the following century, the difficulty will remain between *genetos* and *gennetos*, "made," and "born."

Origen took the right step. He preferred not to heavily rely on the term *gennetos-genetos*, (often uncertain), but on the meaning appearing from the context in Scripture. He derived a solution from the theology of "participation": if the subject can share or possess the Deity perfectly, he is equal to the Father, whether he is called "Son of God", or "first-born of all creatures". If not, he is simply a creature, and shares in the Deity by "participation" only, i.e., in so far a table has something in common with the carpenter who made it.[206] Origen coped with another difficulty, the statement of Jesus in John, that "The Father is greater than I." It can mean that only the Father is God, and that the Son is but a creature, deprived of the divine essence. Origen answered[207] that Jesus spoke *eucharistikos*, in a manner of prayer and thanksgiving, i.e., with the respect and gratitude of a son for his father, not in terms of Greek philosophy dealing with nature and definitions of essences.

Later on, in the Trinitarian controversies of the fourth century, the Arians took advantage of Origen's acknowledgement that Scripture, in these two formulas (Christ as "first-born of all creation", and, "The Father is greater than I") referred to the WORD of God, and they pretended that Origen was supporting their (Arian) meaning, i.e., that the WORD of God was not God, but inferior to God, and a mere creature which did not share in the divine essence. It belongs to every great thinker who leaves a posterity of writings to be "abused" by people engaged in later controversies, who make use of his words, but do not respect his meaning. For this reason, Origen, who was the "pillar of or-

---

[205] Origen, *Dialogue with Heraclitus.*

[206] Origen, *Commentary on John* I 243-251, II 22; *De Principiis*, I, ch. 2, "Christ," Transl. Butterworth p. 15ff.

[207] Origen, *Commentary on John* XIII, 151 SC.

thodoxy" in his life-time, was considered as a heretic (a pre-Arian) by classical theology.

## THE CREED OF NICAEA-CONSTANTINOPLE (325, 381 A.D.)

Athanasius, theologian, later on bishop of Alexandria, loved to portray the Incarnation of Christ as the coming of the divine MODEL, assuming the flesh for the restoration of the divine image in humankind, i.e., for our salvation.

Arius, a priest of Alexandria, trained at Antioch, introduced a new theology in Alexandria, and was condemned by the Council of Nicaea. In order to maintain the unity of God, Arius declared that God is the "Unoriginate," and that whatever is originate cannot be God, but is a creature. Arius was thinking in philosophical terms and definitions. His LOGOS (WORD) was the Logos of the philosophy of the Stoics, for whom the Logos is a part (the "Sovereign part," or Soul) of the world, but nothing besides the world. For Arius, Christ is not God.

We quote the *Thalia* of Arius:[208]

> God Himself, then, in His own nature, is ineffable by all men. - Equal or like or one in glory with Himself, He alone has none. - And Ingenerate we call Him because of Him who is generate by nature. - We praise Him as without beginning, because of Him who has a beginning. - And adore Him as everlasting, because of Him who in time has come to be. - He that is without beginning made the Son a beginning of things originated; and advanced Him as a Son to Himself by adoption. He has nothing proper to God in proper subsistence (*kath'hypostasin*). - For He is not equal, no, not one in essence (*homoousios*) with Him...

The COUNCIL OF NICAEA (A.D. 325) was summoned by the recently converted Emperor Constantine in order to settle the controversy raised in the Eastern world by Arius after his condemnation by the Synod and the bishop (Alexander) of Alexandria.

> The CREED of Nicaea reads: ...*IN JESUS CHRIST, THE ONLY SON OF GOD, BORN FROM THE FATHER BEFORE ALL AGES, GOD FROM GOD, LIGHT FROM LIGHT, TRUE GOD FROM TRUE GOD, CONSUBSTANTIAL (homoousios) WITH THE FATHER, THROUGH WHOM ALL*

---

[208] Athenasius, *De synodis* 15, tr. J. Stevenson, *A New Eusebius* n. 296.

*THINGS WERE MADE, WHO FOR US AND FOR OUR SALVATION CAME DOWN FROM HEAVEN AND WAS MADE FLESH...*

The addition of *homoousios* (consubstantial, of the same substance as the Father) prevented an Arian interpretation of the generation of the Son of God in the sense of the creation of any creature (for, in a sense, all creatures are "from God", but not "of the same substance or nature" as God). Therefore, the Council of Nicaea proclaimed the deity of the Son, or his equality with the Father.

### PROOF AND COUNTERPROOF

The Arians used a series of biblical texts suggesting an inferiority in the Word of God, and interpreted them as an inferiority in nature in the philosophical sense. On the contrary, Athanasius and other Nicaeans interpreted the same texts of the Incarnation, as meaning that, in his human nature, Christ (obviously) is inferior to the Father. Neither of the two parties was prepared to look for an objective interpretation of these texts, which they interpreted "systematically," i.e., according to the formal needs of their own thesis, as usual, unfortunately, in all theological controversies.[209]

Athanasius, in spite of appearance, was not adamant concerning a "word" (the *homoousios*), but opposed all formulas (many creeds!) failing to confess the deity of Christ as the Word of God. More important, theologically, Athanasius insisted on the divine works of Christ as evidence for his deity (miracles, divine teachings, etc. ), and on the unity of the divine Trinity, since Christians are baptized in the name of the Father, of the Son, and of the Holy Spirit. To pretend that the Son is not God is to drop him from the divine Trinity, and to destroy the Trinity itself.

## THE DIVINITY OF THE HOLY SPIRIT

The deity of the Holy Spirit was questioned by second generation Arians for the same reasons as first generation Arians had questioned the deity of Christ. Athanasius and the Cappadocian Fathers answered with the same arguments as for the deity of the Son: the Holy Spirit performs divine deeds (human sanctification, and the inspiration of prophets) and belongs to the Blessed Trinity.

---

[209] A good example of such "systematic exegesis" on the orthodox side is found in the *Theological Orations* of Gregory Nazianzen (LNPF).

The Cappadocian Fathers (from Cappadocia in the center of modern Turkey) are Basil of Caesarea, his brother Gregory of Nyssa, and their friend Gregory Nazianzen. Under their influence, the council of Constantinople, 381 A.D., formulated the definition of the deity of the Holy Spirit:

> AND IN THE HOLY SPIRIT, LIFE-GIVING, WHO PROCEEDS FROM THE FATHER, WHO IS WORSHIPPED TOGETHER WITH THE FATHER AND THE SON, WHO SPOKE THROUGH THE PROPHETS...,

which completes the Creed of Nicaea-Constantinople, our Creed. The later addition in the West during the reign of Charlemagne of the FILIOQUE (the Holy Spirit proceeds from the Father *and the Son*) to the Creed does not represent a real improvement of the theology of the Cappadocians, and it caused a deep and bitter division between the Eastern and the Western Church, which is not healed yet.

The theological contribution of the Cappadocian Fathers is significant. Basil wrote the treatise *On the Holy Spirit* where he proves the deity of the Spirit without declaring It "God". He insists on the "divine works" of the Holy Spirit:[210]

> And the operations of the Holy Spirit, what are they? For majesty ineffable, and for numbers innumerable. How shall we form a conception of what extends beyond the ages? What were His operations before that creation whereof we can conceive? How great the grace which He conferred on creation? What the power exercised by Him over the ages to come?
>
> He existed; He pre-existed with the Father and with the Son before the ages. It follows that, even if you conceive of anything beyond the ages, you will find the Spirit yet further above and beyond. And if you think of the creation, the powers of the heavens (angels) were established by the Spirit, the establishment being understood to refer to disability to fall away from good. For it is from the Spirit that the powers derive their close relationship to God, their inability to change to evil, and their continuance in blessedness.
>
> Is it Christ's advent? The Spirit is forerunner. Is there the Incarnate presence? The Spirit is inseparable. Working of miracles, and gifts of healing are through the Holy Spirit. Demons were driven out by the Spirit of God. The Devil was brought to naught by the presence

---

[210] Basil, *On the Holy Spirit* 19, n. 49, LNPF 8, pp. 30-31.

> of the Spirit. Remission of sins was by the gift of the Spirit, for "ye were washed, ye were sanctified...in the name of the Lord Jesus Christ, and in the Holy Spirit of our God".[211] There is a close relationship with God through the Spirit, for "God sent forth the Spirit of His Son into your hearts, crying Abba, Father."[212]
>
> The resurrection of the dead is effected by the operation of the Spirit, for "Thou sendest forth Thy Spirit, they are created; and Thou renewest the face of the earth."[213] If here creation may be taken to mean the bringing of the departed to life again, how mighty is not the operation of the Holy Spirit, Who is to us the Dispenser of the life that follows on the resurrection, and attunes our souls to the spiritual life beyond?
>
> Or if here by creation is meant the change to a better condition of those who is this life have fallen into sin, (for it is so understood according to the usage of Scripture, as in the words of Paul: "If any man be in Christ he is a new creature",[214] the renewal that takes place in this life, and the transmutation from our earthly and sensuous life to the heavenly conversation which takes place in us through the Spirit, then our souls are exalted to the highest pitch of admiration.

As we see in the quote given above, Basil believed and taught the deity of the Holy Spirit. Through the use of an old local doxology, he also managed to maintain the idea that the Holy Spirit belongs in the divine Trinity. Against the semi-Arians who interpreted as an expression of the Arian theology the usual doxology, "Glory be TO the Father THROUGH the Son, IN the Holy Spirit" in the (Arian) sense of "Praise *to* the Father only as God, *through* the Son as a created mediator, *in* the Holy Spirit as in a kind of spiritual environment", Basil ascribed equality of honor to all the members of the Blessed Trinity: "Glory be *to* the Father, *and to* the Son, *and to* the Holy Spirit."

Basil had a serious reason to abstain from a formal confession of the deity of the Holy Spirit. His enemies, supported by the pro-Arian politics of Emperor Valens, were just waiting for such a declaration in order to have him deposed from his See

---

[211] I Cor. 11:11.

[212] Gal. 4:6.

[213] Ps. 104:30.

[214] 2 Cor. 5:17.

and the important diocese of Caesarea given to an Arian. It would have meant giving up the last fortress to the power of heresy. Circumstances required of Basil both courage and prudence. It was not the same for Gregory of Nyssa and Gregory Nazianzen, who had not much to lose and could speak more freely.

Gregory of Nyssa observed that, in the Blessed Trinity, everything is common, except for the notions of origin, which are: Father, Son, and Holy Spirit. The key is to make the right distinction between nature and mode of existence or origin:[215]

> If one were to ask a husbandman about a tree, whether it was planted or had grown of itself, and he were to answer either that the tree had not been planted, or that it was the result of planting, would he by that answer declare the nature of the tree? Surely not; but while saying how it exists he would leave the question of its nature obscure and unexplained.
>
> So, in the other case, when we learn that he (the Son) is unbegotten, we are taught in what mode he exists, and how it is fit that we would conceive him as existing, but what he is we do not hear in that phrase. When, therefore, we acknowledge such a distinction in the case of the Holy Trinity, as to believe that one Person is the *Cause*, and another is *of the Cause*, we can no longer be accused of confounding the definition of the Persons by the community of nature.

Gregory Nazianzen gave a philosophical form to Gregory of Nyssa's distinctions of origin when he used the Aristotelian category of RELATION in order to explain the characteristics of the divine Persons.[216] The nature is whatever is "common" in the Deity. The Persons are whatever is "relative." Actually, in the Trinity, the "relation" can only be one of origin. In other words, relatively, or as relations, we have the Father, the Son, and the Holy Spirit. Father and Son are relative terms, and this relation is one of "generation." And the Holy Spirit, according to Scripture, "proceeds from the Father": in this case, the relation is one of "procession."

Now, what is the difference between a relation of generation and a relation of procession? Gregory Nazianzen affirms the existence of such a difference on the basis of the

---

[215] Gregory of Nyssa, *Quod non sunt tres dii*, LNPF 5, pp.336.

[216] Gregory Nazianzen, *Theologican Orations* III,16 and *passim.*

difference of terms (generation and procession) found in Scripture, but he refuses to explain the meaning of this difference philosophically, preferring to leave it to the secret of God who did not reveal it.[217] For this reason we speak of the "mystery" of the Blessed Trinity. The Eastern Church, which called Gregory Nazianzen the "Theologian," remained attached to his position.

## THE CHRISTOLOGICAL CONTROVERSIES OF THE FIFTH CENTURY

The controversies described above were "trinitarian," and discussed the nature and distinctions in the Trinity. The controversies of the fifth century were properly "christological," and discussed the way the deity and human nature combined in Christ.

The Christological controversy was inaugurated in the fourth century with the case of Apollinaris, a strong supporter of the Nicaean *homoousios*, and a friend of Athanasius, the champion of the Nicaean faith. But Apollinaris denied the existence of the soul of Christ, saying that the LOGOS of God functioned as a soul in Christ. His Christology was termed a "Logos-body" christology. Athanasius himself condemned his friend at the synod of Antioch (362 A.D.), because of his negation of the soul of Christ, and the Antiochian theologians insisted on the complete character of the human nature of Christ. Athanasius could only follow his own principle: "What is not assumed (of the human nature by the divine Logos) is not redeemed." Was Apollinaris heterodox in his thought also, and not only in his language? Was it wrong to say that in Christ the divine Logos, the model upon which the human logos was created, could substitute for its copy? Was it the same as to say that the lady of the house can substitute for her maid?

Two different notions of the human composition were current in that time: one Semitic and biblical, the spirit animating the flesh; the other Greek and philosophical, the soul governing a body. Interference between these two notions could cause confusion and eventually error. The two notions were concurrently used by Athanasius himself, who sometimes also seemed to ignore the soul of Christ. All of that was a mere affair of language. Sometimes scholars seem to be unaware of this concurrence, or to ignore that the Semitic "flesh" includes both soul and body.

The real Christological controversy burst out in the fifth century between Nestorius, bishop of Constantinople and Cyril, bishop of Alexandria. It was also a conflict of rivalry between the two great Sees of the East: Constantinople, the Imperial

---

[217] Gregory Nazianzen, *Theological Oration* V 8.

residence, and Alexandria, the metropolis of Nicaean orthodoxy in Egypt. Moreover, theological interests and methods of biblical interpretation were not the same in the "School of Aleandria" and the "School of Antioch" (which stretched its influence to the Church of Constantinople).

As a theologian of the School of Antioch, Nestorius, a monk of Syria raised to the See of Constantinople, insisted on the distinction of the two natures in Christ, and incautiously attacked from the pulpit the *Theotokos*, the popular title of the Blessed Virgin as MOTHER OF GOD. He was willing to say *Christotokos* ("Mother of Christ"), or *Anthropotokos* ("Mother of man in Christ"), but the notion of "Mother of God" seemed for him to be blasphemous. It was easy to understand that Mary was the mother of a Son who happened to be the Son of God, just as a shepherdess would become the mother of a king. But the division was deep between the School of Antioch and that of Alexandria, and the *Theotokos* became a symbol of division.

The conflict was carried to bishop Celestine of Rome, who approved the teaching of Cyril of Alexandria, and entrusted him with the mission of notifying Nestorius of his condemnation. It was a terrible diplomatic mistake. Not only did Cyril fulfil his mission without diplomacy, but he added 12 "Anathemas" (condemnations) of his own composition to be signed by Nestorius. These anathemas were not part of the Roman decision, and obliged Nestorius to accept the theological particularities of the School of Alexandria. Nestorius refused to sign them.

Moreover, his theologians found errors in the doctrine of the Anathemas of Cyril. Cyril had repeated a statement of Apollinaris, who had been condemned in 362 as we remember. Cleverly the supporters of Apollinaris had ascribed it to Athanasius, the champion of orthodoxy, using him as an umbrella for the writings of their master. It was there that Cyril found it, thinking it belonged to Athanasius. This statement was "one nature of the Word incarnate." For Cyril, it expressed the concrete being of Christ in the flesh, in the unity of his divine power. Cyril was interested in the divine dynamism of Christ, and in its activity: our salvation and deification. On the contrary, the School of Antioch was interested in a careful distinction of the two natures of Christ. For this School, the "one nature of the Word incarnate" meant a mixture of the two natures, and the loss of something in the human nature of Christ.

The Council of Ephesus, 431 A.D., under the one-sided leadership of Cyril, who did not wait for the arrival of the group from Antioch, proclaimed the *Theotokos*, deposed Nestorius, and approved the doctrine of Cyril of Alexandria. At the so-called "Robber-Synod" of Ephesus, 449 A.D., Monophysitism (the doctrine of one nature of Christ), won an brief victory by way of violence, under the leadership of Dioscorus, Cyril's successor in the See of Alexandria. Flavian, the bishop of

Constantinople, was trodden under foot. Eutyches, the champion of Monophysitism, was reinstated.

The Council of Chalcedon, summoned by Emperor Marcian, 451 A.D., and inspired by the *Tomus to Flavian* (of Constantinople) written by pope Leo the Great (+461), gave the definitive formula of faith. Marcian obtained what he wanted: a formula of faith as short and clear as possible. There are in Christ two natures (the human nature, and the divine nature), and one Person, that of the Word made flesh, just as in the Trinity there are three Persons and one nature. An algebraic formula of the utmost simplicity summarized the orthodox position on the Trinity and on Christology: 1 versus 3, and 2 versus 1. A additional distinction was added in the face of Monothelitism, a resurgence of Monophysitism : there are two wills in Christ, just as there are two natures. Maximus the Confessor was the champion of orthodoxy and suffered in this controversy.

The presence of violence in these controversies between Christians who were probably all sincere and deeply dedicated to Christ is a sad story. It can be explained, though not justified, by many kinds of reasons. It proves that the cause of orthodoxy (right doctrine) is serious, because it has to do with the integrity of faith.

In his *De Trinitate*, in the beginning of the fifth century, Augustine added a chapter to the development of Trinitarian theology. Starting from a Neo-Platonic triad, somehow similar to the Greek diagram of the Trinity, he ended with a psychological diagram. He relied on the idea that, since we have been created according to the image of God, God himself must have some similarity with us, and this consists of three faculties existing in him as Persons: "Memory" (God the Father, source and principle of all), "Word", or Thought (the perfect expression of God), and "Will", or Love (the bond between the two).[218] This theory has become classical in the West, but Augustine himself presented it as a mere hypothesis, a very challengeable suggestion.

The development of classical theology concerning the Trinity and Christology represents the sum of all efforts displayed for the defense of the right faith against successive heresies. In this sense, it is a positive and useful achievement. In other ways, it represents a tendency to build the edifice of doctrine on aspects which are external to the presentation given

---

[218] Augustine, *De Trinitate*, Book 16, ch. 9-25. For the evolution of Augustine's thought from the "linear" (Plotinian) toward the "circular" (Western, or Latin) diagram, see Olivier du Roy, *L'intelligence de la foi en la Trinité chez Augustin* (Paris: Etudes Augustiniennes, 1966).

by the primitive Christian tradition. It is as if theology had built on the basis of the defense of orthodoxy rather than on the faith received from divine revelation, or as if it had built on the fence instead of on the rock of doctrine.

For this reason, we must always look back to the early forms of our faith, even though they seem to lack later distinctions which have become quasi-necessary. They are closer to the Gospel, and life-giving faith. The Trinity reminds us that we call God "Our Father who art in heaven", that God loved us so much that he sent his only Son for our salvation, and that Christ sent to us from the Father the Holy Spirit of divine inspiration and love for our sanctication. As for Christ, we consider him as more than any one of us, but we believe that he is the living Word and Son of God who spoke to us in the flesh, and who gathering us in his heavenly Kingdom, brings us back to the Father.

## QUESTIONNAIRE ON THE GENESIS OF THE CREED

1. What part of the CREED do we inherit from the Old Testament? What does Psalm 95-96 say about God and about our attitude regarding God?

2. How could such personifications as WORD of God, WISDOM of God, JUSTICE, MERCY of God in the Old Testament prepare for a theology of the divine nature of Christ?

3. Although Jesus did not preach about himself, but proclaimed the Kingdom of God, what was the implication of the prophecy of Daniel concerning the SON OF MAN (Daniel 7) when Jesus claimed it for himself before Caiphas' tribunal?

4. Among those who saw and heard Jesus when he was preaching, can you determine several degrees of faith and understanding, going from hostility and rejection to the impression that he was more than human?

5. Do you think that just reading thoughtfully the written word of Jesus in the Gospels, without the assistance of a guide or teacher, can deeply move the heart and lead to a real faith? Sometimes, can the contrary happen?

6. How could the resurrection of Christ confirm, or increase, the faith of the disciples ?

7. Why did early heretics such as the DOCETISTS consider Jesus to be a supernatural being without a real body? What was the answer of the Church?

8. Why did the EBIONITES refuse to affirm Jesus as divine? What was Jesus in their opinion? Why did the Church consider their faith as deficient?

9. How did the MONARCHIANS, by emphasizing the "Economy", or "Mission" of Christ, incline to deny both Christ's divine dignity and Christ's existence as a Person other than the Father?

10. Show that the APOLOGISTS believed in the divinity of Christ.

11. How did the APOLOGISTS, in order to explain the Christian belief in Christ as the Word of God, use and adjust with corrections the notion of the Stoic LOGOS (WORD)?

12. Among the "lower" titles of Christ, select two or three of these titles, and explain how they suit Jesus.

13. Among the "most divine" titles, explain how WORD and SON of God could correct what was deficient (too earthly, or without substance) in each other.

14. How could Origen explain that Christ, through these various titles, makes himself closer to each of us, more effective in our life? How do you like to address Christ in your prayer?

15. What was the advantage and inconvenience of the confession of Christ as a "second God," which ORIGEN tried to impose on the Monarchians?

16. How could the statement of Jesus, THE FATHER IS GREATER THAN I be interpreted in an orthodox sense? in the sense of Arius?

17. How could the statement of Paul, (CHRIST AS) THE FIRST BORN OF ALL CREATION be interpreted in an orthodox sense? in the sense of Arius? What was the solution proposed by Origen ? When can being "made" have the same sense as being "born"?

18. What was right? what was wrong? in Arius' use of the term UNORIGINATE for God?

19. According to Arius, was Christ the WORD properly Son of God? Show that his idea of Christ as the Word is the notion of the Stoic Logos (or Word).

20. How could the use of *HOMOOUSIOS* by the Council of Nicaea in the Creed prevent an interpretation of the WORD of God as nothing more than a dignified creature?

21. On what proofs of the divinity of Christ did Athanasius insist the most?

22. How did Basil prove the deity of the Holy Spirit without declaring that the Spirit was God?

23. Explain how, according to Gregory of Nyssa and Gregory Nazianzen, the divine Persons in the Trinity can be identified as RELATIONS OF ORIGIN?

24. What could be said "for" and "against" the term THEOTOKOS as applied to the Blessed Virgin?

25. What was the understanding of Christ by Cyril of Alexandria? by Nestorius of Constantinople?

26. With what quasi-algebraic formula did the Council of Chalcedon (451 A.D.) define both the divine Trinity and the composition of Christ? What is the advantage? the inconvenience? of this definition?

## BIBLIOGRAPHY

GRILLMEIER, A. *Christ in Christian Tradition from the Apostolic Age to Chalcedon.* Tr. J. Bowden, 2d ed. Atlanta, Ga: John Knox Press, 1975.

KELLY, J.N.D. *Early Christian Doctrines.* London: A.& Ch. Black, 1958.

_____. *Early Christian Creeds*, 2nd ed. London: Longmans, 1960.

NORRIS, R.A.Jr. *The Christological Controversy.* Philadelphia: Fortress Press, 1980.

QUASTEN, J. *Patrology.* 3 vol. Utrecht, Brussels: Spectrum, 1950, 1960. (Of general interest on Early Christian Literature).

STEVENSON, J. *A New Eusebius, Documents illustrative of the History of the Church to A.D. 337.* London: SPCK, 1965.

_____. *Creeds, Councils and Controversies. Documents illustrative of the history of the Church A.D. 337-461.* New York: Seabury 1966.

# CHAPTER XI

# BECOMING A CHRISTIAN IN EARLY CHRISTIANITY

Tertullian said, "one is not born a Christian: one becomes a Christian." We must be baptized in order to benefit from salvation through Christ. But, because of the normal practice of infant baptism, many today seem to assume that the rite is enough to make a Christian. It is enough, certainly, in the case of a child's death, but, as early as possible, a child must acquire a personal faith, be prepared to receive other sacraments, and learn to live a Christian life. Such is the purpose of Christian catechesis (teaching and training related to baptism).

In early Christianity, although infant baptism was known and widely spread in certain geographical areas such as North Africa, the custom of adult baptism generally prevailed, and the pattern of baptism was that of an adult coming to personal faith through conversion or reflection, and then of his or her reception into the Church after a rather long time of instruction and a period of probation. This period of training which culminated with baptism and eucharistic communion was Christian initiation.

In order to explain the early Christian initiation, we begin with a presentation of the *Didache*, the earliest "church order,"or manual, which seems to be very close to the Gospels, and with the description of the sacraments of initiation by Justin in the first half of the second century. After the presentation of a few cases of conversion, both of educated and of uneducated people, we turn to the *Apostolic Tradition* of Hippolytus (beginning of the third century), which provides rituals for baptism, the celebration of the Eucharist, and ordinations. The middle of the third century, with Cyprian, sees the beginning of a long African controversy on the validity of baptism performed by heretics. From the "golden age" of early Christian literature, in the fourth century, we select for a summarized presentation the famous *Catecheses* of Cyril of Jerusalem.

## I. BAPTISM AND EUCHARIST

### BAPTISM AND EUCHARIST IN THE DIDACHE[219]

In 1883, the *Didache* was published by Philotheos Bryennios from a Greek parchment codex of Jerusalem. Until

---

[219] The quotes of the *Didache* are from LCC I, pp.171-179, with the change of "Child" into "Servant."

then unknown, this document is the earliest church order, and seems to have been written in Syria between 100 and 150 A.D. The *Didache* enjoyed a great authority in early Christianity, in some places almost equal to that of the books of the New Testament.

THE "TWO WAYS" (1-6)

The "Two Ways" is an instruction designed for Catechumens, very much in the manner of the Jewish training of proselytes(new converts). It is interesting to notice how it reflects the Jewish origins of the Church (Decalogue), the particular influence of the Gospel (love for enemies, almsgiving, brotherly warning), and the necessity to oppose pagan customs (lust, divination, sorcery, harsh treatment of slaves). There are beautiful expressions of charity to the poor, and the encouraging invitation for those who fail to reach perfection, that at least they should do what they can! We quote a few sentences of the "Two Ways":

> There are two ways, one of life and one of death; and between the two ways there is a great difference. Now, this is the way of life: "First, you must love God who made you, and second, your neighbor as yourself." And whatever you want people to refrain from doing to you, you must not do to them.
>
> What these maxims mean is this: "Bless those who curse you," and "pray for your enemies." Moreover, fast "for those who persecute you." For "what credit is it to you if you love those who love you? Is that not the way the heathen act?" ...If someone strikes you "on the right cheek, turn to him the other too, and you will be perfect." ..."Give to everybody who begs from you, and ask for no return." For the Father wants his own gifts to be universally shared. Happy is the man who gives as the commandment bids him!"...
>
> The second commandment of the Teaching: "Do not murder; do not commit adultery"; do not corrupt boys; do not fornicate; "do not steal"; do not practice magic; do not go in for sorcery; do not murder a child by abortion or kill a newborn infant... Do not slander; do not bear grudges; do not be double-minded or double-tongued. Do not be greedy or extortionate or hypocritical or malicious or arrogant. Do not plot against your neighbor. Do not hate anybody; but reprove some, pray for others, and still others love more than your own life....
>
> Be humble since "the humble will inherit the earth." Be patient, merciful, harmless, quiet, and good; and always

"have respect for the teaching you have been given. Do not put on airs or give yourself up to presumptuousness. Do not associate with the high and mighty, but with the upright and humble. Accept whatever happens to you as good, in the realization that nothing occurs apart from God.

Do not be one who holds his hand out to take, but shuts it when it comes to giving. If your labor has brought you earnings, pay a ransom for your sins. Do not hesitate to give and do not give with a bad grace; for you will discover who He is that pays you back a reward with a good grace. Do not turn your back on the needy, but share everything with your brother and call nothing your own. For if you have what is eternal in common, how much more should you have what is transient!

Do not neglect your responsibility to your son or your daughter, but from their youth you shall teach them to revere God. Do not be harsh in giving orders to your slaves and slave girls. They hope in the same God as you... You slaves, for your part, must obey your masters with reverence and fear, as if they represented God...

If you can bear the Lord's full yoke, you will be perfect. But if you cannot, then do what you can.

BAPTISM, FASTING, AND DAILY PRAYER (6-8)

The ritual of baptism mentions the three Persons, and alludes to the baptism by infusion, if the baptism by immersion --the usual way-- is impossible. Generally baptism is given in running water.

The Christians are forbidden to eat meat sacrificed to idols[220] ; they fast on Wednesdays and Fridays (8) (the Jews fast on Mondays and Thursdays). They pray three times a day (8), reciting the prayer of the Lord.

THE EUCHARIST (9-10)

The *Didache* offers two prayers of genuinely Jewish inspiration. The Jewish background seems to be a prayer of thanksgiving and petition for the land of Israel, Jerusalem and the Temple, good seasons and crops, for the name of the Lord, and for the gathering of Israel from the four corners of the world. The Christian community has made it into a prayer of thanksgiving and petition for the universal Kingdom of God, for the coming of grace, the gathering from the ends of the earth,

[220] Acts 15:29.

the knowledge of God and the spiritual food of eternal life, through the mediation of Jesus, the "Servant of God":[221]

> Now about the Eucharist: This is how to give thanks: First in connection with the cup: "We thank you, our Father, for the holy vine of David, your Servant, which you have revealed through Jesus, your Servant. To you be glory for ever."
>
> Then in connection with the piece (broken off the loaf): "We thank you, our Father, for the life and knowledge which you have revealed through Jesus, your Servant. To you be glory for ever. As this piece (of bread) was scattered over the hills and then was brought together and made one, so let your Church be brought together from the ends of the earth into your Kingdom. For yours is the glory and the power through Jesus Christ for ever."
>
> You must not let anyone eat or drink of your Eucharist except those baptized in the Lord's name. For in reference to this the Lord said, "Do not give what is sacred to dogs." After you have finished your meal, say grace in this way:
>
> We thank you, holy Father, for your sacred name which you have lodged in our hearts, and for the knowledge and faith and immortality which you have revealed through Jesus your Servant. To you be glory forever. Almighty Master, you have revealed everything for the sake of your name, and have given men food and drink to enjoy that they may thank you. But to us you have given spiritual food and drink and eternal life through Jesus, your Servant.
>
> Above all, we give thanks to you for you are mighty. To you be glory for ever. Remember, Lord, your Church, to save it from all evil and to make it perfect by your love. Make it holy, and gather it from the four winds into your Kingdom which you have made ready for it. For yours is the power and the glory for ever. Let grace come and let this world pass away! Hosanna to the God of David!
>
> If anyone is holy, let him come. If not, let him repent. "Our Lord, come!" " Amen."

---

[221] L. Bouyer, *Eucharist. Theoloty and Spirituality of the Eucharistic Prayer*, trans. C. U. Quinn (Notre Dame, IN: University of Notre Dame Press, 1968), ch.5, "From the Jewish *Berakah* to the Christian Eucharist."

Herewith the order given by Jesus at the Last Supper, "Do this in memory of me!"[222] seems to be fulfilled, since, in spite of the absence of the narrative itself of the Last Supper, a thankful recall is made of the spiritual gifts of God and salvation, and a special emphasis is laid on the mediation of Christ in their acquisition.

Worship on Sundays (14) includes the Eucharist, and prescribes confession of sins and reconciliation to neighbor in order to offer up to God a pure sacrifice.[223]

## PROPHETS

Prophets are allowed to give thanks freely (10:7). A substantial section on prophets follows (11-13), which is very interesting for the existence of prophets in the early Church. There are local prophets. Caution is taken regarding those (apostles-prophets, or itinerant preachers) coming from outside, against whose eventual fraud discernment of spirits is necessary. True prophets are men --probably also women-- of prayer. Since the Eucharist (like all prayers in antiquity) is flexible, their thanksgiving is welcome. It is irrelevant to say that they "presided" over the Eucharist: they were "prophets," not "presidents" of the community.

"Bishops and Deacons" are to be elected for the government and service of the community. They seem to correspond to the bishops, presbyters and deacons of I Timothy 3-5 and Titus 1, which explain the qualities required for their election. There were groups of elders presiding over synagogues among the Jews, and it seems that our Christian "presbyters" and "bishops" are essentially the continuation of this structure. In the Church, they presided over the Eucharistic meeting as well as over the life of the community, and the bishop assumed a prominent position.

## DESCRIPTION OF BAPTISM AND THE EUCHARIST BY JUSTIN, c. 150 A.D.

From the middle of the second century we learn about baptism and the Eucharist from Justin:

> We, however, after washing the one who has been convinced and signified his assent, lead him to those who are called brethren, where they are assembled. They then

---

[222] This order does not need to be an order of repetition. It seems that Jesus was asking his disciples to remember (to have a memorial celebration with thanksgiving) the New Testament in his blood in the same manner as they remembered the Old Testament granted through the agency of Moses and a sacrifice.

[223] Malachi 1:11,14.

earnestly offer common prayers for themselves and for the one who has been illuminated and all others everywhere, that we may be made worthy, having learned the truth, to be found in deed good citizens and keepers of what is commanded, so that we may be saved with eternal salvation. On finishing the prayers we greet each other with a kiss. Then bread and a cup of water and mixed wine are brought to the president of the brethren and he, taking them, sends up praise and glory to the Father of the universe through the name of the Son and of the Holy Spirit, and offers thanksgiving at some length that we have been deemed worthy to receive these things from him. When he has finished the prayers and the thanksgivings, the whole congregation presents assents, saying, "Amen."

And on the day called Sunday there is a meeting in one place of those who live in cities or the country, and the memoirs of the apostles or the writings of the prophets are read as long as permits. When the reader has finished, the president in a discourse urges and invites us to the imitation of these noble things. Then we all stand up together and we offer prayers. And, as said before, when we have finished the prayer, bread is brought, and wine and water, and the president sends up prayers and thanksgivings to the best of his ability, and the congregation assents, saying the Amen; the distribution, and reception of the consecrated (bread and wine) by each one, takes place and they are sent to the absent by the deacons.[224]

## II. CONVERSION TO THE CHRISTIAN FAITH

In this section we gather testimonies of conversion to the Christian faith in the second century: first, the conversion of Justin and other apologists who belonged to the intelligentsia, and then that of very simple and poor people. The cases of Marius Victorinus and that of Patricius, Augustine's father, also cast an interesting light on certain aspects of conversion in happier times.

When the Christians were persecuted and despised, a few converts from the Gentiles, who belonged to the world of culture, made themselves "Apologists." They knew Greek philosophy and were able to take advantage of it. Their own culture enabled them to speak boldly, to defend their unjustly persecuted fellow-Christians, and to claim for them equality of rights. To some extent, their language was not that of the Church, full of biblical reminiscences, but it was best for their

[224] Justin, I *Apology*, 64-67, LNPF.

purpose. Their theology became a bridge between the traditional Jewish-Christian theology of the Church, and Greek philosophy. From then on, Christian theology built its thought on a twofold basis: Scripture and philosophy.

THE CONVERSION OF JUSTIN.

In the beginning of his *Dialogue with Trypho*, Justin explains to Trypho, a Jewish Rabbi, how he converted to Christian philosophy:

> Being at first desirous of personally conversing with one of these philosophers, I surrendered myself to a certain STOIC; and having spent a considerable time with him, when I had not acquired any further knowledge of God (for he did not know himself, and said such instruction was unnecessary), I left him and betook myself to another, who was called a PERIPATETIC, and as he fancied, shrewd. And this man, after having entertained me for the first few days, requested me to settle the fee, in order that our intercourse be not unprofitable. Him, too, for this reason I abandoned, believing him to be no philosopher at all.
>
> But when my soul was eagerly desirous to hear the peculiar and choice philosophy, I came to a PYTHAGOREAN very celebrated --a man who thought much of his own wisdom. And then, when I had an interview with him, willing to become his hearer and disciple, he said, "What then? Are you acquainted with music, astronomy, and geometry? Do not expect to perceive any of those things which conduce to a happy life, if you have not been first informed on those points which wean the soul from sensible objects, and render it fitted for objects which appertain to the mind, so that it can contemplate that which is honorable in its essence and that which is good in its essence?"
>
> Having commended many of these branches of learning, and telling me that they were necessary, he dismissed me when I confessed to him my ignorance. Accordingly I took it rather impatiently, as was to be expected when I failed in my hope, the more so because I deemed the man had some knowledge; but reflecting again on the space of time during which I would have to linger over these branches of learning, I was not able to endure longer delay.
>
> In my helpless condition it occurred to me to have a meeting with the PLATONISTS, for their fame was great. I thereupon spent as much of my time as possible

with one who had lately settled in our city --a sagacious man, holding a high position among the Platonists-- and I progressed, and made the greatest improvements daily. And the perception of immaterial things quite overpowered me, and the contemplation of ideas furnished my mind with wings, so that in a little while I supposed that I had become wise; and such was my stupidity, I expected forthwith to look upon God, for this is the end of Plato's philosophy.

And when I was thus disposed, when I wished at one period to be filled with great quietness, and to shun the path of man, I used to go into a certain field not far from the sea. And I was near that spot, which having reached I purported to be by myself, A CERTAIN OLD MAN, by no means contemptible in appearance, exhibiting meek and venerable manners, followed me at a little distance....

- "Does philosophy make happiness?" said he.
- "Accordingly, I said, and it alone... Philosophy is the knowledge of that which exists, and a clear perception of the truth; and happiness is the reward of such knowledge and wisdom."
- "But what do you call God?" said he.
- "That which always maintains the same nature, and in the same manner, and is the cause of all other things -- that, indeed, is God."
So I answered him; and he listened to me with pleasure...

- "There existed, he said, long before this time, certain men more ancient than all those who are esteemed philosophers, both righteous and beloved of God, who spoke by the Divine Spirit, and foretold events which would take place, and which now are taking place. They are called PROPHETS. These alone both saw and announced the truth to men, neither reverencing nor fearing any man, not influenced by a desire for glory, but speaking those things alone which they saw and which they heard, being filled with the Holy Spirit. Their writings are still extent, and he who has read them is very much helped in his knowledge of the beginning and end of things, and of those matters which the philosopher ought to know, provided he has believed them.

For they do not use demonstration in their treatises, seeing that they were *witnesses of the truth above all demonstration and worthy of belief*; and those events which have happened, and those which are happening, compel you to assent to the utterances made by them, although, indeed, they were entitled to credit on

> account of the miracles which they performed, since both glorified the Creator, the God and Father of all things, and proclaimed his Son, the Christ sent by him; which, indeed, the false prophets, who are filled with the lying unclean spirit, neither have done nor do, but venture to work certain wonderful deeds for the purpose of astonishing men, and glorify the spirits of error.
>
> But pray that, above all things, the gates of light may be opened to you; for these things cannot be perceived or understood by all, but only by the man to whom God and his Christ have imparted wisdom..." When he had spoken those and many other things, he went away, bidding me to attend to them; and I have not seen him since. But straightway a flame was kindled in my soul; and a love of the prophets, and of those men who are friends of Christ, possessed me; and whilst revolving his words in my mind, I found this philosophy alone to be safe and profitable. Thus, for this reason I am a philosopher.
>
> Moreover I would wish that all, making a resolution similar to my own, do not keep themselves away from the words of the Savior. For they possess a terrible power in themselves, and are sufficient to inspire those who turn aside from the path of rectitude with awe; while the sweetest rest is afforded those who make a diligent practice of them. If then you have any concern for yourself, and if you are eagerly looking for salvation, and if you believe in God, you may, since you are not indifferent to the matter, become acquainted with the Christ of God, and, after being initiated, live a happy life.[225]

Among the other apologists, Aristides of Athens was converted by the Christian purity of life.[226] Tatian was converted by the reading of Scripture,[227] and the same with Theophilus of Antioch, particularly by the argument of prophecy.[228] Tertullian was converted by the courage of Christian martyrs.[229] Cyprian was converted by the consideration of the

---

[225] Justin, *Dialogue with Trypho* 2-8, ANF 1, pp. 195ff.

[226] Aristides, *The Apology*, tr. ANF 9, pp. 263-279.

[227] Tatian, *The Discourse to the Greeks* 29, tr. ANF 2, pp. 65-83.

[228] Theophilus of Antioch, *Ad Autolycum I*, 14, ANF 3, pp. 53-133, see p.

[229] Tertullian, *Ad scapulam* 5, ANF 3, pp. 105-108.

purity of Christian life as opposed to the immorality of pagan public and private life, and a priest, Caecilius, intervened in his conversion.[230] Cyprian gave all his fortune to the poor, became bishop of Carthage, and died a martyr in 249 A.D.

THE SIMPLE ARE CONVERTED BY THE SIMPLE

Celsus provides precious information concerning Christian evangelization among the simple and the poor. This information is transmitted to us in Origen's *Contra Celsum*, c. 240 A.D., i.e., 70 years after Celsus' *True Doctrine* against the Christians:[231]

> (According to Celsus) their (the Christians) injunctions are like this, "Let no one educated, no one wise, no one sensible draw near. For those abilities are thought to us to be evils. But as for anyone ignorant, anyone stupid, anyone uneducated, anyone who is a child, let him come boldly." By the fact that they themselves admit that these people are worthy of their God, they show that they want and are able to convince only the foolish, dishonorable and stupid, and only slaves, women, and little children...(44)
>
> In private houses also we see wool-workers, cobblers, laundry-workers, and the most illiterate and bucolic yokels, who would not dare to say anything at all in front of their elders and more intelligent masters. But whenever they get hold of children in private and some stupid women with them, they let out some astounding statements as, for example, that they must not pay attention to their father and school-master, but must obey them; they say that these talk nonsense and have no understanding, and that in reality they neither know nor are able to do anything good, but are taken up with mere empty chatter. But they alone, they say, know the right way of life, and if the children would believe them, they would become happy and make their home happy as well. And if just as they are speaking they see one of the school-masters coming or some intelligent person, or even the father himself, the more cautious of them flee in all directions; but the more reckless urge the children to rebel. They whisper to them that in the presence of their father and their school-masters they do not feel able to explain anything to the children, since they do not

---

[230] Jerome, *De viris illustribus* 53.

[231] Origen, *Contra Celsum*, tr. H. Chadwick, (Cambridge, U.K.: Cambridge University Press, 1965), Book 3.

want to have anything to do with the silly and obtuse teachers who are totally corrupted and far gone in wickedness and who inflict punishments on the children. But, if they like, they should leave father and their schoolmasters, and go along with the women and little children who are their play-fellows to the wool-dresser's shop, or to the cobbler's or to the washer-woman's shop, that they may learn perfection. And by saying this they persuade them.(55)

And that I am not criticizing them and more than the truth compels me, anyone may say also from this. Those who summon people to the other mysteries make this preliminary proclamation: Whosoever has pure hands and a wise tongue, and again, Whosoever is pure from all defilements, and whose soul knows nothing of evil, and who has lived well and righteously. Such are the preliminary exhortations of those who promise purification from sins. But let us hear what folk these Christians call. Whosoever is a sinner, they say, whosoever is unwise, whosoever is a child, add, in a word, whosoever is a wretch, the kingdom of God will receive him. Do you not say that a sinner is he who is dishonest, a thief, a burglar, a poisoner, a sacrilegious fellow, and a grave-robber? What others would a robber invite and call?(59)

Why on earth this preference for sinners? (64) - "We say such things (the Christians are supposed to answer) to encourage sinners because we are unable to convert anyone really good and righteous, and that is the reason why we open our doors to the most impious and abominable men..." And yet (Celsus continues) I suppose that it is obvious to everyone that no one could entirely change people who sin by nature and habit, not even by punishment, much less by mercy; for it is very hard to change a nature entirely; but those without sin take part in a better life.(65) The man who teaches the doctrines of Christianity is like a man who promises bodies to health, but turns his patients away from attending to expert physicians because his lack of training would be shown up by them (75). Our teacher (Christian) acts like a drunkard who enters a party of drunkards and accuses sober people of being drunk (76), or like men with ophthalmia in the presence of people suffering from ophthalmia and accusing men with good eyes of having defective eyesight.(77)

Origen, who gives these long quotes, and many others, of Celsus' *True Doctrine*, points out that the apparent strength of Celsus' attacks is the offensive language which he uses, and the deliberately one-sided, negative and contemptuous judgment which he passes on everything in Christianity. Origen calls for more serenity and a better understanding of Christian doctrines and people. Moreover, between Celsus (c.170 A.D.) and Origen (240 A.D.) the Church increased in number, and conversions among cultured people multiplied. Christianity was no longer a religion for workers and the poor, but for cultured people as well.

The chief interest of this text for our purposes is that it shows Christianity growing among the poor and simple workers, who spontaneously spread it among their own folk. They are persecuted by civil authorities, despised by cultured people, subjected, as simple workers or slaves, to their owners'caprice. In spite of this handicap, and perhaps because of it, and without any missionary organization, they let the Gospel shine in their hearts, lives, and words. And the Gospel reaches its target, conquering the hearts and minds of those who are in many ways so close to them and ready for the Christian faith and hope. It was the will of Jesus that the Gospel be preached to the poor: wherever the Church is able with faith in the Gospel to reach or keep the poor, she is on the right track. In some regard, the presence in the Church of the wealthy, powerful and cultured seems to be a bonus.

Celsus misunderstood the power of Christianity. He seems to be offended by the fact that sinners and the poor -- whom Celsus included in the same category as sinners-- entered the Church. How can a sinner by nature or habit, he asks, be transformed? Can Christianity win the world? By such remarks, Celsus acknowledged both the failure of pagan culture to change their hearts, and the success of Christianity with those whom he considered as sinners. A few generations later, Christianity was the religion of the majority, and the Emperor was a Christian.

## THE CONVERSION OF MARIUS VICTORINUS AND OF PATRICIUS

In *Confessions*, Augustine describes the conversion of a famous Roman rhetor, Marius Victorinus, a great joy for the Christians. The point which I want to make in this case is to show the reason why such a worthy man who was a Christian in his heart postponed his baptism:

> Victorinus used to read the Holy Scriptures, most studiously sought after and searched into all the Christian writings, and said to Simplicianus,[232] not openly, but secretly, and as a friend, "Know thou that I am a Christian." To which he (Simplicianus) replied, "I will not believe it, nor will I rank you among the Christians unless I see you inside the Church of Christ." Whereupon,

[232] A Christian priest, future bishop of Milan.

> Victorinus replied derisively, "Is it then the walls that make Christians?" ...FOR HE WAS FEARFUL OF HIS FRIENDS, proud demon-worshippers,... and he thought a storm of enmity would descend upon him.[233]

At the end of the fourth century, in the Western world and particularly in Rome, the upper cultured class remained generally attached to paganism, and the system of education was traditionally pagan. Great courage was necessary for Victorinus, in spite of his moral worth, to break away from the circle of his friends and place himself under the ban of his society, in order to openly become a Christian. But, one day, Victorinus, spontaneously told Simplicianus, "Let us go to church!" Augustine, who then was very much in the same situation, was deeply moved by his example.

Augustine's father, Patricius, did not belong to the world of academia, and was not among the wealthy who ruled his small city of Thagaste in North Africa, but he was a man of good standing, and had a good circle of friends in the city. He was pagan, and so was his society, a pagan by tradition, not by personal conviction. His wife, Monica, was Christian: the Church respected this kind of marriage which, in most cases, led to the conversion of the family and, at least on his death-bed, to the baptism of the husband. It happened in the case of Monica and Patricius.

The point, here, is that, like Marius Victorinus in his own circle, Patricius met with an insuperable obstacle to baptism. Was it necessary, in order to become a Christian according to one's own desire, to break with a society which, after all, did not believe in pagan gods, and was, by its values, very close to the Christians of the same time and place? The solution in such cases was to postpone baptism to the end, and die as a Christian with the Christian hope. The Church seems to have condoned this practice. Patricius was not a hero of the Christian faith, but his family and he himself became Christian.

## III. BAPTISM ACCORDING TO THE *APOSTOLIC TRADITION* OF HIPPOLYTUS.[234]

The *Apostolic Tradition*, under the name of Hippolytus, is a collection of liturgical texts and church observances going back in its primitive form to the beginning of the third century. As is the case with these types of documents, there are problems concerning its primitive contents and its binding

---

[233] Augustine, *Confessions* VIII 3.

[234] The quotes are taken from *Early Sources of the Liturgy*, compiled and edited by Lucien Deiss, tr. by B. Weatherhead, (Staten Island, NY: Alba House, 1967).

authority in any local Church. But the contents reflect actual practice. The *Apostolic Tradition* deals with the ordination of bishops, priests, and deacons, the appointment or recognition of readers, virgins, sub-deacons, widows, healers, confessors, with the "Anaphora" or Eucharistic Prayer, with baptism and its preparation, with the meal of *Agape* and evening prayer, with times of prayer, fasting, communion at home, meetings of clergy, and the cemetery.

## CATECHUMENATE (PERIOD OF CHRISTIAN TRAINING)

There are rules for the acceptance of new catechumens by the Church, concerning their purpose and situation (slave or free, married or unmarried). They come to the teachers with Christians who bear witness for them. A section follows[235] concerning crafts and professions forbidden to Christians, which is closely paralleled in Tertullian's *De idololatria*,[236] and which does not seem to be a rule capable of being strictly enforced. For instance, in both Hippolytus and Tertulllian, a soldier cannot be baptized, but, in *De corona,* Tertullian praises a Christian soldier who refused to wear a crown (the military crown was given to brave soldiers in a pagan religious celebration).

Hippolytus prescribes three years of catechumenate. Catechumens pray by themselves, apart from the faithful; they do not give the kiss of peace, for their kiss is not yet pure. After the prayer of the catechumens, the teacher lays hands upon them and prays, before dismissing them. Catechumens are exorcised daily, but, during the days before baptism, the bishop himself exorcises each of them. Candidates to baptism are examined, "whether they lived piously while catechumens, whether they honored the widows, whether they visited the sick, whether they have fulfilled every good work."

## THE RITUAL OF BAPTISM

> And they (clergy) shall spend all the night in vigil (Easter vigil), reading the Scriptures to them and instruc-

---

[235] Hippolytus, *The Apostolic Tradition*, II 16, "Of new Converts: Of the crafts and professions (forbidden to Christians)."

[236] Tertullian, *De idololatria* 6-23, cf. Tertullian, *De corona* (a Christian cannot be a soldier) ; *De spectaculis* (nor a circus athlete or a gladiator). *De idololatria* covers a large variety of activities : schoolmasters, trade, holidays and feasts, private ceremonies, the case of servants, magistratures, *insignia*, military service and oath, pronouncing the names of the gods, verbal restriction.

ting them (the candidates). And at the hour when the cock crows they shall first pray over the water. And they shall put off their clothes. And they shall baptize the little children first. And if they can answer for themselves, let them answer. But if they cannot, let their parents or someone from their family answer. And next they shall baptize the grown men; and last the women, who shall (all) have loosed their hair and laid aside the gold ornaments.

And at the time determined for baptizing the bishop shall give thanks over the oil and put it into a vessel and it is called the "Oil of Thanksgiving." And he shall take (also) other oil and exorcise over it, and it is called "Oil of Exorcism." ...

And when the presbyter takes hold of each of those who are to be baptized, let him bid him renounce saying: - "I renounce thee, Satan, and all thy pomps and all thy works." And when he has said this let him anoint him with the oil of exorcism saying: - "Let all evil spirits depart from thee." (And also turning to the East, let him say: - "I consent to Thee, O Father and Son and Holy Spirit, before whom all creation trembles and is moved. Grant me to do all thy wills without blame)."

Then after these things let him give him over to the presbyter who stands at the water (to baptize). And let them stand in the water naked. And let a deacon likewise go down with him into the water. And (when) he (who is to be baptized) goes down to the water, let him who baptizes lay hand on him saying thus: - "Dost thou believe in God the Father Almighty?" And he who is being baptized shall say: - "I believe." Let him forthwith baptize him once, having his hand laid upon his head. And after (this) let him say: - "Dost thou believe in Christ Jesus, the Son of God, who was born of the Holy Spirit and the Virgin Mary, who was crucified in the days of Pontius Pilate, and died, (and was buried), and rose again the third day living from the dead, and ascended into the heavens, and sat down at the right hand of the Father, and will come to judge the living and the dead?" And when he says: - "I believe," let him baptize him the second time. And again let him say: - "Dost thou believe in (the) Holy Spirit, in the holy Church, and the resurrection of the flesh?" And he who is being baptized shall say: - "I believe." And so let him baptize him the third time.

And afterwards when he comes up (from the water) he shall be anointed by the presbyter with the oil of thanksgiving saying: - "I anoint thee with holy oil in the name

> of Jesus Christ." And so each one drying himself (with a towel) they shall now put on their clothes, and after this let them be together in the assembly.
>
> And the bishop shall lay his hand upon them invoking and saying: - "O Lord God, who didst count these thy servants worthy of deserving the forgiveness of sins by the laver of regeneration, make them worthy to be filled with the Holy Spirit and send upon them thy grace, that they may serve thee according to thy will; for to thee is the glory, to the Father and to the Son with the Holy Spirit in the holy Church, both now and ever and world without end. Amen." After this, pouring the consecrated oil and laying his hand on his head, he shall say: - "I anoint thee with the holy oil in God the Father almighty and Christ Jesus and the Holy Spirit." And sealing him on the forehead, he shall give him the kiss (of peace) and say: - "The Lord is with you." And he who has been sealed shall say: - "And with thy spirit." And so he shall do to each one severally. Henceforward they shall pray together with all the people.

Then, the Easter Eucharist begins with the Offertory. The neophytes (newly baptized) are given, in addition to the communion, a mixture of honey and milk to drink as a symbol of "the land flowing with milk and honey", an image of paradise.

### THE ANAPHORA

The text of the "Anaphora", or Eucharistic Prayer, is given with the ritual of the ordination of the bishop. The Roman Catholic Eucharistic Prayer n.2 closely repeats Hippolytus.

## IV. CYPRIAN: CONTROVERSY ON BAPTISM

In the middle of the third century, the practice of INFANT BAPTISM had become customary in North Africa. It was the sign of massive conversion to Christianity in that particular area. Usually, when a religious practice becomes traditional, there is a kind of obligation to follow it, which then calls for theological reasons. Cyprian referred to the sin of Adam:

> Adults, if any, rather than babies, should be denied the gift of grace, because of their sins. A baby is not guilty of sin. He only inherits the old disease of death attached to carnal birth and the inheritance from Adam. But the remission of sins is made easier for a baby because the sin which is forgiven is not his own, but that of others. Therefore, the council decided that nobody should be

> refused the grace of baptism, and this decision included children.[237]

Cyprian adds an "irresistible" argument: "Babies have more right than anyone to God's mercy, since they appeal to it by their cries and tears as soon as they are born!" This text shows that there is a beginning of a theology of original sin. It also indicates that the emphasis is laid on the communication of grace by God and Christ through the Church rather than on personal repentance and catechumenate as in the case of adults.

But what is the validity of baptism conferred outside the Church, by a heretic such as Novatian and his clergy? The answer of Cyprian is that such a baptism is invalid, and must be renewed if this person comes back to the Catholic Church:

> Since all heretics and schismatics have no power or jurisdiction, being out of the Church, being revolting people and enemies who erect altar and priesthood against altar and priesthood, their baptism is void.[238]

Cyprian entered into a bitter conflict with the newly elected Roman bishop Stephen, who received into the Catholic Church those baptized by heretics, by the laying of the hand of reconciliation of sinners, without rebaptizing them. Cyprian argued against this practice on the basis of the decision of a Council of Carthage under his predecessor Agrippinus in 220 A.D. Stephen, the new bishop of Rome, defended the practice on the basis of Roman tradition, maintaining that this custom was based on the authority of the apostle Peter. Martyrdom took the lives of the two opponents.[239]

During the fourth century, the dispute resumed between the Donatist Church of Africa which rebaptized Catholics under the pretext that they had been baptized by unworthy ministers, and the Catholic Church which accepted the baptism of heretics. The Catholic Church had been accused of *traditio* (scandalous delivery of sacred books to pagan authorities in time of persecution), and had a hard time in Africa for more than one century, until the brief victory of Augustine.

From the beginning of the Donatist controversy, the Catholic Church in Africa adopted the Roman position, and did not rebaptize heretics. Augustine justified this position, saying that it is not the purity of the minister which confers the Holy Spirit, since the Holy Spirit is not a human gift, but Christ is the

---

[237] Cyprian, Epistle 64 to bishop Fidus, ANF.

[238] Cyprian, Ep. 69 to Magnus, ANF.

[239] Cf. Cyprian, Ep. 70 and 75 from Firmilian of Caesarea, ANF.

author of baptism, and confers the Holy Spirit through the instrumentality of a human minister, even if this minister is a heretic, or Judas himself.

Augustine's theological solution was appropriate, and has become classical theology. However, the case of a valid baptism given to a baby by a minister who may be a sinner and a heretic, for the remission only of original sin, was not the appropriate basis for further theological development about baptism! The Middle Ages suffered from this reduction of sacramental theology to a question of validity. In order to carry on a good discussion about baptism and other sacraments, it is necessary to come back to the right model of Christian baptism: the baptism of adults, after due conversion, repentance and catechesis, completed by their first Eucharistic communion in the holy Church of Christ living according to the principles of the Gospel.

## V. THE CATHECHESIS OF CYRIL OF JERUSALEM

Cyril, bishop of Jerusalem between 348 and 387 A.D. was the most outstanding catechist of the golden age of early Christianity. In order to know what catechumens were taught, we simply give a resumé of his *Baptismal Catecheses*, given before baptism, and of his *Mystagogical Homilies*, given after baptism.

In *Procatechesis* 16, Cyril gives a definition of baptism rich in spiritual symbolism: "Great is the Baptism that lies before you: a ransom to captives; a remission of offenses; a death of sin; a new birth of the soul; a holy and indissoluble seal; a chariot to heaven; the delight of paradise; a welcome to the Kingdom; the gift of adoption!"

### BAPTISMAL CATECHESES.

1. CONVERSION. Catechumens are invited to convert, to have a new heart and a new spirit, to get rid of the "old man" through confession (of sins). If their conscience is free from lies and if they have the right intention, their souls will be regenerated by the Holy Spirit in faith: they will receive a spiritual shield, and be planted in the mystical paradise. The time has come for them to confess their faults, to attend catecheses, to spend 40 days caring for their salvation. The remission of sins is equally given to all, but the participation of the Holy Spirit is granted according to the degree of faith of each one. They must first forgive others if they want to be forgiven by God.

2. REPENTANCE. Premeditated sin is a grievous disease of the soul, as terrible as fire in the hand for those who keep it in themselves, but easy to heal through repentance. Sin may be inspired by the Devil, but also by concupiscence,i.e. evil desire growing from ourselves. Evil desire, like a tender root breaking

a stone, can terribly harm the eye of our soul. In spite of the weakness resulting from our sins, we can be saved, but the assent of our free will is required. Just as a sick man trusts a physician, telling him what is wrong with himself, a sinner must confess his faults to the Lord. Catechumens must confess their faults to the Lord in order to obtain the remission of their past sins, to receive the heavenly gifts, and become coheirs of the saints in the Kingdom.

3. INVITATION TO BAPTISM. Catechumens must rejoice: baptism is compared to the wedding dress, cleansed through conversion, which enables them to join the Bridegroom for the Banquet. Moreover, just as the food offered on pagan altars defiles those who touch it, the water over which the Holy Spirit, Christ, and the Father have been invoked, acquires a sanctifying power. The washing of baptism is twofold: the water purifies the body, but the Holy Spirit seals the soul. We must be born again of both water and spirit: only one of them does not open the Kingdom.

4. BASIC CHRISTIAN DOGMAS. Cyril gives as essential doctrines the articles of the Creed, and insists on the divine dignity of the Holy Spirit (denied by the Semi-Arians of his time), on the free will of the soul (against the idea of being a sinner by nature), on the body as good and beautiful because created by God (against those who despise the body and marriage), on the necessity to avoid all compromise with the paganism through divination, magic and superstition.

5. FAITH. The faithful are rich even in poverty, agreeable to God, and terrible to the Devil. We are the children of Abraham, who believed that God could raise his son from the dead, when we believe in Christ dead and raised from the dead. There is a "dogmatic" faith when we assent to Christian truth, and a "charismatic" faith when, through the gifts of the Spirit, we are made able to perform super-human deeds.

6. THE ONLY GOD. God is transcendent, incomprehensible, and can be seen only by the Son and the Holy Spirit. God cannot be represented as a human (Anthropomorphism) or as material. The pagans worship several gods (Polytheism); others (the Manichees) hold to a twofold deity: one good and the other evil, the author of material things.

7. THE FATHER. The Father is the Father of the Son from eternity, and not in the same sense as he is the "Father" of creatures. When Jesus said, "I ascend to My Father and Your Father", MY means that he is Son by nature, and YOURS that we are sons by adoption. In his goodness and mercy, God granted us the favor of calling him "Father". We can become children of God, or children of the Devil as well, for the divine adoption is offered to our free choice.

8. (FATHER) ALMIGHTY. The Father is almighty, creator, and providence of the universe: not only of the heavens, but also of the earth and of the body. He endures the existence of the Devil in order to defeat him more completely through human victory over him. He tolerates sinners in order to grant them a delay for repentance, not impunity. All riches belong to God, not to the Devil, but the wealthy can be justified if they feed the poor.

9. CREATOR. We can know God through his creatures. People offend the Creator when they put heavenly bodies at the service of astrology, or when, like the Manichees, they despise his works. A glance at the spring season with its flowers proves the beauty of material creatures. But God's wisdom is particularly admirable in the creation of humans in their body and soul. We must worship the Creator.

10. (THE ONLY SON AS) LORD. There are many titles of Christ, which suit the needs of each one of us. For those who need to enter, he is the "Gate;" for those who need an intercessor, he is the "High-Priest," the "Mediator" of their prayers; for sinners he made himself the "Sheep" on the altar. He adjusts to the needs of all as a good "Physician". But he remains "Lord" since he created all things according to the will of the Father, and, then, he exercises his lordship over them. He was "Lord" before his incarnation, for we read in Genesis, "Let *us* make man according to *our* image and likeness."

11. THE ONLY SON OF GOD. There are two generations of Christ: the eternal generation as the Only Son of God, and the "Son of David" according to the flesh. The Son does not become Son, but is eternally Son. He is the subsisting Word of God, unlike the human word which vanishes. And the Father did not change because he begot the Son, nor was he deprived of any part of his divinity. The Son enjoyed his glory together with the Father from eternity. The Father created the world through his Son. He can be compared to a king establishing a city through his son.

12. THE INCARNATION. We are invited to share in the mystical Lamb: in his head (his divinity), and in his feet (his human nature). Without his participating in our nature, we could not reach salvation. God took a human nature because humans wanted to talk to a God with a human face. Moreover, since the Devil was using the flesh as an instrument against us, God made use of the flesh for our salvation. The Devil would not have attacked him, had he known that he was God incarnate, but the flesh of Christ was the bait which attracted the Dragon and caused the liberation of those whom the Dragon devoured and kept prisoners.

13. THE CROSS OF CHRIST. We must be proud of the cross of Christ, which was his triumph over death, and our salvation, our liberation from the bondage of sin and death. The power of the cross of Christ is attested by the fear of the devils. Christ really died, and not only in appearance (as say the Gnostics and Manichees). For this reason, our salvation is real, and not in appearance only. His passion was foretold by the prophets. The death of Christ manifested both God's justice and mercy.

We should eagerly seal our forehead with the "sign of the cross"; we should make it over our bread, our drink, when we enter or when we leave, before sleeping, in bed, when we wake up, when we travel, when we rest. It is the sign of believers, and demons fear it. The power of the cross appears in the conversion of so many Christians in all parts of the world!

14. RESURRECTION AND ASCENSION. The resurrection of Jesus is the "good news" which rejoices the hearts of Christians. It was foretold by the prophets. Against the Manichees who teach a resurrection of Christ in appearance only, we must affirm with Paul that, if Christ did not rise again, our faith is vain and our preaching is empty. Christ's Ascension also was announced in the Old Testament. We shall meet Christ in heaven for the judgment.

15. THE END. The first coming of Christ was under the sign of suffering; the second coming will be under the sign of the divine kingship. Cyril gives a long development about the Anti-Christ who must come before. Then, he enlarges on the judgment: nothing good or evil in our deeds will escape the investigation of the Judge. Everything is recorded: every prayer, every psalm, every marriage duly observed, continence kept for God's sake, and more particularly virginity and purity, but, on the other hand, covetous deeds, false oaths, fornication, blasphemy, sorcery, theft, murder.

16-17 THE HOLY SPIRIT. Since sins against the Holy Spirit shall not be forgotten, we must be cautious in our language, and stick to what the Scripture says about the Holy Spirit, without adding anything of our own. Cyril refuses "to divide the Blessed Trinity" (to eliminate the Holy Spirit from the divine Trinity), and refers to the divine works of the Holy Spirit in the soul. Moreover, the Holy Spirit casts devils away through the breath of exorcists; It intercedes for us, and assists us in martyrdom and whenever we are unjustly treated. It works in each one according to the dispositions of each, and suggests what is right. It provides the suitable gifts to bishops, presbyters, deacons, monks, virgins, and all the faithful. It is the inspirer of all, particularly of the prophets. It seals our souls. It was communicated by the laying on of hands of Moses or of Peter. Catechumens receive the spirit in baptism.

In the New Testament, the Holy Spirit is given many names: Spirit, Spirit of Truth, Paraclete, Spirit of God, Spirit of the Father, Spirit of the Lord, Spirit of God and Christ, Spirit of Christ, Spirit of holiness, Spirit of adoption, Spirit of revelation, Spirit of promise, Princely Spirit, Spirit of Wisdom and other spiritual gifts. The Holy Spirit, who spoke through the prophets, came unto the Blessed Virgin in the Incarnation, and inspired Elisabeth, Zachariah, Simeon. It was in John the Baptist from the womb, came on Jesus at his baptism under the appearance of a dove, came on the Apostles at Pentecost. In a few days, the catechumens will be baptized in water and the Holy Spirit: the water will run on their body outside, but the Holy Spirit will baptize their soul, and penetrate it deeply, just as fire penetrates iron.

Once baptized, the new Christians should beware of lying to the Holy Spirit. They will come to baptism and receive from the Holy Spirit this seal which frightens the demons. Not only shall they receive the pardon of their sins, but they shall be able to perform works which surpass the human capacity. They may be given the charisma of prophecy, or any other charisma, and certainly the ordinary fruits of the Holy Spirit: charity, joy, peace, longsuffering, meekness, goodness, faith, purity.

18. RESURRECTION, CHURCH, ETERNAL LIFE. The hope for the resurrection of the dead is the root of all virtuous deeds. Moreover, the resurrection, together with the judgment and reward, are postulated by divine justice. The resurrection is not a work impossible to God, for it is even easier than creation. All shall rise, but not in the same manner: the righteous in glory will join the angels; sinners with a body capable of suffering forever the chastisement of their sins without being destroyed by the eternal fire.

The "Catholic" Church is spread all over the world ("Catholic" means universal geographically). It also heals all kinds of sins, and owns all forms of virtues and spiritual gifts ("Catholic" in the sense of carrying every form of spiritual activity). Eternal life is the plenitude of heavenly gifts. We obtain it through faith, martyrdom, renunciation, obedience to the commandments.

THE MYSTAGOGICAL HOMILIES

1. RENUNCIATION OF SATAN. Facing the West, the neophytes[240] have renounced Satan with his works, pomps, and service. His "works" are all sins; his pomps are the passion of theatre, or eating meat offered to idols, which is sharing with devils; his service is all gestures of idolatry and superstition, for instance the use of amulets on children or the sick, which are the cult of the devil. Then, turning to the East, they have pronounced their allegiance to Christ: they must be diligent now, for the Devil, like a roaring lion, is wandering around them.

[240] Neophytes: the "newly baptized."

Cyril also compared the Devil to Pharaoh, and Christ to Moses, and our fight against evil, and our salvation, to the Exodus of the people of God from Egypt.

2. BAPTISM. The stripping off of clothes symbolized the taking off the "old man" with his sins in order to follow Christ and to triumph together with him. The anointment of the whole body with exorcised oil was, like the oil on the whole body of athletes, a good protection against the attacks of evil spirits. The immersion in the baptismal pool, and the emerging from water, three times, means that, together with Christ, the neophytes died, were buried, and raised again for a new life. Through baptism they died and were born again, and the water of salvation for them appeared to be both a tomb and a mother's womb (in Greek just as in English, "tomb" and "womb" sound almost the same). Christ died in reality: the neophytes only in symbol, but he conquered for them the reality of salvation which he conferred upon them.

3. THE HOLY CHRISM. Their anointment with the holy oil of Chrism has made them new "Christs" ("Christ" means "anointed"). Chrism is an oil of joy, a perfumed oil which symbolizes the gift of Christ, the Holy Spirit. It is not common oil since, just as the Eucharistic bread, after the invocation of the Holy Spirit, is not common bread, but the body of Christ, the oil of Chrism is no longer common oil, for the faithful owe to it their name of "Christians." Moreover, just as in the Old Testament high-priest and king were anointed, the holy oil of Chrism confers on the Christians priesthood and kingship in Christ. Finally, the anointment made on their forehead, ears, nostrils, etc. means that they are given spiritual senses as a shield against the enemy and as a step toward the possession of a "spiritual body."

4. THE EUCHARISTIC FOOD. Cyril insists on the real presence of the body and blood of Christ in the bread and wine after the invocation of the Holy Spirit. Receiving this spiritual bread, the faithful become one body and one blood with Christ, and are "Christ-bearers."

5. THE EUCHARISTIC RITE. Cyril comments on the spiritual meaning of gestures and prayers at Mass. The deacon brings water to the bishop and presbyters for the washing of their hands before the offering. The washing of the hands symbolizes the purification from sins (the hands are the symbol of deeds).

The kiss of peace symbolizes reconciliation between the brethren and the rejection of all hatred.

The priest invites the congregation to abandon all worldly care, and to keep their hearts in heaven with the merciful God. Then, he invites them to give thanks to the Lord, and he pronounces the great Prayer of Thanksgiving, or *Anaphora*, first praising God for the creation of heaven and earth, of the sea, the sun, moon, and stars; then, of the angels, archangels, etc. When he mentions the Cherubim and Seraphim, who surround the throne of God and sing their hymn: "Holy, Holy, Holy, Lord God of Sabaoth," the congregation repeats the same hymn, thereby joining the heavenly choirs.

Then, the transformation of the bread and wine to the body and blood of Christ takes place. It is accomplished by the power of the Holy Spirit who has been invoked, and who sanctifies and transforms whatever he touches.

Then, the priest makes the intercessions for the peace of the Churches, the welfare of the universe, the emperors, the armies, the allies of the Empire, the crippled, the afflicted, all those in need, and the dead: patriarchs, prophets, martyrs, apostles, and all the saints.

Then, the congregation recites the Lord's Prayer, on which Cyril comments briefly. Great is God's mercy, who allows us to call him "Father." We ask that among us his name be sanctified, that God --not sin-- reign over our mortal bodies; that we get the "substantial bread" which feeds the soul and penetrates the whole human being; that we forgive those who offended us so as to be forgiven our sins by God; that we might not be overcome by temptation, but kept free from the bondage of the Wicked One.

Then, the deacon proclaims, "Holy things for the holy!", and the congregation answers, "One is holy, One is Lord..." And, while the cantor sings, "Taste and see how good is the Lord," the congregation comes forward for the communion, which is received in the hand, and each one comes to the cup. After receiving the body of Christ, one answers, "Amen!", and the same after receiving the blood. The Communion helps the faithful to progress in virtue and to avoid sin.

## QUESTIONNAIRE

1. In the "Two Ways" of the *Didache*, find evidence of the Decalogue (the "Ten Commandments" in the Old Testament), then, of precepts of properly Christian inspiration.

2. In the same "Two Ways" find warnings against sins which are more characteristic of pagan society.

3. Discuss the conclusion of the "Two Ways": "If you can bear the Lord's full yoke, you will be perfect. But if you cannot, then, do what you can!"

4. If you had to write a "Two Ways" for the training of converts of our time, what would you emphasize in, delete from, add to, the text given by the *Didache*?

5. Can we say that the Eucharist of the *Didache* conforms to the precept of Jesus at the Last Supper, "Do this in memory of me"? Is the memory of Jesus and of the redemption obvious in the Eucharistic Prayers of the *Didache*?

6. Since the Christian "Old Man" who talked to Justin did not himself rely on philosophical arguments, on what did he rely in order to support his faith in God and Christ?

7. What do we learn about the conversion to Christianity of simple or poor people from the bitter criticism of Celsus?

8. From Celsus' criticism of the Christians, can we discover the failure of philosophy and education to change the hearts and morals of many in his time? What seems to explain the success of the Christians with the simple and the poor?

9. Discuss the statement of Victorinus: "I am a Christian in my heart; is it then the walls that make Christians?"

10. What do you think of the case of Patricius (Augustine's father who was baptized on his death bed): is it hypocrisy? cowardice? apostasy? cunning calculation?

11. Describe the ritual of baptism in Hippolytus' *Apostolic Tradition*. Explain how meaningful are some details of this ritual.

12. Discuss the case between bishop Cyprian of Carthage and bishop Stephen of Rome concerning the validity of baptism conferred by heretics.

13. What was the theological solution given by Augustine in support of the validity of baptism conferred by heretics or sinful ministers?

14. Explain how this controversy on baptism left an impoverished image of baptism to the theologians of the following ages.

15. Comment upon Cyril of Jerusalem's definition of baptism found in *Procatechesis* 16. Do you prefer it to the definition which you learned in your catechism?

16. According to ch.2 ON REPENTANCE, what is the origin of temptation, the danger of foul thoughts, and the remedy suggested by Cyril?

17. How does Cyril explain the spiritual effectiveness of water in baptism (ch.3, INVITATION TO BAPTISM), of oil in the ANOINTMENT, or Confirmation (ch.3, ON THE HOLY CHRISM, in the *Mystagogical Homilies*), of bread and wine

in the Eucharist (, ch. 4, ON THE EUCHARISTIC FOOD, in the *Mystagogical Homilies*)?

18. Show that, according to Cyril of Jerusalem (ch. 13, THE CROSS OF CHRIST, in *Baptismal Catecheses*), the cross of Christ has a particular power, and that the sign of the cross is in constant use in daily Christian life. For Cyril, is it a sign of fear, or a sign of joy?

19. According to Cyril of Jerusalem (ch.16-17, THE HOLY SPIRIT, in *Baptismal Catecheses*), what are the works of the Holy Spirit? What are the common fruits of the Holy Spirit in those who do not receive the particular gifts of prophecy or miracles?

20. How can Cyril of Jerusalem compare baptism to both a "tomb" and a "womb" (ch.2, BAPTISM, in *Mystagogical Homilies*)?

21. Compare the ritual of the Eucharist in your Church and that of Cyril (ch.5,ON THE EUCHARISTIC RITE, in *Mystagogical Homilies*).

## BIBLIOGRAPHY

BOUYER, Louis. *The Eucharist: Theology et Spirituality of the Eucharistic Prayer*, tr. C. U. Quinn. Notre Dame, IN: University of Notre Dame Press, 1968.

CYRIL OF JERUSALEM. *Catechetical Homilies*, LNPF, LCC.

____. *Lectures on the Christian Sacraments*, ed. by F.L. Cross. London: SPCK, 1951.

DIX, Gregory. *The Treatise on the Apostolic Tradition of St. Hippolytus of Rome*, ed. by Gregory Dix, reissued with corrections by H. Chadwick. London: SPCK, 1968.

HAMMAN, A., ed. *Baptism*; *The Mass*; *The Paschal Mystery. Ancient Liturgies and Patristic Texts*, 3 vol. Staten Island, NY: Alba House, 1969.

JEREMIAS, Joachim. *Infant Baptism in the First Four Centuries*. London: SCM, 1960.

____. *The Origin of Infant Baptism*. London: SCM, 1960.

RICHARDSON, Cyril C., ed. *Early Christian Fathers*. (the same as LCC 1).

WILKEN, Robert L. *The Christians as the Romans saw them*. New Haven: Yale University Press, 1984.

YARNOLD, E. *The Awe-Inspiring Rites of Initiation. Baptismal Homilies of the Fourth Century*. Middlegreen: St.Paul Publications, 1971.

# CHAPTER XII

# MARTYRDOM

The Christians had been persecuted for almost three centuries, until the Edict of Milan, 313 A.D. The persecution was not always active, and there were long periods of calm, but the sword was still hanging over the head of the Christians as long as Christianity was an "illicit religion."

Persecution was an unfair and cruel punishment. Following the advice of Christ (Mat. 19:23), Christians tried to escape when it could be done without denying their faith. The apologists of the second and third century did their best to clear their fellow-Christians from accusations of all kinds and to prove that they were good citizens, good servants of God and of humanity.

Yet, Christians were proud of the courage of their martyrs and of their confessors (those who openly profess their faith before a judge in time of persecution). Martyrdom was for the Christians a victory over the forces of evil in the world and over human weakness. It was also faithfulness to God and Christ unto death, the highest evidence of love. Finally, it was the incomparable way to the glory of the Kingdom of God.[241] Their confession of faith and their suffering were considered as evidence of divine assistance as well as submission to the divine will. Baptized and purified in their blood, martyrs were honored as saints. Every year the community, on the day of their death, celebrated their "birthday" to the Kingdom. Relics of martyrs were held as precious.

We shall successively give: 1) an account of persecution in history and law; 2) the testimonies of Tacitus; 3) the martyrdom of Polycarp, and a section of Ignatius' letter to the Romans; 4) an account of Origen's *Exhortation to martyrdom*; 5) sections of Cyprian's letters concerning martyrs and the lapsed; 6) fragments of the *Passion of Perpetua;* 7) reflections on martyrdom.

## I. PERSECUTION IN HISTORY AND LAW[242]

---

[241] Matt. 16:24-27.

[242] For the section, "Martyrdom in Law," I rely on Jacques Moreau, *La persécution du Christianisme dans l'Empire Romain* (Paris: PUF, 1956).

BEFORE THE BIRTH AND DEVELOPMENT OF CHRISTIANITY. Rome seems to have been very liberal regarding freedom of belief and religious practice. But because Rome had a great sense of dignity and was afraid of the dangers of moral subversion from the strange practices of Eastern cults and magic, repeated action was taken against Chaldean and Egyptian mystery religions, and even against philosophers who denied the existence of the gods.

DURING THE FIRST CENTURY. Pilate permitted and enforced the sentence of the Jewish authorities condemning Jesus to death. The case of Paul is similar to that of Jesus, although he appealed to the court of Caesar (c. 59 A.D.).

According to Suetonius, c. 50 A.D., Emperor Claudius expelled the Jews from Rome because of agitation caused by a certain "Chresto" (Christ?). On the other hand, there is no reference to the Christians in the same Claudius' *Epistle to the Alexandrians* concerning the rights --or the limitation of the rights-- of the Jewish communities in Alexandria.

Emperor Nero initiated the persecution against the Christians when he himself was suspected of starting the great fire of Rome (64 A.D.). He accused the Christians, who were hated by the mob, and he perpetrated cruel torments against them in his own gardens. Clement of Rome (c. 95 A.D.) echoes this persecution of Nero, and refers to the death of Peter and Paul, without mentioning the circumstances and time of their martyrdom. The persecution of Nero seems to have been confined to Rome, without occasioning the publication of any decree properly speaking. However, the so-called "Rescript of Nero" was a dangerous antecedent for the persecution of the Christians.

Under Domitian (91-98), Flavia Domitilla, a niece of Consul Flavius Clemens, was executed, according to Eusebius, and many Christians were exiled to Island Pontia. According to Suetonius and Dio Cassius, Flavius Clemens was accused of atheism and sentenced to death, and similarly Consul Glabrio for "disinterest in public duties." According to Hegesippus, Domitian stopped the persecution which he had started and which does not seem to have been important. In many places, however, there were riots against the Christians, and, under the pressure of the populace, Roman authorities were forced to pass judgment on, and punish, Christians. These persecutions were local, and varied in regard to their duration and the number of victims. The Revelation of John reflects such a persecution in Asia.

PERSECUTION UNDER THE ANTONIANS (96-192). Emperor Trajan (96-117) is important in the history of persecutions because of his correspondence with Pliny the Younger, a governor of Bythinia (on the Black See, North of modern Turquey) who asked him for advice concerning the persecution of Christians (c. 112 A.D.). The province of Bythinia had just passed from the mild authority of the Senate to that of the Emperor. There are many Christians, Pliny says, and denunciations, both regular and anonymous. Against the Christians there is no other accusation but their name and their profession of faith. The practice, which Pliny adopted and which Trajan considered as appropriate, was to sentence to death those who refused to sacrifice to the gods, and to set free those who yielded. A Roman governor, Trajan added, was not expected to prosecute Christians by his own initiative, and should reject anonymous denunciations as "unworthy of our time."[243]

Under Trajan, Simeon of Jerusalem and Ignatius of Antioch died as martyrs, probably because of local pressure.

Emperor Hadrian (117-138) was not a persecutor, although pope Telesphorus was martyred during his reign. Justin quotes a decree of Hadrian,[244] forbidding the persecution of Christians, and threatening their denouncers (who benefited from the seizure of possessions).

Under Antoninus (138-161), in spite of the general peace of the Church, we find several martyrs. The Stoic philosopher Emperor Marcus Aurelius (138-161) despised Christians. Although following the moderate policy laid down by Trajan, he allowed local action against Christians, and martyrs multiplied. In 177 A.D., we have the martyrs of Lyons,[245] Polycarp in Smyrna; the progroms mentioned by Tertullian in Rome ("When the Tiber overflows...you shout, The Christians to the lion!"); Justin martyred in Rome.

It seems that Montanism (illustrated by Tertullian in the West), offered a style of Christianity more offensive to the Roman administration: they were conscience-objectors in a time when the Emperor needed soldiers against barbarian attacks on the Danube, and they jockingly disregarded the laws encouraging higher birth rates that were to remedy the lack of men which was a danger for the Empire.

Commodius (180-193) was inconsistent in his attitude, sometimes tolerant and even favorable to the Christians, other times a persecutor, although persecution was more a local affair than an action of the ruler.

PERSECUTION UNDER THE SEVERIANS (193-235). Emperor Septimus Severus (194-211) and the other Severians were not persecutors, although several martyrdoms occurred during their reign. They were syncretists (welcoming and com-

---

[243] Pliny the Younger, *Ep.* X,96-97.

[244] Justin, *2 Apology*, end, in Eusebius, *Ecclesiastical History* IV,9.

[245] Eusebius, *Eccl. Hist.* V,1.

bining various religions), particularly Alexander Severus (222-235). He was the son of Julia Mammaea, a tolerant and cultured woman who encouraged Philostratus to write his *Life of Apollonius of Tyana,* the Pythagorean "saint," and invited Origen, the great Christian theologian and exegete, to talk to her concerning the Christian faith. In the personal shrine of Alexander Severus were the figures of Abraham, Orphaeus, and Jesus.

However, in 202, Septimus Severus forbade both Jewish and Christian proselytism, i.e., conversion,[246] and the Christian communities were scrutinized by Roman police. There were martyrs in Rome, Gaul, Alexandria, Carthage. Origen's father died a martyr in Alexandria, and Perpetua and Felicity in Carthage. Converts and those who converted them were threatened by laws against proselytism.

Caracalla (211-218) granted Roman citizenship to everyone in the Empire (212). Under Caracalla, Christian cemeteries became property of the Church, a fact which proves that the Church was, then, more than "non-existing in law."

Maximinus (235-238), a rough Thracian soldier turned emperor, hated Christians who were favored under the former administration and reluctant to do military duty. He persecuted the heads of Churches,[247] although only for a short time, and few people died. Pontianus and Hippolytus (the pope and the anti-pope) were exiled. There was also a local persecution in Cappadocia (modern Turkey).

The Gordian Emperors (238-248) resumed the tolerant policy of the Severians. Philippus the Arab particularly was favorable to the Christians.

THE PERSECUTION OF DECIUS. Emperor Decius (248-253) was the first great persecutor. A soldier, like Maximinus, he hated Christians for the same reasons. Pope Fabian died in January 250. In the middle of year 250, everyone in the Empire was obliged to sacrifice to the pagan gods and to obtain a certificate of sacrifice. Many Christians did not actually sacrifice, and just managed to get a certificate, or *libellum*, from authorities. But many indeed sacrificed, and became apostates. Their reconciliation after the persecution posed a delicate problem to the Church in many places, especially in Africa. Many also suffered in jail or were martyred.

Emperor Valerian, at first granted peace to the Church. But, between 257 and 259 (when he became prisoner of his Parthian enemies), he persecuted Christians. His purpose seems to have been that of lessening their influence on the state and to confiscate the possessions of Churches in a time of bankruptcy

---

[246] *Historia Augusta*, Severus XVI 9.

[247] Eusebius, *Hist. Eccl.* VI 28.

for the Empire. In 257 A.D. a law, enforced in 258, obliged clergy to sacrifice: the sentence was death in case of refusal. Christian senators and knights were degraded; high class ladies were exiled and their possessions confiscated spolia; officials were sentenced to hard work. But Christians proved to be stronger and more determined in their trial than under Decius. Cyprian was beheaded. Pope Sextus of Rome and many Christians died in this persecution.

Emperor Gallian (253-268) was first associated with his father Valerian, and became the only Emperor from 260 to 268. When Valerian was prisoner, Gallian issued a decree of tolerance: cemeteries were returned to the Church, and bishops were able to represent their Church at court for the recovery of their possessions. However, the Church remained "religio illicita" (an illicit association), and was only tolerated. The same tolerance was granted to Christians in the army. The Church enjoyed 50 years of peace until the fourth century when persecution burst out again.

THE PERSECUTION OF DIOCLETIAN AND THE VICTORY OF CONSTANTINE. Emperor Diocletian (284 to his resignation in 305) and his associate Maximianus restored the imperial power and order, but they also tried to restore pagan religion. They made the adoration of the Caesars compulsory. In 293, Galerius and Constantius Chlorus were associated to the Augusti as Caesars. Galerius influenced Diocletian to initiate a persecution. First, Christians were persecuted in the army: in 300, every soldier was obliged to sacrifice, and similarly every official in the administration.

The first edict of persecution (Feb. 23d, 303) -torn into pieces by a Christian- prescribed the destruction of churches and forbade cult meetings. Christians were not allowed to go to court. High-ranking Christians lost their status, and emancipated Christians were returned to servitude. This persecution was not intended to be bloody, but such hard proscriptions could only lead to blood shed. A second edict (Spring 303) attacked the clergy, making them responsible for political trouble resulting from the persecution. A third edict was issued: Christians who retracted their faith were to be set free, but those who persisted were to be tormented. Diocletian's sickness (304-305) enabled Galerius to issue a fourth edict (304) compelling every citizen in the Empire to sacrifice. Those who refused were to be judged and sentenced to death or to hard labor in a mine.

The persecution was enforced or neglected according to the personal dispositions of the local ruler. Constantius Chlorus (Gaul, Britain) simply destroyed churches without persecuting persons. Maximianus (Spain, Italy, Africa) violently persecuted the Christians, but for a short time. In Africa, Christian "sacred books" were to be delivered to local authorities, but the *thurificatio* (offering of incense to a pagan deity) and *sacrificatio* (sacrifice) were not enforced. In the States of

Diocletian (the East: Arabia, Cappadocia, Pontus, Phrygia, Syria, Phoenicia, Egypt), persecution was hard and atrocious.[248] In the States of Galerius himself (countries along the Danube), persecution was hard, but not important because of the small number of Christians. Nowhere was the fourth edict rigorously enforced.

In 305, Diocletian and Maximianus resigned. Galerius and Constantius Chlorus became Augusti. Finally, the new Tetrarchia consisted of Galerius, Constantine (the son of Constantius Chlorus), Maxentius and Licinius. Constantine and Maxentius were not persecutors. Galerius, sick, renounced the persecution. Licinius, who suceeded him, married Constantine's sister, and became tolerant of Christians.

Only Maximus Daia continued the persecution, violently and methodically. He forbade Christian meetings even in cemeteries, and encouraged cities to ask for more repression of Christians. At the same time, he tried to reorganize pagan worship according to the hierarchical patterns of the Church. He published Apocryphal *Acts of Pilate*, etc. Maximus Daia was defeated by Licinius in April 313.

On June 13th, 313, in Nicomedia, Licinius published an edict returning to the Church freedom of worship and the possessions confiscated during the last persecutions. This edict is known as the "EDICT OF MILAN," and later on, ascribed to Constantine. After the defeat of his rivals, Constantine became the only Ruler (324).

## II. TESTIMONY OF TACITUS

### TACITUS, THE NERONIAN PERSECUTION (after the great fire of Rome, 64 A.D.)

> But all human efforts, all the lavish gifts of the Emperor, and the propitiations of the gods, did not banish the sinister belief that the conflagration was the result of an order (of Nero). Consequently, to get rid of the report, Nero fastened the guilt and inflicted the most exquisite tortures on a class hated for their abominations, called Christians by the populace. Christus, from whom the name had its origin, suffered the extreme penalty during the reign of Tiberius at the hands of one of our procurators, Pontius Pilate, and a deadly superstition, thus checked for the moment, again broke out not only in Judaea, the first source of the evil, but also in the City (Rome), where all things hideous and shameful from every part of the world meet and become popular.

---

[248] Eusebius, *Hist. Eccl.* VIII 12.

> Accordingly, an arrest was first made of all who confessed: then, upon their information, an immense multitude was convicted, not so much of the crime of arson, as of hatred of the human race. Mockery of every sort was added to their deaths. Covered with the skins of beasts, they were torn by dogs and perished, or were nailed to crosses, or were doomed to the flames. These served to illuminate the night when daylight failed.
>
> Nero had thrown open his gardens for the spectacle, and was exhibiting a show in the circus, while he mingled with the people in the dress of a charioteer or drove about in a chariot. Hence, even for criminals who deserved extreme and exemplary punishment, these arose a feeling of compassion: for it was not, as it seemed, for the public good, but to glut one man's cruelty, that they were being destroyed.[249]

## III. MARTYRDOM OF POLYCARP, AND IGNATIUS' EPISTLE TO THE ROMANS

Polycarp, bishop of Smyrna in Asia Minor, was a great figure of the Church of the second century. First he is a bond between the apostolic times and the Church of the Fathers through Irenaeus of Lyons. Then, we find him in Rome, supporting against pope Anicetus the cause of the Quartodeciman tradition, i.e., the Jewish practice of having Easter on Nisan 14. The relation of his martyrdom reflects the quality of his faith in Christ, that of his pastoral life, and his liturgical inspiration. We are also reminded that, since martyrdom is impossible to human forces alone but successful with the help of divine grace, a Christian must be sure that, in his individual case, it is clearly the will of God, and not human presumption. We learn from circumstances (for instance, the fact of being arrested) that it is effectively the will of God, therefore an act of obedience. The presumptuous who denounce themselves to persecuting authorities are running to failure.

> ...Now blessed and noble are all the martyrdoms which have taken place in accordance with the will of God... Some were so torn by the scourges that the structure of their flesh to the inner veins and arteries was exposed to view; but they endured it, so that even the bystanders were moved to pity and lamentation. Some reached a pitch of noble endurance that no one of them let cry or groan escape him, showing to us that in the hours of

---

[249] Tacitus, *Annals* XV 44:2-8, tr. J. Stevenson, *A New Eusebius*, p. 2.

their torture Christ's martyrs were absent from the flesh, or rather that standing by their side their Lord conversed with them. So, giving heed to the grace of Christ, they despised the torments of the world, by a single hour purchasing eternal life...

A certain Quintus by name, a Phrygian, lately arrived from Phrygia, when he saw the beasts, was afraid. It was he who had forced both himself and certain others to come forward of their own accord. After very earnest entreaty he had been persuaded by the Proconsul to take the oath and offer incense. Therefore, brethren, we do not commend those who surrender themselves, for not such is the teaching of the Gospel.

Now the most admirable Polycarp so soon as he heard the news showed no dismay, but wished to remain in town. The majority, however, prevailed on him to withdraw. And withdraw he did, to a little farm not far from the city. There he spent his time with a few companions, occupied night and day in nothing but prayer for all men, and for the Churches throughout the world, as indeed was his constant habit. And while praying he fell into trance three days before his apprehension, and he saw his pillow burned by fire. And he turned and said to his companions, "I must needs be burned alive."

As his pursuers were persistent, he shifted his quarters to another farm. Immediately the pursuers arrived (at his first hiding place) and, on failing to find him, they seized two slave-boys. One of these confessed under torture. For indeed it was impossible for him to evade pursuit, since they that betrayed him were of his own household. Accordingly, having the lad with them, on Friday at about supper-time they went out, constables and mounted men, with their usual equipment, hurrying as against a thief. Late in the day they came up in a body and found him in a cottage lying in an upper room. He could have escaped thence to another place, but he refused, saying, "God's will be done." So, on hearing of their arrival, he came down and conversed with them, while they wondered at his age and constancy, and at there being so much haste about the arrest of such an old man. Upon this he gave orders for something to be served for them to give him an hour, that he might pray undisturbed. On their granting him this he stood up and prayed, being so full of the grace of God, that for the space of two hours he could not hold his peace, and the hearers were astonished, and many were sorry that they had come after so venerable an old man.

After remembering all, both small and great, high and low, who had ever come his way, and all the Catholic Church throughout the world, at last he brought his prayer to an end. The time had come for departure. They set him on an ass and brought him into the city... As Polycarp was entering the stadium, there came a voice to him from heaven, "Be strong, Polycarp, show yourself a man." The speaker indeed no one saw, but the voice was heard by those of our friends who were present. Then he was brought forward, and great was the din as they heard that Polycarp was arrested. So he was brought before the Proconsul, who asked him if he were Polycarp? He said, "Yes", and the Proconsul tried to persuade him to deny his faith, urging, "Have respect to your old age," and the rest of it, according to the customary form, "Swear by the genius of Caesar; change your mind; say, Away with the Atheists!" Then Polycarp looked with a stern countenance on the multitude of lawless heathen gathered in the stadium, and waved his hands at them, and looked up to the heaven with a groan, and said, "Away with the Atheists!" The Proconsul continued insisting and saying, "Swear, and I release you; curse Christ." And Polycarp said, "Eighty-six years have I served him, and he has done me no wrong: how can I blaspheme my King who saved me?"

The Proconsul continued to persist and to say, "Swear by the genius of Caesar;" he answered, "If you vainly imagine that I would swear by the genius of Caesar, as you say, pretending that you are ignorant who I am, hear plainly that I am a Christian. And if you are willing to learn the doctrine of Christianity, appoint a day, and listen." The Proconsul then said, "Persuade the people." Polycarp then said, "You, indeed, I should have deemed worthy of argument, for we have been taught to render to authorities and powers ordained by God, honor as is meet, so long as it does no harm, but as for those, I do not think them worthy of making my defence to them." The Proconsul said, "I have wild beasts; if you will not change your mind I will throw you to them." Then Polycarp said, "Bid them to be brought; change of mind from better to worse is not a change that we are allowed; but to change from wrong to right is good." Then again said the Proconsul to him, "If you despise the beasts, unless you change your mind, I shall have you burnt." But Polycarp said, "You threaten the fire that burns for an hour, and after a little while is quenched; for you are ignorant of the fire of the judgment to come, and of everlasting punishment reserved for the ungodly. But why delay? Do what you wish."

While speaking these words and many more he was filled with courage and gladness: his face grew full of grace, so that not only did it not fall agitated at all that was being said to him, but on the contrary the Proconsul was amazed, and sent his own herald to make proclamation in the middle of the stadium thrice, "Polycarp has confessed himself to be a Christian." No sooner was this proclaimed by the herald that the whole multitude, both of Gentiles and of Jews dwelling at Smyrna, with ungovernable rage and a loud voice began to yell --"This is the teacher of Asia, the father of the Christians, the destroyer of our gods, the man who teaches many not to sacrifice or worship..."

This happened with great speed; the mob in a moment got together logs of faggots from the workshops and baths... When the pyre had been made ready, Polycarp took off his upper garments, and untied his girdle. He endeavoured also take off his shoes, though he had never been in the habit of doing this, because every one of the faithful was eager to be the first to touch his bare body. Because of the goodness of his life he had been treated with every honor even before his head was white. Forthwith then all the gear adapted for the pyre was put about him. They were on the point of fastening him with nails, but he said, "Let me be as I am: he that gives me power to abide the fire will grant me too without your making me fast with nails to stay at the pyre unflinching." So they did not nail him, but they bound him. He put his hands behind and was bound, like a godly ram out of a great flock for an offering, a whole-burnt offering made ready and acceptable to God. Then he looked up to heaven and said:

"O Lord God Almighty, Father of thy beloved Child, Jesus Christ, through Whom we have received full knowledge of thee, the God of Angels and powers, and of all creation, and of the whole family of the righteous, who live before thee! I bless thee, that Thou hast granted me this day and hour, that I may share, among the number of the martyrs, in the cup of thy Christ, for the resurrection to everlasting life, both of soul and body in the immortality of the Holy Spirit. And may I, today, be received among them before Thee, as a rich and respectable sacrifice, as Thou, the God who lies not and is truth, hast prepared beforehand, and shown forth, and fulfilled. For this reason I also praise Thee for all things, I bless Thee, I glorify Thee through the everlasting and heavenly high Priest, Jesus Christ, thy beloved Child, through whom be glory to Thee with him and the Holy Spirit, both now and for the ages that are to come, Amen." (14)[250]

## IGNATIUS OF ANTIOCH: HIS DESIRE OF MARTYRDOM (*Ep. to the Romans*)

Like the apostle Paul, bishop Ignatius of Antioch was led to Rome under a guard of ten soldiers, and was permitted to stay for a while in Churches on his way. Like Paul also he wrote precious letters to these Churches. In Smyrna he was received by Polycarp. In the present letter, he begs the Christians of Rome --to whom he certainly ascribes more influence than they had in the palace-- not to intervene in his behalf. He has been received as a martyr. As a preacher, he has been a Christian in words. But now, he must be a Christian in deeds, i.e., imitate the passion of Jesus Christ.

> ...For if you are silent concerning me (if you do not intercede for me in order to prevent my death in martyrdom), I shall become a "man of God;" but if you show your love to my flesh, I shall again have to run my race. Pray, then, do not seek to confer any greater favor upon me than that I be sacrificed to God while the altar is still prepared; that, being gathered in love, you may sing praise to the Father, through Jesus Christ, that God has deemed me, the bishop of Syria, worthy to be sent forth from the East unto the West. It is good to set from the world unto God, that I may rise again to him... Only request on my behalf both inward and outward strength, that I may not only speak, but truly will; and that I may not only be called a Christian, but really be found to be one...
>
> Suffer me to become food for the wild beasts, through whose instrumentality it will be granted me to attain God. I am the wheat of God, and let me be ground by the teeth of the wild beasts, that I may be found the pure bread of Christ... May I enjoy the wild beasts that are prepared for me; and I pray they may be found eager to rush upon me, which also I will entice to devour me speedily, and not deal with me as with some, whom, on fear, they have not touched. But if they be unwilling to assail me, I will compel them to do so. Pardon me: I know what is for my benefit. Now I begin to be a disciple. And let no one, of things visible and invisible, envy that I should attain to Jesus Christ. Let fire and the cross; let cutting off of members; let shatterings of the

---

[250] *The Apostolic Fathers*, tr. Kirsopp Lake, The Loeb Classical Library, Vol.2, pp.313-333 abbreviated.

> whole body; and let all the dreadful torments of the devil come upon me: only let me attain to Jesus Christ...
>
> Suffer me to obtain pure light: when I have gone thither, I shall indeed be a "man of God." Permit me to be an imitator of the passion of my God.. If any has him within himself, let him consider what I desire, and let him have sympathy with me, as knowing how I am straightened... Even should I, when present with you, exhort you to it (to intervene on my behalf), be you persuaded not to listen to me, but rather give credit to those things which I now write to you... My love has been crucified, and there is no fire in me desiring to be fed; but there is within me a water that liveth and speaketh, saying in me inwardly, Come to the Father. I have no delight in corruptible food, nor in the pleasures of this life. I desire the bread of God, the heavenly bread, the bread of life, which is the flesh of Jesus Christ, the Son of God who became man after the seed of Abraham; and I desire the drink of God, namely his blood, which is incorruptible love and eternal life...[251]

## IV. ORIGEN, *EXHORTATION TO MARTYRDOM.*

Son of a martyr, Origen lived for many years under the threat of martyrdom. He visited confessors --some among his disciples-- in jail and assisted them in their martyrdom. Origen himself suffered for the faith in jail during the persecution of Decius (250 A.D.). He died soon afterwards without receiving the crown of martyrdom.

In his *Exhortation to Martyrdom*, Origen exhorts his friends in jail against the temptation of surrendering: a long desired union with God will be granted to them, and an eternal reward is waiting for them, if only they accept to suffer an hour. They should give thanks for this grace of God. On the other hand, they should know that God is a "jealous God," who does not condone idolatry and apostasy. Jesus will acknowledge before his Father only those who confessed his name upon earth. A disciple brought to trial has no escape but martyrdom. A confessor should not look back at his possessions, even at his children --God will provide for them--, lest he give place to the devil. A martyr is a follower of Christ, who takes up his cross after Christ: such is our engagement at baptism when we promise faithfulness to Christ. Martyrs are watched by both angels and humans: they must not fail and join the fallen angels.

Origen quotes intances of martyrdom in full text from both the Old and the New Testament.

---

[251] Ignatius of Antioch, *To the Romans*, tr. ANF 1, pp.73f.

There is no reason why Christians should fail: "they can drink the chalice of salvation if they call upon the name of the Lord."

Answering an objection, Origen interprets the trouble of Jesus at Gethsemani not as an evidence of weakness, but as a hesitation concerning knowledge of the will of God, i.e., whether it was, or was not, the kind of death expected from him by God.

Martyrdom is a baptism of blood for the remission of the sins committed after the baptism of water. It is also a work of atonement, "a sacrifice for many."

Martyrdom can be considered as the bliss of Christ. In martyrdom we are sure of building on the rock (on Christ), and we prove to be "the good tree" spoken of in the Gospel. Martyrdom is superior to mere justification (through baptism), since it is exaltation and glory together with Christ.[252]

Origen kept a nostalgia for the time of persecution. He said:

> There were real faithful in the past, when Christians were martyred, when, coming back from the cemetery after burying martyrs, we went to our assemblies, and the whole Church was present, without trembling, and catechumens were trained in the closeness of martyrdom and of the death of those who confessed the truth "unto death," without being "frightened," or shaken in their faith in the living God.[253]

## V. MARTYRS AND THE LAPSED ACCORDING TO THE EPISTLES OF CYPRIAN

Cyprian was bishop of Carthage during the persecution of Decius (250 A.D.), and died as a martyr under Valerian (258A.D.). His withdrawal from the city during the persecution --Cyprian followed the advice of the Gospel-- provided members of his clergy who envied his authority with an opportunity to take over the government of his Church, and even to give him a successor. For awhile, before he could come back, Cyprian governed his divided Church from a distance, through epistles.

The question of the *lapsed* (those Christians who had sacrificed to the gods, or simply obtained a certificate of sacrifice from civil authorities) was particularly delicate. Cyprian's opponents won the minds of certain confessors who

---

[252] A resume of Origen, *On Martyrdom.* Cf translation in ACW 19.

[253] Origen, *Homilies on Jeremiah* IV 3.

wrote recommendations for lapsed individuals, sometimes without even identifying these individuals. Paul the martyr, they said, had reconciled all the lapsed by the merits of his own passion. But Cyprian required from the lapsed a time of penance which would prove the sincerity of their repentance. Cyprian was able to remedy this confusion through agreement on a common policy about penance for the lapsed between bishops in Africa and overseas, particularly with the clergy and bishop of Rome. Cyprian's treatise *On the Lapsed* was written in the heat of this controversy.

However, Cyprian was not a hard man, but compassionate, and willing to be as liberal as possible. Before a year was up, the lapsed were reconciled because of a danger of contagious disease and of the threat of a new persecution: how could the Eucharistic blood of Christ be refused to Christians expected to pour their own blood for Christ?

Cyprian's *Epistle 10.* Cyprian praises the confessors for their courage: Mother Church is proud of her children! In the camp of God, the soldiers of Christ are eager to fight. Some of them have already won the crown of martyrdom. Those who were tormented proved to be stronger than their executioners. The contest was a beautiful spectacle offered by the Lord, for the death of the righteous is precious in the eyes of God,[254] and martyrdom is a contest for the crown of justice.[255] Mother Church is mourning, indeed, over the apostasy of many, but she is strengthened by the fidelity of her confessors. There were in the past white crowns only, the crowns of virtue: the purple crowns of martyrdom are now offered to us.

Cyprian's *Epistles 38,39.* Cyprian is writing to his clergy and brethren concerning ordinations. Since he is away from them, he cannot consult them and examine together with them the conduct and merit of each one of the candidates. However, the testimony of the Lord in their particular cases makes human testimony unnecessary. Aurelius, one of the candidates, is a virtuous man, and has confessed Christ twice: in exile and in suffering. Because of his young age, he is made a reader, and it befits a confessor to read the Gospel of Christ! Celerinus, another confessor, was hesitant to join the clergy, but he was warned in a vision to yield. He is recommended by his courage in his trial, and by the merits of his family which counts several martyrs. Aurelius and Celerinus have been selected for the priestly dignity. They shall receive the monthly wages together with the priests, but will sit with the priests only when they are old enough.

Cyprian's *Epistle 57*, about the lapsed. After one year of penance, Cyprian thinks that the lapsed (those who sacrificed

---

[254] Ps. 115:15.

[255] 2 Tim. 4:7-8.

to the gods during the persecution) ought to be reconciled, i.e.,granted peace and admitted to the Eucharistic communion. They have not left the Church, and, from the very day of their fall, they have done penance with lamentations and prayers. They should be granted peace without delay so as to be strong in the upcoming persecution. They need the help of the Eucharist, not because they are sick (as the "Viaticum" given to the sick and dying), but because they need to be strengthened: who could, indeed, impose on a Christian to give his blood in confession, if he is refused the communion of the blood of Christ? For the same purpose Cyprian celebrates the Eucharist daily.

Cyprian answers the objection that a martyr who is baptized in his own blood is forgiven his sins, and, therefore, does not need to receive the peace from the bishop since he received it from God. The answer is that the Eucharist --which a sinner can receive only if he has been granted peace by the bishop-- is necessary to strengthen the soul of martyrs: how could the Spirit of the Father speak in the confession of a Christian who has not recovered it in the gift of peace?

Cyprian's *Epistle 58.* Cyprian cites examples of martyrdom in both the Old and the New Testament. Christ, our Lord, suffered first, and those who want to join him must obey and imitate him, therefore, they must consent to suffering. Since the Son of God suffered in order to make us sons of God, we cannot refuse to suffer in order to persevere as sons of God. The world, which loves its own, hates the Christians who do not belong to the world. Since martyrdom is a spectacle given to the angels, the lapsed must be given their weapons, and recover what they had lost in a former contest. Martyrdom is a festivity, the day in which we join Christ and the saints, in which the glory of God will shine upon us. On the contrary, those who yield to the will of the Devil shall be sent to the everlasting fire.[256]

## VII. THE PASSION OF ST. PERPETUA.

The Passion of Perpetua is an account made by Perpetua herself, a young woman arrested for her faith, of her own confession and suffering in the jail, and of those of her companions, particularly Felicity, a slave-woman, and a deacon Saturus. Tertullian may be the compiler who put the whole story together. Because of the emphasis laid on the role of the Holy Spirit and on the gift of prophecy, this group of confessors may belong to the Montanists (a sect of charismatics of the second century with a tendency to excessive severity). But we find the same assistance of the Holy Spirit and the same gift of prophecy in other martyrdoms. According to the word of Jesus, the dis-

[256] A translation of Cyprian's *Epistles* can be found in ANF and in the Fathers of the Church (Deferari).

ciples should not worry about being brought to a tribunal and tried for their faith, for the Holy Spirit will inspire in them the right answer.

The visions of Perpetua are very interesting for their contents: not only do they manifest the experience of heavenly things integrated by the confessors in the events of their life, but these visions show features which are characteristic of feminine experience and mark them with the seal of authenticity.[257]

> PERPETUA AND HER COMPANIONS ARE PUT INTO JAIL. In a brief space of time we were baptized; and the Spirit intimated to me that I was not to expect anything else from my baptism but sufferings of the flesh. A few days later we were received into the prison, and I shuddered because I had never experienced such gloom. O awful day! fearful heat arising from the crowd and from the jostling of the soldiers! Finally I was racked with anxiety for my infant there. Then Tertius and Pomponius, blessed deacons who were ministering to us, arranged by bribery for us to go forth for a few hours and gain refreshment in a better part of the prison. I suckled my child, who was already weak from want of nourishment... I then arranged that my child should remain with me in the prison. And immediately I gained strength, being relieved from anxiety about the child; and my prison suddenly became to me a palace, so that I preferred to be there rather than anywhere else....
>
> THE VISION OF THE LADDER. And I prayed, and this vision was shown to me: I see a brazen ladder of wondrous size reaching up to heaven; narrow, moreover, so that only one could go up it at once, and on its sides every kind of iron instrument fixed --swords, lances, hooks, daggers-- so that if one went up carelessly, or not fixing one's attention upwards one would be torn, and pieces of one's flesh would be left on the iron implements. There was also lying under the ladder a dragon of wondrous size, which laid snares for those climbing it, and frightened them from the ascent.
> Now Saturus (the deacon) went up first. He had given himself up voluntarily after our arrest on our account, because he had taught us the faith, and he had not been present on the occasion of our trial. When he got to the top of the ladder he turned and said to me, "Perpetua, I am waiting for you; but take care that that dragon does not bite you." And I said, "In the name of Jesus Christ he shall not hurt me." And the dragon, as if afraid of me, slowly thrust his head underneath the ladder itself;

---

[257] We give abbreviated sections of the translation of T.H. Bindley (London: SPCK, 1900).

and I trod upon his head as if I were treading on the first step. And I went up and saw a large space of garden, and in the midst a man with white hair sitting, in the garb of a shepherd, tall, milking sheep; and a white-robbed host standing round him. and he lifted his head and saw me, and said, "Welcome, child;" and he called me and gave me a piece of the cheese which he was making, as it were a small mouthful, which I received with joined hands and ate; and all those around said "Amen." And at the sound of the word I awoke, still tasting something sweet. This vision I told at once to my brother, and we understood that we were about to suffer martyrdom, and we began to give up every earthly hope....

(AT THE TRIBUNAL) my turn came. And my father appeared on the spot with my boy, and drew me down from the step, praying to me, "Pity thy child." Then Hilarian the procurator... said, "Spare thy father's grey hairs; spare thy infant boy. Sacrifice for the safety of the Emperor." And I replied, "I do not sacrifice." "Art thou a Christian?" asked Hilarian; and I said, "I am." And when my father persisted in endeavouring to make me recant, he was ordered down by Hilarian and beaten with a rod. And I felt it as keenly as though I had been struck myself; and I was sorry for his miserable old age. Then he pronounced sentence against us all, and condemned us to the beasts; and we joyfully went down to the prison. (The child is taken off from her), but God willed it that neither the child any longer desired the breasts, nor did they cause me pain.

THE VISION OF THE EGYPTIAN GLADIATOR. In my dream, I wondered why the beasts were not sent to me. And a certain Egyptian of terrible aspect came forth against me along with his assistants, ready to fight with me. There came also to me comely young men as my assistants and helpers. And I was smoothed down and changed my sex. And they began to rub me down with oil, as is customary for a contest. And I see that Egyptian opposite rolling in the dust. And a certain man came forth, of wondrous size, whose height was greater than the amphitheater, wearing a loose purple robe with two broad stripes over the middle of his breast, and embroidered shoes wrought of gold and silver. He carried a rod like a fencing-master, and a green branch on which were golden apples. Calling for silence he said, "This Egyptian, if he conquer her, shall kill her with the sword, but if she conquer him she shall receive this branch." And he went away. And we approach each other, and begin to exchange blows. He was trying to catch me by the feet, but I was striking his face with my heels. And I was borne aloft in the air, and began to strike him as though I were not treading upon the ground. And when I saw we were wasting time I joined my hands and interlocked my fingers. Then I caught him by the head, and he fell on his face and I trampled on his head. And the people began to shout, and my assistants to sing psalms. And I went to the fencing-master and received the branch. And he gave me a kiss, and said to me, "Daughter, peace be with thee." ...And I understood that I was destined not to fight against the beasts, but against the Devil; but I knew that victory would be mine.

SATURUS' VISION OF THE HEAVENLY TEMPLE. And we approached a place, the walls of which were as though they were built of light, and before the door four angels were stationed, who robed those entering with white garments. And we entered in, and heard a chorus of voices saying incessantly, "Holy, holy, holy!" And we saw in that place as it were an old man sitting, with snowy hair but a youthful countenance, whose feet we saw not. And on his right hand and on his left four elders; and behind them many more elders were standing. And entering in with wonder we stood before the throne. And the four angels raised us up, and we kissed him, and with his own hand he passed across our face. And the rest of the elders said to us, "Let us stand." And we stood and gave the sign of peace. And they said to us, "Go and play." And I said to Perpetua, "You have your desire;" and she said to me, "Thanks be to God, that, however happy I was in the flesh, I am happier here now."

A MEANINGFUL ANSWER OF FELICITY. Felicity gave birth in jail, and one of the jailers said to her, "What will you, who cry out so much now, do when thrown to the beasts?"... She replied, "Now it is I who suffer; but then there will be Another by my side who will suffer for me, because it is for him that I shall be suffering."

THE DAY OF MARTYRDOM. When they were brought to the gate, and were compelled to put on costumes, the men that of the priests of Saturn, and the women that of devotees of Ceres, Perpetua fought against this disgrace, saying, "We have so far come to this willingly, lest our liberty should be taken away; we have pledged our life that we will do no such thing; this is the very bargain we have made with you." Injustice recognized injustice: the Tribune allowed them to be led in simply in whatever attire they were. Perpetua sang a psalm, already trampling on the head of the Egyptian. Revocatus and Saturninus uttered warning threats to the spectators, and told Hilarian, "You may judge us, but God will judge you."...

Now for the young women the devil prepared a mad cow... And so they were brought forth, stripped and enclosed in nets. The crowd shuddered, seeing one, a delicate girl, and the other fresh from childbirth with dripping breasts. In such plight they were called back and clothed with loose garments. Perpetua was tossed first and fell on her loins, and sitting up she drew back the tunic, which had been torn from her side, to cover her thigh, mindful of her modesty rather than of her sufferings. This done she tied up her loosened hair; for it was not becoming for a martyr to suffer with dishevelled hair, lest she should seem to be mourning in her glory. So she arose, and when she saw Felicity tossed, she approached her and gave her her hand and lifted her up. Both stood equally firm, and, the cruelty of the crowd being conquered, they were called back to the gate *Sanavivaria*... There Perpetua, as if awaking out of sleep (so completely was she in the Spirit and in ecstasy), began to look around and, to the utter astonishment of every one, said, "I wonder when we are going to be led forth to that cow." And when she had heard that it had already happened she did not at first believe it, until she saw some marks of the tossing on her body and her dress. Then having sent for her brother, she addressed him and the catechumen, saying, "Stand fast in the faith and let all love each other; and let not our suffering be a stumbling block to you."

THE DEATH OF SATURUS AND OF PERPETUA... At the end of the show, when a leopard was let loose, Saturus poured forth from one bite so great a quantity of blood that the people shouted out to him as he turned round what amounted to a testimony to his second baptism, "Well washed; well washed!" Thereupon, already half dead, he was laid along with the others in the accustomed place for the throat-cutting... They had already before this mutually exchanged the kiss, in order to complete the martyrdom by the solemn rite of the peace. The rest were unable to move and received the sword in silence. Saturus was the first to yield his spirit; for he was waiting for Perpetua. As for Perpetua, she guided the uncertain hand of the clumsy gladiator to her own throat... O most brave and blessed martyrs! O truly called and elect for the glory of our Lord Jesus Christ!

## VIII. REMARKS ON MARTYRDOM

Certain people say, or at least think, that our martyrs are fanatics, and that they love glory, or foster an insane desire of suffering and death. In order to make their point, they quote the words of the martyrs, particularly those of Ignatius of Antioch, which they take out of context. They ignore that baptism includes a promise to be faithful to Christ which may require suffering and death.

Sometimes it seems that our martyrs accept suffering because they refuse to yield on a detail which ought not to be given such importance. For instance, the Maccabean martyrs, who were Jews, died because they refused to eat a bite of pork meat. And Polycarp refused to swear by the genius of Caesar. Was throwing a grain of incense on an altar an act of faith in the gods for a Christian, while it was almost an indifferent gesture for a pagan? Actually, the gesture or word asked for by the enemy of our faith, and refused by a Christian believer, is more than mere detail. What is at stake is the Christian faith in the absolute sense. For a Christian, there is no hesitation: Christ will acknowledge before his Father those only who acknowledged him, and deny those who denied him.

There are martyrs even in our times --maybe more than ever in Christian history, for instance in the last fifty years in Russia, China, Spain, Central or South America, Africa, without mentioning other countries. Just like the early Christians, the Christians of today, when the faith itself (not status or privilege) is at stake, have proved to be faithful unto death like genuine believers.

Early Christianity also had its apostates. Although resulting from weakness, apostasy was not just treated as a bad memory of the past, but required repentance, and all sins can be forgiven by God. Mother Church did not grant them a cheap and deceiving peace, but combined her severity and her mercy in the process of their reconciliation, as we see in the Epistles of Cyprian and in his treatise *On the Lapsed*.

We may be surprised by the hatred of the populace for the Christians from the beginning, in spite of the commandment of love which governed Christian behavior. Even in our times, the Christian faith is a disturbing agent in a society well established in its persuasions and privileges. As a religion, Christianity necessarily enters a manner of competition with other religions, and particularly with such modern forms of religion as the totalitarian regimes of Fascism or Marxism. In antiquity, the existence of pagan religion under its thousand forms, and more particularly its taboos, was a dreadful obstacle to the presence of Christianity. For not only did the Christians disregard the gods, but their behavior offended them, and their readiness to touch a corpse --a relic-- without customary purifications was considered by the pagans as a cause of pollution for all those who met them. Pagan life was a network of superstitions, and Christianity appeared as a profanation. The Christians were not wrong when they contended that, through idolatry and superstition, the pagans were prisoners of the Devil. Christianity came as a revolution, and emancipated the world from the terrible bondage of superstitious practices which pervaded domestic and social life.

The cruelty of martyrdom also requires some explanation. First, the narratives transmitted to us are those of outstanding cases, where cruelty seems to have passed the common measure. Probably many Christian martyrs died the same miserable death like thousands and thousands poor wretches sentenced to death unjustly, and for reasons which today would hardly lead them to jail. Many of them were given as a spectacle to the crowd which delighted in shows of "gladiators." Ancient society was cruel. Sometimes modern society shows the same instincts.

Modern society, at least in our highly civilized countries, has lost --fortunately-- the experience of suffering, and it even attempts to hide the dreadful aspects of death. Modern medicine remedies many illnesses, and generally almost suppresses suffering. For this reason, suffering in its bare reality, and sometimes death itself, appear as a scandal. It was not the same in antiquity, not even fifty years ago! Suffering was part of common life, and death generally implied lots of suffering. No wonder that death could be considered as atonement for sins, if, of course, it was offered up as such. In this context, martyrdom appears to be closer to human experience.

Motivation was high in Christian martyrdom. Not only did a martyr, at the cost of one hour of suffering, win eternal life and the kingdom of heaven, but he, or she, was obeying the will of God, and was thereby sure of the divine assistance in the ordeal. Martyrs admitted that, for a mere human cause and with mere human means, they would have given up, and not endured such sufferings, but, being sure of the will of God, they were sure also of his assistance. We read that those who denounced themselves often failed, for they were obeying the human will, not that of God.

We now reach the heart of the question. A martyrdom is not exactly a human achievement, but a divine work. The Holy Spirit is working in martyrdom, and strengthening the soul of the martyr who lifts his heart up to God in prayer. Martyrs sing psalms, show courage and joy, often are ecstatic, i.e., seem to forget physical suffering because their soul is full of the divine presence. Their answers to the judge and their whole behavior shows spiritual intelligence and determination. They speak, and suffer, as if Another --Felicity said-- was by their side, and assuming their suffering.

The evidence of divine power in martyrs sometimes reaches the hearts of unbelievers, who convert to the Christian faith in spite of the threat attached to it. But the Christian community rejoices at the victory of her martyrs, and sees in it the victory of God over the enemy, and the most powerful encouragement. They keep and honor the relics of their martyrs; later, these relics may become object of superstition, but they remain an object of trust. When the persecutions were over, the Christians kept a memory of these privileged hours when they came back to church after one of their brethren had just won the crown of martyrdom, and the power of the Spirit of God was still filling their hearts.

As for the confessors, who came back from jail to the community after the persecution, their prestige was high, for they too, in their courageous confession, proved to have acted under the inspiration of the Holy Spirit. After the sad spectacle of apostasy and division, Cyprian was happy to see a young confessor reading the Gospel in his church! Confessors had a role in the reconciliation of sinners. Because of their merit, and probably more because of the spiritual gift which they had manifested in their confession, their opinion concerning a repenting sinner had a great weight. Certain confessors abused this authority, for instance in Carthage, when they turned against bishop Cyprian. Finally, when a confessor was to be made a priest, the bishop did not lay his hand on him, for it would be inappropriate to lay hands on one who was already in possession of the Holy Spirit.

## QUESTIONNAIRE

1. Ignatius has been categorized as an insane man, a fanatic, a poet, a mystic: what do you think?

2. Why is it so important for the author of the *Martyrdom of Polycarp* to be sure that martyrdom is the will of God and not of human will ( i.e., martyrdom is imposed by circumstances, and Christians should not denounce themselves to civil authorities)?

3. Can you interpret Polycarp's divine voice saying to him, "Be a man!", and a similar statement from Ignatius? What kind of "man"? Why not say, "a true disciple" (which you find also)? Is it an exaltation of human will contradicting what we find in question 2 ?

4. Is there a difference between antiquity and today regarding suffering which made martyrdom not that much worse than ordinary suffering?

5. Do you find evidence in the texts for a divine help granted to martyrs? Describe it. Can we say that martyrs suffered less because they were praying, singing, in ecstasy (their mind was elsewhere, with Christ in heaven)? Did they believe that the "will of God" also implied the assurance of the "help of God"?

6. What were the reasons motivating martyrdom on the part of Christians?

7. What were the reasons motivating the persecution of Christians on the part of the pagans?

8. Can you compare the prayer of Polycarp on the pyre to the Eucharistic prayers at Mass? Can we do something similar in case of personal suffering?

9. How can you explain Tertullian's maxim, *Sanguis martyrum semen Christianorum* (the blood of martyrs is the seed of new Christians)?

10. In your opinion, what would Christians do today in case of persecution? What have they done in the recent past?

11. Explain the main points made by Origen in his *Exhortation to Martyrdom*. Do you find the same in Cyprian's Epistles?

12. What was the importance of the acts of Nero and of Trajan regarding persecution? Why were Christians a "religio illicita" (illicit religion)? What should they have done in order to be tolerated by the Pontifex Maximus (the Minister of cults)? Was Rome in principle and fact tolerant of religions?

13. When did persecution become violent locally, and then generally in the Roman Empire? How can you explain the reaction of the mob to Christianity? of the Emperors?

14. Was it a serious thing to say, "Caesar is Lord," or to swear by the genius of the Emperor?

15. Do you find some evidence of the principle of "non-violence" in the behavior of the Christians which, when made more obvious, may have partly been the cause of certain persecutions?

16. Were there questions of money involved in denunciations of Christians to the authorities?

17. Mention some names of martyrs.

18. What do you think of Perpetua's struggle against the will of her pagan father, and regarding her baby?

19. Explain that Perpetua is a "prophet," but a prophet very feminine in her style?

20. Did the Christian community help the confessors in jail?

21. Explain Perpetua's vision of the "bronze ladder".

22. Explain Perpetua's vision of the contest against the Egyptian gladiator?

23. What feelings could the suffering and death of Perpetua, and her behavior generally, suggest to a pagan who is not vicious but is a lover of truth, although he may not share our beliefs and may be full of prejudice against the Christians?

24. Is not there an abuse of the term "martyr" today? Make the difference between "martyr" in the Christian sense, and "martyr" of a human cause?

## BIBLIOGRAPHY

ATHENAGORAS. *A Plea for the Christians.* ACW, or LCC 1, pp. 300-340.

BINDLEY, T.H., trans. *The Epistle of the Gallican Churches Lugdunum and Vienna, with an appendix containing Tertullian's Adress to Martyrs, and The Passion of St. Perpetua.* London: SPCK, 1900.

CYPRIAN. *The Lapsed*, tr. M. Bevenot. ACW 25, 1957.

EUSEBIUS OF CAESAREA. *Ecclesiastical History.*

FREND, W. H. C. *Martyrdom and Persecution in the Early Church.* New York: Doubleday, 1967.

JUSTIN, I Apology. LCC 1, pp. 242-289.

MOREAU, Jacques. *La persecution du Christianisme dans l'Empire Romain.* Paris: PUF, 1956.

ORIGEN. *On Prayer. Exhortation to Martyrdom.* ACW, 1954.

TERTULLIAN. *Apology.* ANF.

## CHAPTER XIII

## EARLY MONASTICISM

Christian monasticism properly speaking, i.e., a movement of withdrawal from the world to a desert or a cloister, began with Antony at the end of the third century, and flourished in the fourth century. Since then it has developed as part and parcel of the Church.

Monasticism was not a substitute for martyrdom, in a Church of half-converted Christians attracted by the conversion of Emperor Constantine. According to this opinion, disgusted by the low morals of the newly established Church after Constantine, the Christian elite took refuge in the desert. In fact, monasticism was the ripe fruit of a spiritually productive Church, which had antecedents in past generations and was not born from discontent. Although some of the great monastic characters and probably many simple monks joined the movement in order to escape the harassing burden of paying taxes and assuming civil or military duties, their presence does not explain the existence or the ideals of monasticism.

Monasticism was born from a need for contemplative life and perfection, which is inherent in Christianity from the beginning. This need for contemplative life, and certain forms of monastic community or heremetical life, existed in Judaism before Christianity (cf. Qumran on the shore of the Dead Sea, and the "Therapeutae" of Philo of Alexandria's *De contemplativa vita*). There had been recluses in the Egyptian temples. And, in the Hellenistic world, the Pythagoreans, and their schools of philosophy worked as pious communities of ascetics in search of virtue.

Christian monasticism is directly rooted in the prophetic character of the apostolic Church. This prophetic character is a spiritual impulse toward contemplative life, which consists of prayer, dedication of one's time to God, renunciation of the world, fasting, mastery over the passions, continence (renunciation to sexual pleasure), and especially meditation on Scripture. Gifts of healing (physical and moral) and of revelation (divine inspiration in counselling people or interpreting Scripture) were frequent, and more typical than the "gift of tongues."

Paul lived according to these ideals, which he explains in I Cor. 7. It was not the common way of life, since it tended to include sexual continence for the sake of the kingdom of heaven. This does not mean that married people cannot enjoy the gift of prophecy: they could be inspired, have visions, and be rich in love and virtue. But it seems that elderly people, especially among the group of the holy widows, and a few younger men or women living in continence, were a rich field for the blossoming of prophetic gifts. The reason is that contemplative life --the life of prayer and meditation-- required time and dedication, and was more accessible to elderly people, particularly if they were poor and lonely.

After the "Age of the Holy Widows" during the two first centuries, came the time of the holy virgins, first a few of them, found among the widows, then, a privileged group in the Church. There are groups of virgins in the second half of the third century, as we see from the treatise of Cyprian *On the dress of virgins*, and from the *Banquet of the Virgins* of Methodius Olympus. In the fourth century, treatises on virginity multiplied: Athanasius, Basil, Gregory of Nyssa, Chrysostom, Ambrose, Jerome, and Augustine.

Men were more likely than women to enter active life, to work, get married, support a family. There were prophets among men and women. When the title "prophet" disappeared, the prophetic way of life and gifts were observed in the holy widows, the holy virgins, and in certain holy men, fewer in number, sometimes identified as "servants of God." The title of "disciple" seems to have been confined to those who followed Jesus in the beginning, and to those of the apostolic age. In the Gospels, the ideals of "discipleship" are not the way of life of the crowd, but the perfection offered to a few. Jesus also spoke of the "eunuch for the sake of the Kingdom," but it was an image, and not a title.

The men who identified themselves as "servants of God" seem to have been more generally men who were able to spend all their time on, and dedicate their life to, the meditation of Scripture. Naturally they often became "doctors," or "teachers." Sometimes they became "servants of God" after a "second conversion" from average or low Christian life to the ideals of perfection and contemplative life. Most of the Fathers of the Church were unmarried men dedicated to God. Clement of Alexandria, Origen, Augustine, Ambrose, Pelagius, Paulinus of Nola were "servants of God." This does not mean that bishops, priests and deacons were not married, but it explains why most of the early Christian writings were the work of celibate men. It also explains the quantitative disproportion in Christian literature of our information concerning the ideals of virginity versus that of Christian marriage.

After warning the reader against misunderstandings arising from a difference of culture between the early monks and our modern civilization, and from the mental risk inherent in the spiritual challenge of a life on the margin of nature, we present two writings of the third century on virginity: Cyprian, *The Dress of Virgins*, and (in appendix) Methodius Olympus, *The Banquet of the Virgins*. Then, come Antony and Pachomius, founders respectively of heremitic and of cenobitic (conventual) monasticism in Egypt. A few sayings of the desert fathers illustrate the spirituality of these saints. The *Conferences* and *Institutes* of Cassian, which explain their teachings, are summarized in appendix. Unfortunately, in such a brief study, it was impossible to find for Basil the place which he deserved. We present the *Benedictine* Rule because of its influence on the West. Finally, following the study of R. Metz, we explain the development of female monasticism and the symbolism of their vows.

## I. WARNINGS BEFORE READING EARLY MONASTIC WRITINGS

A few remarks are necessary in order to understand the phenomenon of monasticism before coming to the texts. We must clear up certain obstacles, and prepare the reader for an intelligent evaluation of their ethics and of certain supernatural aspects of their life.

Before the fourth century, the Church lived under the threat of persecution, and consisted of relatively small communities. These small communities provided the right environment for those who loved prayer and meditation, and communities benefited from their presence. A document such as the *Shepherd of Hermas* in the middle of the second century already attested in the Roman community the existence of a number of questions about the spiritual life: the question of the acquisition of virtue, of the discernment of spirits, of the pitfalls of spurious holiness. The Encratist movement, with its excessive severity, supported the ideals of continence and the pursuit of perfection, which it proposed to enforce by church-law and to impose on all. *Didascalia Apostolorum,* a Church manual of the third century, described a Christian community where, in spite of human weaknesses, spiritual gifts and Christian virtues blossomed. Long before the existence of convents, the *Banquet of the Virgins* of Methodius extoled in biblical images the beauty of holy virginity.

The development of monasticism under its new forms (monasteries and hermitages) during the fourth century led to a new experience. This new experience can be compared to laboratory research. In laboratory research, the object is subjected to harsh treatment, colored, magnified, etc., in order for a significant result to be seen. And the scientist must muster all his attention and remove all possible obstacles in order to be prepared to observe this result.

The whole experience of early monastic life is colored by representations of a long struggle against the "Enemy," a figure of evil in which the supernatural and the demonic seem to be materialized or personalized beyond measure. What should a modern observer do? Should we just reject what our culture is not inclined to admit? Are we too negative in our views about miracles and demons, to the point of losing part of the sense of the spiritual contest? There is in these mythical or popular images of the Devil and of miracle a kind of "existentialism," a concrete and living representation of the struggle for spiritual life, which we miss today with our dull abstractions. In any case, a student of early Christian literature should not take a negative approach regarding supernatural phenomenon and the Devil, but should sympathize with the data of his or her research, in order to understand their language. Let the student, therefore, "suspend his or her judgment" regarding scientific or philosophical reality, and accept the object the way it comes, i.e., as phenomenology, just as he or she would welcome exotic civilizations, or the popular religion of the Middle Ages. If he or she comes to the data of early monasticism with the wrong criterion, i.e., with a modern scientific and philosophical approach, he or she will "throw out the baby with the bathwater."

All the discussions, and often negations, of the miracles found in the lives of the saints of the early Church, which characterize scholarship in the beginning of the 20th century, reflect the influence of this misunderstanding. It is one thing to acknowledge an amplification of miracles under the influence of time and intermediaries, and quite another thing to systematically reject as impossible every supernatural phenomenon. The error is to impose on the phenomenon a scientific or philosophical meaning, instead of taking it on the phenomenological level where it stands, i.e., on the level of appearances, representations, concrete imaginative experience of events, living communication with God: the "living God" of phenomenology! The ethical and spiritual contents and message of early monasticism was embedded in this phenomenology, i.e., in the culture of their time and place.

A second warning: the results of this kind of laboratory of spiritual life, which the monastery is, derive from a violent treatment of the soul. When monks leave society, and cut down on food, sleep, sex, even personal will, certainly they find the resistance of the "Enemy." Perhaps they win the contest, but they don't reach a cheap peace, for they live on the margin of human nature, perhaps closer to pure spirits than to people. They may also fail in their purpose, for many pitfalls, failures, and psychological reactions are found in their way towards perfection. They may become spiritually crippled, mentally encumbered, mistaken in their judgments. Finally, they may indulge themselves in pride, which is a form of impiety toward God and of contempt for others.

The struggle against the Devil is necessary. The Devil does not seem to care very much for beginners who are concerned with material goods and the passions of the flesh. But he opposes the more advanced, whose struggle is more directly with supernatural powers, according to Paul.[258] This doctrine, traditional in the Church, was developed by Origen in the third century, and by others.

In the context of monastic life, the war against the Devil involves lots of diabolical devices: appearances, noises, persecutions by evil spirits. Antony is the champion of this kind of war:

---

[258] Eph. 6:12.

he was also the first hermit, in his refuge in the Egyptian wilderness, who dared to attack the Devil. Later on, especially in Syria, we do not observe the same "insolence" of the Devil. There is more discretion in his methods of attack, or a less "mythical" approach to the contest by the monks. The struggle against the Devil progressively becomes more spiritual, although to some extent preserving the same material kind of manifestation.

The material aspect of this struggle does not prove the presence of madness or deception in Antony and others. There is a basis for these kinds of manifestations in the Gospels themselves. We may notice that the Devil generally works in an imaginative context of reality, making use of what he finds inside a human person, not outside. For instance, visions are not seen by everyone present at an event.

The struggle of the monk, which began with the fight against the passions of the body, ends with the fight against the passions of the soul. In the beginning, a monk must resist hunger; at the end, he must resist pride. His constant companion, the Devil, changes his method of attack according to the spiritual situation of the monk. The Devil may renounce violence and foul advice, and turn into an "angel of light." Like a conscience-director he gives good advice, indeed, but always the second best advice, i.e., he urges the monk to do the good thing which has bad consequences. For instance, in order to break down the physical resistance of the monk, he suggests to him more prayer and fasting than the latter can bear.

In principle, the struggle of the monk ends with victory and peace, without damage of the mind, but with both virtue and simplicity. We see Antony, the pioneer of hermits, and many monks of the desert, reaching a delightful sense of humanity, the same as we can also observe in many old monks today. They do not appear as a threat, but are humble, understanding, loving, shining with divine grace. To some extent they return to the world, and, like Antony, welcome disciples who come to them attracted by the fragrance of genuine holiness.

We must notice that the structure itself of community life in monasteries teaches the virtues of socialization. The system of monastic community life is called cenobitism, contrary to hermitism, which is life in solitude. Pachomius, the initiator of cenobitism, allowed a monk to become a hermit only after he had been trained in the virtues of community life, and Benedict maintained this principle in his *Rule*. However, Basil, the Father of Eastern monasticism, adopted cenobitism as the way of contemplative life.

Concerning the sources of monasticism, we insisted on the pre-existing Christian tradition of men and women living according to the ideals of virginity and contemplative life. We must now insist on a second source, the most important of all: the meditation on Scripture and the recitation of Psalms. Nobody can underestimate the influence of Scripture on monastic morals since, according to their principle of "constant prayer," monks were always uttering sentences of Scripture.

We must also consider Stoicism as an important source of inspiration for monastic life, not particularly because monks read Stoic literature --they do not mention it--, but because Stoicism was the most powerful ethical system of philosophy in Hellenistic times. The Stoics taught the doctrine of the eradication of the passions and of the acquisition of virtue. Because of their influence, Philo noted in the first century that hundreds of halls were filled daily in Alexandria by people eager to hear lectures on virtue. Heroism in virtue was deemed worthy of the highest praise and of deep esteem. It is through the heroism of its martyrs and the virtues of its simple members that Christianity won the admiration of its enemies. Monasticism hammered on the same nail, and conferred on Christianity a spiritual power which made it invincible.

## II. CYPRIAN, *DE HABITU VIRGINUM* (*The Dress of Virgins*).[259]

Cyprian's *De habitu virginum* offers a well developed mystical and ascetical doctrine of holy virginity as a marriage to Christ, angelic life, victory over the flesh, and renunciation of luxury and the self.

An uninformed reader may question the necessity of so many warnings given in this treatise, but we must remember that these virgins lived in the world, among pagans and Christians who too often adopted the same worldly practices.

Although a virgin must please the Lord only, yet often she remains exceedingly attached to her earthly possessions and to the care of her body. Married women may have an excuse in the necessity to please their husbands, but virgins cannot cast the blame on husbands for their extravagance in dress and adornment, and should follow the advice of Paul and Peter who prescribed moderation to rich women in this regard. When virgins dress their hair sumptuously and walk so as to draw attention in public, and attract the eyes of the youth, they cannot be excused on the pretense that they are chaste and modest in mind: they cause others to perish as if they were offering them a sword or poison.

Ornaments and garments and the allurements of beauty are not fitting for any but prostitutes and immodest women. Therefore, let chaste and modest virgins avoid the dress of the unchaste, the manners of the immodest, the emblems of brothels and the ornaments of harlots. Cyprian refers to Scripture.[260]

---

[259] Cyprian, *De habitu virginum*, 249 A.D.,tr. ANF 5, pp. 430-436. We give a resume.

[260] Revelation 17:1; Isaiah 3:16.

According to Cyprian, the "sons of God" of Gen. 6:1-13 are the Devil and his angels, and they taught women about magic and make-up. Actually Cyprian is repeating an argument of Tertullian in *De cultu feminarum*. Using Tertullian's statement against make-up and hair-dye, Cyprian repeats that God has not created sheep with scarlet or purple fleece. What we find here is Stoic reasoning: the work of nature, which is the work of God in creation, ought in no manner to be adulterated. To do so is a fault against nature, and a sin against God.

However, it seems that Cyprian is going beyond Stoicism. In the resurrection, he says, God may not recognize these virgins. They ought not to be counted among virgins, but like infected sheep and diseased cattle, should be driven away from the holy and pure flock of virginity lest by living together they should pollute the rest with their contagion and ruin others even as they have perished themselves. Cyprian's severity seems to find some justification in what follows. Some virgins were not ashamed to be present at wedding parties, where lust was a reality. Others frequented promiscuous baths where they were seen naked and could see men naked. According to Cyprian -- he was not exaggerating-- the danger was serious because of the mores of pagan society. Cyprian added, "For this reason, the Church frequently mourns over her virgins."

Cyprian does not speak of the particular duties of virgins in the community, for such communities of virgins did not yet exist, and nothing but more freedom to serve the Lord distinguished these virgins from the other faithful. Just like others, they are invited, if wealthy, to help the poor, and so to obtain the powerful intercession of the poor for their own perseverance in the virtues of holy virginity.

For METHODIUS OLYMPUS, *The Banquet of the Virgins* (c.270-290), which is a good example of spirituality for holy virgins at the end of the third century in the Near East, see the resumé given in Appendix I to this chapter.

## III. ATHANASIUS, *THE LIFE OF ANTONY*.

The year 270 marks the beginning of the anchorite movement (those who live in seclusion for religious reasons); about this time the great Antony went into the desert and drew flocks of pilgrims and ascetics to him. Antony is the first great ascetic we know by name. Jerome, in his largely fictional *Life of Paul the Hermit*, attempted to place a man in the desert before Antony, but his work was suspect even in his lifetime. The *Life of Antony* bears all the marks of authenticity and was composed about the year 356 by Athanasius, bishop of Alexandria (328-373), or by a member of the bishop's circle and under his direction.

Antony came from a well-to-do family and was born about 250 in Middle Egypt in a little town not too far from the banks of the Nile. The language was Coptic. When his parents died, he placed his sister in the keeping of some pious women, distributed his goods to the poor, and began a life of asceticism outside of his native village, in an old tomb. Some fifteen years later he moved to the outer mountains at Pispir on the East bank of the Nile, about fifty miles south of Memphis. Here he lived in a deserted fortress. The period at Pispir lasted about twenty years and during this time monks began to surround the great master of the spiritual life.

He is said to have led a delegation of monks to Alexandria during the persecution of Maximinus Daia. Later he departed from Pispir and headed across the desert toward the Red Sea. He finally settled at the foot of Mt. Colzim, 70 miles beyond the Nile river. By the time of his death in 356, at the age of 105, monasticism had become an established phenomenon throughout the Christian world.

### ANTONY'S SETTLEMENT IN A FORTRESS; HIS FIGHT AGAINST THE DEVIL AND HOW HE BECAME A FATHER OF MONKS

> Antony hurried to the mountain. On the far side of the river he found a deserted fort which in the course of time had become infested with creeping things. There he settled down to live. The reptiles, as though someone were chasing them, left at once. He blocked up the entrance, having laid in bread for six months - this the Thebans do and often loaves keep fresh for a whole year - and with water in the place, he disappeared as in a shrine. He remained there alone, never going forth and never seeing anyone pass by. For a long time he persisted in this practice of asceticism; only twice a year he received bread from the house above.
>
> His acquaintances who came to see him often spent days and nights outside, since he would not let them in. They heard what sounded like riotous crowds inside making noises, raising a tumult, wailing piteously and shrieking: "Get out of our domain! What business have you in the desert? You cannot hold out against our persecution." At first those outside thought there were men fighting with him and that they had entered it by means of ladders, but as they peered through a hole and saw no one, they realized that demons were involved; and filled with fear, they called out to Antony. But he was more concerned over hearing them than to pay any attention to the demons. Going close to the door he suggested to them to leave and to have no fear. "It is only against the timid," he said, "that the demons conjure up spectres. You, now, sign yourselves and go home unafraid, and leave them to make fools of themselves."

So they departed, fortified by the sign of the Cross, while he remained without suffering any harm whatsoever from them. Nor did he grow weary of the contest, for the assistance given him through visions coming to him from on high, and the weakness of his enemies brought him great relief in his hardships and gave him the stamina for greater zeal. His friends would come again and again, expecting, of course, to find him dead; but they heard him singing: "Let God arise and let his enemies be scattered; and let them that hate him flee from before his face. As smoke vanishes, so let them vanish away; as wax melts before the fire, so let the sinners perish before the face of God." And again: "All nations compassed me about; and in the name of the Lord I drove them off."

So he spent nearly twenty years practicing the ascetic life by himself, never going out and but seldom seen by others. After this, as there were many who longed and sought to imitate his holy life, some of his friends came and forcefully broke down the door and removed it. Antony came forth as out of a shrine, as one initiated into sacred mysteries and filled with the spirit of God. It was the first time that he showed himself outside the fort to those who came to him. When they saw him, they were astonished to see that his body had kept its former appearance, that it was neither obese from want of exercise, nor emaciated from his fastings and struggles with the demons: he was the same man they had known before his retirement. Again, the state of his soul was pure, for it was neither contracted by grief, nor dissipated by pleasure nor pervaded by jollity or dejection. He was not embarrassed when he saw the crowd, nor was he elated at seeing so many there to receive him. No, he had himself completely under control - a man guided by reason and stable in his character.

Through him the Lord cured many of those present who were afflicted with bodily ills, and freed others from impure spirits. He also gave Antony charm in speaking; and so he comforted many in sorrow, and others who were quarelling he made friends. He exhorted all to prefer nothing in the world to the love of Christ. And when in his discourse he exhorted them to be mindful of the good things to come and of the goodness shown us by God, who spared not his Son, but delivered him up for us all, he induced many to take up the monastic life. And so now monasteries also sprang up in the mountains and the desert was populated with monks who left their own

> people and registered themselves for citizenship in heaven.[261]

ANTONY'S ADDRESS TO THE MONKS: DISCERNMENT OF SPIRITS

Antony first recommends to his disciples never to give up monastic discipline, but rather to consider each day as a new beginning. He gives as a reason for entering monastic life the comparison between material and spiritual goods:

> Why not give up our possessions for virtue's sake so that we may inherit a kingdom besides? Therefore, let none of us have even the desire to possess riches. For what does it avail us to possess what we cannot take with us? Why not rather possess those things which we can take along with us - prudence, justice, temperance, fortitude, understanding, charity, love of the poor, faith in Christ, meekness, hospitality? Once we possess these we shall find them going before us, preparing a welcome for us in the land of the meek.

Antony particularly warns against wrath and lust, two temptations more frequently mentioned in monastic literature.

Demonology is very important in the theology of Antony. Demons are fallen angels who had been created as good by God. They deceived the Greeks by their lies, and now, out of envy, they leave nothing undone to hinder the Christians from entering heaven. With the practice of prayer and ascetic discipline a Christian may receive through the Holy Spirit the gift of discerning spirits, and become able to recognize them from their characteristics and from their tricks.

Demons first send evil thoughts, a kind of attack which will fail if we turn to prayer, fasting, and faith in the Lord. Then, demons change their tactics and march to the attack again. They devise apparitions in order to frighten the soul, transforming themselves and mimicking women, beasts, reptiles, and bodies of huge size and hordes of warriors. Antony warns: "but even so we must not cower at these their phantoms, for they are nothing and quickly vanish, especially if a person fortifies himself with the sign of the Cross."

The third kind of demoniac attack is even more strange. They pretend to prophesy and to foretell future events. They show themselves taller than the roof and burly and bulky.

The demons, then, seem to play the role of spiritual directors, who suggest good ideas, but always the second best, that is, the wrong idea:

---

[261] Athanasius, *The Life of Antony*, tr. R.T. Meyer, (ACW 10, 1950), 10-14.

> Often they even pretend to sing Psalms without appearing, and to quote sayings from Scripture. Sometimes, too, when we are reading they at once repeat like an echo what we have read. When we go to bed they rouse us to prayers; and this they carry on continuously, scarcely permitting us to sleep at all. At other times again they put on the guise of monks and simulate pious talk, having in mind to practice deception by their assumed likeness and then to drag off the victims where they will. But we must not pay attention to them, even if they rouse us to prayer, even if they advise us not to eat at all, even if they pretend to accuse and revile us for what they once approved. It is not for the sake of piety or for truth's sake that they do this, but in order to bring the guileless into despair; and to represent the ascetical life as worthless, and to make men disgusted with the solitary life as something coarse and all too burdensome, and to trip up those who live such a life in spite of them.

Antony gives the rule for the discernment of spirits. We find this rule already in Hermas in the middle of the second century.[262] With Antony it becomes traditional in Christianity:

> A vision of the holy ones is not turbulent, but it comes so quietly and gently that instantly joy and gladness and courage arise in the soul. For with them is our Lord who is our joy, and the power of God the Father. And the thoughts of the soul remain untroubled and unruffled, so that in its own bright transparency it is able to behold those who appear. A longing for things divine and for the things of the future life takes possession of it, and its desire is that it may be wholly united to them if it could but depart with them. But if some, being human, are seized with fear at the vision of the good, then those who appear dispel the fear by love, as did Gabriel for Zachary, and the angel who appeared to the women at the holy sepulchre, and the angel who spoke to the shepherds in the Gospel: *Fear not*. Fear in these cases is not from craveness of the soul, but from an awareness of higher beings. Such, then, is the vision of the holy ones...
>
> When, therefore, you have a vision and are afraid, if then the fear is taken from you immediately and in its place comes ineffable joy and contentment; and courage and recovery of strength and calmness of thought, and love of God, then be of good cheer and pray - for your joy and

---

[262] *Shepherd of Hermas*, "Mandatum" 6, 2, 1-4.

your soul's tranquillity betoken the holiness of him who is present.

On the other hand, the attack and appearance of the evil ones is full of confusion accompanied by crashing, roaring, and shouting: it could well be the tumult produced by rude boys and robbers. This at once begets terror in the soul, disturbance and confusion of thoughts, dejection, hatred of ascetics, indifference, sadness, remembrance of kinfolk, and fear of death; and then a desire for evil, a disdain for virtue, and a complete subversion of character... And let this also be a sign to you: when the soul remains in fear, it is enemies that are present.

According to Antony, Demons have no real power over us, and their only power consists in that they take advantage of the conditions of mind in which they find us. If they see us rejoicing in the Lord, they are defeated and they turn away. Antony suggests first to boldly ask the apparition: "Who are you? And from whence are you coming?" And if it is a vision of holy ones they will assure you, and change your fear into joy. But if the vision should be from the devil, immediately it becomes feeble, beholding your firm purpose of mind."[263]

## IV. A FEW SAYINGS OF THE DESERT FATHERS[264]

I,11. A brother asked an old man, saying, "What things are there so good that I may do and live?"... "According to Scripture," Abbot Nestero said, "Abraham was hospitable, and God was with him. And Elias loved quiet, and God was with him. And David was humble, and God was with him. What therefore you find that your soul desires in following God, that do, and keep your heart."

I,15. Abbot Pastor said, "If a monk will hate two things, he can be free from this world: relaxation of the body, and vain glory."

II,1. Abbot Antony said, "Fish die, if they tarry on dry land: even so monks that tarry outside their cell or abide with men of the world fall away from vow and quiet."

---

[263] *The Life of Antony*, 16-44.

[264] From H. Waddell, *The Desert Fathers*, (Ann Arbor, MI: University of Michigan Press). Certain sayings are abbreviated.

II,2. Abbot Antony said, "Who sits in solitude and is quiet has escaped from three wars: hearing, speaking, seeing: yet against one thing shall he continually battle: that is, his own heart."

II,9. A certain brother came to abbot Moses seeking a word from him. And the old man said to him, "Go and sit in your cell, and your cell shall teach you all things."

III,22. One of the brethren asked abbot Isidore, saying, "Wherefore do the devils fear you so mightily?" And the old man said to him, "From the time that I was made a monk, I have striven not to suffer anger to mount as far as my throat."

IV,49. Abbot Hyperichius said, "The monk that cannot master his tongue in time of anger will not be master of the passions of his body at some other time."

IV,51. He said again, "It is better to eat flesh and to drink wine than to eat the flesh of the brethren by backbiting them."

IV,62. A monk met the handmaids of God upon a certain road, and at the sight of them he turned out of the way. And the abbess said to him, "Had you been a perfect monk you would not have looked so close as to perceive that we were women."

V,4. A certain brother, who was harassed by a demon of lust, came to an old man and related to him his imaginings. But on hearing them, and himself being free, the old man was wroth, and declared that the brother was vile and unworthy to wear the habit of a monk, inasmuch as he admitted such thoughts to his mind. And the brother, hearing this, despaired of himself: and he left his own cell and took the road back to the world. But by God's providence abbot Apollo met him...(When he heard his story), Abbot Apollo counselled him, saying, "Think it no strange thing, my son, nor despair of yourself. For I myself, at my age, and in this way of life, am sorely harried by thoughts just as these. Wherefore be not found wanting in this kind of testing, where the remedy is not so much in man's anxious thoughts as in God's compassion. Today at least grant me what I ask of you, and go back to your cell."

VII,5. A certain brother who lived in solitary was disturbed in mind, and consulted abbot Theodore of Pherme. The old man said to him, "Go, humble your spirit and live with other men." So he went away to the mountain, and dwelt with other men. And afterwards he came back to the old man and said to him, "Nor in living with other men have I found peace." And the old man said, "If you cannot be in solitude, nor yet with men, why did you will to be a monk? Was it not that you should have tribulation? Tell me now, how many years have you been in this habit?" And the brother said, "Eight." And the old man said, "Believe me, I have been in this habit seventy years, and not for one day could I find peace: and you would have peace in eight?"

VII,32. The Fathers used to say, "If temptation befall you in the place you do inhabit, desert not the place in the time of temptation: for if you do, wheresoever you go, you shall find what you want to leave behind before you."

VIII,19. Syncletica said, "A treasure that is known is quickly spent: and even so any virtue that is commented and made a public show is destroyed. Even as wax is melted down before the face of fire, so the soul enfeebled by praise loses the toughness of its virtues."

IX,2. A certain brother had sinned, and the priest commanded him to go out of the church. But Bessarion rose up and went out with him, saying, "I too am a sinful man."

IX,6. A brother asked abbot Pastor, saying, "If I should see my brother's fault, is it good to hide it?" The old man said to him, "In what hour do we cover our brother's sins, God shall cover ours: and in what hour we do betray our brother's shames, in like manner God shall betray our own."

X,40. A brother asked abbot Pastor, saying, "I have sinned a great sin, and I am willing to do penance for three years." But the abbot Pastor said, "That is a good deal." And the brother said, "Do you order me one year?" And again the old man said, "That is a good deal." Some who stood by said, "Up to forty days?" The old man said, "That is a good deal." And then he added, "I think that if a man would repent with his whole heart and would not reckon to do again that for which he now repents, God would accept a penance of three days."

XI,2. When abbot Agatho was dying, he remained for three days motionless, holding his eyes open. And the brethren shook him, saying, "Father, where are you?" And he answered, "I stand in sight of the divine judgment." And they said, "Are you afraid?" And he said, "Here I have toiled with what strength I had to keep the commandments of God: but I am a man, and I do not know whether my works have been pleasing in his sight."

The brethren said to him, "And have you no confidence that your works are according to God?" And the old man said, "I do not presume, until I have come before God: for the judgments of God are other than the judgments of men." And when they would have questioned him for further speech, he said to them, "Show me your love and speak not to me, for I am busy." And this said, straightway with joy he sent forth his spirit.

XI,43. A brother said to an old man, "I see no war in my heart." And the old man said to him, "You are like a chariot-gate, and whatsoever will may enter and go and come where he pleases, and you do not know what is going on.

XII,2. The brethren asked abbot Agatho, saying, "Father, which virtue in this way of life is most laborious?" And he said to them, "Forgive me, but to my mind there is no labor so great as praying to God."

XIII,7. A brother came to a certain solitary; and when he was going away from him, he said, "Forgive me, Father, for I have made you break your rule." He made answer and said, "My rule is to receive you with hospitality and send you away in peace."

XV,28. Abbot Mathois said, "The nearer a man approaches to God, the greater sinner he sees himself to be. For the prophet Isaiah saw God, and said that he was unclean and undone."

XV,68. The Devil appeared to a certain brother, transformed into an angel of light, and said to him, "I am the angel Gabriel, and I am sent unto you." But he said, "Look to it that you were not sent to some other: for I am not worthy that an angel should be sent to me."

XVI,19. They used to tell of a certain brother, how he was neighbor to a certain great old man, and that he used to go in and steal whatever the old man had in his cell. The old man saw him, but he would not upbraid him, but forced himself to work the harder with his hands, saying, "I think that my brother is needy."... Now when the old man came to die, the brethren stood around him. And gazing on him who thieved, he said to him, "Come close to me." And he held his hands and kissed them, saying, "I thank these hands, my brother, since because of them I go to the Kingdom of God." And he, cut to the heart, did penance and became an upright monk, taking pattern from the deeds of that great old man.

V. CENOBITISM : THE RULE OF PACHOMIUS, according to Palladius, *The Lausiac History 32:*[265]

> Pachomius, a monk of Tabennesi in the desert of Thebaid, Egypt, was a man of the kind who live rightly, and he was deemed worthy of prophecies and angelic visions. He was extremely kind and brotherly. One time when he was sitting in his cave, an angel appeared to him and told him: "So far as you are concerned, you conduct your life perfectly. It is vain for you to continue sitting in your cave. Come now, leave this place and go out and call the young monks together and dwell with them. Rule them by the model I am now giving you. And the angel gave him a bronze tablet.
>
> You will let each one eat and drink as suits his strength; and divide up their tasks in accord with their respective strengths, and not hinder any one from fasting or eating. Make separate cells in the cloister and let there be three monks to a cell. Meals, however, should be taken by all in one house. Let them recline at full length. Let each one have a coat of worked goatskin; they may not eat without it. On Saturday and Sunday when they go to communion, they may loosen their girdles and go in with the hood only.
>
> He arranged them in 24 groups, and to each group he assigned a letter of the Greek alphabet, beginning with alpha, beta, gamma, delta, and so on. When he asked questions or carried on the community business, he would ask the prefect: How is the alpha section? How is zeta doing? Or again: Give greetings to ro. He fitted the letters to each order according to their state of life and disposition; but only the more spiritual knew the meaning of each symbol.
>
> A strange monk of another monastery may not eat or drink or stay with them unless he is really on a journey... He commanded that they pray twelve prayers each day. When the group was about to eat, he commanded them to sing a psalm in addition to each prayer. When Pachomius objected to the angel that the prayers were too few, the angel said: "I arranged it this way so that even the little ones might keep the rule, and not grieve. Now those who are perfect need no rule, for they have offered themselves entirely to the contemplation of God in their cells."

---

[265] Palladius, *The Lausiac History*, tr. R.T. Meyer, (ACW, 1965). Abridged by author.

Monks work at every sort of handicraft and from their surplus they provide for the monasteries of women and the prison. They even keep swine. When Palladius objected to this practice, they answered him: With us it is an old custom that pigs are nourished with the refuse and vegetable left-overs. The pigs are killed and their flesh is sold, but their feet are given to the sick and the old, as the territory is poor but heavily populated. (Pachomius preferred to see food not eaten by fasting monks to be thrown to the pigs --thereby not wasted-- than to see young monks deprived of the quality of food which their health required).

Regarding their work, one works the ground as husbandman, another works as gardener, another as smith, another as baker, another as fuller, another as weaver of large baskets, another as shoemaker, another as copyist, another as weaver of tender reeds. (Palladius has also seen carpenters, tailors, and camel drivers.)
The monks appointed to serve for the day rise up early and go to the kitchen or the refectory. They are employed until meal time in preparing and setting the tables, putting on each table loaves of bread, preserved olives, cheese made of cow's milk, and small vegetables. Some (groups of monks) come and eat at the sixth hour, others at the seventh, others at the eight, others at the ninth, others at the eleventh, still others at late evening, some every other day, so that every group knows its own proper hour.

They all learn the Holy Scripture by heart.

The monastery of women, on the other side of the river, lives under a similar rule.

In order to wipe out the impression that Pachomius was only a kind of colonel or administrator, we add a passage of *The Life of Pachomius*[266] which shows him as a humble person, taking a motherly care of his novices, and respecting the freedom of their soul:

Pachomius welcomed new disciples, gave them the monk's habit, and bid them to renounce the world, their family, and themselves, and to follow Christ, carrying their cross after him. He prepared their food, sowed vegetables and watered them. He answered when people

[266] A.J. Festugière, *Les Moines d'Orient* (4 vol., Paris: Éditions du Cerf, 1961), IV, 2, "La première vie grecque de Pachomius," ch.24.

came. He himself took care of sick novices, staying at night with them. Making his novices free from material tasks, he exhorted them to learn their monastic vocation from the text of Scripture, particularly from Psalms and the Gospels. He explained to them the word of God and taught them the zeal for good deeds. But he preferred to assume all the menial jobs than to give orders. Teaching them by his example, silently he let them progress towards understanding. It happened that some preferred to live below the ideals of monastic life: Pachomius imposed on them the law of common prayer and the other rules. They left, and the others improved.

## VI. *THE RULE OF ST. BENEDICT*[267]

The *Rule of St. Benedict*, inspired by Cassian and the *Rule of the Master*, became the monastic rule of the Western Church. As a classic of monasticism, it is necessary to read it completely, but we will give selections. Its success comes from its brevity, simplicity, and congeniality with the Western mind.

PROLOGUE:

> Therefore we intend to establish a school for the Lord's service. In drawing up its regulations, we hope to set down nothing harsh, nothing burdensome. The good of all concerned, however, may prompt us to a little strictness in order to amend faults and to safeguard love. Do not be daunted immediately by fear and run away from the road that leads to salvation. It is bound to be narrow at the outset. But as we progress in this way of life and in faith, we shall run on the path of God's commandments, our hearts overflowing with the inexpressible delight of love. Never swerving from his instructions, then, but faithfully observing his teaching in the monastery until death, we shall through patience share in the sufferings of Christ that we may deserve also to share in his kingdom. (45-50)

QUALITIES OF THE ABBOT:

> To be worthy of the task of governing a monastery, the abbot must always remember what his title signifies and act as a superior should. He is believed to hold the place of Christ in the monastery, since he is addressed by a title of Christ... therefore, the abbot must never teach or

---

[267] *The Rule of St.Benedict in Latin and English*, (Collegeville, MN: Liturgical Press, 1981).

decree or command anything that would deviate from the Lord's instructions. On the contrary, everything he teaches and commands should, like the leaven of divine justice, permeate the minds of his disciples. Let the abbot always remember that at the fearful judgment of God, not only his teaching but also his disciples' obedience will come under scrutiny. (ch.2:1-6)

Anyone who receives the name of abbot is to lead his disciples by a twofold teaching: he must point out to them all that is good and holy more by example than by words, proposing the commandments of the Lord to receptive disciples with words, but demonstrating God's instructions to the stubborn and the dull by a living example. If he teaches his disciples that something is not to be done, then neither must he do it... (ch.2:11-13)

In his teaching, the abbot should always observe the Apostle's recommendation, in which he says: "Use argument, appeal, reproof."[268] This means that he must vary with circumstances, threatening and coaxing by turns, stern as a taskmaster, devoted and tender as only a father can be. With the undisciplined and restless, he will use firm argument; with the obedient and docile and patient, he will appeal for greater virtue; but as for the negligent and disdainful, we charge him to use reproof and rebuke. (ch.2:23-25)

OBEDIENCE:

The first step of humility is unhesitatating obedience, which comes naturally to those who cherish Christ above all. Because of the holy service they have professed, or because of dread of hell and for the glory of everlasting life, they carry out the superior's order as promptly as if the command came from God himself. (ch.5:1-4)

THE SLEEPING ARRANGEMENTS OF THE MONKS:

The monks are to sleep in separate beds. They receive bedding as provided by the abbot, suitable to monastic life. If possible, all are to sleep in one place, but should the size of the community preclude this, they will sleep in groups of ten or twenty under the watchful care of seniors. A lamp must be kept burning in the room until morning. They sleep clothed, and girded with belts or cords; but they should remove their knives, lest they accidentally cut themselves in their sleep. Thus the monks will always be ready to arise without delay when

---

[268] 2 Tim. 4:2.

> the signal is given; each will hasten to arrive at the Work of God before the others, yet with all dignity and decorum. (ch.22:1-6)

THE GOOD ZEAL OF MONKS:

> Just as there is a wicked zeal of bitterness which separates from God and leads to hell, so there is a good zeal which separates from evil and leads to God and everlasting life. This, then, is the good zeal which monks must foster with frequent love... supporting with the greatest patience one another's weaknesses of body or behavior, and earnestly competing in obedience to one another. No one is to pursue what he judges better for himself, but instead, what he judges better for someone else. To their fellow-monks they show the pure love of brothers; to God, loving fear; to their abbot, unfeigned and humble love. Let them prefer nothing whatever to Christ, and may he bring us all together to everlasting life. (ch.72:1-11)

## VII. THE CONSECRATION OF VIRGINS: RITE AND MEANING

Tertullian, Cyprian, Methodius Olympus in the third century, and all later tradition, call women who vow their life to God according to the ideals of virginity "Brides of Christ." In the fourth century in Rome, the consecration of virgins was understood as a spiritual marriage to Christ. For instance, Pope Innocent, in his *Letter to Victricius of Rouen*, mentions virgins "who have spiritually married Christ, and deserved to be veiled by the bishop."

The minister of almost all these consecrations of virgins was the bishop. Bishops defended this privilege against priests and especialy against abbesses in order to protect the freedom of the virgin. No requirement of age is found in the fourth century. Ambrose says that the veil should be given only when the virgin is mature in virtue. However, Jerome knew in Rome girls who made a vow of virginity when they were 10 years old, and sometimes parents consecrated a daughter even before her birth. The rule of 12 years (the age for marriage) became usual and lasted until the Council of Trent, which imposed 16 years. Basil required 16 or 17 years.

The vow could be taken early (when they were 12 years old), but the consecration itself was postponed to a later age. Two tendencies existed in the second half of the fourth century: the one favored 40 years of age; the other only 25 years. The age of 25 became the rule in Rome in the fifth century, after the adoption of the African rules. With the development of monastic communities of men and women, a time of probation was imposed before taking the habit. Caesarius of Arles imposed one year on women; Benedict one year on men; Gregory the Great two years on men, and even three on soldiers. Emperor Justinian imposed three years on all.

The laws concerning consecrated women derived from the notion of their consecration as a marriage to Christ. The virgin's union to Christ implied unity, fidelity, indissolubility. Augustine opposed the legal character and consequences of this definition, and refused to consider as properly adulterous (i.e. liable to heavy punishment, even the death sentence) a virgin who was unfaithful to her vow of religion.

The ceremony of the consecration of a virgin was called "marriage," and borrowed rites from the ceremony of marriage. In the fourth century, in a ceremony of marriage, the couple was given a blessing and the bride took the veil. Similarly, the consecration of a virgin consisted of a blessing and of the *velatio*, or imposition of the veil. The ceremony was performed on a great feast of the year, during the Mass, before the congregation. The bishop explained to the virgin and to the congregation the meaning of the ceremony. The virgin (probably) expressed her resolution to belong to Christ. The bishop recited a blessing over her, and gave her the veil. Probably the bishop laid his hand on her head. The veil was the same as that of married women.

This ritual is attested in a strange manner by a curious event. A girl from a rich Roman family, who was threatened to be given in marriage by her parents against her own will, cunningly joined the virgins at the altar, caught the hand of the priest and asked him for the blessing of the consecration of virgins, and, then, put her head under the altar as under a veil. She was trying to copy the ritual of the *velatio*.

During the Middle Ages, the ritual of the consecration of virgins adopted the accompanying details of the ritual of marriage, and later on borrowed from the ritual of ordinations. Today traditional religious congregations of women have come back to the ancient ritual and notion of the marriage to Christ, which is a beautiful expression of mystical love. Others, however, find it irrelevant to wear the dress of a bride in their very renunciation of marriage.

Early holy virgins lived at home independently without habit, superior, rule or convent. However, during the fourth century more and more virgins renounced their independence and accepted to live in communities of nuns. Pachomius, the founder of cenobitic life for men, also founded monasteries of women. Basil founded monasteries of women, and his sister, Macrina, organized one of them in their family house. Paula and Eustochium, the Patrician ladies who followed Jerome from Rome to Bethlehem, founded a community of women, and many rich ladies did the same. Hegeria visited many convents of women in Asia Minor, and she may have been the superior of a convent of women in Gaul or Spain. In the time of Augustine, there are many convents of women in Africa (his sister was the head of a convent of women in Hippo), and the same is true of Italy: in Milan in the time of Ambrose, in Colonia near Rome where Ambrose's sister was superior of a convent, in Rome itself with Irene, the sister of Pope Damascus, and with the great ladies known through Jerome's correspondence, who organized convents in their own houses. The number of nuns increased, and, according to Gregory the Great, they were about 3000 in Rome at the end of the sixth century. Gregory himself founded a convent of virgins.[269]

## APPENDIX I

### METHODIUS OLYMPUS, *THE BANQUET OF THE TEN VIRGINS* (c. 270-290 A.D.).

The most interesting point of this series of topics on the spirituality of holy virginity is the way these early groups of virgins were able to speculate on the symbolism of biblical images. We give a resume. In the house of Arete (virtue), ten virgins in turn praise the advantage of virginity.

1. MARCELLA comments on Mt. 19:12, "the Eunuch for the sake of the Kingdom," and the reference to the "sons of the resurrection who don't marry but live like the angels of God." Virginity is the crowning in Christ (who lived in virginity) of a long progress of humankind from the depravation described in Rom. 1-3. Virginity is the source and first fruit of immortality. Virginity is perfection, wisdom, a perfect offering, the salt of the earth. Those who now follow Christ, the model of virginity, shall sit together with him in heaven.

2. THEOPHILA comments on Gen. 1:28, God's command, "Grow and multiply." She notes that, although virginity remains the ideal of Christianity, marriage is a lawful way of life. Procreation, according to the divine disposition, shall last until the end of the world, but shall not exist in the kingdom of heaven. Theophila adds that there is nothing wrong with the sons of adultery, and that they will be included in the edifice. Only their parents are guilty.

3. THALIA comments on Eph. 5:28-32, where Paul compares the union between Christ and the Church to the marriage of Adam and Eve (Gen.2:23-24). Just as Eve was born from the side of Adam, the Church was born from the side of Christ pierced by the spear on the cross, and we are purified by the bath of

[269] René Metz, *La consécration des Vierges dans l'Eglise Romaine* (Paris: PUF, 1955).

regeneration in baptism. Without Christ's humiliation in the Incarnation, there would have been no birth of the Church from his side on the cross, and no gift of the Holy Spirit for us.

4. THEOPATRA comments on Ps. 136, "Upon the rivers of Babylon." The rivers of Babylon symbolize the waves of corruption in this foreign world, whereas the holy river of Ps.1 symbolizes the watering of the just. Purity is the antidote of corruption and the best way to reach immortality. But we must turn our eyes upwards where Christ is found, who is our joy and the crown of immortality promised to the chaste.

5. THALLUSA comments on the Vow of the Nazirite (Num. 6:2), which she interprets as the sacrifice of virginity. This sacrifice includes the offering of senses, mind, and reason, and is also symbolized by the sacrifice of the covenant with Abraham (Gen. 15:9, allegorical symbolism of the victims). It is the offering of our progress in virtue and of our purification through the successive ages of life, until we make the last offering, when God shall call us to him.

6. AGATHE comments on the parable of the Ten Virgins. The Bridegroom is Christ, the Word of God, crowned with immortality. The five torches of the wise virgins symbolize the five senses, which are the gates of wisdom when they are pure and virginal; the oil is wisdom and justice; the lamps must burn until the morning as a symbol of the necessity for the Church to keep chastity until the return of Christ. The sleep of the foolish virgins symbolizes the reign of the Anti-Christ. The waking up of the virgins symbolizes the judgment, and the reward for chastity shall be sharing in the virginity of the Bride of Christ and singing with the heavenly choirs.

7. PROCILLA comments on the fiancée of Song of Songs, who can be either holy virgins, or the Church, or again the flesh of Christ in the Incarnation. The lilies among the thorns symbolize purity of soul. Christ only looks at the beauty of the soul, for we read (Ps. 45:14), "All the glory of the King's daughter is from inside." There are many mansions in heaven, according to the merit of the faith of each, but only the choir of the virgins will be admitted into the "Nuptial Chamber."

8. THECLA comments on the "Sign of the Woman" in Revelation 12:1-7. Virginity is equal to God, therefore, herself divine. *Partheneia* (virginity), indeed, includes *partheia* (equality with God). The wings of virginity are not made for the earth but for heavenly and angelic life. At the resurrection, the virgins will be the first who join Christ and receive the crown, and they will dance in front of God. The "sign of the woman" who is clothed in sunshine with the moon underfoot, and twelve stars round her head, and who is pregnant with a male son, but

threatened by a dragon, refers to the Church, our Mother, who begets as spiritual those already born as carnal. The dragon is the Devil. The sentence, "Thy youth is renewed like the eagle's" suits the woman, who crushes the head of the dragon, i.e., intemperance and sensuality, and, after her victory, soars upwards to the heavens.

9. TYSIANE comments on the feast of Tabernacles (Leviticus 23:39-43), which symbolizes the Resurrection. We shall celebrate this heavenly feast with our bodies once made incorruptible, if, in the present life, we adorn them with the palms of purity. The palms used in the feast of Tabernacles are taken from *agnus castus*, a tree which symbolizes chastity (*agneia* is "purity").

10. DOMINA comments on Judges 9:8-15, the parable of the Trees looking for a King, and finally choosing a bush as the best candidate. The Devil is able to corrupt every tree of virtue, except for chastity, which is figured by the thorny bush, and is the enemy of pleasure.

ARETE gives the crown to THECLA, and all the virgins together sing a hymn to Christ, their heavenly Spouse, and in honor of the Church, his Bride. They celebrate the biblical champions of virginity, and extol virginity as the way back to paradise and to heaven.

## APPENDIX II

CASSIAN, *The Institutes*, & *The Conferences*, a resumé:

In the beginning of the fifth century, Cassian, the founder of two monasteries near Marseilles (southern coast of France), wrote the *Institutes* and *Conferences*, wherein he compiled and organized the rich information which he had gathered during his journey through the prestigious monasteries of Egypt.

### *THE INSTITUTES.*

Book I, THE VESTURE OF THE MONKS. A monk is a soldier of Christ: the belt symbolizes his willingness to fight the combat of continence and chastity; the hood symbolizes the simplicity and innocence of a child, which suits a monk; the short sleeveless tunic is a symbol of mortification and of renunciation of worldly activity; the linen scarf symbolizes the readiness of the monk to work, for it retains the tunic from floating away; the goat-skin symbolizes firmness in virtue; the staff symbolizes discipline of life against temptations, and is the sign of the cross against the

Devil. The monastic habit should be practical, modest, uniform, traditional, adjusted to local needs.

Books II & III deal with liturgical matters.

Book IV, ADMISSION AND TRAINING OF CANDIDATES. For ten days a postulant stays outside, begging the permission to enter, and proving his patience under insult, contempt and rebuke. Once admitted, he must say whether he has renounced all his possessions, to the last penny. For a whole year he must live apart from the brethren, in the guest-house, under a brother in charge of guests and strangers, and learn service and humility. Afterwards, he enters the community and is entrusted to an elder monk in charge of the training of ten brethren. This training aims at breaking the will of the new monk through commands which contradict his inclinations. He must also reveal all his thoughts to his elder. And he must punctually obey the detail of the rule.

In case of disobedience, or neglect, or grumbling, he is subjected to a spiritual punishment. In the case of more blamable faults, such as public insult, contempt, violent contradiction, lack of self-mastery, familiarity with women, anger, arguments, revenge and quarrels, choice of a particular work, avarice, possession of superfluous things, eating at other hours and in hiding, etc., the remedy may be physical beating, or, much worse, dismissal from the community.

Book V, THE SPIRIT OF GREEDINESS. Cassian begins his explanation of the eight capital vices with greediness. Since physical needs are not the same for all, there is no uniform rule concerning food. But a monk should never eat to satiety, for excess in eating causes lust, and, by subjecting the flesh, he obtains freedom of the will. He improves his mind through fasting, reading, vigils, and reaches the compunction of the heart. Fasting, which purifies the heart, should, however, yield to charity. The training of a monk can be compared to that of an athlete of the Olympic games.

Book VI, THE SPIRIT OF FORNICATION. For the acquisition of chastity, bodily fasting is not enough, but we must practice the contrition of the mind and the meditation of Scripture. Against the spirit of fornication, the work of our hands is also a great help. Of course, we must drive away from our imagination every memory of women. Cassian sees in the absence of images of women and lustful things in our dreams the sign that we are in possession of chastity.

Book VII, THE SPIRIT OF AVARICE. Avarice is almost incurable, and becomes the source of all other evils. It begins with the possession of a small amount of money, saved for apparently good purposes, and hidden, for which we lie, commit perjury, steal, disobey the rule and our superiors, offend humility, criticize our fellow-monks, work insatiably, miss meetings of prayer and vigils, neglect the work assigned to us, and think of cohabitation with women and of life in the world. The Apostolic Church (Acts of Apostles 4-5) lived in complete renunciation of riches.

Book VIII, THE SPIRIT OF ANGER. Justice and spiritual light in the heart are impossible with anger, as we read in Scripture, "My eye has been dimmed with anger." The remedy to anger is to remember the statement of Paul, that "the sun should not set upon our anger, lest we give an opportunity to the devil,", and again, "Be angry, but do not sin!" (in such a way as to be led to action by anger). Actually, the Lord does not want us to keep anger even for a short time, for he wants us to be able to offer the sacrifice of praise ceaselessly, which is impossible if we hate our brethren. Often solitaries in the desert become angry for a small thing, for a pen, a knife, or the stone for kindling fire.

Book IX. THE SPIRIT OF SADNESS. Sadness is an obstacle to contemplation, weakens the soul, banishes joy from our prayer, keeps our attention away from the meditation of Scripture, makes us less gentle with our brethren, and leads us to a painful feeling of despair. Sadness can be compared to worms and mites eating our soul. Sadness comes from anger, or from some kind of disappointment. There is a good kind of sadness, when we repent from our sins. This sadness is obedient, kind, patient, humble, meek and sweet, as coming from the love of God and aiming at our salvation. The evil kind of sadness is bitter, impatient, hard, revengeful, desperate, barren. It paralyzes the soul and turns it away from salvation, prayer and all spiritual things. The remedy is the consideration of the good things promised by God.

Book X. THE SPIRIT OF ACEDIA. "Acedia" is a disgust for spiritual things and particularly for our cell, which usually occurs around the hour of sext (noon), and lasts until none (3 p.m.). We find labor tedious, our whole life useless, and we think that there should be better monasteries elsewhere, or that we could direct others with good spiritual profit. We feel tired and hungry, but the sun is still high in the sky. We would like to visit brethren, or the sick, or relatives. And if we leave our cell, our disease only increases in strength, so far as we even forget the goal of our monastic profession. The remedy is activity. The Egyptian Fathers do not allow young monks to stay idle, but they evaluate their progress in patience and humility from their assiduity to work. They train them to works of charity, sending them to Lybia to feed the poor in time of starvation, or to towns to feed those in jail. They consider that, in their case, handiwork is a true and reasonable sacrifice which we can offer up to God. They say that a monk who works is only tempted by one demon, but an idle monk by many. Abbot Paul, who lived in the desert of Porphyra and could not sell his handiwork, worked every day and burnt the whole product at the end of the year: his only purpose in working was to preserve his purity of heart.

Book XI, THE SPIRIT OF VAINGLORY. Vainglory ("*kenodoxia*") does not attack the flesh of the monk as the other vices do, but his spirit, and takes advantage of his virtue in order to destroy him. Every virtue, even humility, every good deed, even fasting and prayer, meditation and spiritual science, obedience and silence, can become a pretext of vain-glory at the instigation of the Devil. The beauty of their voice, the rank of their parents, or the fact that they have despised a military carrier and honors can incite beginners to vainglory. It even brings someone to desire the priesthood or deaconate. Accordingly, the Egyptian Fathers advise monks to avoid bishops as well as women.

Book XII. THE SPIRIT OF PRIDE. This spirit attacks the perfect rather than beginners who are still entangled in the humiliations resulting from the fight against the passions. Pride was the sin of Lucifer, who, confiding in himself, and despising the grace of God, made himself equal to God: he considered that he could reach perfection by himself. As being the first sin, pride became the principle of all other sins, of envy in the Devil, and of all vices in men, his victims. The remedy to pride is its opposite, humility, of which the Lord gives a great example in the Incarnation. Another remedy is thanksgiving, when we ascribe our progress in virtue to the grace of God and not to our merit, although we know that our efforts are necessary for the acquisition of virtue. Another remedy is obedience to our spiritual guides, instead of trusting our own judgment. Against carnal pride, a lower kind of pride, the remedy is to consider oneself as inferior to all, to be patient, and to imitate the passion of the Lord.

## *THE CONFERENCES*

I. ON THE MONK'S GOAL, BY ABBOT MOSES. Cassian proves the superiority of contemplative life over active life. Contemplative life is the life of the saints in heaven, even before the resurrection.

II. ON DISCRETION, OR DISCERNMENT, BY THE SAME. Cassian explains how a monk, particularly a young monk, should disclose his thoughts and sins to the elder who is his spiritual director: a bad thought is emptied of its venom when brought to the fore.

III. ON THE THREE RENUNCIATIONS, BY ABBOT PAPHNUCE. They are the renunciations of external goods, of our past life in the world, of our vices and passions, finally, of things present and visible for the sake of future and invisible goods.

IV. ON THE CONCUPISCENCE OF THE FLESH AND OF THE SPIRIT, BY ABBOT DANIEL. Cassian gives a deep analysis of the darkness and abandonment of the soul as a trial sent from God.

V. ON THE EIGHT CAPITAL VICES, BY ABBOT SERAPION. Cassian examines their interrelations and remedies.

VI. ON THE MURDER OF THE SAINTS, BY ABBOT THEODORE. Cassian discusses the spiritual advantage which can be derived from evil, even from moral evil.

VII. ON THE SPIRITS OF EVIL, BY ABBOT SERENUS. Cassian notes that the spirits of evil are more subtle than they were before, i.e., less violent and material, and more spiritual and insidious. Cassian, then, discusses the notion of "being delivered to Satan" (certain cases of demoniac possession): it is for a good purpose, not for the loss of the person. We must pray for demoniacs (those possessed by an evil spirit), and, if possible, give them the communion. Cassian (ch.32) describes several forms of demoniac possession: phenomenologically they do not widely differ from what we can see in psychiatric hospitals, but the spiritual context is different.

IX. ON PRAYER, BY ABBOT ISAAC. Cassian analyses the various forms of prayer mentioned in I Tim. 2:1, "obsecration, promise, demand, thanksgiving," and comments on the Lord's Prayer. Obsecration is the cry of the soul of a sinner who is touched by compunction and implores his pardon. Cassian gives a good description of "compunction," a state of the soul which combines tears and joy, fear and love.

(Through "compunction," the memory of our past sins brings the soul to renew in itself feelings of repentance with fear and shame, humble begging of pardon, invocation of God's mercy, thanksgiving for the love of God, and the immense joy of feeling God's presence. It is one of the main ways for monks to find contact with the living God in prayer. Because of the abundance of tears in compunction, they were nicknamed "Weepers.")

XI, ON PERFECTION, BY ABBOT CHEREMON. Cassian discusses the question of fear and love.

XII. ON CHASTITY, BY THE SAME. Same doctrine as *Institutes VI* "On fornication."

XVI. ON FRIENDSHIP, BY ABBOT JOSEPH. We observe an interesting transposition, on the high spiritual level of monastic life, of Aristotle's classical analysis of friendship in the *Nichomachaean Ethics*.

XVI,2. ON RESOLUTIONS, BY THE SAME. We are told (together with Cassian himself and his companion) that we should not absolutely stick to our own promises, but sometimes change our mind in order to be, with more flexibility, more faithful also to the will of God.

XIX. ON CENOBITIC AND HEREMITIC LIFE, BY ABBOT JOHN. Contrary to normal expectation, abbot John, after living many years as a hermit, came back to community life in his monastery. He does not contest the perfection of heremitic life, but he found by experience that, instead of a total freedom for contemplation, his time was consumed by the many cares and anxieties of daily life (gardening, cooking, etc.). In the convent, he had plenty of time for contemplation. Moreover, in the convent, a monk benefits of brotherly warning and exercises in the virtues of social life, two advantages which are lacking in heremitic life.

## QUESTIONNAIRE ON EARLY MONASTICISM

1. According to Cyprian's *De habitu virginum*, what is the particular dignity of the way of life of the holy virgins, which raises them above the spiritual status of average married people?

2. Do you find in the same treatise of Cyprian signs of Stoic reasonings ("What is not according to nature is morally wrong and sinful")? Do you agree with him on the examples which he gives? Is it always wise to use the Stoic principle in order to determine what is right or wrong?

3. Do you find some similarity between the interventions of demons in the Gospels, and the very vivid interventions of demons in the *Life of Antony*?

4. Are demons and angels more relevant in a less cultured form of Christian life? Can we simply say that the devil today has managed to persuade people not to believe in him? Can we reject angels and demons as a whole as obsolete superstition? Is there a middle position in this regard?

5. Can we say that the belief in the existence of demons contributes to make our spiritual fight more dramatic and realistic than a mere fight against the wind-mills of abstraction when we define evil as a mere lack of required goodness, or merely as self-injury?

6. What do you think of Antony's rules for the discernment of spirits: the manifestations of evil spirits cause turmoil and sadness, whereas those of good spirits bring about peace and

joy? Does this observation correspond to something in the experience of your own conscience?

7. In the absence of an "elder" as we find in early monastic life, or of a friend or spiritual director, is it a good and effective idea to bring forth our bad thoughts to the judgment of God in our conscience?

8. Are these evil spirits necessarily "persons"? Or are they often simply vices, i.e., perverted instincts which have developed as a kind of cancer of the soul and acquired power and independence? Cf. Cassian.

9. What kinds of temptations seem to have developed in monks of antiquity because of the harsh treatment which they imposed on themselves? What do you think of the relevance of such a challenge?

10. What is depicted in the *Sayings* as particularly dangerous for the spiritual life of monks?

11. What are, in your opinion, the *Sayings* which are the more moving?

12. What is the advantage of heremitic life (life in solitude) according to Pachomius or Cassian?

13. What is the advantage of cenobitic life (life in community) according to Pachomius or Cassian?

14. Would you, like the *Rule of Pachomius*, approve the method of breaking the personal will of young people entering monastic life today?

15. Do you find a good balance in the notion of the abbot in the *Rule of St. Benedict*?

16. Among the images of the spiritual life of holy virgins in Methodius Olympus' *Banquet of the Ten Virgins*, select three images which you consider as better than others.

17. Do you find that a spirituality (style of dedication to God) of "servant of God" is more suited to men, whereas a spirituality of "bride of Christ" is more suited to women in holy virginity?

18. Do you personally know any monastics? In what type would you classify them? Have you found the monastic full of wisdom, benevolence, shining joy, truly human?

19. Would it be a good idea today to return to the notion of old age as the natural age of contemplative life? Could not also

good divorced men or women, or unmarried men or women be interested in a kind of community life?

## BIBLIOGRAPHY

ATHANASIUS. *The Life of Antony*, tr. R.T. Meyer. ACW 10, 1950.

BASIL. *Ascetical Works: The Morals; The Long Rules*, tr. Sr. Monica Wagner. FC 9, CUA, 1962.

BENEDICT. *The Rule of St. Benedict, 1980 in Latin and English*. Collegeville, MN: The Liturgical Press, 1981.

BROWN, Peter. *The Body and Society: Men, Women, and Sexual Renunciation in Early Christianity*. New York: Columbia University Press.

CASSIAN. *Institutes & Conferences*. LNPF, 2d ser., vol.11.

_____. *Conferences*, selections. LCC 12.

CHADWICK, Owen. *John Cassian, A Study in Primitive Monasticism*, 2nd ed. Cambridge, England: Cambridge University Press,1968.

CHAPMAN, John. *St. Benedict and the Sixth Century*. London: Longmans, Green & Co., 1929.

CHITTY, Derwas J. *The Desert a City: An Introduction to the study of Egyptian and Palestinian Monasticism under the Christian Empire*. Oxford: Blackwell 1966.

CLARKE, W.K. Lowther. *St. Basil the Great, A Study in Monasticism*. Cambridge, England: Cambridge Univ. Press, 1913.

CYPRIAN. The Dress of the Virgins. ANF 5, pp.430-436.

GREGORY OF NYSSA. *The Life of St. Macrina*, tr. W.K.L. Clarke. London: SPCK, 1916. Also recently in Classics of Western Spirituality.

METHODIUS OLYMPUS. *The Banquet of the Ten Virgins*, tr. H. Musurillo. ACW, 1958.

METZ, René. *La consécration des Vierges dans l'Eglise Romaine*. Paris: PUF, 1954.

ORIGEN. *The Song of Songs: Commentary and Homilies*. ACW, 1957.

*The Rule of the Master.* Kalamazoo, MI: Cistercian Publications.

WADDELL, Helen. *The Desert Fathers.* Ann Arbor, MI: Ann Arbor paperback, 1957.

# CHAPTER XIV

## CHRISTIAN COMMUNITY LIFE

Once made a Christian through instruction and baptism, what was the style of life of the faithful in the local Church, or parish? The present chapter tries to answer this question. And since there are many aspects to this question, the answer also is many-faceted. The best way to keep the right balance and unity is to start with the example of a Christian community of average size, when the Church had already reached its maturity of structure and spiritual experience. A gigantic Church of the kind found in large cities such as Rome, Milan, Carthage, Alexandria, Antioch, and Constantinople in the Christian Empire offers many features which are peculiar to the importance of its position and number, but not typical of the average local Church. To start with such a large Church would be as mistaken as to study American life according to the patterns of New York, Washington D.C., or Los Angeles. Fortunately, we possess a Church manual belonging to an unknown, average-size Syrian Church of the second half of the third century. This manual was written by a bishop as a guide for other bishops. It is the so-called *Didascalia Apostolorum*.

We successively deal with the questions which follow:

1) We first describe Christian community life according to the *Didascalia*. Then, in order to complete our information, we cast a glance in several directions. 2) The soul of the community consisted of devoted people, chiefly elderly, among whom blossomed charisma and who ministered to their fellow members through intercession and friendly warning, as attested in Clement of Alexandria. 3) Christian family life is well illustrated in detail by Tertullian's treatise *To his Wife*, which also shows how Christian practices were a liberation from the tyranny of pagan superstition. Augustine's pastoral position on conjugal life, in spite of his reputation of pessimism concerning sex, is not a condemnation, but sound realism and wisdom.

4) *Shepherd of Hermas* teaches Christian ethics, first of all, parental duties, and shows a great awareness of the problems of spiritual life for the individual and the community. 5) Encratism was supported, on the one hand, by Tertullian, Novatian, etc., and opposed, on the other hand, by the *Didascalia*, Hermas, and Clement of Alexandria. Encratism (from *encrateia*, self-mastery) taught renunciation, but unwisely tried to impose its own patterns on everyone, and refused to reconcile repenting sinners, thus making Christian life impossible for married people and the average faithful.

6) The process of healing from sin could be private and by ordinary means such as fasting and almsgiving. It could also

be managed by a priest privately. Theodore of Mopsuestia describes the priest as a physician of souls in private. 7) The penitential system, visible, official, stern, is well known from Tertullian, Cyprian, Basil, Chrysostom, Ambrose, Augustine, the bishops of Rome, and Caesarius of Arles. It became so oppressive with time that, like laws which pretend to maintain their efficiency by more severity, it progressively fell into disuse. Bishops with a pastoral sense such as Caesarius laid the emphasis on the penitential character of daily life, and allowed communion to people of good will.

Generally speaking, it is unfair to claim that the Church degenerated once it became part of the Empire after Constantine. The Church proved to be successful in the training of the masses, an achievement which seemed impossible to Celsus who acknowledged the failure in this regard of the Schools of philosophy.

## I. *DIDASCALIA APOSTOLORUM*.[270]

### PREAMBLE.

Just like all church manuals in early Christianity, the *Didascalia* depends on a model found in I Timothy and Titus, the so-called "Pastoral Epistles," which appear in the Pauline collection of writings, and which belong to the New Testament from the beginning. They may represent the situation of Pauline Churches of the second generation, after they have reached their "normal" structure. It is a synagogal structure, with a college of elders (presbyters) elected, and ordained with a laying on of hands. This basic structure is completed by the presence of a bishop (there was a president in the synagogue), and of deacons (servants, or ministers, absent from the Jewish synagogue probably because of the small number of its members and of their ability to take care of the poor directly as neighbors).

There are various ranks among the faithful. The most interesting of all is that of the widows of the Church: destitute and holy widows who were supported by the community and lived according to the patterns of contemplative life (prayer, fasting, daily worship, spiritual influence).

### REQUIREMENTS FOR THE APPOINTMENT OF A BISHOP.

The *Didascalia* develops the passage of I Timothy 3 concerning the bishop, and also borrows vocabulary and images from the liturgy of the Temple of Jerusalem. Ignatius of Antioch's ideal of the bishop as over and above the whole com-

---

[270] *Didascalia Apostolorum*, tr. R. Hugh Connolly (Oxford: Clarendon Press, 1929), selections, abridged.

munity and presbyters influenced the *Didascalia*. The bishop is the father of the community after God, their mediator with God, their high-priest, leader and king.

> The pastor who is appointed bishop and head among the presbyters in the Church in every congregation is chosen a blameless man, not less than 50 years of age, instructed and apt to teach, younger possibly if the congregation is a small one, merciful, peacemaker. Let his hands be open to give; and let him love the orphans with the widows, and be a lover of the poor and of strangers. His alms must be wisely distributed, for instance, passing by a widow who is able to nourish herself, he will give to a woman who is not a widow, but is in want, whether by reason of sickness, or of the rearing of children, or of bodily infirmity.
>
> And let the bishop be also without respect of persons, and let him not defer to the rich nor favor them unduly. And let him be scant and poor in his food and drink, that he may be able to be watchful in admonishing and correcting those who are undisciplined.
>
> And let him be assiduous in his teaching, and constant in reading the divine Scriptures with diligence, that he may interpret and expound them fittingly. And let him compare the Law and the Prophets with the Gospel in such a way as to show their accord. But before all let him be a good discriminator between the Law and the Second Legislation (precepts added by human authorities to the divine commands), so that he does not impose on the brethren or on himself heavy burdens and become a son of perdition (4).

THE ADMINISTRATION OF PENANCE AND FORGIVENESS.

In a long section (4-10), *Didascalia* deals with penance and forgiveness. Instead of an impersonal display of legislation and procedure, the bishop of *Didascalia* suggests an attitude which combines sternness with mercy toward a sinner, and first insists on the necessity, in order to rebuke a sinner, of keeping himself and the community blameless and pure from sin:

> But if the bishop is not of a clean conscience and, for the sake of the presents which he receives, spares one who impiously sins, and suffers him to remain in the church: such a bishop has polluted his congregation with God; yea, and with men also, particularly with the young or those immature in mind. But if he (who impiously sins) sees that the bishop and the deacons are clear of reproach, and the whole flock pure; first of all he will

not dare to enter the congregation, because he is reproved by his conscience; but if he comes to the church in his arrogance, and he is rebuked by the bishop, and looking upon all present finds no offence in any of them, neither in the bishop nor in those who are with him: he will then be put to confusion, and will go forth quietly, in great shame, weeping and in remorse of soul; and so shall the flock remain pure. Moreover, when he is gone out he will repent of his sin and weep and sigh before God, and there shall be hope for him. (5)

Do thou, O bishop, judge: first of all strictly; and afterwards receive (the sinner) with mercy and compassion, when he promises to repent. Receive him that repents without hesitating ever; and be not hindered by those who are without mercy. But when thou hast seen one who has sinned, be stern, and command that they put him forth; and when he is gone forth, let them be stern with him, and take him to task, and keep him outside the church; and then let them come in and plead for him. And then, do thou, O bishop, command him to come in, and examine him whether he be repentant. And if he is worthy to be received into the church, appoint him days of fasting according to his offence, two or three weeks, or five, or seven (6). You have received authority to forgive sins.

Those that deserve rebuke, rebuke and afflict; but unto conversion and not unto destruction. Him that is broken by his sins, cure him with the exhortation of admonition, lighten him of his transgressions, comfort him and show him that there is hope for him. Heal him and bring him into the church. Visit and count thy flock, and seek that which is gone astray. Leave the 99 upon the mountain, and go seek that one which is gone astray. Do not use force, and be not violent, and pass not sentence sharply, and be not unmerciful. Like wild beasts, the heathen and heretics will devour as meat the man driven out of the church without hope (7).

So neither do we communicate with these (baptized sinners) until they show the fruits of repentance. But let them by all means come in, if they desire to hear the word, that they not wholly perish; but let them not communicate in prayer, but go forth without (before the prayer of the faithful and the Eucharist). As you baptize a heathen and then receive him, so also lay hand upon this man, while all pray for him, and then bring him in and let him communicate with the Church. For the imposition of hand shall be for him in the place of (a new) baptism: for whether by the imposition of hand, or by baptism, they receive the communion of the Holy Spirit (10).

THE TRIBUNAL OF THE BISHOP.

Let the bishop and the deacons be of one mind; and do you shepherd the people with one accord. For you ought both to be one body, father and son. And let the deacon make known all things to the bishop, even as Christ to his Father. But what things he can, let the deacon order, and all the rest let the bishop judge. Yet let the deacon be the hearing of the bishop, and his mouth and his heart and his soul; for when you are both of one mind, through your agreement there will be peace also in the Church.

Let your judgments be held on the second day of the week (Monday), that if perchance any one should contest the sentence of your words, you may have space until the Sabbath to compose the matter, and may make peace between them that are at odds and reconcile them on the Sunday. Now let the presbyters and the deacons be ever present in all judgments with the bishop. Judge without respect of persons (10).

PLACES IN CHURCH.

And for the presbyters let there be assigned a place in the eastern part of the house; and let the bishop's throne be set in their midst, and let the presbyters sit with him.

And again let the laymen sit in another part of the house toward the east. For it should be, that in the eastern part of the house the presbyters sit with the bishop, and next the laymen, and then the women; that when you stand up to pray, the rulers may stand first, and after them the laymen, and then the women also. For it is required that you should pray toward the east.

But of the deacons let one stand by the oblations of the Eucharist; and let another stand outside by the door and observe them that come in; and afterward, when you offer (the offerings of the faithful) let them minister together in the church.

Those who are young sit apart, if there be room, and if not they stand up; and those who are advanced in years sit apart. And let the children stand on one side, or let their fathers and mothers take them to them; and let them stand up. And let the young girls also sit apart; but if there is no room, let them stand up behind the women. And let the young women who are married and have children stand apart, and the aged women and widows sit apart.

> And let the deacon also see that no one whispers, or falls asleep, or laughs or makes signs. For if it should be, that with decency and decorum they watch in the church, with ears attentive to the word of the Lord (12). Warn the people to be constant in assembling in the church, and not withdraw themselves but always to assemble, lest any one diminish the Church by not assembling, and cause the Body of Christ be short of members (12).

THE APPOINTMENT AND CHARISMA OF WIDOWS.

Holy widowhood is called the "glory of widowhood," i.e., the promotion to the rank of contemplative life for those who fulfill the requirements of I Timothy 5, and are abandoned and destitute. Like the Old Testament, the Church assists and honors widows according to the divine precept.[271]

In the *Didascalia*, holy widows are clearly recognized as charismatics: their prayer of intercession is seen as powerful, and they pray over the sick with a laying on of hands in order to heal them. The paradigm of the holy widows in Scripture are the widow of Sarepta, and Anna, daughter of Phanuel. The example of Anna is particularly interesting since, according to Luke,[272] she was a widow and had spent many years praying and fasting in the Temple. Moreover, she enjoyed the gift of prophecy.

The widows of the *Didascalia* can be appointed when they are 50 years old (60 in I Timothy). The bishop receives gifts from the faithful and distributes them to each one of the widows, mentioning the name of the donor that she may pray for this person by name. The widows must obey the bishop or deacon when asked to go and pray over somebody, but not decide by themselves with the secret hope of getting presents from unworthy donors.

Widows should not teach, or answer questions on such delicate items of the Christian faith as the Incarnation and the Redemption --women have not been sent to teach, but to pray. Let then a widow know that she is the altar of God! Since an altar does not move, widows should not run about among the houses of the faithful in order to receive alms. The *Didascalia* then gives a development on the behavior of bad widows, who are led by avarice and the love for gossip.

Holy widows are ascribed the gift of healing. Two interesting texts respectively point to the power of their prayer of intercession, and to their use of the laying on of hands.

---

[271] Ex. 23:22-24.

[272] Luke 2:36-38.

> A widow who wishes to please God sits at home and meditates upon the Lord day and night, and without ceasing at all times offers intercession and prays with purity before the Lord. And she receives whatever she asks, because her whole mind is set upon this.
>
> But you, O widow who are without discipline, see your fellow widows or your brethren in sickness, and have no care to fast and pray over your members, and to lay hand upon them, and to visit them, but feign yourself to be not in health, or not at leisure; but to others who are in sins or are gone forth from the Church, because they give much, you are ready and glad to go and visit them (14-15).

THE APPOINTMENT OF DEACONS AND DEACONESSES.

The *Didascalia* does not deal with the ordination of deaconesses, but simply with the question of their appointment, and justifies their usefulness since their institution was not yet widely spread. There is no reason to deny them the benefit of ordination as certain scholars do. The fact that the need of a woman deacon is mentioned for the visit of sick Christian women in pagan houses, and for the baptismal anointment of women, does not mean that these are their only duties, but that a woman is more particularly suitable in such cases. Finally the fact that they do not serve at the altar does not mean that they are not ordained. The objection to their ordination arises from another church order, the *Apostolic Tradition* of Hippolytus, which specifies that ordination with laying on of hands is to the service of the altar. The objection from the *Apostolic Tradition* can be challenged on two grounds. First, we should remember that the "liturgy" of a deacon, in the ancient Greek sense of *leitourgia*, is not necessarily related to worship and altar, but points to the service of the community and of the bishop, very much in the manner of a modern "social worker." In this sense, on a Sunday, a deaconess would simply, because she is a woman, not serve at the altar, but, like the other deacons who do not serve at the altar, she would serve among the community of the faithful. Second, the chief reason for the existence or non-existence of deaconesses is geographical. Deaconesses were absent from Egypt and from the Western Churches, but common in the Eastern Churches. The reason was local tradition and the special need for deaconesses in the large communities of Asia Minor, which was the most populated part of the Roman world.

> Those who please you (bishop) out of all the people you shall choose and appoint as deacons: a man for the performance of most things that are required, but a woman for the ministry of women.

> For there are houses where you cannot send a deacon to the women, on account of the heathen, but may send a deaconess. Also, because in many other matters the office of a woman deacon is required. In the first place, when women go down into the water, those who go down into the water ought to be anointed with the oil of anointing; and where there is no woman at hand, and especially a deaconess, he who baptizes must of necessity anoint her who is being baptized. But where there is a woman, and especially a deaconess, it is not fitting that women should be seen by men; but with the imposition of hands do you anoint the head only. Let a woman deacon anoint the women. But let a man pronounce over them the invocation of the divine Names in the water. And when she who is baptized has come up from the water, let the deaconess receive her, and teach and instruct her how the seal of baptism ought to be kept unbroken in purity and holiness... Our Lord and Savior also was ministered by women ministers (16).

THE CARE OF ORPHAN CHILDREN.

Adoption is recommended for orphans. The *Didascalia* suggests that a family without children might adopt an orphan, or that "whoever has a son might adopt a girl, whom he would later on give to his son as wife." The bishop must see that the orphan girls make the right marriage, and that the boys learn a craft, and receive the wages which they deserve in order to support themselves and to prepare for the future (17).

ALMS ARE REFUSED FROM IMPIOUS SINNERS: A LIST OF "SOCIAL SINS."

The *Didascalia* criticizes careless bishops who feed the "altar" of God (orphans and holy widows) with gifts from sinners who oppress the poor or make money on vice and on pagan worship, but who propose to conciliate God with such gifts and thereby obtain the favor of the Church.

> For bishops receive gifts to use for the maintainance of orphans and widows, from rich persons who keep men shut up in prison, or ill-treat their slaves, or behave with cruelty in their cities, or oppress the poor; or from the lewd, and those who abuse their bodies; or from evil-doers; or from forgers; or from dishonest advocates, or false accusers; or from makers of idols; or from workers of gold and silver and bronze who are thieves; or from those who alter weights or measure deceitfully; or from inn-keepers who mingle water with their wine; or from dishonest tax-gatherers; or from soldiers who act lawlessly; or from murderers; or from spies who procure

> condemnations; or from any Roman officials, who are defiled with wars and have shed innocent blood without trial: perverters of judgments who, in order to rob them, deal unjustly and deceitfully with the peasantry and with the poor; and from idolaters; or from the unclean; or from those who practise usury, and extortioners. (Then, *Didascalia* suggests a collection among the faithful) (17).

The *Didascalia* sees in the use of these alms for the sustenance of orphans and widows a desecration of the "altar of God." The offering of alms by good people is a sacrifice, particularly if they are destined to such a living "altar of God."

CONJUGAL RELATIONS.

Concerning defilement, it is interesting to observe that the *Didascalia* has a very positive view of conjugal relations, and refuses to consider them as a ritual impurity preventing access to the Eucharist or any kind of worship, or requiring a ritual purification by washing:

> There are men and women who for such reasons refrain themselves from prayer and from receiving the Eucharist, or from reading the Scriptures, supposing themselves to be unclean, and deeming it necessary either to absent themselves from church for a season or to have recourse to ceremonial baptisms (ablutions) (26).

The *Didascalia* answers that the spouses do not lose the presence of the Holy Spirit, and remain pure without the help of any levitical purification. And the same is true of contact with a dead person or a tomb, since they also offer the Eucharist and read Scriptures in cemeteries.

## II. THE HEART OF THE COMMUNITY

The Christian community honored widows and the elderly, and supported them in their material needs through the ministry of the deacons when they were destitute. Religious meals (*Agape*) were organised for them, in which clergy and community participated.[273] In return, widows and the elderly assumed an important role in the life of the community: they were the praying part of the community in the daily worship -- those in active life generally came on Sunday. And, together with the presbyters, they accomplished spiritual ministries of intercession before God and of counselling for their fellow

[273] Tertullian, *Apology* 39.

Christians. Sometimes it is not easy to distinguish them from the presbyters properly speaking. The elderly were the contemplatives and the sages of the community, and to join them was a kind of promotion.

The holy widows of the *Didascalia Apostolorum* fulfilled a spiritual ministry of prayer and healing. Tertullian[274] introduces sinners confessing their sins before such a group of presbyters and elderly:

> It requires that you habitually nourish prayer by fasting, that you sigh and groan day and night to the Lord your God, that you prostrate yourself at the feet of the presbyters and kneel before the beloved of God, making all the brethren commissioned ambassadors of your prayer for pardon.

According to the same Tertullian, old women who have the experience of marriage and children --not virgins-- are the natural advisers of the young women in the Christian community.[275]

Clement of Alexandria refers to weak members who also beg the praying community for help:

> He should say, I have come into sanctuary, I can suffer nothing. And if he has the fear that he may fall, he may say, Brother, lay your hand on me lest I sin, and he will receive help both spiritually and physically.[276]

In his sermon, *Who is the rich man who shall be saved*,[277] Clement provides precious information about these spiritual ministries of the elderly:

> Collect for yourself an unarmed, unwarlike, bloodless, passionless, stainless host, pious old men, orphans dear to God, widows armed with meekness, men adorned with love. Obtain with your money (alms) such guards, for body and soul, for whose sake a sinking ship is made buoyant, when steered by the prayers of the saints alone; and disease at its height is subdued, put to flight by the

---

[274] Tertullian, *On Penance* 9-10, tr. ACW, cf. *On Monogamy* 11.

[275] Tertullian, *On the Veiling of Virgins* 9.

[276] Clement of Alexandria, *Stromaton* III, 1,2, (LCC).

[277] Clement of Alexandria, *Quis dives salvetur* 34-35, (ANF 2).

> laying on of the hands; and the attack of robbers (devils) is disarmed, spoiled by pious prayers.
>
> (These spiritual ministries are:) intercession for the pardon of sins; comforting the sick; weeping and groaning for you (sinner) to the Lord of all; teaching you some of the things useful for salvation; admonishing with confidence; counselling with kindness; and all can love truly without guile, without fear, without flattery, without pretence.

Holy widows and pious elderly Christians enjoy the rank of contemplatives in the community, and often the possession of charisma for the service of their fellow members.

## III. FAMILY LIFE

From Tertullian again, in the treatise which he wrote *To his Wife* in order to dissuade her from a second marriage after his death, particularly of a marriage with a pagan husband, we learn interesting details on daily life for a Christian couple.[278] Tertullian first describes the inconvenience of a marriage with a pagan husband:

> What condition shall be hers with a pagan husband? She will not be able to fulfil her religious duties. When she wishes to go to church, he bids her to join him at the public baths earlier than usual. When she proposes to fast, he orders a large meal for the same day. When she needs to be out, the servants of the household have never been bidden more work than this time. What pagan husband will ever allow his wife to visit the brethren from street to street, and to enter the poorest places? Who will endure her to leave at night and join a meeting, when it is appropriate? Who will allow her to be out all night long for Easter? Who will let her, without any suspicion, share in the Lord's Supper, which is the subject of many attacks from the pagans? Who can endure her to get into the jails in order to kiss the chains of the martyrs, to wash the feet of the saints, to give them and to get from them the kiss of peace? or to share in the bread and wine, in the agapes, and to spend her days long in prayer? If a brother from abroad happens to come, how will he be welcomed in the house of a foreigner of faith? Everything will be closed, loft and cellar.

---

[278] Tertullian, *To his Wife*, Book II, 4-5,8,(ANF). Abridged.

Our exercises cannot be hidden: the more you conceal them, the more you make them suspect, and occasion curiosity and envy from the pagans. Is it possible, tell me, to be hidden when you make the sign of the cross over your bed and your body, when you blow in order to cast out the evil spirit, when you wake up at night to pray? Would they not suppose that you are practicing magic? Would you be unobserved by your husband when you eat something secretly before the meal? And when he comes to know that it is bread, shall he not assume that it is this bread so slandered by the pagans? Since he cannot get into a mystery which he does not know, he will be alarmed and suspicious. He will imagine murder and poisoning (4-5 ANF).

Far better is the marriage of two Christians:

Whence are we to find words enough fully to tell the happiness of that marriage which the Church cements, and the oblation confirms and the benediction signs and seals; which angels carry back the news of (to heaven), which the Father holds for ratified? For even on the earth children do not rightly and lawfully wed without their fathers' consent. What kind of yoke is that of two believers, partakers of one hope, one desire, one discipline, one and the same service? Both are members, both fellow servants, no difference of spirit or flesh; nay they are truly *two in one flesh*. Where the flesh is one, one is the spirit too. Together they pray, together prostrate themselves, together perform their fasts; mutually teaching, mutualy exhorting, mutually sustaining. Equally are they both found in the Church of God; equally at the banquet of God; equally in straits, in persecutions, in refreshments.

Neither hides anything to the other; neither shuns the other; neither is troublesome to the other. The sick is visited, the indigent relieved, with freedom. Alms are given without danger of ensuing torment; sacrifices attended without scruple; daily diligence (discharged) without impediment; there is no stealthy sighing, no trembling greeting, no mute benediction. Between the two echo psalms and hymns; and they mutually challenge each other which shall better chant to their Lord. Such things when Christ sees and hears, he rejoices. To these he sends his own peace. Where two are, there is he himself. Where he is, there the Evil One is not (8, LCC).

It is noticeable, maybe merely incidental, that children do not appear in this description of marriage in his treatise. If asked whether conjugal life is pure by itself with the exception of sin, probably Tertullian would have answered positively, in the case of a first marriage, because of the divine blessing. But he condemned second marriage, and, because of the sinful inclination of the flesh, he qualified marriage as a lawful fornication.

AUGUSTINE ON CONJUGAL LIFE.

Because of his pessimism about human nature, Augustine is often put on the "black list" of theologians of marriage. He, indeed, insisted on the persistence after baptism of "concupiscence," a disorder of the flesh inherited from Adam together with the original sin. In addition, it seemed that, according to Augustine, no human act, even virtuous deeds, escaped some measure of imperfection or of sin, since our acts should be motivated by a pure love of God and of his will.

My contention is that, on the contrary, Augustine showed a very positive understanding of marriage as both a theologian and a pastor. And if I am right, we can assume that generally married people could feel spiritually comfortable in the early Church.

In *De bono conjugali* (11:24) Augustine said that in a lawful marriage intercourse with the intention of begetting children is perfect and not sinful at all. Let us presume that he meant what he said, and that this also belonged to his system of thought. He knew that young couples want offspring, and in antiquity this necessity was felt as more imperative because of the high proportion of early deaths. It would be foolish to suppose that he required an explicit act of will in this matter before each intercourse. For him, as a philosopher and not a picky moralist, the willingness to have offspring was included in the will of nature, and represented what a couple wants to achieve in their life.

The question of the pleasure attached to intercourse was different: according to the philosophy of his time, Augustine held that pleasure, as a companion and an incentive of a good action, can be desired together with it, but should not itself become the purpose of our acts. Augustine fought the Epicurean idea of considering pleasure as an end in itself.

If the purpose of the couple actually was pleasure and not offspring, Augustine, following the Stoic reasoning, saw a disorder in relation to the natural law, and a sin. But the same natural law also suggested the answer: this is a small sin, not usually a grievous one. Intercourse, only for the sake of pleasure within the limits of a lawful marriage, protects marriage against breaking up.[279] Thereby conjugal fidelity is maintained, and the procreation of children encouraged. The

[279] Augustine, *De continentia* 12:27.

couple assume their responsibility as parents, a very noble task. Age and the difficulties of life will teach them more gravity and temperance. God's providence thus takes advantage of human weakness for its own purposes.

Augustine is tolerant of human weakness, but he resolutely condemns practices preventing the formation and continuance of the human fetus. He condemns a marriage indulging itself in such practices as a prostitution, although recognizing that the wife may not bear the same guilt as the husband. He knows that she is the victim of brutal devices, which were often lethal for the mother as well as the fetus.

## IV. RESPONSIBILITY FOR OUR BRETHREN: *THE SHEPHERD OF HERMAS*[280]

The *Shepherd*, written in the first half of the second century, looks like a note book of a revival preacher. It belongs to the literature of prophecy in the early Church. It is very interesting for the doctrine of the Church, sacraments, ethics, penance, prophecy, the discernment of spirits. It is a beautiful piece of early Christian literature, fascinating to read.

### RESPONSIBILITY FOR FAMILY.

We limit our report to a few ideas only. First, as a former slave who became rich, Hermas has been neglectful of his duties as a husband and a father. His wife is too talkative: we hope that was her only defect! But his children have lost the sense of moral duty, and, it seems, are apostates. After his conversion to a serious Christian life, Hermas is concerned for a sin of thought he committed long ago when he was a slave, and looked with lust at his mistress who was bathing in a river. This small sin took a disproportionate importance in his mind, and blinded him to far more important sins of omission. In a vision, Hermas saw an old lady who first warned him regarding his domestic duties:

> God is not angry with you on account of this (sin of thought against chastity), but that you may convert your household, which has committed iniquity against the Lord, and against you, their parents. And although you love your sons, yet you did not warn your household, but you permitted them to be terribly corrupted.

---

[280] The quotes are from the Loeb Classical Library, tr. K. Lake, *The Apostolic Fathers*, vol.II.

> On this account the Lord is angry with you, but he will heal all the evils which have been done in your household. For, on account of their sins and iniquities, you have been severely destroyed by the affairs of this world. But now the mercy of the Lord has taken pity on you and your household. But be of good courage and comfort your house. For as a smith hammers out his work, and accomplishes whatever he wishes, so shall righteous daily speech overcome all iniquity. Cease not therefore to admonish your sons; for I know that, if they will repent with all their heart, they will be enrolled on the Books of Life with the saints (I,3).

A MISSION TO THE CHURCH: THE PREACHING OF PENANCE.

The old lady continued to be seen by Hermas and to deliver her messages to him. This time, he will communicate a booklet to Clement ("Clement" maybe a symbol for the present bishop) and to Grapte, a lady involved in the care of widows. The object of the booklet is the opening of a mission of revival, which will start with a good examination of conscience of the various categories of sinners, and end with forgiveness and spiritual health. As befits this style of preaching, the mission is offered only once, and there will be no forgiveness for those who lose this unique opportunity. However, delays after delays are granted, and probably will always be.

The old lady herself is the Church. In the first vision, she appears as a crippled old lady with white hair and sitting on a chair: an image of the Christian community, weak and crushed down under the weight of her sins. Progressively she recovers her strength and youth, and appears as a young bride, the Pauline image of the Church and the biblical image of the people of Israel.

In the third vision, the Church appears under the image of a tower in the process of being built, and rising from water. The lady herself gives the comments. The builders are the angels, and Christ is introduced as the Archangel. The stones taken from the water (of baptism) are not all in good condition and not ready to enter the construction as are the "square stones" which represent apostles, bishops, teachers and deacons of old, or the martyrs who suffered for the Lord's sake, or even "those whom God has approved of, for they walked in the straight ways of the Lord and practiced his commandments."

The stones which are rejected and cast away by the angels symbolize those who have sinned, but wish to repent. They are not sent far away, but left near the building, where they will find a place after they repent. The stones which are sent far away are the children of iniquity and they believed in hypocrisies. But they too may repent and enter the building. The stones which have cracks symbolize "those who are in disaccord in their hearts with one another, and are not at peace among themselves."

The stones which are round and white are "those who have believed and share in righteousness, but have also the riches of this world. When, therefore, tribulation comes, on account of their riches and business, they deny the Lord."

> For as a round stone cannot square unless portions be cut off and cast away, so also those who are rich in this world cannot be useful to the Lord unless their riches be cut down. Learn this first from your own case. When you were rich, you were useless; but now you are useful and fit for life.

After the "Visions," come the "Commandments given by the "Shepherd," or angel of penance, which deal with ethical problems, for instance, the case of the adulterous partner in marriage, or the possession of particular virtues under the name of spirits, and the discernment of these spirits. Good observations are given for the discernment of true and false prophecy (II,11). It proves the importance of charisms in the Roman Church of the second century. The subtlely of the psychological analysis of spiritual problems foreshadows the *Life of Antony* and the *Conferences* and *Institutes* of Cassian, for instance, concerning sadness as a propensity to sin, and cheerfulness as readiness for good deeds (II,9).

The third part consists of "parables," which deal with great images of charity, with the attitude toward sinners, and with the necessity to catch the opportunity offered to be rejuvenated in soul. The most remarkable of the parables is the allegory of the vine and the elm tree:

> The vine produces fruit, and the elm is an unfruitful tree; but unless the vine be trained upon the elm, it cannot bear much fruit when extended at length upon the ground; and the fruit which it does bear is rotten, because the plant is not suspended upon the elm. When, therefore, the vine is cast upon the elm, it yields both from itself and from the elm.
>
> The similitude is for the servants of God --for the poor man and for the rich. The rich man has much wealth, but is poor in matters relating to the Lord, because he is distracted about his riches; and he offers very few confessions (praise) and intercessions to the Lord, and those which he does offer are small and weak, and have no power above. But the rich man helps the poor in all things without hesitation; and the poor man, being helped by the rich, intercedes for him, giving thanks to God for him who bestows gifts upon him. Both accordingly accomplish their work... Blessed are they who have riches, and who understand that they are from the Lord (III,2).

For those who are not rich, but would be able to give alms if they were more organized and could save money, Hermas suggests the idea of combining fasting and almsgiving:

> In that day on which you fast taste nothing except bread and water, and you shall reckon the price of the expense for that day which you are going to keep, of the food which you would have eaten, and you shall give it to a widow or an orphan or to some other destitute, and then you shall thus fulfill the fast as I commanded you, your sacrifice shall be acceptable to God, and this fast shall be written down to your credit, and the service which is thus done is good and joyful and acceptable to the Lord. You shall therefore keep these things thus with your children and all your house, and if you keep them you shall be blessed, and all who hear them and keep them shall be blessed and shall obtain from the Lord whatever they ask (III,5).

The third parable compares the sinner and the just one -- in no wise distinguishable upon earth-- to the trees of a forest in winter, and the fourth parable to the trees in summertime. The idea is that nobody should condemn others, even a sinner, and reject them from the Church, because God only knows what is going on in the human hearts, and whether he will repent and be saved (III,3-4). According to the parable of the willow tree, everyone in the Church is given a chance of repentance and forgiveness under the image of a branch apparently dried which, if planted in the ground and kept moist, can recover life and blossom again. Similarly, through penance, sinners can be roused to life again (III,8).

These parables address a particular situation in the Church of the second and third century, known as the crisis of "Encratism," a party of supporters of an abusively severe discipline in the Church and intolerant of sinners, even though they be repenting sinners.[281] Hermas supports the possibility of a "second penance," i.e., of forgiveness of sins committed after baptism, and the possibility of a "second marriage" in case of widowhood.

---

[281] Concerning the crisis of Encratism and the interpretation of early documents related to it, see P. Nautin, *Lettres et Ecrivains Chrétiens des IIe et IIIe siècles* (Paris: Éditions du Cerf, 1961), ch.3-6, pp.65-165.

## V. ENCRATISM AS BASIC TO THE MONTANISM OF TERTULLIAN

Tertullian turned to Montanism, which was both a prophetic and Encratist sect. He supported their condemnation of second marriage, their denial of the power of bishops to forgive what he called "irremissible sins," and their system of fasting and abstinence. The "irremissible sins" of Tertullian were murder, apostasy, and fornication, which he saw as symbolized in the prohibitions of the apostolic council of Jerusalem: blood, meats sacrificed to gods, and adultery. These sins were generally forbidden by bishops in churches all over the world. However, bishops were allowed by Tertullian to forgive "sins against people, i.e., sins which we consider as often very grievous, for instance, sins against human self-respect and against justice and social duties. Why could "sins against God" not be forgiven by bishops, according to Tertullian? Perhaps because they were committed against a "sacred" thing, therefore more directly against God, and because they kept from this connotation the character of a "sin unto death." Concerning the "power of the keys" (the power to forgive sins), Tertullian denied it to bishops, and, against the general opinion, maintained it had been given only to the apostles. And he mocked the "peremptory edict" of a certain "Supreme Pontiff," perhaps the bishop of Rome, or more probably a bishop of Carthage, who forgave adultery in order to attract the wicked to his "school."[282]

Tertullian was aware of the fact that Montanism --the "New Prophecy"-- required more from its followers than Moses from ancient Israel, or Jesus or Paul from the generation of the gospels. He was not short of an answer, and explained that, although Jesus was able to ask for more than Moses could, for instance, concerning divorce, he was unable to require the full measure of spiritual perfection, for instance, the ideal of continence, since the Holy Spirit had not yet been sent, who should perfect the work of Jesus. But the Holy Spirit was sent by now, and the full discipline inherent in Christianity could be exacted.[283]

One understands that Tertullian was wrong to try to "improve" upon the gospel, and to correct Jesus and the Apostle! Encratism is a systematization of certain ideals of the gospel, which eliminates the rest of the gospel, and becomes a burden imposed on the shoulders of others who cannot bear it. There is enough diversity, or enough "contradiction," in the gospel, to suit every Christian worthy of the name. The pastoral sense of the Church --the care of souls-- won the victory over Encratism. But

---

[282] Tertullian, *De pudicitia.*

[283] Tertullian, *De exhortatione castitatis* ; *De monogamia*, tr. ANF 3.

Encratism, under one form or another, is an endemic disease in the Church, and part of the dialectic of Christian ethics. It has won many victories since then!

## VI. THE PROCESS OF SPIRITUAL HEALING: PRIVATE

Although the modern system of confession to a priest and absolution given in the sacrament of penance did not exist in early Christianity, and developed in the Middle Ages, there were many ways to obtain the remission of sins, which are still good even today!

There was the practice of friendly warning, which was possible among a devoted small number, but became difficult with many. The kiss of peace previous to the offering of the faithful was the sign of peace, i.e., forgiveness of offences between Christians, which made their sacrifice and prayer acceptable. Meditation, prayer, fasting, and almsgiving were ways of forgiveness. In the fourth century, in his *Festal Letters*,[284] Athanasius explained how Lent, as a time of common fasting and prayer, purified the faithful for their Paschal communion. The essential was confession to God directly, with humility and a broken heart.[285] Sometimes, the faithful needed the counselling of an "expert" who could evaluate their guilt and suggest the remedy. We have seen above the presbyters and the community of pious elderly people receiving such confessions and providing intercession and exhortation.[286]

On the basis of this ordinary practice, we shall observe the role of the presbyters and bishop in private and public penance. But, first, we give two short texts of Cyprian and of Origen on the usual means of remission of sins.

Origen, *Homily on Leviticus 2:4* The seven remissions of sins:

> But perhaps those who listen to us in the church may say that with us there is only one pardon of sins, which is given in the rites of initiation through the grace of the laver. You have heard of the number of sacrifices for sin (kinds of victims) in the Law. Listen now to the many remissions of sins in the gospel.

---

[284] Athanasius, *Festal Letters*, LNPF 2d ser.4, pp.506-553, cf. J. Quasten, *Patrology* vol.3, p.53.

[285] Cf. Ps.51.

[286] Clement of Alexandria and Tertullian, cf. p.000 above.

> There is that first by which we are baptized unto the remission of sins. The second remission is had in the sufferings of the martyrs. [The third is almsgiving; the fourth is forgiveness of offences, the fifth is friendly warning[287]], the sixth is charity, which covers a multitude of sins. And there is yet a seventh, although hard and laborious, the remission of sins through penance, when the sinner bathes the couch in tears, and the tears become one's bread by day and night, and when one is not ashamed to show one's sin to the priest of the Lord, and to seek the remedy.[288]

Cyprian, *On Works and Alms 2-3*: Almsgiving is a remedy for sin):

> The Holy Spirit speaks in the sacred Scriptures, and says, "By almsgiving and faith sins are purged",[289] not those sins which had been previously contracted, for those are purged by the blood and sanctification of Christ. Moreover we say again, "As water extinguishes fire, so almgiving quenches sin."[290] Here also is shown and proved that, as in the laver of saving water the fire of Gehenna is extinguished, so by almsgiving and works of righteousness the flame of sin is subdued.
>
> The deep and profound darkness of avarice has blinded your carnal heart. You are the captive and slave of your money; you are bound with the chains and bonds of covetousness; and you whom Christ had once loosed, are once more in chains. You keep a patrimony which burdens you with its weight; and you do not remember what God answered to the rich man, who boasted with a foolish exultation of the abundance of his exuberant harvest: "You fool, said he, this night your soul is required of you; then whose shall those things be which you have provided?" Why do you watch in loneliness over your riches? Why for your punishment do you heap up the burden of your patrimony, that, in proportion as you are rich in this world, you may become poor to God? Divide your returns with the Lord your God; share your gains with Christ; make Christ a partner with you in your

---

[287] Origen, Commentary on Matthew XIII 31.

[288] P.F. Palmer, *Sacraments and Forgiveness* (Westminster, MD: The Newman Press, 1959) p.35-36.

[289] Prov.16:6.

[290] Eccl.3:30.

earthly possession, that he also may make you a fellow heir with him in his heavenly Kingdom.

PRIVATE HEALING BY A PRESBYTER.

Bishop Theodore of Mopsuestia recommended communion to the Eucharist as the way to obtain spiritual strength and forgiveness for those having sinned against their will from the weakness of the human nature, and praying God in great repentance. He relied on the words of Jesus at the Last Supper: "My body... my blood... for the remission of sins." Sins thus committed contrary to our deep desire were considered as involuntary. But, in the case of a great sin, contrary to the commandments, if the sinner persists in evil and refuses to repent, he should abstain from receiving the communion. Once he acknowledges his sin in his conscience, he must repent, then, look for the medicine provided by God for those sick in their soul. Theodore advises this repenting sinner to confess his sin secretly to a priest, who will diligently and in all confidentiality heal him from his sin:

> Because God who greatly cares for us gave us penitence and showed us the medicine of repentance, and established some men, who are priests, as physicians of sins, so that if we receive in this world through them healing and forgiveness of sins, we shall be delivered from the judgment to come --it behoves to us to draw nigh unto the priests with great confidence and to reveal our sins to them, and they, with all diligence, pain and love, and according to the rules laid down from the beginning, will give healing to sinners. And they will not disclose the things that are not to be disclosed, but they will keep to themselves the things that have happened, as fits true and loving fathers, bound to safeguard the shame of their children while striving to heal their bodies.[291]

## VII. THE SYSTEM OF PENANCE: PUBLIC

The seventh remission of sins mentioned by Origen is the way of hard penance, in which the repenting sinner confessed the sin to the priest and sought the remedy. Obviously Origen was referring to the system of public penance. By itself, public penance did not always mean that the bishop compelled the

[291] Theodore of Mopsuestia, *Commentary on the Lord's Prayer and on the Sacraments of Baptism and the Eucharist*, tr. Mingana (Woodbrooke Studies, Cambridge, 1933), pp. 117-122.

sinner to publicly confess his sin and to accept the shame and all the trials of public penance, from excommunication to absolution. In *Homily 2 on Psalm 37*, Origen presented the case of a sinner who, fearing the severity of the Last Judgment, stepped into the middle of the assembly and spontaneously confessed his sin, asking the faithful for their intercession, even looking for shame in order to be spared the shame of his condemnation at the tribunal of God. Probably more frequent was the case of the sinner who resented the sentence of excommunication and slandered the bishop instead of repenting. The best pages on public penance, excommunication and recovery of peace are certainly found in the section of *Didascalia Apostolorum* quoted above[292]

TERTULLIAN'S DESCRIPTION OF PUBLIC CONFESSION.

Tertullian gave a very vivid and moving description of the *exomologesis* (public confession of sins and public penance):

> By *exomologesis* (confession) we confess our sins to the Lord, not indeed as if he were ignorant of it, but inasmuch as by confession satisfaction is settled, of confession repentance is born, by repentance God is appeased. And thus *exomologesis* is a discipline for human's prostration and humiliation, enjoining a demeanour calculated to move mercy. With regard also to dress and food, it commands the penitent to lie in sackcloth and ashes, to cover his body in mourning, to lay his spirit low in sorrows, to exchange for severe treatments the sins which he has committed; moreover, to know no food and drink but such as is plain --not for the stomach's sake, to wit, but the soul's; for the most part, however, to feed prayers on fastings, to groan, to weep and roar unto the Lord his God; to roll before the feet of the presbyters, and kneel to God's dear ones; to enjoin on all the brethren to be ambassadors to bear his prayer for mercy. All this *exomologesis* does, that it may encourage repentance, may honour God by its fear of the danger incurred, may, by itself pronouncing against the sinner, stand in the stead of God's indignation, and by temporal mortification discharge eternal

[292] *Didascalia Apostolorum*, ch.5-7, pp. 36-76. Quote above pp.000

> punishment... While it accuses, it excuses; while it condemns, it absolves.[293]

This practice may seem to us to be distasteful and almost cruel, and public exposition of guilt reminds us too much of certain modern systems of repression. If we want to understand Tertullian's *exomologesis*, we must overcome these impressions, and know that certain cultures require the exteriorization of feelings, like a kind of theatrical attitude. Just as sin in a small society, a village for instance, often occasions scandal, the pressure of that society demands an adequate remedy to the scandal by an act of public repentance. Moreover, this public self-accusation was intended as an anticipation of the judgment of God while the divine judge might still be moved to mercy by the sinner's humble repentance and by the intercession of the holy members of the community.

GREGORY THE WONDERWORKER: THE FIVE GRADES OF PUBLIC PENANCE.

> The grade of "Mourner" takes place outside the door of the church; here it is proper for the sinner to stand, and to beseech the faithful as they enter to pray for him. That of "Hearer" is inside the door, in the narthex; here it is proper for the sinner to stand as long as the catechumens remain, and then go forth. For he (Gregory) says, when he has heard the Scriptures and the instructions, let him be put forth and not be counted worthy of the prayer. The grade of "Faller" is had when he stands within the door of the nave, and goes forth with the catechumens. That of "Bystander" when he takes his stand with the faithful and does not go forth with the catechumens. Last is that of "Participant" in the holies.[294]

These grades are ordinary practice and reappear elsewhere. Basil of Caesarea gives the penalties incurred for grievous sins: he deals with the cases of sinful clerics, an adulteress, the willful homicide, the involuntary homicide, the fornicator, the thief, the apostate.[295]

These steps of penance before re-admission to communion are very long, and the whole system seems to be very

---

[293] Tertullian, *On repentance* 7, 9, J. Stevenson, *A New Eusebius* 158, p.186.

[294] *Canonical Epistles of Basil*, Canon 11 in P.F. Palmer, *Sacraments and Forgiveness*, p.64.

[295] *Canonical Epistle of Basil 217.*

heavy on sinners. Probably the key to the solution is found in the last canon (74), which allows the bishop, seeing the good disposition of the repented sinner, to reduce these periods of penance by reason of the power of the keys. Cyprian reduces to one year of penance repenting apostates who were threatened by a plague or a persecution. In the *Didascalia Apostolorum* we read of a penance of three weeks or no more than seven weeks.[296] In a monastic environment, which itself is penitential, we have seen an old abbot reducing three years of penance to three days. Certainly, in the hands of pastors concerned with the care of souls and preserving the necessary flexibility, the system of public penance could work. And the forty days of Lent represented a formula of public penance for the whole community.

However, the system of public penance, instead of maintaining flexibility, underwent a process of stiffening, and became less and less practical.

OBLIGATIONS OF A RECONCILED PENITENT.

According to Pope Siricius, *Epistle to Himerius 5*,[297] after public penance, a reconciled penitent was still obliged to live in continence, to abstain from military service, from business, from the games, and from marriage or intercourse. In case of relapse, penitents were excommunicated for their whole life, although granted the *Viaticum* (communion) on their death-bed. After their reconciliation, they remained "penitents," and lived a kind of monastic life in the world.

Cyril Vogel shows in detail the excessive rigidity of this system of penance in Gaul. Pope Leo in Rome suggested that young people should not be admitted to public penance. However, certain Christians submitted to public penance even for small sins, which was not required by church law. Innocent I mentions this practice with praise in his *Epistle to Decentius of Gubbio* (416 A.D.). In the sixth century, public penance was open to those who simply wanted to "convert" to an ascetic and contemplative style of life without entering a cloister: the life of the penitents provided them with the right status.

Caesarius of Arles (first half of the sixth century) a pastor very dedicated to the care of souls, managed to take advantage of the system of public penance as a way to provide absolution on the death-bed, and granted communion on feast days to those who were not without sin, but who were people of good will, giving alms to the poor, and performing good deeds.

The whole system of public penance became obsolete and disappeared almost completely. The Middle Ages, under the

---

[296] *Didascalia Apostolorum*, ch.6, p.52.

[297] P.F. Palmer, *Sacraments and Forgiveness*, p.111.

influence of the Irish monks, inaugurated a new system: graded penance, which made absolution almost immediate. It evolved into the modern system of confession to a priest in the sacrament of penance.

The present decline in the practice of confession, a great loss indeed, should not be a cause of discouragement for the Church. There are other ways to obtain the pardon of ordinary sins, and the history of the sacrament of penance shows a diversity of forms.

## QUESTIONNAIRE

1. What is the moral behavior expected in a bishop according to the *Didascalia Apostolorum?*

2. What is the status, and the liturgical and social functions of deacons and deaconesses according to the *Didascalia Apostolorum?*

3. What do you learn from the *Didascalia Apostolorum* concerning the role of the bishop as a "physician of souls" in the process of healing sinners? What is the method of excommunication and reconciliation? Why is it so important that the bishop be blameless?

4. What do we learn from the *Didascalia Apostolorum* concerning the tribunal of the bishop? Do we find something of this kind in the churches of Paul and in the synagogue? Is this kind of peace and reconciliation possible in churches today?

5. Is the *Didascalia Apostolorum* for, or against, the views of the Encratists (excessive severity for sinners, abstinence from meat and wine, and contempt for sexual life)?

6. What do we learn concerning the status in church, and the spiritual gifts, of the holy widows of the *Didascalia Apostolorum?*

7. What are the ideas of the *Didascalia Apostolorum* concerning the dignity, the maintenance, and the preparation for life of orphans? What do you think of these ideas?

8. Can you, from the list of people whose money cannot be accepted "on the sacred altar of widows and orphans," explain the position of the *Didascalia Apostolorum* concerning grievous sins, particularly those against social justice?

9. What were, according to Clement of Alexandria, the spiritual ministries fulfilled by pious elderly people? Can elderly people today seriously help in counselling?

10. How could the life of prayer offered to pious elderly people in early Christianity be considered a kind of "promotion"? Can we imagine such a promotion for elderly today, instead of treating them like kindergarden kids?

11. What interesting detail does Tertullian's treatise *To his Wife* reveal to us concerning Christian life? What seems to be strange to you among these things?

12. In your opinion, would Augustine be a good counsellor for young people in trouble with their marriage?

13. How does *Shepherd of Hermas* depict the Church and the various categories of Christians in his time?

14. What is the meaning of *Hermas'* parable of the wine and the elm tree, and his idea concerning fasting and almsgiving?

15. What is the meaning of *Hermas'* parable of the trees in winter, and of the branches of the willow tree given to everyone? Was Hermas an Encratist?

16. How is *Shepherd of Hermas* a "prophetic book"? Do you find "prophetic" features in other texts, for instance, in the *Martyrdom of Polycarp* and in the *Passion of Perpetua*? Is such a kind of experience still frequent today?

17. What were the excessive views of the Encratists, including the Montanists and Tertullian, concerning sin and forgiveness? Are there "Encratists" today? Are there "irremissible sins"?

18. What are, according to Cyprian and Origen, the ways to obtain the forgiveness of sins? Are these ways still available today?

19. How, according to Theodore of Mopsuestia, did priests heal sinners privately and confidentially? Can we compare our modern confession with this method?

20. Discuss the method of *exomologesis* (public confession of sin and penance) found in Tertullian's *De paenitentia*.

21. What were the steps of public penance according to Gregory the Wondermaker and Basil of Caesarea? What was the meaning of each of these steps?

22. How did the system of public penance stiffen, become excessive in severity, and disappear from use in the Church? Why, in your opinion, did it evolve in this direction?

23. What would you suggest for the future as a good method of spiritual healing, and a good use of the priest's power of the keys? Is the Church bound to the present system?

## BIBLIOGRAPHY


*Apostolic Tradition of St Hippolytus of Rome*, tr. G. Dix, reissued with corrections by H. Chadwick. London: SPCK, 1968.

Didascalia Apostolorum, tr.R.H. Connolly. Oxford: Clarendon Press, 1929.

GREGORY THE GREAT. *Pastoral Care.* ACW 1950.

GRYSON, R. *The Ministry of Women in the Early Church*, tr. J. Laporte & M.L. Hall. Collegeville, MN: The Liturgical Press, 1976.

LABRIOLLE, P.de. *La crise montaniste* ; *Les Sources de l'histoire du Montanisme*, Paris: E. Leroux, 1913.

LAPORTE, J. *The Role of Women in the Early Church.* New York: Edwin Mellen Press, 1982.

_____. "The Elderly in the Life and Thought of the Early Church," *Ministry with the Aging*, ed., W.M. Clements. San Francisco: Harper & Row, 1981, pp.42-48.

LIENHARD, J.T. *Ministry, Message of the Fathers of the Church.* Wilmington, DL: Glazier, 1984.

MEER, F. van der. *Augustine the Bishop.* London, New York: Sheed & Ward, 1962.

NAUTIN, P. *Lettres et écrivains chrétiens des second et troisième siècles.* Paris: Éditions du Cerf.

PALMER, P.F. *Sacraments and Forgiveness, History and Doctrinal Development of Penance, Extreme Unction and Indulgences.* Westminster, MD: The Newman Press, 1959.

TERTULLIAN, *De paenitentia*; *De pudicitia*, tr. W. P. Le Saint. ACW 28, 1959.

_____. *Treatises On penitence and On purity.* ACW 28, 1959.

_____. *Treatises on Marriage and Remarriage: To his Wife, An Exhortation to Chastity, Monogamy.* ACW, 1951.

THEODORE OF MOPTUESTIA. *Commentary on the Lord's Prayer and on the Sacraments of Baptism and the Eucharist*, tr. Mingana. Woodbrooke Studies 6. Cambridge, 1933.

VOGEL Cyril. "Sin and Penance, A Survey of the Historical Evolution of the Penitential Discipline in the Latin Church," *Pastoral Treatment of Sin* by P. Delhaye and others, English translation. New York: Desclee, 1968. Pp. 177-282.

## CHAPTER XV

## THE CONVERSION OF AUGUSTINE

Augustine (354-430), bishop of Hippo in North Africa (modern Algeria), is the leading theologian of the Western Church. Together with Gregory the Great, Augustine was the source and authority on which Aquinas relied as representing Christian tradition. Augustine remains as influential today as he was in all periods of serious theological reflection.

The most appropriate way to enter the wonderful spiritual temple of Augustine's theological thought, for a student, is to begin with the famous narrative which Augustine gave of his own conversion, the *Confessions*. We shall follow this way, and see how Augustine grew in, and, then, was liberated by the grace of God from the fetters of the flesh. *Confessions* also tells us about successive periods of Augustine's life spent in Manicheism, then, in the Ciceronian (Academic) scepticism, and again, in the discovery of the Neo-Platonists, who brought him back to the Christian Trinity of the prologue of John's Gospel. However, we find direct and substantial information about his "philosophical conversion" in the dialogues and treatises which he wrote during his retreat at Cassaciacum near Milan, and which reflect his philosophical discussions and reflections. We shall discuss these successive aspects of the conversion of Augustine, and say something of the real attitude of his mother Monica.

Augustine wrote *Confessions* in his forties when he was priest and bishop in Hippo, North Africa. According to Peter Brown, the kernel of this writing seems to be an exchange of letters between Augustine and Paulinus of Nola which started as correspondence between Augustine's friend Alypius, and Paulinus.[298] These Christian laymen dedicated to a holy way of life and to meditation on scripture, often also to continence, called themselves *servants of God*, and were scattered all over the world. There was a desire to know one another, to communicate, to receive and give advice and exhortation, to live in spiritual communion with each other. One of the first steps in this kind of exchange was to ask the addressee for an account of his conversion, i.e., to explain how the grace of God had worked in his heart and transformed his life. Such accounts naturally took the form of a long prayer of thanksgiving. In order to show the effects of the grace of God, it was necessary to explain how bad they were before, and some exaggeration--in all sincerity--was possible in this regard.

All these characteristics appear in Augustine's *Confessions*: the form of a long prayer of thanksgiving in 13

---

[298] P. Brown , *Augustine of Hippo, A Biography* (Los Angeles: University of California Press, 1967), pp.160-163.

books, a painstaking proof that he was a great sinner in his past life, the unceasing reference to the grace of God and its wonderful power. In *Confessions*, the defense of the Christian truth is included in the texture of the life of Augustine. By the grace of God, who intervened in his life, Augustine was rescued from the error which kept him prisoner in the sect of the Manichees. Then, again by the grace of God, he was made free from the more insidious bondage of the Platonic philosophy, in the golden palace of which he might have spent the rest of his life satisfied, without coming back to Christ and the Church. Augustine gave thanks to God for all these graces, and more particularly for the way God delivered him from the passions of the flesh, healed his soul and granted him the favor of living a life of continence for the sake of contemplation.

Books X to XIII, the second part of *Confessions*, which consist of speculations on creation, do not offer the same personal character as the first part. But they point to the importance of the Bible as the book of the works of God for the salvation of humankind as a whole. A personal conversion is only an individual attempt, isolated, therefore uncertain and fragile, unless we turn to the Bible and situate ourselves in the general act of salvation devised by God in his providence, and functioning from the beginning of human history.

## I. BOOKS I & II: THE FIRST YEARS OF AUGUSTINE

In the first book, Augustine deals with the sins of his childhood. He does not remember anything of this period, but he has observed the behavior of babies: "No one is clean of sin, not even the infant who has lived but a day upon earth," says Augustine, remembering the biblical saying, "How can one be just in God's sight, or how can any woman's child be innocent?"[299] Was it a sin to desire the breast with tears, to turn to violent anger, to beat, to bite, to try to hurt his nurse? The innocence of a child is the weakness of his body, but there is no innocence in his soul. The word of David is right: "I have been born in iniquity; my mother conceived me in sin."[300]

At school, where the child learned the art of offensive language, Augustine was lazy and was beaten. His first prayer to God was to be spared such beatings at school. But he disobeyed his parents and teachers because of his love of playing.

As a baby he was marked with the sign of the cross and given salt on his tongue. That is, he was made a catechumen in view of his future baptism, but his parents postponed his baptism because they wanted to provide him with a good education, which would have been impossible in the case of an early mar-

---

[299] Job 25:5.

[300] Ps.51:7.

riage. We must remember that, according to Roman law, boys were allowed to marry, and did, when they were fourteen years old, the girls when twelve and a half. Those who were bound by marriage at that early age obviously were unable to attend further education. Augustine suddenly became very sick, with much fever, and asked his mother for baptism in order to be purified from his sins, but she preferred to wait, and the child survived. The reason was that, as long as he was not baptized, he could live a disorderly life, since he was not subject to the laws of the Church. Tertullian, two centuries earlier, had advised postponement of baptism for children and even for a young widow until the time of maturity or settlement in life.

During his adolescence, Augustine studied Greek which he hated and never mastered, and Latin which was his native language and which he loved. But the religion which he learned at school was mythology, i.e., legends --often licentious-- about the gods, and how they possessed all the human passions. Immorality was not considered wrong in school studies. Only incorrect language was wrong! Augustine heard about the Trojan Horse, and the Loves of Dido. He was a good student, and destined by his parents to higher education.

Augustine stole food and drink from the cellar of his parents, and lied to his companions. There is no innocence, indeed, in childhood! The only difference between the sins of children and the sins of adults is the importance of the "matter" of sin. Augustine affirms he was looking for pleasure in creatures, rather than in God.

Augustine's sixteenth year was marked by his discovery of concupiscence, i.e., the disorder of the flesh with the sexual drive. The drive was so strong that, years later, Augustine wished he had married like his companions, for marriage is the remedy to concupiscence and its dangers. During that year, his parents kept him at home in Thagaste because they could not afford to send him to school at Madaura. Augustine manifested his puberty: his father rejoiced, in the hope of soon becoming a grandfather, but his mother worried, and sternly warned him against fornication and particularly against adultery. The same year, Augustine was involved in an small theft of pears: they were not even good! But Augustine noted that this sin revealed a great malice since it was evil for the sake of evil!

In all these years of youth, Augustine was actually a good boy according to usual standards. But, seen from the point of view of his recent conversion in his thirties, the guilt attached to the disorders of the first years of life became the symbol of the sinful life from which God rescued him by his grace. Augustine systematically represented his past life as evil. It is biased, but his purpose is clear and candid. Augustine wants to celebrate the efficacy of the grace of God throughout his life, in order to give thanks to God for his conversion and to edify the servants of God, the readers of his first communications.

## II. BOOKS III-V: CARTHAGE

In Carthage, the great African metropolis, Augustine studied literature in order to become a rhetor (public speaker, professor of literature), or eventually enter the Roman administration, a career for which humanities as well as law prepared one. He loved to study, and hated the kind of students who disturbed the classroom and often made teaching impossible. The ambiance of the big city was very different from that of his native village of Thagaste. Augustine lived with a concubine. In fact, he stayed with her for 15 years, and with her had a son, Adeodatus. He loved her, but he could not grant her the status of a wife.

He read Cicero's *Hortensius*, a lost exhortation to philosophy, and felt the love for "immaterial wisdom": he prayed to God, and turned to Scripture, but he was disgusted with its rough language, and with the authoritarian character of the teaching of the Church. He was proud for having read, without the guidance of a teacher, the *Categories* of Aristotle.

Augustine was persuaded to join the Manichees, and became a "hearer," i.e., a low member of the sect. In this rank, he was not subjected to the same asceticism as the "elect," or "perfect," who abstained from wine, meat, and marriage. The "hearers" fed the "elect" who, in return, interceded for them before God. Augustine became a propagandist of the sect, and a very efficient one, since he converted all his friends to Manicheism.

Manicheism was a Persian sect which, although outlawed and persecuted by Roman authorities, spread all over the Roman world during the fourth century. It taught a kind of theosophical system of Christianity in which the doctrine of salvation through Christ was mixed with mythological figures and with a dualism of good and evil powers. The Old Testament was contemptuously rejected, together with the creation of the material world, as the work of a lower God, a God of justice and wrath, the God of the Jews. But the God of Jesus, the Father, a God of love, was acknowledged as the true God.

The version of Manicheism which spread in the Western world and was known by Augustine seems to have been characterized by a basic materialism, an emphasis on astronomy and astrology, and a strong vindication of the rights of human reason versus the Catholic appeal to faith. Such a system pleased young Augustine, who was philosophical and in search of a clear and rational understanding of the world. It also suited his personal experience of the overwhelming power of the flesh.

Actually, the Manichees did not believe in two gods, or two worlds, one good, the other evil. In their system of the world, on the lowest level of the *anthropos* (the individual person) and of the cosmos (the world, a counterpart of humanity), there was matter: the heavy, dark, stormy, powerful, evil element. This matter was closer to the passions of the flesh than to the purely chemical modern notion of matter. On the highest level, there was a tenuous element, quiet, quasi-immaterial, beautiful and bright like a blue sky, but passive, the Good, or God.

The spiritual struggle of the *anthropos* was to find a way between the two opposite elements, to escape the power of matter and the flesh, and to absorb as much as possible the higher element, the good light of God. For this reason, the Manichees taught a doctrine of the "Three Seals," that of the mouth, of the hand, and of sex, which prevented the sins of the tongue (lying, swearing, blasphemy), of the hand (murder, war, military service, hunting), and of sex (adultery, fornication, even marriage itself was forbidden as evil).

The "elect," who abstained from wine, meat, and sex, fulfilled in the world a mission of salvation which consisted of gathering and returning to their heavenly source by eating the particles of divine light which the sunshine had scattered in plants all over the world.

Manicheism proposed to teach a perfectly rational system of the world and of humanity, and professed to appeal only to reason and not to faith. For this reason, and because of its Persian origin --remember the Magi of Matthew,[301] who were guided by a star-- Manicheism heavily relied on astronomy and astrology, its ancient version. Astrology was considered as a scientific art of knowing future events and destiny. The claim of astrology was that the destiny of each individual was determined by a conjunction of stars. Although claiming a scientific character, astrology was the weakness of Manicheism, and subject to objection.

Augustine's friend Nebridius challenged astrology with the "argument of the wheel" (distances between stars in the outer sphere can hardly be distinguished by an observer on the earth at the center of the world) which destroyed the pet dogma of the Manichees. Vindicianus, a physician and proconsul in Carthage who crowned Augustine as the winner of a poetry contest, also warned him against astrology. Augustine's mother Monica refused to admit him under her roof in Thagaste because he was a heretic. A bishop, with whom she wanted Augustine to have a discussion, told her that, as had been the case with himself in the past, Augustine too would sooner or later become aware of the errors of Manicheism and renounce them. The bishop added, "How can the son of so many tears be abandoned by God?"

Augustine began to have objections to Manichaean teachings, which the Manichees of Carthage could not answer. But Faustus, a Manichaean bishop whom they held in high esteem, would come, they said, and resolve all the problems of Augustine. Two years later, Faustus came, but he did not try to answer Augustine's questions. He wisely confessed that he did

---

[301] Matt. 2:1-13.

not know these matters, and asked Augustine for help in rhetoric. Augustine liked Faustus as a person and appreciated both his sincerity and his willingness to learn from a young man.

Although remaining a member of the sect, Augustine progressively lost confidence in the Manichaean truth. He also was scandalized when he saw certain elects, who were supposed to live in celibacy, visiting brothels. Hypocrisy is the worst crime in the eyes of young people. They do not see in hypocrisy "the last homage which vice pays to virtue!"

Augustine moved to Rome. He had heard that Roman students were more serious with their studies than their fellows in Carthage: he did not yet know that these good students cut the last class in order to leave without paying their fees to the teacher! He left his mother Monica (and probably also his concubine and son), and sailed to Rome, where he lived in the house of a Manichee. For one year he benefited from the hospitality of this "brother," who even took care of him when he was sick. Manichaean hospitality was not a empty word, and the strength of the sect was a network of friendship all over the world.

## III. BOOKS VI-VIII: MILAN

In Rome, Augustine attracted the attention of Symmachus, a prefect of Rome and famous rhetor, who offered him a job of imperial rhetor in Milan, the imperial residence. Symmachus was a cousin of Ambrose, the illustrious bishop of Milan. Symmachus was the champion of paganism, and Ambrose that of Christianity. According to the predominant influence of either the pagans or the Christians, they managed to have the statue of Victory removed, or restored, at the entrance of the Roman Senate. Perhaps, with the choice of a Manichaean as rhetor, Symmachus intended to embarass his cousin Ambrose!

Augustine taught rhetoric to the young Milanese aristocracy, and delivered official speeches and panegyrics before civil authorities. His mother Monica, his concubine, his son Adeodatus, and his friends joined him in Milan. Very soon Augustine was disgusted with his prestigious job. He envied a poor drunkard who, at least, could express himself frankly, while he, an imperial rhetor, was obliged to praise people whom he despised for their vices.

He resigned his job of imperial rhetor, giving as a reason the bad condition of his throat in the cool temperature of northern Italy, and retired with his friends to the estates of a benefactor at Cassaciacum. His intention, actually, was to make a change in his career, and to enter the Roman administration. But he was from a very modest origin, almost a foreigner, and high positions in the administration were the privilege of the Roman aristocracy. The way to join it was through marriage, and good aristocratic families were quite willing to give a daughter to a promising young man like Augustine.

Monica found for him an "heiress," but Augustine had to wait two more years because she was too young for marriage. Monica dismissed her son's concubine, who returned to Africa, swearing she would never know a man again. Now Monica could rejoice, for her son would be married, and could be baptized. And he would be successful in life. Her reasoning was not yet that of a saint, nor of a wicked person, but just that of a good middle class mother. Augustine wept, for he loved his concubine. Many scholars see in Augustine's tears a sign of weakness under the irresistible authority of a domineering mother. I think they are wrong, and that Augustine is a great character, who cannot be labelled as a psychiatric case. More than once he resisted his mother. Actually, the three of them, Monica, Augustine, and the concubine agreed on the same principle, which was that his union with the concubine was not a marriage, and would have to end when Augustine found the right person to be his wife. Augustine wept, but he does not even tell us the name of his concubine! The whole affair seems rather disgusting. In my opinion, however, it is not different from the behavior of a graduate student who, having achieved the goal of his studies, divorces the wife who supported him with her work during his years at the university, because now she does not suit his high social position![302]

Augustine was deeply influenced by Ambrose's preaching. Ambrose interpreted Scripture figuratively, as was usual in the Alexandrian method in which he was well trained. Thereby he avoided the pitfalls of literal interpretation, and always derived spiritual meanings from Scripture. Ambrose's figurative interpretation revealed to Augustine the beauty and depth of Scripture, and delivered him from the contempt which he inherited from the Manichees for the Old Testament.

Augustine read Neo-Platonist books, which "a proud man" lent him, probably books of Plotinus and Porphyry in the translation of Marius Victorinus. These books were teaching very much the same doctrine of the divine Trinity as the prologue of the Gospel of John, "In the beginning was the Word, and the Word was with God, and the Word was God..." They taught the illumination of the soul by God, and the creation of the world, but Augustine noted that he did not find in these books the doctrine of the Incarnation of Christ and of the Cross.

The scant information which Augustine gives in *Confessions* about the intellectual preparation for his conversion must be completed with his "philosophical treatises," i.e., his dialogues with his friends in their retreat at Cassaciacum. Confessions provides information concerning his moral preparation, i.e., the struggle with the flesh, and the victory of faith in Christ. We will now deal with these two aspects.

---

[302] P. Brown, *Augustine of Hippo*, p.63.

## IV. CONVERSION OF THE MIND: THE "PHILOSOPHICAL TREATISES"

When Augustine abandoned Manicheism, he did not immediately fall into tears in the arms of his mother, surrendering to her Catholic faith! He acknowledged himself a Christian, since he had "tasted salt and been marked with the sign of the cross" at his birth but, intellectually and morally, he was still very far from baptism.

Even since his first enthusiastic reading of *Hortensius*, he was a disciple of Cicero. As such, he was a Platonist, but a Platonist of a particular kind. The Academy (the School of Plato) had long ago turned to skepticism: the denial of the power of the senses and of the mind to reach objective truth. As a Ciceronian, therefore, Augustine was a skeptic, and as a former Manichee, he was a materialist, and could not conceive of the deity and of the soul as immaterial. We remember that, for the Manichees, the difference between heaven and earth was one of density. Like all materialists, he could hardly conceive of any reality other than matter.

The "philosophical treatises" are a series of dialogues or investigations which Augustine wrote in his retreat at Cassaciacum. They were the fruit of his discussions with his friends, and reflected the successive steps of his intellectual conversion. Since in the *Confessions* Augustine just briefly referred to such discussions, we fill in this gap with a short analysis of this series of philosophical treatises.

### CONTRA ACADEMICOS.

His discovery of Neo-Platonism appeared in his first refutation of the skepticism of the Academy, the *Contra Academicos*. The argument of the skeptics was the uncertainty of our reasoning and the unreliable nature of our senses. The skeptics proved the uncertainty of our reasoning by the disagreement between philosophers on important matters. Against the reliability of our senses, they referred to the 10 "tropes" of Aenesidemus, for instance, a rod seems to be broken when dipped into water; a tower seems to move when we sail in a boat; a rough surface seems warmer to the hand, etc.

In his answer, Augustine starts from the principle that, since happiness is the human goal, and there cannot be happiness without the possession of the truth, our mind should be able to reach real knowledge. Our senses don't lie, but faithfully transmit the appearance of things. Radical skepticism is but a philosophical theory, which does not apply to the ordinary realities of life, for instance, in court, where witnesses are heard. And the most radical skeptics cannot deny that there is an object of wisdom, since they agree on discussing it. They even define error!

Then, Augustine explains away the skepticism of the Academy as a variation of the School of Plato. Since the Stoics, because of their materialism, refused to acknowledge the existence of the Platonic Forms (the Intelligibles as opposed to the sense-perceptibles), and since they pretended to explain everything as a product of matter, the Academy relied on skepticism in order to undermine their false confidence in material things.

Skepticism, therefore, was the exoteric (public) teaching of the Academy, but recently, the genuine teaching of Plato (the Forms), which had been kept as a secret (esoteric) doctrine of the school, had been taught again, first under the form of a compromise by Antiochus of Ascalon, then, openly. Augustine is alluding to the success in his time of Neo-Platonic philosophy as taught by Plotinus and his disciple Porphyry. There was a circle of such "Platonists" in Milan, and one of them lent books to Augustine. Why Augustine labels him as a "proud man" is another question which we may explain later on.

### DE BEATA VITA.

In *De beata vita* ("On happiness"), Augustine explains that we find perfect and everlasting happiness in the possession of Wisdom, and that those who indulge into vice and turn away from God are not happy. "Wisdom," which is true and divine knowledge, is also the "Son of God." Accordingly, the divine Wisdom --not humanity-- is the "measure of the soul," or a guide of right behavior. The plenitude, or perfect happiness of the soul is possible only when we are in the possession of God. But there is an experience of God in the present life. This experience grows in intensity from a simple hearing of the "voice of God" which is just a divine warning in our conscience, to the "vision" of God, which is the full possession of wisdom, and perfect happiness.

### DE ORDINE.

In *De ordine* (On order, or divine providence) Augustine discusses the relation of evil to the general order of the world as determined by God's providence. A noise of water falling from the roof brings the friends to discuss the presence of evil and error in a world ordered by God. Just as this noise has an explanation, error and evil contribute to the beauty and order of the universe. God is just and good, and he loves order and hates evil. He is not the cause of evil, but is able to take advantage of evil and to integrate it into the order of his providence. And, like the existence of executioners and prostitutes, evil is a confirmation of virtue. The order of the world and divine providence are a guide leading to God.

## SOLILOQUIA.

In *Soliloquia* (book I), a dialogue of the soul alone with God as the Truth, Augustine enlarges on the idea of knowing the Truth from experience by the eye of the soul once purified. Then the Truth may present itself to our sight. In book II, continuing his argumentation against the skeptics, Augustine notes that the immortality of the soul depends on the eternity of God himself, and on the fact that the truth is found in both God and in the human soul. In order to prove the last point, Augustine outlines a demonstration of the existence of the Truth which might persuade a skeptic. He starts from the unstable character of error as compared to the truth, and, from this, passes to positive arguments. Reason is the source of arts and sciences, first of all, grammar and dialectics, which are admitted by all. The Academicians, who are also called mathematicians, are those who do not doubt the reliability of numbers, which share in the stability of the intellegible object (a geometrical figure is more "true" than the perishable material object). Therefore, we can accept the idea of the immortality of the soul which is in possession of perfect science and eternal Truth.

However, since a skeptic will never be persuaded by reasoning, Augustine appeals to the "testimony of the soul" which spontaneously affirms that she is not the same thing as the body, and cannot imagine that she would perish together with the body, and not think any longer.[303]

## DE IMMORTALITATE ANIMAE.

In *De Immortalitate animae*, Augustine proves that the soul is immortal. He relies on the *Phedo* of Plato, which shows that our soul can always find strength and youth in the highest Forms to which she can always return and on which she can feed. For this purpose we only have to purify our soul from the passions and to adhere to the Good. Augustine drops the Platonic theory of reincarnations. And he insists on the indestructibility of the soul, which cannot be destroyed by external or by internal causes, for instance by sleep or folly, and which is the cause of her own motion. If the soul is not rationality by itself, at least, she is intimately united to the rational principle which is immortal. Thereby she is able to directly contemplate the divine Truth with which she is acquainted.

---

[303] Tertullian, *The Testimony of the Soul*, ANF 3, pp.175-181

## DE QUANTITATE ANIMAE.

In *De quantitate animae*, Augustine explains that, since the soul produces incorporeal objects (as we do when, with a line and a point, we create objects which possess the third dimension), the soul is herself incorporeal. Moreover, the soul does not grow externally, in quantity, but internally. The soul does not really grow with time, but in worth, with eventual ups and downs. Sensation is common between people and animals, but knowledge is the affair of the human soul only.

Augustine distinguishes seven degrees in the growth of the soul: mere *animatio* (life), *sensus* (sensation), *ars* (school disciplines), *virtus* (moral virtues), *tranquillitas* (silence of the soul), *ingressio* (attention to God), *contemplatio* (God shows himself to the soul).

## DE MUSICA.

In *De musica*, after five books on technical aspects of poetry, book VI deals with the higher and higher implications of sound. Sound is based on vibrations, or number. The memory does not only welcome "material numbers," but also "spiritual and eternal numbers." These spiritual numbers are proper to the soul, and enable her to master the body, now but particularly in the incorruptibility of the resurrection, as they did before the fall, but they depend themselves on the subjection of the soul to the higher authority of God. From an elementary reaction of our senses to external sound, the soul progressively reaches the level of intellectual or moral judgment, which is based on the Platonic Form of Equality, Beauty, Truth, i.e., the divine, which communicates something of its life to a purified soul. In this treatise, Augustine supports his thesis of "absolute idealism": since sensation is a reaction of the soul to data from outside, not only our reasonings, but also our sensations, together with the pleasure or pain attached to them, are essentially an act of the soul.

## DE MAGISTRO.

*De magistro* deals with teaching or communication. We need signs (words) in order to think and to communicate with the outside, but these signs are not enough if they cannot feed on the data provided by reminiscence or direct evidence. Moreover, on the higher level of "spiritual numbers" (things of the soul implying a relation with God), we do not understand such things through communication from outside properly, but because the Truth is sitting inside over our mind, Christ, the Wisdom of God. And the internal Teacher reveals it according to our capacity and our good dispositions.

DE VERA RELIGIONE.

In the treatises examined above, Augustine, more and more distinctively insisted on the relevance of learning "from authority," i.e., through faith, from the Church. In *De vera religione*, he affirms that Socrates and Plato would approve the Christian doctrine on God, beatitude, the purification of the soul, and on Christ as the Human assumed by God, who converted the nations by persuasion. The Catholic Church is the true Church, which is not destroyed by, but benefits from, the attacks of her enemies, and proves to be both tolerant and effective with sinners.

Christianity is a religion of authority, since we receive our doctrines from god, but faith is only the beginning of understanding. Like children, we begin with *historiae*, or the examples of people in Scripture, but we progress toward God by reason, when we discover God through his creation, and pass from visible to invisible things. Augustine develops a theology of sin, the Redemption, the resurrection, the life of virtue, faith and reason.

DE LIBERI ARBITRIO.

In *De liberi arbitrio*, Augustine deals with the question of the free will. As created by God, human free will is good, but its motion may be evil. The free will is a "middle good," i.e., a good thing which can be used for evil. The free will is the cause of its own motion to evil. We cannot accuse divine foreknowledge, which is the consequence, not the cause of our misdeeds. Again, because of our free will, the devil has no right over humankind, and his quasi-right over sinners is redeemed for those who believe in Christ. As the fruit the blindness due to slothful error and passion, the sins committed after the original sin remain acts of the human free will and fully responsible. However, every creature, even sinners in a certain manner contribute to the beauty of the universe. Augustine also deals with the "inner," or "spiritual" sense, which is our communication with the divine Wisdom. In return, the "inner sense" perceiving the "spiritual numbers" hidden in things stands as a kind of proof for the existence of God.

DE UTILITATE CREDENDI.

In *De utilitate credendi*, Augustine vindicates the Catholic appeal to faith, and refutes the Manichees who criticize faith and reject the Old Testament: faith is a step towards understanding. Augustine enlarges on the several methods of Scriptural interpretation: the analogical meaning (agreement between Old and New Testament); the allegorical meaning (things of the Old Testament symbolize things of the New testament, or spiritual things); the historical meaning (the events of the Old

Testament for themselves). Just like the interpreter of Virgil, the interpreter of the divine Scriptures must sympathize with them, and not take a hostile attitude.

But, since God in his providence has not left us without an authority on which we can rely, we must look for this authority, which we find in the Catholic Church. The claim of the Catholic Church that it is the true Church preferable to all heresies is not only antiquity and miracles, but that, according to the divine promise, it is spread all over the world, and has changed the hearts of many. On the one hand, Augustine can even say that now he believes in Scripture, not because of the authority of Scripture itself, but because he believes in the Church which is the accomplishment of Scripture. On the other hand, he says that there is a connaturality between divine Wisdom and the Sage, and that Wisdom has her own way of persuasion. But the Incarnation adds to the persuasive power of divine Wisdom in Christ.

## V. FROM THE TRINITY OF PLOTINUS TO THE CHRISTIAN INCARNATION

As we can see from the "philosophical treatises," Augustine's notion of the world and humanity is completely reversed. From Manichaean materialism he has passed to idealism. Actually, he has adopted the neo-Platonic philosophy of Plotinus, with its strong mysticism. Instead of granting, with the Manichees, all power to the material and stormy element, and passivity to the good and divine, now Augustine, with the new philosophy, acknowledges the power of the good. The supreme Good, or Beauty, or the One God, is like a shining sun pouring light and energy everywhere. This energy, as it were, overflows: it feeds our intellectual life and, on a lower level, confirms the virtues of our moral life, establishing its mastery over the body and the passions.

Conversely, when we turn upwards toward the good, we first acquire self-mastery and moral virtue. Then, purified from the passions, we adhere to the Intelligibles through the exercise of reason, and acquire strength and unity of soul. We are directed to the One, mysterious source of all energy, center of the universe and of humanity, an inner reality, where we find our perfection in a sublime purification from multiplicity, i.e., from whatever is not God.

Augustine is willing to recognize in the Triad of Plotinus: the "One," "Intelligence," and "Soul," the Christian Trinity: "Father," "Son" or "Word," and "Spirit."[304] However, in Plotinus, he does not see any mention of the Incarnation, i.e., of the practical way to ascend toward the One. Porphyry, he says,

---

[304] *Confessions* VII, 9; cf. P. Brown, *Augustine of Hippo*, pp.98-100.

thought of the necessity of such a way, but, because of his unbelief, he did not know that God had provided it in Christ.[305] Augustine accused the Platonist who lent to him Platonic books of being a "proud man." Probably he meant a man who wanted to reach God and perfection without the assistance of Christ. Augustine understood from his own experience the sad reality of human weakness and the invincible power of the flesh. The philosophy of Plotinus, in spite of its truth, was a theoretical, not a practical redemption.

We can now turn to the other aspect of Augustine's conversion, the conversion of the flesh, which we find fully developed in *Confessions*.

## VI. THE CONVERSION OF THE FLESH: RETURN TO THE *CONFESSIONS*

Augustine could not live for two years without sexual life: he found a mistress. But he would soon forget both marriage and mistress. He converted to the style of life of a "servant of God," living in continence and contemplation. How did such a change happen?

When he decided to change from education to administration, his purpose was less to acquire power and wealth than to acquire a rank in society which would provide him with studious *otium* (leisure time). Many members of the aristocracy found their delight in culture, and spent part of their time reading and editing books of classical literature. They enjoyed contemplative life.[306]

When his philosophical reflection led him back to the Christian faith, Augustine gave up the hope of a leisurely life because he discovered another way to reach the same goal, and a better goal, indeed. It was a life of meditation on Scripture, and of dedication to this ideal in asceticism. Ambrose lived in celibacy. Augustine confesses that, when he arrived in Milan, he did not understand the meaning of this way of life.[307]
But all the great names in Christian literature pointed to the same way of life: Simplicianus, the spiritual father (and later successor) of Ambrose, Jerome, Basil, Chrysostom, and particularly Paulinus of Nola. Paulinus renounced a governorship and wealth in order to live a life of continence and contemplation at Nola near the tomb of a martyr, and his wife followed his example.

Augustine read the epistles of Paul, and found the explanation for his case. There were two conflicting wills in

---

[305] *City of God* X 32.

[306] P. Brown, *Augustine of Hippo*, pp. 115-116.

[307] *Confessions* VI, 3.

him, the will of the flesh and the will of the spirit, and, with the help of the grace of God, he had to get rid of the "old man" in himself, or the "body of death," with the help of the grace of God, in order to put on the "new man," re-created according to the divine image found in Jesus.[308]

Simplicianus told Augustine the story of the conversion of Marius Victorinus, a famous rhetor, whose statue was placed in the Roman forum in his lifetime. Having himself been an imperial rhetor, Augustine could not be ashamed of following such an example.

Ponticianus, an African member of the imperial administration, who was just arriving from Treves, an imperial residence like Milan, on seeing that Augustine was reading the epistles of Paul, told him about a curious event which took place near Treves. Two distinguished members of the Roman administration, on a trip in the neighborhood, visited the cabin of a hermit and discovered a copy of the *Life of Antony*. One of them did not even come back to the city, and adopted monastic life. Augustine also read the *Life of Antony*, and wondered how simple and uncultured people like Antony and many others were able to become ascetics, and he, in spite of his culture and philosophy, was still walking in the marshland of the passions. He prayed for the gift of chastity and continence. He very much wanted to adopt this higher way of life. But he was unable to make a decision, and his passions mocked him: "You cannot do without us, and if you try, you will soon come back to us, for you need us."

Here took place the famous scene in the Milanese garden.[309] Augustine was weeping in distress, in spite of his great desire for a virtuous life of continence. He heard the voice of a child singing, *Tolle, lege*! (Take, and read!). Interpreting this voice as a heavenly warning, he took the book of Paul, and opened it at random. He fell upon Romans 13:13-14, which exactly suited his case:

> Let us behave with decency as befits the day: no revelling or drunkedness, no debauchery or vice, no quarrels or jealousies! Let Jesus himself be the armour that you wear; give no more thought to satisfying the bodily appetites.

Immediately Augustine found certitude, light, peace. Alypius used the same device of opening the book of Scripture, and joined his friend in conversion. Both came to Monica to tell her the news, and Monica exulted and blessed God.

---

[308] *Confessions*, VII,21.

[309] *Confessions* VIII, 12.

It was the day and hour. Augustine does not describe his baptism. The scene of the garden has been diversely interpreted. P. Courcelles argued that it is an artificial piece, for which Augustine found his inspiration in parallel literature concerning divine warning through an innocent child.[310] Whatever parallels there be in classical literature, Courcelles did not understand the psychological truth of the scene of the garden, and its importance in the conversion of Augustine. It was the drop of water which makes the vessel overflow. It was the tiny bit of emotion which changed the dispositions of Augustine's soul. It was the work of grace. I mean "grace" according to the understanding of Augustine: a concrete event which God uses in order to change our mind, not a "grace" in the modern abstract sense of the term as a kind of invincible divine fluid carrying the human will where it does not want to go.

There are parallels to the scene of the garden in our time, for instance, in the conversion of Paul Claudel, the famous French poet, in the beginning of our century. He converted on a rainy and dull Christmas day when, entering the cathedral of Notre Dame in Paris, he heard the voice of the children's choir singing the *Adeste fideles* announcing the birth of Jesus. It was artistic emotion, indeed, but there is no division between artistic emotion and religious emotion, since both are born from an inspiration from on high, and can find a powerful ally in the mysterious depths of our soul.

And once we become cheerful and optimistic in our spiritual life, everything becomes much easier. We love virtue and find pleasure in it. And what we love, that we achieve easily. Augustine read in Paul that the Holy Spirit of God pours love into our hearts, and this love is a divine power which fills our soul and enables us to win battles against the passions of the flesh and of the mind. Such is the basis of Augustine's future theology of grace as he will develop it against the Pelagians in *De natura et gratia, De spiritu et littera, De gratia et liberi arbitrio*, etc.[311]

Augustine remembered the warning of his passions before his conversion: "You will come back to us." Until the end of his life he was careful to avoid temptations: he never attended wedding parties, and did not allow a woman to live under his roof. He managed to have his priests and deacons live together with him in his episcopal house according to his ideal of a priest living in celibacy:[312] it was the beginning of a custom which has

---

[310] P. Courcelles, *Recherches sur les Confessions de St. Augustin* (Paris: De Boccard, 1950), p. 200.

[311] *De natura et gratia* 57.

[312] *The Life of Augustine* by Possidius, 25-27, *Early Christian Biographies*, tr. R.J. Deferrari, FC 1952.

been observed as a general law in the Western Church. With a great compunction of heart, and for several days, he recited on his deathbed penitential psalms which he had written on the wall.

## VII. THE VISION IN OSTIA[313]

The wishes and prayers of Monica were fulfilled, her son had come back to the Catholic faith and was baptized. He was now a servant of God, and she could communicate with him better than ever before. Since Augustine renounced his secular ambition, they had no reason any longer to stay in Italy, and they decided to return to Africa.

Because of the presence of pirates on the Mediterranean sea, their voyage to Africa was delayed, and they spent several months in Ostia, the harbor of Rome. Monica's health was declining, and she died in Ostia. She had always wished her body to be buried next to the body of her husband Patricius. However, she died with joy because her chief vow was fulfilled, the conversion of her son.

A few days before her death, mother and son engaged in a spiritual conversation about life after death. Its account is known as the "Vision in Ostia" and is the description of an "ecstasy," i.e., an experience of heavenly life following a purification of the soul from all lower thoughts:

> If to any one the tumult of the flesh were silenced -- silenced the phantasies of earth, waters, and air-- silenced, too, the poles; yea, the very soul be silenced to herself, and go beyond herself by not thinking of herself --silenced the fancies and imaginary revelations, every tongue, and every sign, and whatever exists by passing away, since, if any should hearken, all these say, "We created not ourselves, but were created by him who abides for ever": If, having uttered this, they now should be silenced, having only quickened our ears to him who created them, and he alone speak not by them, but by himself, that we may hear his words, not by the fleshy tongue, nor angelic voice, nor sound of thunder, nor the obscurity of a similitude, but might hear him --him whom in these we love-- without these, as we two now strained ourselves, and with rapid thought touched on that eternal wisdom which remains over all. If this could be sustained, and other visions of a far different kind be withdrawn, and this alone ravish, and absorb, and envelop its beholder amid these inward joys, so that his life might be eternally like that one moment of knowledge

---

[313] *Confessions* IX 10.

> which we now sighed after, were not this "Enter into the joy of your Lord"?[314]

P. Henry notes the similarity between the "Vision of Ostia" and the ecstasy of Plotinus, and P. Courcelles concludes to a literary dependency.[315] They are right, fortunately. It is fitting that the same philosophy of the mystical experience (union with God) bring about similar effects in Plotinus and in Augustine, and in a thousand others. However. Augustine's ecstasy remains faithful to the biblical belief of a radical distinction between our soul and God, which finds expression in a dialogue with God through the words of a psalm. This distinction is not as clear in Plotinus where the issue is with the search for unity as a transcendent source within, a principle of unity which could be identified with the self.

In *Confessions*, Augustine has a beautiful formula for the expression of the experience of God in the soul: "God, *intimior intimo meo, superior summo meo*": the God who is within myself, and more present to myself than I myself am; the God who is above myself, whom I touch with the summit of my soul.[316]

## AN OVERVIEW OF AUGUSTINE'S TEACHING

Augustine fought against Manicheism in public conferences, and in writings more particularly when their leaders realized the devastating power of his rhetoric.

He fought against Donatism, an African schism, one century old and well established as a kind of national church, but rejecting the communion of the Catholics in Africa and overseas, and rejected from their communion. The Donatists logically, but abusively, derived from the ecclesiology of Cyprian the idea that baptism given outside the church (their own church) could not provide salvation, and they re-baptized Catholics. The Catholics rejected the legitimacy of the donatist hierarchy, and condemned as blasphemous the practice of re-baptizing. In spite of their wishes, the two parties had been fighting too fiercely and too long to be able to achieve the common goal of unity. Augustine took a large part in this long campaign. From his contribution we inherit the recognition of the importance of the notion of "universal church" and the idea that the real author of baptism is

---

[314] Tr. A. Fremantle, *A Treasury of Early Christianity.*

[315] P. Courcelles, *Recherches sur les Confessions de St. Augustin*, pp.222-228.

[316] *Confessions* III 7.

not the minister -- who may be a schismatic, a sinner, a Judas -- but Christ.

Following the "linear diagram" of the Triad of Plotinus: the One, Intelligence, Soul, Augustine discovered in the prologue of the Gospel of John a parallel: God, Word, Holy Spirit. In his philosophical treatises and in his *De Trinitate*, he continued his metitation on the Plotinian Triad, which he knew from philosophy, and on the Christian Trinity, which he knew from the creed of Nicaea-Constantinople. From the observation of a sun shining over the earth and providing it with life, Augustine progressively passed to the investigation of what is inside this "sun," in other words, of the internal life of the Divinity. The Father conceives his Son or Word, and the Holy Spirit constitutes the bond of love or will existing between these two. We observe a similar process in our soul when we think or produce an internal word, and approve it with love or will. The difference is that, when God expresses and wills himself, his Word and Love are substantial and eternal as co-equal with him. Since this diagram proposes to describe the internal life of the Trinity, independent of God's relation to the world, we call it the "circular diagram."

Against the accusations of the pagans, who related the sack of Rome by Alaric (410 A.D.) to the law of Theodosius forbidding sacrifices to the gods, Augustine started his gigantic apology, the *City of God*. After refuting the pagan objection to the Christian God, Augustine dealt with the gods and superstitions of the pagans. Then, he discussed the philosophical notions of God of the Stoics and especially of the neo-Platonists. He was particularly interested in the demonology of Porphyry, in whom he recognized a philosopher looking for the "way" (the Incarnation), but unable to accept it. Then, Augustine dealt with beatitude -- the destiny of all rational beings -- and followed the successive ages of the "City of God" from the creation of the angels to the age of grace with Christ and the Church, and with the problems related to the resurrection. The *City of God* is like a gigantic catechesis, that is, whatever a cultured person might have needed in order to complete his/her conversion to a Bible opened toward the world, after being attracted to the Church by divine providence. The small treatise *De catechizandis rudibus* explains how the theme of the "Two Cities" belonged to the catechesis.

When Caelestius, a "servant of God" like his master Pelagius, arrived in Africa after the sack of Rome in 410, he engaged in theological discussions with the Africans, and mocked the African practice of infant baptism which was the exception in Italy. It was the beginning of the controversy of original sin. In theology, appeal to Scripture is the rule. Augustine represented Adam as not simply the originator of sin in humankind, but as the originator of "original sin," existing in babies and requiring infant baptism. He interpreted in this sense Romans 5:15 where he read that all humans were found in Adam and sinned in

Adam. The original sin is not simply, Augustine noted, a matter of forgiveness, but really a wound in the human nature, which appears in the weakness of the flesh. Augustine was aware of the anthropological obscurities attached to its tranmsmission, but insisted on the fact of our wounded will.

Baptism purifies and heals the soul of a baby and that of an adult as well. But, in the case of an adult, the human will can always return to evil, and daily prayer must continually ask God for grace: a particular grace for a particular good deed, because we have opened the wound of the human nature. In spite of this gloomy view, the theology of grace of Augustine is not pessimistic, but becomes essentially optimistic once we understand that the grace of God consists of the many events, small or great, of our life which are constantly given us as help or warning, and that the Holy Spirit makes everything possible and cheerful by pouring love into our hearts.

## QUESTIONNAIRE

1. In what sense does Augustine identify himself in *Confessions* as a "servant of God"?

2. How did Augustine proceed when he wanted to introduce a new candidate to the Christian faith and doctrine? What was the role of personal events, and that of the Bible, in this catechesis?

3. What is the real purpose of Augustine in his terrible description of the sinful gestures of babies?

4. Why did Augustine's parents postpone his baptism to adult age? Was infant baptism a current practice?

5. From all we learn in the first chapters of *Confessions*, was Augustine a bad, or a good child and young man?

8. Pass judgment on Monica as a mother and as a Christian mother.

7. Was Augustine seriously afflicted with a "mother-complex"?

8. For what purpose did the "servants of God" tell their stories to each other?

8. What do you think of the sad destiny of Augustine's concubine?

10. Explain the rank of a "hearer," and that of an "elect" in the sect of the Manichees.

11. Describe the Manichaean system of the world and of humanity.

12. What was the advantage and the weakness of astrology in the Manichaean system?

13. How could Augustine accede to a high position in the Roman administration?

14. What were the arguments of the skeptics against the reliability of human thought? (*Contra Academicos*)

15. How does Augustine answer the skeptics?

16. How does Augustine describe the appearance of Neo-Platonism?

17. How does Augustine answer the argument of the existence of evil? (*De ordine*)

18. What do you think of the proof for the existence of Wisdom-God in *Soliloquia*?

19. Explain Plato's proof for the immortality of the soul in Phedo. What does Augustine keep? What does he drop? (*De immortalitate animae*)

20. Show that the "degrees of growth" mentioned by Augustine represent an itinerary of the soul toward God (*De quantitate animae*).

21. What is philosophical "idealism"? (*De musica*)

22. How can Augustine say that, in a sense, we don't learn anything from a teacher? (*De magistro*)

23. How does Augustine prove that the true religion is the Catholic Church? (*De magistro*)

24. How can Augustine say that divine foreknowledge is the consequence, not the cause of our deeds? (*De liberi arbitrio*)

25. How can Augustine say that he now believes in the holy scriptures because he first believes in the Catholic Church? (*De utilitate credendi*)

26. Show that, although Plotinian Deity is energetic (not passive as was the Manichaean Deity), we are still unable with it to change from evil to virtue (*De utilitate credendi*).

27. Can you make a connection between continence and contemplative life from the consideration of discipleship, prophetism, holy widowhood, etc., in the early Church? Is con-

templative life necessarily bound to continence? What does the case of the "servants of God" add to this discussion?

28. What considerations could Augustine derive from the story of the conversion of Marius Victorinus, and from the Life of Antony?

29. How could a child's voice have such an effect on the conversion of Augustine? Is this superstition, or exaggeration?

30. From the "Vision in Ostia" explain how in ecstasy a direct experience of God follows a purification of the soul which goes beyond the purification from the passions. Why is silence necessary for such an experience?

31. How can Augustine say that an instant of ecstasy proves the hope for eternal bliss?

32. What does Augustine mean when he says that God is *intimior intimo meo, superior summo meo* ?

## BIBLIOGRAPHY

### THE WORKS OF AUGUSTINE

*City of God.* Translation by David KNOWLES. Pelican Classics, 1100p. (integral).

*Confessions.* New York: Doubleday Image Books, 1960.

See also *Augustine* in the following Series:

*A Select Library of Nicene and Post Nicene Fathers. The Fathers of the Church.*

*Ancient Christian Writers.*

*Library of Christian Classics.*

### BOOKS ON AUGUSTINE

BROWN, Peter. *Augustine of Hippo, A Biography.* Los Angeles: University of California Press, 1967. (Best)

Van der MEER, F. *Augustine the Bishop*, tr. Battershaw et al. New York: Sheed & Ward, 1961. (Best)

PORTALIE, E. *A Guide to the Thought of St. Augustine.* Chicago: Regnery, 1960. (Important for Augustine's theology).

O'Meara, J.J. *The Young Augustine.* Paris: Etudes Augustiennes, 1954.

TeSELLE, E , *Augustine the Theologian.* New York: Herder & Herder, 1970.

FREND, W.H.C. *The Donatist Church: A Movement of Protest in Roman North Africa.* Oxford, 1952.

BURNABY, J. *Amor Dei: A Study of the Religion of St. Augustine.* London, 1938.

du ROY, O. *L'intelligence de la foi en la Trinité selon saint Augustin, Genèse de sa théologie trinitaire jusqu'en 391.* Paris: Etudes Augustiniennes, 1966.

ALFARIC, P. *L'evolution intellectuelle de S. Augustin.* Paris, 1918.

DECRET, F. *L'Afrique Manichéenne (IVe-Ve siècles).* 2 vol. Paris: Etudes Augustiniennes, 1978.

MONCEAUX, P. *Histoire littéraire de l'Afrique Chrétienne.* Vol. V, *Donatism.*

COURCELLE, P. *Recherches sur les Confessions de Saint Augustin.* Paris: De Boccard, 1950.

WIDENGREN, George. *Mani and Manicheism.* Tr. Ch. Kessler. New York: Weidenfeld & Nicolson, 1965.

MATTHEWS, A.W. *The Development of St. Augustine from Neoplatonism to Christianity 386-391 A.D.* University Press of America, 1980.

# CHAPTER XVI

## UNITY IN EARLY CHRISTIANITY

This chapter proposes to explain succintly the struggle for unity in early Christianity, in the East as well as in the West. It goes far beyond the question of the authority of the papacy.

Following chronological order, it begins with the unity of the church in the New Testament and the first decades of the second century, as seen under its charismatic, mystical, and structural aspects. Then, it discusses the crises of the second century: gnostic, quatuordeciman (dispute on the date of Easter), Encratist-Montanist, and the use of the criterion of apostolic tradition in these controversies. It also explains the importance of communion and excommunication in such conflicts. Finally, it shows how these conflicts reveal the existence of a subtle network of authority among the churches. The discussion of unity in the third century focusses on Tertullian and Cyprian, both of the African church. The fourth century is the time of the Arian crisis, of repeated councils with imperial interference, of condemnations motivated by partisan concerns. It is also the time of the development, under the authority of metropolitan churches (in the capital of a country), of jurisdiction and of a system of appeal.

In Rome and the Western Church, claim was made to the rights conferred by Jesus on Peter as confirmation of the authority of the Roman bishop. Further reflection on texts in the gospels led to the development of a Petrine doctrine, namely, the Roman bishop inheriting from Peter a privileged magisterial, priestly, and judicial authority in the whole church. The Donatist and the Pelagian controversies during Augustine's lifetime illustrated both the affirmation of the Petrine doctrine and the weaknesses of its actual implementation. In the following centuries, the growth of the See of Constantinople as a "second Rome" challenged the old Rome and raised the question of the "primacy," a problem which can only exist when there are rivals.

The papacy became the guaranty of church unity in the West, developed a system of laws and an administration through "decretals" (papal epistles turning into laws) and a curia (secretaries in Rome), and strenghtened its influence outside Italy through "apostolic vicars." Eventually the papacy reached its eminent status in the Middle Ages, and struggled to maintain it during the Reformation and modern times. On the other hand, the Greek churches lived under the authority of their heads - the Patriarchs. The growth of nationalities and the pressure of Islam weakened the unity, and caused divisions among the Eastern Patriarchs. A situation of schism (religious division), fed with bitter conflicts, deepened between East and West. In times of emergency, the East expressed its willingness to accept papal authority, but such artificial unity did not suit

Eastern people and clergy, who enjoyed their own unbroken tradition and had never been subject to Rome.

## I. CHARISMATIC AND SYNAGOGAL CHURCH IN NEW TESTAMENT TIMES

The first question is: Why the church at all? According to A. Harnack,[317]

> "the preaching of Jesus was simple: the kingdom of God, a better righteousness embodied in the law of love, and the forgiveness of sins. He declared his Father to be their Father. He also declared himself to be Messiah. He taught them to surrender to him, which prompted them to leave all and follow him. He also taught them to think of him and of his death in the breaking of the bread and the drinking of the wine, and to say that his death took place for the remission of sins."
>
> "Now we find a Church as a political union and worship organization, a formulated faith and a sacred learning; but one thing we no longer find is the old enthusiasm and individualism which had not felt bound by subjection to the authority of the Old Testament. Instead of enthusiastic independent Christians, we find a new literature of revelation, the New Testament, and Christian priests."

Harnack's evaluation of the early church reflects the views of liberal Protestantism at the end of the last century. Since then, scholars have considerably clarified the early development of the church from the time of Jesus to the end of the formation of the New Testament in the beginning of the second century.

According to R. Brown,[318] the church is presented as a mystical entity in the Epistles to the Colossians and to the Ephesians: the church is the Body of Christ, of which we are the members, and a heavenly temple built on Christ, of which we are the living stones. In the "pastoral epistles" (I,II Timothy, and Titus), the emphasis is laid on the necessity of approved teachers and on the ordination of deacons, presbyters and bishops as ministers and supervisors of the community. Luke, in his Gospel and Acts, insists on the continuity of the Christian community after Christ as a community of the Spirit. Interested as he is in the continuity of the charismatic community, he even omits the

---

[317] A. Harnack, *History of Dogma*, vol.I, pp.43-46.

[318] R. Brown, *The Church, the Apostles left Behind* (New York: Paulist Press, 1984), 156p.

mention of the death of Peter and of Paul. The Gentile communities addressed by Luke, which do not observe circumcision and the prescriptions of the law of Moses, consider Paul as the spiritual guaranty of their membership in the church.

Matthew's community was predominantly Jewish, but, while Jewish conversions became scarce, the proportion of Gentile conversions increased, and raised a problem of identity. The controversy between Christians and Pharisees in the Matthean community is projected back into the time of Jesus, whose historical discussion with the Pharisees is inflated by Matthew. With a remarkable sense of harmony and unity, Matthew manages to keep Jewish-Christian traditions, and to integrate the new members coming from Greek culture. He enlarges on the teaching of Jesus, insists on the continued invisible presence of Jesus in the church, and warns against the danger of clericalism when ministers abuse their authority and condemn the lost sheep instead of looking out for them.

According to R. Brown, the fourth Gospel idealizes the image of Jesus. Although incarnate in a real flesh, really dying, and rising again for our salvation and future resurrection, Jesus is introduced as a pre-existent and eternal being (the Word of God) standing beyond human nature. Jesus cannot show weakness or ignorance, and knows the thoughts of others before they speak. The fourth gospel likes to present Jesus as the divine life-giver who feeds us with his word and sacraments.

R. Brown sees in the Epistles of John a corrective added to the Gospel of John a decade later, after a painful schism divided the Johannine community. This schism, Brown conjectures, was caused by the failure of the new generation to recognize the salvific importance of the teaching of Jesus and of his death for the remission of our sins. They tended toward a merely spiritual form of religion in which Jesus was seen as a divine power sending his Paraclete (comforting Spirit) as a source of mystical life in the heart of the faithful. The Epistles of John severely remind the secessionists of the traditional teaching on the redemption through the death of Christ. The Book of Revelation also reflects traditional views of the redemption.

The Paraclete, as a divine assistant of Jesus, should keep the faithful on the right way and in unity. But are all "charismatics" really inspired by the Spirit of God? Their disagreements prove the existence of wrong inspiration, and the necessity of rules for the discernment of spirits. R. Brown shows that, a decade after the Epistles of John, c. 100 A.D., Ignatius of Antioch, in order to remedy "heresy," i.e., disagreement and division, advocated the "rule of one" in the church, namely, obedience to a "monarchical" bishop presiding locally over the college of presbyters and the whole community.

IGNATIUS OF ANTIOCH.

In his letters, Ignatius preached unity and obedience to all the churches he visited on his way to Rome where he expected to be martyred. To the *Ephesians*, Ignatius wrote:

> If anyone is not inside the sanctuary, he lacks God's bread. And if the prayer of one or two has great avail, how much more that of the bishop and the total church. He who fails to join in your worship shows his arrogance by the very fact of becoming a schismatic. It is written, moreover, God resists the proud. Let us, then, avoid resisting the bishop so that we may be subject to God... You must avoid them (heretics) like wild beasts.[319]

To the *Magnesians* he wrote:

> Because he embodies the authority of God the Father, show him (your young bishop) every mark of respect... I exhort you to strive to do all things in harmony with God: the bishop is to preside in the place of God, while the presbyters are to function as the council of the Apostles, and the deacons, who are most dear to me, are entrusted with the ministry of Jesus Christ... Just as the Lord, therefore, being one with the Father, did nothing without Him, either Himself our through the Apostles, so neither must you undertake anything without the bishop and the presbyters... At your meetings there must be one prayer, one supplication, one mind, one hope in love, in joy that is flawless, that is Jesus Christ, who stands supreme. Come together, all of you, as to one temple and one altar, to one Jesus Christ --to Him who came forth from one Father and yet remained with, and returned to, one.[320]

References could be multiplied to the Epistles of Ignatius concerning the mystical as well as the hierarchical aspect of church unity. Of course, it would be wrong to interpret the quotation given above as meaning that the bishop is in possession of full authority, or that deacons are superior to presbyters because they symbolize Christ whereas presbyters are simply assimilated to the apostles. The bishop is compared to God almighty because God is one, and the bishop is the guaranty of unity in the church. And the presbyters are a college similar to that of the apostles, which collectively rules the community and

---

[319] Ignatius, *To the Ephesians* 5, 7, tr. J.A. Kleist, ACW 1,1946.

[320] Ibid. 3,6,7.

presides over worship. Actually, the college of presbyters corresponds to the elders of the synagogue after which the church was patterned.

About the same time, c. 95 A.D., the *Epistle of Clement of Rome to the Corinthians* preached unity to the community of Corinth with images borrowed from the human organization of the Roman army, from the divine order of the universe, and from the levitical hierarchy where everyone has to serve in his own rank. Clement urged the rebels, who dismissed the presbyters and took their place, to repent and submit to these presbyters established by the apostles or by Christians of the apostolic times in order to prevent strife[321]

Scholars have been particularly interested in the development of episcopacy (the order of bishops), and distinguished a type of community living under a "monarchical bishop" from another type preserving several presbyter-bishops, as seems to have been the case in Corinth and probably also in Rome according to the *Epistle of Clement.* Scholars have been less interested in the presbytery as such, i.e., the college of elders invested with authority by the community and collectively presiding over its activities.

However, I think that we should pay more attention to the Jewish synagogue, whose structure basically consists of a community and an appointed council of elders. Synagogues do not know or need deacons. But we hear of a "head of the synagogue," the necessary chairman, or number one, of every community and council. In the church, for many reasons, the "chairman" acquired a particular importance. But the structure of the church is essentially synagogal. Historically, we can say that the model of the church pre-existed in the Jewish synagogue, and that, if the Jewish synagogue had massively converted to Christianity, there would have been no need for a church and a new clergy. Jesus remained faithful to synagogal service and preached in synagogues. He did not see it as a derogation to his preaching of the kingdom. Paul and the apostles also frequented the local synagogue, as long as they were permitted. But, when they were shunned from the Jewish community, for this reason, they opened another "synagogue" in the same locality, which they called a "church," *ecclesia*, a synonym of the term *synagoge*.

Basically, the question of the unity of the church was the same as that of the unity of the synagogue itself on both the local level and the universal level. Judaism found its unity in both the synagogal institution, the temple of Jerusalem, and the Law of Moses. Christians found their unity in the church, local and universal, in Christ as their temple, and in Scripture, both Old and New Testament. Communities of charismatics existed in the beginning, certainly without much organization and

[321] *Clement's First Letter*, LCC 1, pp.43-73.

hierarchy, as we see in I Corinthians, but this does not necessarily mean that the synagogal system was rejected by the apostles as contrary to the freedom of the kingdom. As the synagogue was for the Jews, the church and its organization was a necessity for Christian communities. The first basis of Christian unity consisted in the very simple and flexible structure of the synagogal institution.

The *Shepherd of Hermas*,[322] in the first half of the second century, manifested both the mystical and the organizational aspect of the church. The church is seen as a white-haired and crippled lady sitting in an armchair, who, from vision to vision, recovers the glamor of her youth, and finally appears as a beautiful bride. The preaching of penance has rejuvenated the church of Rome weakened by permissiveness and cowardice. The faithful obtain through repentance the remission of their sins. Now they are progressing in virtue, and show more courage under the threat of persecution. The mystical image of the bride is biblical (cf. the Bride of Song of Songs, and Hosea's unfaithful wife), and symbolizes Israel. In Ephesians, the church is the bride of Christ, who loved her unto death, and wants her to remain forever beautiful and without wrinkles (Eph. 5:20-32).

*Abercius.*

The image of the bride became classical as a representation of the church, either local or universal. For instance, we find it again in Abercius' epitaph, in the beginning of the second century. Abercius, a Christian from Phrygia (south of the Black Sea), in poetic verses, celebrates as the great event of his life his visit to the Roman church:

> I am a disciple of the chaste Shepherd (Jesus), who feeds his flock of sheep on mountains and plains, who has great eyes that look on all sides. He taught me...faithful writings. He sent me to Rome, to behold a kingdom and to see a queen with golden robe and golden shoes. There I saw a people bearing the splendid seal (of baptism)... (There) and everywhere faith led the way and set before me for food the fish (a symbol for Christ as Son of God and Savior) from the spring mighty and pure, whom a spotless Virgin caught, and gave this to friends to eat, always having sweet wine and giving the mixed cup with bread.[323]

---

[322] *Shepherd of Hermas.* Among other English translations, *The Apostolic Fathers*,vol.2, The Loeb Classical Library.

[323] J. Quasten, *Patrology* I, p.172.

Other images expressed the mystical identity of the church in which its unity is deeply rooted, for instance, the image of the vine and branches in John, or that of the temple built with living stones and maintained together by Christ as the key-stone in I Peter (also the tower of Hermas), or that of the army under its general in *I Clement*, or that of the people of Israel with the understanding that the new Israel is the Church, or finally that of the body and members in Paul's I Corinthians. But the image of the bride is the most striking of all, and gives a new meaning to the image of the body since we are the members of Christ who is the head of the church, his beloved bride.

We see also from the epitaph of Abercius, that the eucharist as the bread of Christ in the following centuries becomes a symbol and a bond of unity between the faithful everywhere. It means sharing in the same Christ and Savior. The bread gathered from the hills in Abercius' epitaph, and from the four corners of the earth in the *Didache*,[324] is also a symbol of the faithful gathered in Christ. There is no better expression of Christian unity. Already in the second century, as a sign of communion, bishops sent a portion of the eucharistic bread to other churches, and the bishop of Rome in the fourth century sent it to the priests who celebrated in churches within the city walls.[325] Travellers from foreign churches were provided with *letters of communion* which gave them access to the eucharist and hospitality in the churches they would visit.[326] Bishops kept an up-to-date list of churches and their bishops with which they were "in communion," i.e. in unity[327] For the faithful because of their sins, or for a bishop or a church because of heresy or schism, "excommunication" meant exclusion from eucharistic communion and from unity. It was resented as a painful wound which called for healing, and communion was generally restored as soon as possible. The Roman church stood among other churches as the chief center of communion.[328]

## II. CRISES OF UNITY IN THE SECOND CENTURY

During the second century many "Gnostic" schools grew on the margin of the main churches and claimed the right to

---

[324] *Didache* 9.10.

[325] Innocent the First, *Ep. to Decentius* 4.

[326] L. Hertling, *"Communio" Church and Papacy in Early Christianity* (Chicago: Loyola University Press, 1972), pp.28-29.

[327] Ibid. p.34.

[328] Ibid. p.53.

teach their own doctrines, or, to some extent, total institutional independence as schismatic churches. Marcion organized a structured church which lasted for several centuries. Valentinus, Basilides, and others, who were the heads of "theological schools" in Italy, Egypt, and the Greek world, had been expelled from the church for their teaching in spite of their desire to stay in the church.

*Irenaeus.*[329]

Among other orthodox writers (Justin, Hippolytus, etc.) who refuted the "Gnostics," Irenaeus (a Syrian who had known Polycarp --Polycarp is said to have known John the Evangelist) lived in Rome and became bishop of Lyons in Gaul c. 170 A.D. He wrote a large and substantial refutation of the teachings of many Gnostic groups. Recently a rich collection of such Gnostic writings has been discovered in Nag-Hamaddi in Egypt, which provided a good knowledge of these early theologies rejected by the church.

Against the Gnostic claim of orthodoxy and of the possession of books going back to the apostolic age, Irenaeus relied on the uninterrupted tradition of teaching found in the apostolic churches, chiefly in Rome where both Peter and Paul taught and died. Irenaeus used the argument of apostolic tradition. He proved that the teaching of the Gnostic schools did not go back to the apostles, but only to Marcion, Valentinus, or Ptolemaeus, etc., their founders, and that their so-called apostolic books were artificially related to such figures as Theudas who had left no memory. On the contrary, Irenaeus gave a list of Roman bishops going back to the great apostles, and attested the continuity of teaching. He affirmed that he could do the same for other apostolic sees: we wish he would have!

In this context he makes a statement which became famous in the question of Roman authority:

> Since it would be very tedious, in such a volume as this, to reckon up the successions of all the churches, we do put to confusion all those who, in whatever manner, whether by an evil self-pleasing, by vainglory, or by blindness and perverse opinion, assemble in unauthorized meetings, by indicating that tradition derived from the apostles, Peter and Paul; and also by pointing out the faith preached to men, which comes down to our time by means of the succession of the bishops. For it is necessary that every church, that is, the faithful everywhere, should resort to (? agree with?) this church, on account of its pre-eminent authority (*propter potentiorem principalitatem*), in which the apostolical tradition has

[329] J. Quasten, *Patrology* I, pp. 287-313.

> been preserved continuously by those who exist everywhere.[330]

Mountains of comments have been written about this Roman *principalitas* mostly with the apologetic purpose of supporting, or contesting, the cause of papal authority. In my opinion, this text did not prove the primacy of Rome or even the magisterium of the Roman church over the world, since these questions were not those of the time. But it proved that, if genuine apostolic teaching can be found in many other sees, because of the teaching in Rome of the two princes of the apostles, Peter and Paul, and because of the continuity of this teaching owing to the uninterrupted succession of the Roman bishops, the Roman tradition was the best reference for orthodoxy in the world against the credibility of the Gnostic schools and of their scriptures.

## BIRTH OF A HIERARCHY AMONG CHURCHES.

The Church of the second century not only faced difficulties from outside (pagan persecutions and the growing of Christian sects), but also from inside (especially the influence of Encratism). Encratism was an excessive standard of severity which tended to condemn the use of marriage and to prevent the reconciliation of sinners. It also prescribed abstinence from meat and wine. This excessive severity unjustly imposed a heavy burden on lay people, and was a cause of division, eventually of discouragement, in the Christian community. Encratism was the pressure of a party in the church, of the type of people who believe that they are right because they claim unbalanced severity.

We follow P. Nautin in the following discussion.[331] There were bishops, and confessors (those coming back from jail after a persecution), who supported the cause of Encratism, and claimed a church of the pure. Others avoided this abusive and dividing attitude and, as good shepherds, cared for the weaker ones. Dionysios of Corinth was this type of "liberal" in the good sense of the word. Pinytos, bishop of Cnossos, was an encratist who attached the obligation of continence to baptism. Dionysios wrote to the church of Cnossos against Pinytos, who answered respectfully as to a bishop of a higher authority. Pinytos maintained his encratist positions, and was not deposed by his community. Later on, in Asia Minor, at the request of Bacchylides and Elpistus, neighboring bishops, Dionysios of Corinth

---

[330] J. Stevenson, *A New Eusebius* 96.

[331] P. Nautin, *Lettres et Ecrivains Chrétiens des IIe et IIIe siècles* (Paris, 1961), pp. 13-104.

similarly wrote to the church of Amastris criticizing the rigorist attitude of their bishop Palmas. In order to protect himself from the threat of deposition urged by Dionysios, Palmas wrote to bishop Soter of Rome (166-174 A.D.) as the most powerful ally and as a supporter of severity. Soter wrote to Dionysios a letter of reprobation based on "falsified" fragments of his letter to Palmas. Dionysios sent the real document to Soter, and maintained the principle of the reconciliation of repenting sinners. In this case, we observe several levels of ecclesiastical hierarchy, respectively represented by Bacchylides and Elpistus, Palmas, Dionysios, Soter.

In the *Letter of the Churches of Viena and Lyons to the Churches of Asia and Phrygia* (c. 175 A.D.), Irenaeus insisted that the Gallic martyrs did not condemn their weak fellow Christians, thereby inviting the Phrygian (Montanist?) confessors to be peacemakers instead of playing the agressive game of the encratist party. We find Irenaeus again at the end of the century trying to reconcile bishop Polycrates of Ephesus with pope Victor of Rome (189-198 A.D.). Victor broke the communion with Polycrates and threatened to excommunicate "all the Asian churches" (probably the Asians staying in Rome). The matter of the conflict was the date of Easter. From Polycrates' letter to Victor[332] we learn interesting things about the particular claims of Rome and of Ephesus to apostolicity. Victor claimed he was the heir of the tradition of Peter and Paul whose tombs were in Rome, but Polycrates claimed the possession of prestigious saints in the area of Ephesus: Philipp and his daughters who were prophetesses, Sagaris, Melito the Eunuch bishop of Sardis, John himself in Ephesus. All celebrated Easter on the 14th of the Jewish month of Nisan (whence their name of "Quatuordecimans").

We see Polycrates arguing against Victor of Rome on the basis of the apostolicity of his own tradition in Ephesus: an apostolic church against another apostolic church! However, the Quatuordecimans were a small minority, without much weight, and did not survive the council of Nicea (325 A.D.). Irenaeus advised Victor to grant peace and communion to the Quatuordecimans because such had always been the Roman attitude. Irenaeus referred to Pope Anicetus sharing in the eucharistic celebration with Polycarp, the bishop martyr of Smyrna then on a visit to Rome, whom he had failed to persuade to renounce the quatuordeciman practice.

The conflicts show that, in the second century, before the institution of metropolitan sees, there existed a subtle network of dependency between churches. We also observe that the bond of communion, and ultimately the unity of the universal church, relied on the Eucharist, on communion granted of the eucharistic bread. Among all these churches, the see of Rome appeared as

---

[332] Eusebius, *Eccl. Hist.* V, 23-25.

the best source of recommendation and of communion on the level of bishops. We see also that the understanding of the relative authority of these many churches and of that of Rome is a matter of nuance and context.

## III. THIRD CENTURY: CYPRIAN OF CARTHAGE

Tertullian (end of the second, beginning of the third century), recast the argument of Irenaeus referring to the apostolic churches as the guaranty of the apostolic tradition of teaching. Tertullian named it the "argument of prescription," and explained it in his *De Praescriptione*. *Praescriptio* was a legal argument by which a contender could be disqualified before a tribunal, and his claim discarded from consideration. Against the abuse of scripture made by heretics in their propaganda and controversies, Tertullian invoked the argument of prescription: the use of Scripture by heretics may be rejected because Scripture did not belong to them but to the churches taught by the apostles to whom Christ entrusted his gospel.

Later in his life, Tertullian himself adhered to the Montanist sect and fought the catholic church. He supported the Encratist views of the Montanists and acknowledged their prophets. But he had been such a great spokesperson of the Christian faith that he was not treated as a heretic, but was honored with the title of "Master" by Cyprian, the bishop-martyr of Carthage. Tertullian was recognised as a good servant of the church rather than an offender of unity.

The great champion of church unity in the third century is Cyprian (bishop of Carthage, 248-258 A.D.), with his treatise *De unitate Ecclesiae* (*On Church Unity*).[333] Cyprian had to fight for unity in his own church of Carthage, divided by schism during the Decian persecution. Cyprian's withdrawal from Carthage in circumstances where it would have been suicidal to stay was used as an excuse by his enemies for the appointment of another bishop, and his enemies persuaded a certain number of the confessors to join them against Cyprian. They also obtained the support of apostates whom they readmitted to communion without penance on the basis of the intercession of confessors and martyrs for their forgiveness. Cyprian came back and managed to restore his authority and the unity of his church. In order to reach a common agreement concerning apostates and other grievous sinners, he consulted other bishops of Africa and overseas, especially the Roman clergy. Divisions also existed in the Roman church, and mutual recognition between Cyprian and Pope Cornelius was not reached smoothly.

---

[333] *St. Cyprian, The Lapsed. The Unity of the Church*, tr. M. Bevenot, ACW 25, 1957.

In these circumstances, Cyprian wrote his two major treatises. In *On the Lapsed* he imposed on apostates and grievous sinners a time of penance which would publicly attest the seriousness of their repentance and justify their re-admission to communion. Actually Cyprian reduced this time of penance to less than a year because of epidemic and of persecution, since former apostates who might again be forced to pour their blood for Christ should not be refused the communion to his blood and the assistance of the Holy Spirit.

Cyprian's second major treatise is *On the Unity of the Catholic Church*. It was intended for his own church and for the council of the African bishops to whom it was read. But it was also sent to the church of Rome and probably to other churches overseas. Cyprian's famous reference to the see of Peter (ch.4) remains a crux of interpretation:

> It is on one man (Peter) that he builds the church, and although he assigns a like power to all the apostles after his resurrection,[334] yet, in order that the oneness might be unmistakable, he established by his own authority a source for that oneness having its origin in one man alone. No doubt the other apostles were all that Peter was, endowed with equal dignity and power, but the start comes from him (Peter) alone, in order to show that the church of Christ is unique (ACW).

This text, known as the "second edition," may have been read to the African council of bishops. The so-called "first edition" speaks explicitely of the "chair of Peter" and of the "primacy given to Peter in such a way that there is but one church and one chair." It suits a text sent overseas to the Roman church which owns the chair of Peter and his tomb. In that case, the local Peter is the bishop sitting on the very chair of the great Peter.

Before discussing the meaning of the reference to Peter in *On the Unity*, we must consider what Cyprian said concerning unity in the same treatise and elsewhere. In ch.5 of *On the Unity*, Cyprian explained his theory of a corporate authority in the church relying on the unity of the order of bishops, actually on councils of bishops as they existed in Africa from the beginning of the third century and took place yearly: "The authority of the bishops forms a unity, of which each holds his part in its totality." Cyprian illustrated the unity of the church as residing in the unity of its order of bishops with the images of one sun and many rays, of one tree and many branches, one spring and many channels, finally, of one mother and many children.

In ch.6, Cyprian depicted the church as the undefiled bride of Christ: "whoever breaks with the church and enters on

---

[334] John 20:21-23.

an adulterous union, cuts himself off from the promises made to the church." Like the ark of Noah, the church is the only place of salvation. In ch.7, Cyprian compared the unity of the church to the undivided coat of Christ, which the soldiers at the cross did not dare to tear into pieces. Heretics, Cyprian said (ch.10) have no sense of what a bishop is, and they vainly dared to baptize or to offer the sacrifice (ch.11-15). Cyprian boasted he had been lawfully elected, after the death of his predecessor, in time of peace, by the unanimous will of the people, and the devil himself had confirmed the validity of his ordination by more than once claiming that he should be thrown to the beasts (*Ep.* 59).

The reference to Peter did not always have the same meaning in Cyprian. In several epistles (33, 43, 66, 73) the text of Matthew 16:18-19 ("Thou art Peter...") was interpreted in the sense of the local bishop as the Peter of the local church against schismatics on the local level: the local bishop was the center of unity, and owned the power of the keys for the remission of sins. The "second edition" might be interpreted in this sense. But certainly the "first edition" referred to the see of Rome. Certainly Cyprian acknowledged the capital importance of the see of Rome for the unity of the universal church. For instance, in *Ep.* 44 and following, Cyprian explained to Cornelius the reasons for which he delayed acknowledging his election: a doubt concerning the Roman bishop was a serious problem, since the see of Peter was the womb and the root of the universal church and the basis of unity (*Ep.* 48). On the other hand, Cyprian resented the obligation to report elections and judgments taking place in Africa; for him, communion with Rome did not involve menial subjection to a Roman jurisdiction, and did not justify the Roman habit of welcoming appeals from Africans against the tribunal of their bishops. Augustine had the same reaction.

The reference to Peter in *On the Unity* obviously was a recasting of the famous statement of Irenaeus given above. But there was a shift in the meaning. In Irenaeus, agreement with Peter and Paul was sought for in Rome against heretical masters about apostolic teaching. In Cyprian, the problem is less orthodoxy than schism, i.e., "the priestly unity," *unitas sacerdotalis*, as we read in *Ep.* 59. Cyprian mystically identified clergy to the levitical priesthood of the Temple, although nothing was changed in their traditional status regarding elections, rank and ministries. The crime of schism was raising altar against altar, priest against priest, sacrifice against sacrifice, sacrament against sacrament, thereby cutting the faithful off from the unity of life in Christ. As a breaking of communion with the altar, schism is a question of priestly unity, and, just like communion itself, priestly unity is connected with Peter and Rome.

Cyprian, who supported this idea, was soon destined to suffer from it in his dispute with Stephen, the new Roman bishop. Pushing to its logical conclusion his reasoning on the unity of the church as the one place of salvation and of spiritual life, Cyprian maintained that Christians already baptized by heretics and coming to the Catholic church ought to be re-baptized because their baptism was void. But the practice of Rome in such a case was to suffice with the laying on of hands which was customary in the reconciliation of sinners before granting them peace and communion. A bitter conflict followed between Cyprian and Stephen, which ended only with their martyrdom. Stephen appealed to a Petrine tradition, which Cyprian duely contested as unhistorical. Cyprian relied on the decision of an African council under his predecessor Agrippinus 20 years earlier.[335]

The dispute on the validity of baptism given in a schismatic church poisoned the life the African church during the two following centuries. We owe to Stephen and the Roman practice the right of considering as our brothers and sisters in Christ all Christians baptized in other "denominations." We could not do it if we followed Cyprian in his conclusions, which were derived from a proper principle, but were wrong in spite of their logic.

## IV. THE FOURTH CENTURY: DEVELOPMENT OF METROPOLITAN JURISDICTION

The council of Arles (314 A.D.) approved the Roman position on the baptism of heretics as defined by Stephen. It also dealt with the case of Donatism, an African schism which started during Diocletian's persecution. The Donatists contended that they were the church of the pure and of the martyrs, whereas the Catholic church in Africa was polluted and spiritually dead because of the alleged sins of its *traditores*, bishops or clerics who surrendered (*tradere*) sacred books to pagan authorities during the persecution. Both the Catholic bishop of Carthage, Caecilianus, and the Donatist bishop of Carthage, Donatus, appealed to Emperor Constantine, who deferred the case to Pope Milthiades in order to decide who was the legitimate bishop of Carthage. In that case, Milthiades seems to have followed the Roman tradition regarding the validity of the baptism of heretics, and condemned Donatus who, following the tradition of Cyprian, was guilty of "re-baptizing." Constantine, disappointed by Milthiades because he expected a judgment on the validity of their respective ordinations, carried the case to Arles, but the bishops of this council refused to part from the decision of the pope. Arles is in southern Gaul, where the authority of the pope was respected.

The council of Nicaea (325 A.D.) approved the metropolitan system:

---

[335] *Epistle* 75, of Firmilian of Caesarea, among the Epistles of Cyprian.

> Let the ancient customs prevail which are in Egypt and Libya and Pentapolis, according to which the bishop of ALEXANDRIA has authority over all these places. For this is also customary to the bishop of ROME. In like manner in ANTIOCH and in the other provinces, the privileges are to be preserved to the churches. But this is clearly understood that if anyone be made a bishop without the consent of the metropolitan, the great synod declares that he shall not be a bishop.[336]

The council of Sardica (343 A.D.) made Rome a supreme court of appeal among bishops:

> If any bishop has had judgment passed upon him in any case, and consider himself to have good reason for judgment being given afresh upon it, if you agree, let us honour the memory of the most holy Apostle Peter; let there be written letters to the Roman bishop either by those who tried the case or by the bishops who live in the neighbouring province. If he decide that judgment be given afresh, let it be given afresh, and let him appoint judges...[337]

The council of Constantinople (381 A.D.) added a new major metropolitan to the three recognized in Nicaea: "the bishop of Constantinople shall have the privileges of honor after the bishop of Rome, because it is new Rome." The council of Chalcedon (451 A.D.) confirmed this privilege of Constantinople.[338]

For the exercise of jurisdiction and the hearing of appeals, Christianity was divided by the council of Nicaea into three parts respectively, under the authority of Rome, Alexandria, and Antioch. In order to honor the "new Rome," the council of Constantinople added to the three the bishop of Constantinople, thus creating a rival to the pope. Both claimed Roman primacy. This unfortunate rivalry turned the Roman privilege, essentially an instrument of unity, into a cause of division. The separation between the Western and the Eastern church is the consequence both of the political division of the Roman Empire, and of the religious division between the pope

---

[336] Canon 6 of Nicaea, J. Stevenson, *A New Eusebius* 300, p.360.

[337] J. Stevenson, *Creeds, Councils and Controversies. Documents illustrative of the History of the Church A.D. 337-461* (New York: Seabury, 1966), 12, p.19.

[338] Ibid., n.101 p.147 (Canon of the Council of Constantinople); n.219, p.333 (Canon 28 of Chalcedon).

of Rome and the patriarch of Constantinople. The decision of the council of Sardica to make Rome a supreme court of appeal was the work of a council consisting of Westerners only. It was rejected by the East, although occasionally bishops who were condemned in the East appealed to Rome and, for this reason, recognised this right of Rome. The most famous example is Chrysostom.

## V. THE CHAIR OF PETER IN THE WEST: OPTATUS AGAINST THE DONATISTS

We may have noticed that Irenaeus' reference to the church of Rome as in possession of apostolic tradition in the name of Peter and Paul, the princes of the apostles, has lost with Cyprian the name of Paul in order to focus on Peter. This change was significant. It meant that the matter now was not a question of apostolic teaching for which two witnesses are better than one, but a question of priestly unity, *unitas sacerdotalis*, for which the emphasis is on Peter only as the first bishop of Rome and, in some regards, "still present in the Roman bishop."

### OPTATUS OF MILEVI.

The historian of Donatism in the fourth century, Optatus of Milevi, referred to the bishop of Rome as to the "Chair of Peter" when he tried to bring the Donatist bishop of Carthage, Parmenianus, back to the unity of the catholic church.[339] Actually, Optatus took the five Donatist claims of being the true church, and applied them to the catholic church centered in Rome.[340] He proved that a schismatic (Donatist) bishop has no right to appropriate these claims against the Catholics.

These claims, or "adornments" of a true church, are: the *cathedra* (a lawful right to the see), the *angel* (a bishop sent by God, able to confer the spirit upon baptismal water), the *spirit* (of adoption who makes sons of God in baptism), the *fountain* (of holy baptism which does not need to be repeated), the *seal* (of the catholic creed without which one cannot open the true fountain of baptism), and the *navel* (the altar with a holy priesthood performing the mysteries).

Concerning the *cathedra* (chair), Optatus wrote: "You cannot deny what you know that upon Peter first in the city of Rome was bestowed the episcopal *cathedra*, on which sat Peter, the head of all the apostles (for which reason he was called Cephas = Peter), that, in this one *cathedra*, unity should be preserved by all lest the other apostles might claim --each for himself-- separate *cathedras*, so that he who should set up a

---

[339] Optatus, Books I-VII.

[340] Optatus, *The Donatist Schism*, Book II:iv, PL XI.

second *cathedra* against the unique *cathedra* would already be a schismatic and a sinner."[341]

Augustine tirelessly repeated Optatus' teaching: the remedy to the national schism of the Donatists is to turn to the church scattered all over the world, the church heir of the promise of Christ, which cannot be polluted by communion with particular sinners. The Donatists were wrong when they re-baptized, and Cyprian whom they followed in this regard, was wrong. But Cyprian, who believed in councils and was a Catholic, instead of stubbornly sticking to his local tradition about the baptism of heretics, would have accepted the decision of a general council. The church is one, holy, catholic (universal) and apostolic, and communion with Rome is the sign of unity.

INNOCENT I (402-417 A.D.).

In the Pelagian controversy, Pope Innocent seemed to give the best expression to the mission of the Roman see concerning doctrine and judgment. He answered the council of Carthage, 417 A.D.:

> You have decided that *it was proper to refer to our judgment*, knowing what is due to the Apostolic See, since all we who are set in this place desire to follow the very apostle from whom the very episcopate and whole authority of this name has emerged; following whom, we know how to condemn the evil and to approve the good. So also, you have by your priestly office preserved the institutions of the fathers, and have not spurned that which they decreed by a sentence not human but divine, that *whatever is done, even though it be in distant provinces, should not be ended until it comes to the knowledge of this see.*[342]

Innocent adds in a similar letter to the council of Milevi in the same year: "Especially as often as questions of faith are to be ventilated, I think that our brothers and fellow bishops ought to refer to none but Peter."[343] Actually, the pope is not on top of the affair as he claims to be, but barely follows the Africans on Pelagianism, grace, and original sin.

---

[341] Optatus, *The Donatist Schism*, Book II:iv.

[342] Augustine, *Epistle* 181, *Documents illustrative of Papal Authority A.D. 96 to 453*, ed. by E. Gilles (London: SPCK, 1952), p.201.

[343] Augustine, *Ep*. 182, tr. Giles.

## VI. THE PETRINE PRIVILEGE

Innocent is making use of the petrine privilege. Already Pope Siricius, in his *Epitle to Himerius*, 385 A.D., assumed Peter's responsibility when he spoke against the practice of re-baptizing Arians:

> In view of our office, we are not free to dissemble or to keep silent, for our zeal for the Christian religion ought to be greater than anyone's. We bear the burdens of all who are heavy laden, or rather *the blessed apostle bears them in us*, who in all things, as we trust, protects and defends those who are heir of his government.[344]

Innocent himself, in his *Episthe 25 to Decentius*, (416 A.D.), trying to impose the Roman customs on other churches in the West, wrote:

> Who does not know or observe that it (the church order) was delivered by Peter the chief of the apostles to the Roman church, and is kept until now, and ought to be retained by all, and that nothing ought to be imposed or introduced which has no authority, or seems to derive its precedents elsewhere? -especially since it is clear that in all Italy, the Gauls, Spain, Africa, Sicily and the adjacent islands, no one formed these churches except those whom the venerable apostle Peter or his successors made priests.[345]

According to Innocent, the "petrine privilege" supposed that Peter was the founder and first bishop of Rome, that he was the author of the customs existing in Rome in the time of Innocent, and that he was still active in his successor who exercised the petrine authority at least over the churches founded by Peter himself or by the Roman church. It was much more than the static presence in Rome of genuine apostolic teaching against the pretensions of heretics. It was even more than the idea of a center and source of communion, and of unity in communion. It was also more than a supreme court of appeal for bishops all over the world. It was the idea that the See of Rome was still the See of Peter, and that the pope had the last word in religious matters, at least in relation to local councils. Finally it meant that the Roman customs have a special authority, and should replace other local customs elsewhere.

---

[344] *Epistle to Himerius*, tr. Giles, 108.

[345] Innocent the First, *Ep. to Decentius*, 2, tr. Giles, 175.

Leo the Great (440-456? A.D.) expressed the same petrine doctrine, and gave its scriptural foundation:

> The Lord has placed the principal charge on the blessed Peter, chief of all the apostles, and from him as from the head wishes his gifts to flow to all the body (of the universal church), so that any who dare to secede from Peter's solid Rock may understand that he has no part or lot in the divine mystery (the union of Christ with the church).[346]

As we see, here Leo refers to Mt. 16:18: "You are Peter, and upon this rock (Rock in Greek = Peter) I will build my church." Leo intervenes in the life of churches wherever needed, especially in matters of recruitment and ordination of bishops. The authority and customs of Rome must be adopted everywhere in the West. Leo was a living Peter.

A long way had come when the pope could speak like Leo did with the authority of Peter. It is difficult, or unrealistic, to derive the authority of the pope from the words of Jesus to Peter in the gospels, as did the theologians of the past. Whatever be the "trajectory of Peter" in the New Testament, well described by R. Brown and associates in *Peter in the New Testament*, it does not lead to a pope exercising a universal authority in matters of doctrine and practice. In the first centuries, we meet with the fact of Roman influence, not with a doctrine of the papacy. But the Roman influence, in need of foundation, was subsequently confirmed with proofs from Scripture: the petrine texts of the gospels (Mt. 16:18-19; John 21). These texts are interpreted as evidence for the authority of the bishop of Rome.

Generally, as soon as a theological problem is raised, reference is made to Scripture. But, just as the accepted answer seeks a scriptural justification, it also confers on the text of Scripture a new meaning which it did not originally have. Finally, on the basis of the doctrine developed from such interpretations, doctrinal conclusions and practical consequences are derived which lead to a kind of inflation. Such is the process which we observe in the development of the papacy of the first centuries. The accumulation of papal letters (decretals) became a source of precedents in law, and the creation of a curia added to the papal administration.

The weaknesses accompanying the growth of papal authority were themselves meaningful. I do not mean the short duration of many pontificates, or the presence of insignificant characters, or, even less, the case of popes Liberius (352-366 A.D.) and Vigilius (537-555 A.D.) who yielded to violence and

---

[346] Leo the Great, *Ep.* 10 to the bishops of the province of Viena in Gaul, tr. Giles.

were unjustly condemned by history. I mean weaknesses which, in some regard, are essential to the papal system and therefore should last. I take, for example, the behavior of the popes involved in the Pelagian controversy in the first half of the fifth century.[347] According to the petrine privilege, Innocent affirmed the right of the pope, not only to be consulted, but to have the last word on Pelagianism, original sin, and the theology of grace. But his letter was far less impressive if we consider that he was actually adopting the theological work and decision of the African councils. In other words, he wanted to affirm the petrine privilege, but his gesture sounded like pure bravura.

Pope Zozimus (417-418 A.D.) affirmed the same petrine privilege, but adopted the opposite position, accepting ambiguous confessions of faith from Pelagius and Celestius, and requesting the Africans to change their sentence against them. Zozimus wanted peace and reconciliation, but, later on, when Emperor Honorius exiled Pelagius and Celestius as causing scandal, Zozimus condemned them, and compiled a *tractoria* consisting of Roman documents against Pelagianism, which he obliged the bishops of Italy to undersign. His successor, Boniface (418-422 A.D.), did not take an active part in the repression, but Celestinus (422-432 A.D.), who succeeded him, started a hard campaign against the eighteen bishops of Italy who refused to sign the *tractoria*, and he approved the Augustinian theology of grace. In the discussion of these questions, the conflict vanished with time and a better sense of balance.

Actually, the petrine privilege was tempered by the fact that the Roman bishop exercised it as a judge. Pelagianism was a cause brought to the tribunal of the pope, and was differently handled by successive popes according to their personal opinions, the information which they received, and the pressure of circumstances. It is much better for a judge to hesitate, and even to change his mind, than to answer in the manner of a teacher. The magisterium of a bishop, even of a Roman bishop, is an affair of preaching and teaching, but a controversy is an affair of information and judgment for which time and flexibility are necessary. The solution is definitive only at the end, when the right balance has been reached.

Actually the exercise of the petrine privilege seemed to benefit more than to suffer from the shift of positions often happening between predecessor and successor to the See. The following case suggests interesting observations in this regard. Gregory the Great (590-604 A.D.) inherited from his predecessor, Pelagius II, the approval by pope Vigilius of Emperor Justinian's condemnation of the *Three Chapters*, a series of selections from three orthodox Byzantine theologians of the past whom the oversuspicious Emperor condemned as erroneous

---

[347] For the following, see G. de Plinval, *Pélage: ses écrits, sa vie et sa réforme* (Paris: Payot, 1943).

teaching. Vigilius gave his consent under imperial pressure, while in jail in Constantinople. Gregory might have dropped the *Three Chapters* for the reason given above. But, under the consideration that these selections, like all such selections, reflected error, Gregory preferred to stick to the condemnation pronounced by a predecessor. Repeatedly --and vainly-- he tried to obtain their condemnation from Western bishops, and referred in that case to the authority of Peter.[348] Gregory was persuaded that he should not contradict his predecessor, and this understanding of the petrine authority deprived him of the flexibility which would have spared him unnecessary worries and injustice toward those theologians.

## VII. THE CONTROVERSY ON THE PRIMACY

Leo ignored the canon of the council of Constantinople (381 A.D.) which extolled the See of Constantinople as the new Rome, almost to the same dignity as that of his own See.[349] The Roman See did not recognize this canon. Against Leo's wishes, the council of Chalcedon (451 A.D.) re-affirmed the rights of the See of the new Rome (canon 28), and provided it with a large area of jurisdiction in the East. Leo claimed that canon 28 was contrary to the council of Nicaea (325 A.D.) which established the jurisdiction of the three great Sees, and that Alexandria and Antioch were thereby degraded to the third and fourth rank. Leo noted that, in any case, Anatolius, the bishop of Constantinople could not turn his See into an apostolic See.[350]

In order to put a limit to the growing influence of the See of Constantinople, Leo maintained active relations with the Eastern bishops and with the court of the Emperor. He also established an "apostolic vicar" in Salonica, who would exercise the papal jurisdiction throughout Illyricum, the contested area located between Rome and Constantinople. Gregory the Great followed the same ecclesiastical politics as Leo, and almost generalized the system of the "apostolic vicars".[351] He refused to the Empress the skull of Paul which would have provided

[348] F.H. Dudden, *Gregory the Great, His Place in History and Thought*, 2 vol. (New York: Longmans, 1905), vol.1, pp. 199-211, 446-454; vol.2, p.23. (The Lombard queen Theodelinda among the supporters of the *Three Chapters*).

[349] Leo the Great, *Ep.* 106 to Anatolius, bishop of Constantinople, 452 A.D. (Giles, Document 268).

[350] Leo the Great, *Epistles* 98-108 (LNPF).

[351] Gregory the Great, *Epistles* II:19,20,23; III:6.

Constantinople with a major apostolic relic,[352] and Constantinople was reduced to claim the uncertain patronage of the apostle Andrew.

The dispute about the primacy was no small matter, since John, the bishop of Constantinople, and his successors, ascribed to themselves the title of "universal bishop," thereby attesting their claim to be the real Rome.[353] The place of the "universal bishop" was the imperial city, not the old Rome, abandoned by the emperor and half deserted. Gregory protested that the bishop of Constantinople was making himself the sole bishop in the world, and affirmed that the bishop of Rome had always avoided this title.[354] The principle affirmed by Cyprian was that, in the Catholic church, there is no "bishop of bishops."

Once more, the popes appealed to the petrine privilege: the tombs of Peter and Paul were in Rome, not in Constantinople, and the pope inherited his right to the primacy from Peter, not from the Emperor. In order to foster devotion to the See of Peter, Gregory encouraged pilgrimages to the tombs of the apostles. He also made a large use of the "pallium," a woolen garment left overnight in contact with the bones of Peter, and which the pope conferred on all archbishops who proved faithful to the See of Peter[355]

The popes also reformulated the petrine doctrine in such a way as to include the Sees of Antioch and of Alexandria in the same dignity, under the authority of the bishop of Rome, the heir of Peter. The new formula went back to Damasus (366-384 A.D.), and was used against the claims of Constantinople by Leo[356] and Gregory, who wrote to Eulogius of Alexandria:

> Wherefore, though there are many apostles, yet with regard to the principality itself, the See of the prince of the apostles alone has grown strong in authority, which in the three places (Rome, Antioch, Alexandria) is the See of one. For he himself (Peter) exalted the See (Rome) in which he deigned even to rest and end the present life. He himself (Peter) adorned the See (Alexandria) in which he sent his disciple as evangelist (Mark, Peter's disciple). He himself (Peter) established the See (Antioch) in which, though he was to leave it, he

---

[352] *Ep.* IV:30.

[353] Gregory the Great, *Ep.* VI:18-21, 43; VII:27, 31, 33; IX:122.

[354] Gregory, *Ep.* V:20, 43.

[355] For instance, *Ep.* VII:58; IX:11, 107.

[356] Leo the Great, *Epistles* 129 to Proterius of Alexandria.

> sat for seven years. Since, then, it is the See of one, and one See, over which by divine authority three bishops now preside, whatever good I hear of you, this I impute to myself.[357]

Gregory relied on this doctrine of Peter as the founder, directly or indirectly, not only of the Western churches, but also of the major Sees of the East, in other words, as the founder of the church and as the source of the priesthood and of the Roman customs.

We do not have to enter a discussion of the Middle Ages and the modern papacy. Although relying on Scriptúre and tradition, they answered their own problems very much their own way. Gelasius' famous theory of the "two swords"[358] became a reality in the Middle Ages only, and the so-called *Donation of Constantine*[359] reflected the situation of the West a few decades before Charlemagne. The separation between the East and the West was a long process, and the chief cause of the tragic breakdown of church unity. So-called ecumenical councils since then have never included a real or free participation of the East. In spite of excommunications and even of accusations of heresy, the Eastern and the Western church have lived faithful to Christ in respect of their apostolic and early traditions. With the spirit of ecumenism in the last decades, they have forgotten much of their mutual contentions, and come very close to full communion. The churches of the Reformation, even more eagerly, developed the same spirit of ecumenism and desire for unity. May the hierarchy once established in order to preserve Christian unity recover enough flexibility to accomplish this mission today, and restore communion and unity! May the laity press the issue of church unity and not raise obstacles in its way!

## QUESTIONNAIRE

1. How did Jewish unity locally and internationally rely on the synagogal institution, on the Temple of Jerusalem, and on the

---

[357] Gregory the Great, *Epistles* VII:40.

[358] Gelasius, *Epistle to Emperor Anastasius I*, 494 A.D. (tr. in J. Barry Coleman, ed., *Readings in Church History* I, 29).

[359] *The Forged Donation of Constantine, c.750-850*, tr. S. Z. Ehler & J. B. Morrall, *Church and State Through the Centuries* (Westminster: Newman Press, 1954), doc.44, pp. 16-22.

Law of Moses? Can we conceive of a similar unity in the very early church?

2. How does R.E. Brown, in *The Church the Apostles Left Behind*, show concern for unity in the communities of Luke, Matthew, and John?

3. How does Ignatius of Antioch resolve the problem of unity in the local church?

4. Ignatius compares the bishop to God, the deacon to Jesus, and the presbyters to the apostles. What does that mean, and not mean?

5. What happened in the church of Corinth in the time of Clement of Rome, at the end of the first century?

6. Mention, and interpret, several "mystical" images of the church (cf. Hermas, Abercius, etc.).

7. What could be the use of lists of bishops in churches, and of letters of communion in the hands of Christian travellers?

8. Why did Irenaeus recommend to be in agreement with the apostolic churches, particularly with Rome?

9. Can you put in progressive order the churches of Corinth, Amastris, Cnossos, Gortyna, Rome, Ephesus? Do you see among churches in the second century a network of dependency and unity?

10. What was, according to Irenaeus, the nice example given to Victor by his predecessor Anicetus and by Polycarp?

11. How is the "chair of Peter" in Rome, for Cyprian, a source of unity in the church? How do councils also serve the cause of unity?

12. What would have happened to ecumenism, had the view of Cyprian on baptism and the church prevailed over that of Stephen?

13. Why did Innocent insist in his letters to the African councils on the role of the Roman See?

14. What did the popes of the 4th and 5th centuries mean when they said that Peter was still active in the Roman See?

15. Can we consider the increase of papal authority in these centuries as partly due to the interpretation of the petrine texts

in the gospels, for example, the keys given to Peter, and the church built on Peter as the Rock?

16. Was it better that the pope appear as a "judge" rather than as a "teacher" in the controversy of Pelagianism (cf. Popes Innocent, Zozimus, Boniface, Celestine)?

17. What do we learn concerning the delicate balance between flexibility and tradition on the See of Rome from the affair of the *Three Chapters* under Gregory the Great?

18. What is the meaning and implication of the controversy on the "primacy"?

19. What advice would you give to the hierarchy of the Roman church, of the Byzantine church, and of certain churches of the Reformation, in order to restore church unity? Can we consider all these communities as church?

## BIBLIOGRAPHY

BROWN, R.E. *The Church the Apostles Left Behind.* New York: Paulist Press, 1984.

CAMPENHAUSEN, H.V. *Ecclesiastical Authority and Spiritual Power in the Church of the First Three Centuries.* Stanford: Standford University Press, 1969.

CONGAR, Y. "De la communion des Eglises à une écclésiologie de l'Eglise universelle." *L'Episcopat et l'Eglise universelle.* Ed. by Y. Congar & B. D. Dupuy. Unam Sanctam 29. Paris: Le Cerf, 1962, pp. 227-260.

CYPRIAN. *St. Cyprian: The Lapsed ; The Unity of the Catholic Church.* Tr. M. Bevenot. ACW 25, 1957.

DUDDEN, H. *Gregory the Great, his Place in History and in Thought.* 2 vol. New York: Longmans, 1905.

GILES, E., ed. *Documents illustrative of Papal Authority AD 96 to 453.* London: SPCK, 1952.

HERTLING, L. *Communio, Church and Papacy in Early Christianity.* Tr. with an Introduction by J. Wicks. Chicago: Loyola Univ. Press, 1972.

JALLAND, T.G. *The Church and the Papacy.* London: SPCK, 1944

_____. *The Life and Time of Saint Leo the Great.* London: SPCK, 1941.

NAUTIN, P. *Lettres et Ecrivains Chrétiens des IIe et IIIe siècles.* Paris: Le Cerf, 1961.

OPTATUS. *The Works of St. Optatus Against the Donatists.* Tr. O. R. Vassall-Phillips. London, 1917.

*Papal Primacy and the Universal Church.* Ed. by P. Empie et T. A. Murphy. Lutherans and Catholics in Dialogue IV. St. Louis: Augsburg Publishing House, 1974.

*Peter in the New Testament, A Collaborative Assessment by Protestant and Catholic Scholars.* Ed. by R. E. Brown, K. P. Donfried, J. Reumann. St. Louis: Augsburg Publishing House, 1973.

PLINVAL, G. de. *Pélage, ses écrits, sa vie et sa réforme.* Paris, Lausane: Payot, 1943.

WILLIS, G.G. *St Augustine and the Donatist Controversy.* London: SPCK, 1950. Cf. The Abbot of Downside. "St Augustine's Teaching on Schism." *Downside Review* 69, 1957.

## CHRONOLOGY

## THE BIBLICAL TIMES

The period of the Patriarchs Abraham, Isaac, Jacob (traditions on the Patriarchs in Genesis): late 15th century B.C. onward.

Moses, the Exodus from Egypt, and the Wilderness period: probably under the Egyptian kings Sethos I (1317-1304 B.C.) and Ramesses II (1304-1237 B.C.).

The establishment of the Hebrew tribes in Canaan: early 14th century to second half of 13th century B.C.

Period of Judges: 1200-922 B.C. (the Philistine threat).

King Saul: 1020-1000 B.C.

King David: 1000-c.961 B.C.

King Solomon: c.961-922 B.C. (writing of J and E traditions of Pentateuch).
Division of the kingdom into Israel (North) with Jeruboam, and Judah (South) with Roboam: 922 B.C.

King Omri in Israel (building of Samaria): 876-869 B.C.

King Achab in Israel (869-850 B.C.), battle of Qarkar (853 B.C.) where Achab and 12 kings were defeated by the Assyrian army. Queen Jezabel supports the Syrian Baals and persecutes the faithful of Iahweh (the traditional God of Israel). Resistance of prophets Elijah and Elishah.

King Jehu (842-815 B.C.) overthrows the Omri dynasty, and restores the cult of Iahweh. Prophets Amos and Hosea preach against social injustice and indifference to cults of other gods, which characterized a period of material prosperity.

Prophet Isaiah (Is. 1-39 only: vision of Isaiah: 742 B.C.; end of the activity of Isaiah I: 701 B.C.) preached in Jerusalem under the kings of Judah Jotham 741-735 B.C.; Achaz 735-715 B.C.; Hezekiah 715-687 B.C. This period includes the fall of Samaria 722 B.C.

King Manasseh (640-642 B.C.) established pagan cults in Jerusalem.

King Josiah (640-709 B.C.), on the discovery of a law book

(part of Deuteronomy?) started a Yahwist reformation, and died in the battle of Megiddo against Egypt.

King Jehoiakim (609-598 B.C.) of Judah became an Egyptian vassal, then, a vassal of Babylon. A revolt against Babylon led to the fall of Jerusalem under the power of King Nebuchadnezzar, 597 B.C.

His successor, King Zedekiah's revolt against Babylon led to the destruction of Jerusalem and of its Temple in 586 B.C.

Jeremiah preached between 627 B.C. (beginning of Josiah's reign), and the fall of Jerusalem, 587 B.C.

Deuteromomy (document D) was probably written before the Exile.

Prophet Ezekiel preached in Babylon during the period of Exile (597-538 B.C.)

The Priestly document (P) of the Pentateuch, the Second and Third Isaiah, especially the Poem of the Suffering Servant (Is.53), Lament, the "Deuteronomic" history (Sacred history revised according to the religious principles of Document P), were written during or afterf the Exile. The whole Pentateuch was completed in 400 B.C. The Wisdom literature (Proverbs, Ecclesiastes) is the work of royal scribes and cultured believers under the monarchy of Israel. Wisdom of Solomon was written in Greek and may be the work of a Jewith authof in Alexandria c.50 B.C., before Philo of Alexandria.

Job and the book of Psalms seem to belong to the pre-exilic and exilic times.

The Persian king Cyrus defeated the last Babylonian king Nabonides in 539 B.C., and granted their freedom to exiles of many nations, including Israel. Zorobabel, the high priest Josuah, and the two prophets Haggai and Zechariah worked at the restoration of the temple in Jerusalem, which was completed in 515 B.C.

Nehemiah (445 B.C.) obtained from the king of Persia, Artaxerces, the permission to rebuild the walls of Jerusalem, and tried to purify the Jewish community: he imposed the practice of resting on the Sabbath, and forbade inter-marriage with pagan women. Ezra, who came latefr from Babylon to Jerusalem in a mission of the same type as that of Nehemiah, continued his religious politics, and had the book of the Law read to the entire community. He established a sort of theocracy under the protection of the Persian king, in which the high priest was invested with supreme authority.

Alexander the Great (336-323 B.C.) conquered Greece, Asia Minor, Palestine, Persia, Egypt. Palestine remained caught between its two powerful successors, the Ptolemees in Egypt and the Seleucides in Syria.

The Macchabean revolt (166-164 B.C.) led to the re-dedication of the Temple which had been profaned (167 B.C.) by the pro-Greek party under the influence of the Syrian king Antiochus IV Epiphanes (175-163 B.C.).

The book of Daniel --fictitiously described as a Jew in exile at Babylon-- actually was a literary attack against king Antiochus Epiphanes and his persecution of the Jewish faith.

The Macchabean Rulers of Jerusalem, Judas and Jonathan (166-142 B.C.) restored the city, the temple and worship of Iahweh.

The Asmonean Rulers (142-63 B.C.) maintained and extended the Jewish state of Judah: Simon (141-134 B.C.), Alexander Janneus (103076 B.C.), Salome Alexandra (76-67 B.C.), Aristobulus II (67-63 B.C.), but alienated the earliest supporters of the Jewish movement, the Pharisees.

The Roman general Pompey captured Jerusalem (63 B.C.) and profaned the Temple. Antipater was made high priest, and inaugurated a kind of clever collaboration with the Roman power.

Herod (40 B.C.-4 A.D.) was made "King of the Jews" (40 B.C.), captured Jerusalem (37 B.C.), and rebuilt the Temple of Jerusalem (20-? B.C.)

Birth of Jesus (8-6 B.C.?)

Sons of Herod: Archelaus, Philip, Herod Antipas.

Census of Quirinius (6 A.D.): Judaea is placed under Roman procuratorship.

Under Tiberius (14-37 A.D.) Pontius Pilate (26-36) is made procurator: ministry of John the Baptisg and of Jesus; crucifixion of Jesus (30?)

Caligula (37-41), Claudius (41-54), Nero (54-68), Vespasian (69-79) are Emperors in Rome. The Jews revolt against Rome (66-73): Jerusalem and the Temple are destroyed (70 A.D.).

## THE CHRISTIAN TIMES

Martyrdom of Stephen, and conversion of Paul (36-38).

Paul's first missionary journey (47-49; "council of Jerusalem" (49); Paul's further missionary journeys (50-58); Paul in Corinth (51-52); Paul's arrest in Jerusalem (58); the great fire in Rome and the Neronian persecution (64).

The first Jewish war (66-73); Fall of Jerusalem to Titus (70).

Vespasian emperor (Flavian dynasty 69-96); Titus emperor (79).

Domitian emperor (81); Nerva emperor (dynasty of the Antonines) (c.95); Trajan emperor (98). Letter of Trajan to Pliny concerning the persecution of Christians (111).

Epistle of Clement of Rome to the Corinthians (c.95).

Hadrian emperor (117) (rescript in favor of Christians?)

The Second Jewish war (132-135).

Antoninus Pius emperor (138); Marcus Aurelius emperor (161); Commodius Augustus, then emperor (177, 180).

Martyrdom of Polycarp at Smyrna (161/9); of Justin at Rome (163/7); Martyrs of Lyons (175/7), Irenaeus becomes bishop of Lyons.

"Quatuordeciman" controversy over date of Easter, under Pope Victor (189-190).

Clement teaching at Alexandria (193).

Septimus Severus sole emperor (dynasty of the Severi) (194); Caracalla emperor (212); Elagabalus emperor (218); Alexander Severus emperor (222); Maximinus emperor (235); Gordian III emperor (238).

Appearance of Montanism (c.170); Tertullian's *Apologeticum* (197); Tertullian becomes a Montanist (207-208); Tertullian's *Adversus Praxean* (213).

Callixtus pope (217-222); reform of penance; condemnation of Sabellius; schism of Hippolytus; Pope Pontian and the antipope Hippolytus deported to Sardinia (235).

Origen head of the Catechetical School at Alexandria (202-2-3); Origen ordained priest (231); Origen visits Julia Mammaea at Antioch (232); Origen writes *Exhortation to Martyrdom* (235); literary activity of Origen in Caesarea of Palestine until his suffering as a Confessor of faith, and his death after the Decian persecution (253-54).

Mani begins his preaching in Persia (242); Gregory the Wondermaker begins his missionary work in Cappadocia and Pontus; Novatian writes his *De Trinitate* (c.245).

Cyprian'sconversion (c.245); Cyprian becomes bishop of Carthage (248); Cyprian writes *De unitate Ecclesiae* against schismatics ; holds councils in Carthage to deal with the problem the "lapsed" (251); baptismal controversy between Cyprian and Stephen of Rome (255-256); martyrdom of Cyprian at Carthage during the persecution of Valerian (257-258).

Condemnation of Paul of Samosata at the synod of Antioch (268).

Diocletian emperor (284); Maximian is made Augustus (285/6); Constantius and Galerius are made Caesars in West and East respectively (293); Diocletian's four edicts of persecution (303-304); Diocletian abdicates (305).

Battle of the Milvian Bridge: Constantine master of the West (312); Battle of Tzirallum: Licinius master of the East (313); The "Edict of Milan," proclaimed by Licinius in Nicomedia, 2-13-313, grants tolerance to the Church; Battle of Andrinople (330); death of Constantine (337); the Empire is divided between his three sons.

Synod of Alexandria: condemnation of Arius (323); Council of Nicaea (325); Athanasius bishop of Alexazndria (328); council of Tyre condemning Athanasius and rehabilitating Arius (335); exile of Athanasius to Trier.

Constans (pro-Arian) sole emperor (340-350); Dedication council at Antioch (341); council of Sardica (342).

Constantius (pro-Arian) sole emperor (351); second exile of Athanasius (356); Synods of Sirmium (357-359); Synods of Ariminum-Seleucia (359-360).

Foundation of Tabenessi by Pachomius (323); death of Pachomius (346); death of Antony (356).

Julian emperor (361-363); general amnesty, and return of Athanasius to Alexandria; Apollinarius concemned at Alexandria (362); death of Athanasius (373).

Valentinian emperor in the West, and Valens in the East (384).

Basil bishop of Neo-Caesarea in Cappadocia (370-379); Gregory of Nyssa bishop (371); Gregory Nazianzen bishop (372).

Gratian emperor in the West (375); Theodosius emperor in the East (379); sole emperor (394); death of Theodosius (395).

Second ecumenical council in Constantinople (381).

Pope Damasus of Rome (366-386); Jerome in Bethleem (389).

Chrysostom bishop of Constantinople (398); Synod of the Oak (Theophilus of Alexandria obtains the condemnation of Chrysostom) (404); death of Chrysostom (407).

Ambrose bishop of Milan (373); altar of Victory controversy (384); the massacre of Thessalonica (Ambrose's intervention) (390); death of Ambrose (397).

Conversion of Augustine (386); Augustine bishop of Hippo (395); *Confessions* (400); Sack of Rome by Alaric (410); Conference of Carthage and concenmation of Donatism (411); condemnation of Pelagius by the synod of Carthage (411-412); Augustine's *De spiritu et littera* (413); synod of Jerusalem (justification of Pelagius) (415); Pope Zozimus of Rome (417-418); Augustine's *De Trinitate* (415); Augustine finishes *City of God* (427); The Vandals in Africa (429); death of Augustine (430).

Nestorius bishop of Constantinople (428); Cyril bishop of Alexandria (412-444); Council of Ephesus (431); Eutyches (Monophysitism) condemned at Constantinople (448); "Robber Synod" of Ephesus (victory of Eutyches and of Dioscorus of Alexandria over Flavian of Constantinople) (449); "Tome" of Pope Leo (440-461) on Christology; Fourth ecumenical council (Chalcedon) against Monophisitism (451).

Benedict issues his *Rule* (540); death of Caesarius of Arles (542); Gregory the Great pope of Rome (590-604); Gregory sends a mission to England (597).